W9-CDU-689

Asia Pacific in the
New World Politics

Asia Pacific in the New World Politics

■

edited by
James C. Hsiung

Lynne Rienner Publishers ■ Boulder & London

WINGATE UNIVERSITY LIBRARY

Published in the United States of America in 1993 by
Lynne Rienner Publishers, Inc.
1800 30th Street, Boulder, Colorado 80301

and in the United Kingdom by
Lynne Rienner Publishers, Inc.
3 Henrietta Street, Covent Garden, London WC2E 8LU

© 1993 by Lynne Rienner Publishers, Inc. All rights reserved

Library of Congress Cataloging-in-Publication Data
Asia Pacific in the new world politics / edited by James C. Hsiung.
    p.   cm.
    Includes bibliographical references and index.
    ISBN 1-55587-323-5 (alk. paper)
    ISBN 1-55587-355-3 (pbk.: alk. paper)
    1. Asia—Politics and government—1945– . 2. Pacific Area—Politics
and government. 3. World politics—1989– . I. Hsiung, James Chieh,
1935– .
DS35.2.A7978   1993
950.4'29—dc20   93-12747
                                                          CIP

British Cataloguing in Publication Data
A Cataloguing in Publication record for this book
is available from the British Library.

Printed and bound in the United States of America

∞   The paper used in this publication meets the requirements
       of the American National Standard for Permanence of
       Paper for Printed Library Materials Z39.48-1984.   5 4 3

To those instrumental in ending the Cold War,
and to the memory of those who grieved and perished in it

■ Contents

■ Illustrations

■ Preface

Few studies on Asia Pacific approach it from a global perspective. This one attempts to do just that, placing the region in the context of worldwide trends. It is written with two sets of conditions in view: the end of the Cold War, and the beckoning of the twenty-first century.

The reader may already be familiar with the economic clout and vast potential of the Asia Pacific region. Still, it is appropriate to offer a brief comment on its strategic relevance to the United States, drawing on the lessons that can be derived from a retrospective view of post-1945 world politics.

It is often said that our century was defined by three global wars—the two world wars and the Cold War—and that the United States, in the last half-century, fought three wars across the Pacific—the Pacific War (1941–1945) with Japan, and the Korean and Vietnam wars.[1] When these events are mentioned in the literature, it is typically to show how global international relations affected events in Asia Pacific. But what is not readily apparent—much less appreciated—is how past events in Asia Pacific likewise helped shape or reshape events elsewhere, sometimes events of momentous proportions. One example is the impact of the Korean War on global politics. As one author put it, without the Korean War, many of the characteristics associated with the Cold War—higher defense budgets, a militarized NATO, great Sino-U.S. hostility followed by post-1972 China–card playing, and U.S. security commitments throughout the world—probably would not have developed the way they did.[2]

The Vietnam War is another example in the same category. There is no need to rehash its well-known effects on domestic politics in the United States and on the conduct of regional relations. I shall only mention its influence on international relations theory. The fact that the preponderant military power of the United States failed to stop the North Vietnamese from engulfing South Vietnam remains a puzzle to many. From the consequent scholarly soul-searching, however, have come important insights that have increased our understanding of the nature of power, and its limitations; David Baldwin's "paradox of unrealized power" and Jeffrey Hart's "three measures of power" are two examples.[3]

There is a paradox concerning the place of Asia Pacific in U.S. strategic thinking, however. Every recent U.S. president has asserted that the United States is a "Pacific power." It is nevertheless true that, like the former Soviet Union, the United States tended to subordinate the Pacific to the Atlantic in its strategic thinking about foreign policy. The chapters in this book show how the kaleidoscopic changes in world politics since the late 1980s, along with three decades of phenomenal economic success of Asia Pacific nations, have brought a new age of geoeconomics. If things should turn out as this book anticipates, the twenty-first century will witness the rise of a non-Western bloc (i.e., Asia Pacific) to share the world stage with two Western blocs—one European and one (post-European) North American—on an equal footing and with similar values. That eventuality will change priorities for U.S. foreign policy thinking. More important, it may change the very nature of international relations in the state-centric Westphalian system we live in.

The term "Asia Pacific" used in this volume refers generally to Japan, China, the four Asian NIEs (newly industrializing economies: South Korea, Taiwan, Hong Kong, and Singapore), and Southeast Asia, including Indochina and members of ASEAN (the Association of Southeast Asian Nations). In the literature, Canada, the United States, Mexico, Australia, and New Zealand, among others, are sometimes included in the broader term "Pacific Basin," but this volume offers no separate chapters on the roles of these countries in the security and econopolitical life of Asia Pacific.

A few brief words about the organization of the book are in order. Chapter 1 begins with a definition of what constitutes the end of the Cold War and proceeds to identify the major attributes that characterize the so-called post–Cold War era on the larger world scene. It then explores how global changes manifest themselves at the Asia Pacific regional level and whether there are regional deviations from the global norm.

Each of the next eight chapters, 2 through 9, focuses on a country or area, looking at the general question of how new circumstances brought on by a new era will affect international relations within the Asia Pacific region. There are chapters assessing how the new era bears on Japan (Gordon), China (Hsiung), and Taiwan (Clark). Two chapters survey bilateral relations: between Russia and Japan (Berton) and between the Philippines and South Korea (Celoza and Sours). The chapter by Berton also evaluates the former Soviet Union's role in the region. One chapter (Gordon) covers members of ASEAN. One chapter (Chow) explores the prospects of regional integration in Asia Pacific, and does so in the global context of the trends of competitive trade-bloc formation. Two chapters discuss the United States' changing role, with its challenge for theory (Chan) and possible strategic responses (Denoon).

The book ends with two concluding chapters that, while drawing upon the findings of the previous chapters, also focus on the transition from the end of the Cold War to the coming of the twenty-first century. Chapter 11 provides a retrospective of Asia Pacific's rise as a solid economic force, with a view to assessing how it will fare in the post–Cold War era. The final chapter measures the bequests of our century and speculates on the global and regional balance of power in the new century. It also compares the evolving relative strengths of the three competing trading blocs (Europe, North America, and Asia Pacific) over time, in an attempt to answer the compelling question of whether there is going to be a "Pacific Era."

Except for Chapter 10, by Peter Chow, all chapters grew out of papers presented on two consecutive panels I chaired at the 1992 annual conference of the International Studies Association (ISA), in Atlanta. The panels' common theme ("Post–Cold War International Relations in Asia Pacific") fit the general theme of the ISA conference: "Prospects for Progress in a Changing International Environment." I wish to acknowledge the warm support given by the ISA 1992 Program Committee chairman, Professor James Lee Ray of Florida State University, in endorsing the two panels for the annual conference.

The contributors to this volume demonstrated a superb self-discipline and sense of responsibility in submitting their panel papers and then the final drafts of their chapters on time and, in some cases, even well ahead of time. Steve Chan consistently finished his work months before the deadline, despite his sabbatical spent in Singapore part of the year. Bernard Gordon, who spent a term visiting at Kobe University, Japan, nonetheless finished two chapters on time. This hard work made my job as coordinator and editor much easier; I wish to thank all the contributors. I owe a special debt to Peter Chow for adding a chapter on regional integration as an original contribution to the book, meeting the deadline despite a family loss.

In the preparation of portions of this book, I was ably aided by my research assistant, Mr. Li Wei, at New York University. I also received generous comments and encouragement from my colleagues, among them Leah Haus and Steven Brams, as well as David Denoon. To them, and others who have helped, I owe my sincere thanks.

—JCH

■ NOTES

1. James A. Leach, "A Republican Looks at Foreign Policy," 71 *Foreign Affairs* 3:27 (Summer 1992).
2. Robert Jervis, "The Impact of the Korean War on the Cold War," 24 *Journal of Conflict Resolution* 4:563–592 (December 1980).
3. David Baldwin, "Power Analysis and World Politics," 31 *World Politics* 2: 161–194 (1979), develops the point about the nonfungibility of power and finds power to be not an undifferentiated mass but situation-specific. The U.S. nuclear force may be adequate to deter a Soviet missile attack, but was inadequate for deterring the North Koreans from capturing the Pueblo. Jeffrey Hart, "Three Approaches to the Measurement of Power in International Relations," 30 *International Organization* 2:289–305 (Spring 1976), defines power as control over resources, actors, and events. If control over resources cannot convert to control over events, he notes, then power, no matter how immense, is to no avail. Either Baldwin's or Hart's formulation would explain why, despite its vast high tech power, the United States failed in Vietnam.

■ Acronyms

AFTA	Asian Free Trade Area
APEC	Asia Pacific Economic Cooperation forum (formed in 1989—members are the U.S., Australia, New Zealand, Canada, Japan, China, Taiwan, South Korea, Hong Kong, and the ASEAN nations)
ASA	Association of Southeast Asia
ASEAN	Association of Southeast Asian Nations (Thailand, Malaysia, Singapore, Indonesia, Philippines, Brunei)
CIS	Commonwealth of Independent States (former Soviet Union)
EAEG/EAEC	East Asian Economic Group/Caucus
EC	European Community
GATT	General Agreement on Tariffs and Trade
IAEA	International Atomic Energy Agency
IMF	International Monetary Fund
KMT	Kuomintang (ruling party of Taiwan, aka Nationalists)
LDP	Liberal Democratic Party (ruling party of Japan)
MIA/POW	missing in action/prisoner of war
MITI	Ministry of International Trade and Industry (Japan)
MNCs	multinational corporations
NAFTA	North American Free Trade Agreement
NATO	North Atlantic Treaty Organization
NIC/NIE	newly industrializing country/economy (South Korea, Taiwan, Hong Kong, and Singapore)
NPT	Nonproliferation Treaty (1968)
OECD	Organization for Economic Cooperation and Development
PBEC	Pacific Basin Economic Council
PECC	Pacific Economic Cooperation Conference
PKO	peacekeeping operation
PRC	People's Republic of China (mainland China)
R&D	research and development
ROC	Republic of China (Taiwan)
SEATO	Southeast Atlantic Treaty Organization
ZOPFAN	zone of peace, freedom, and neutrality

■ 1

Asia Pacific in the Post–Cold War Order
James C. Hsiung

This chapter will address how the advent of the post–Cold War era will affect the balance of power in the Asia Pacific region. At the start, it is necessary to discuss what effects the post–Cold War era will bring to the *global* balance of power.

■ DEFINING THE END OF THE COLD WAR

That the Cold War has ended is now accepted as an indisputable fact. But it is neither clear exactly *when* was the genesis of the end of the era that had prevailed since the conclusion of World War II nor certain *what* the "end of the Cold War" really implies. The year 1991 is generally considered the watershed that marked the beginning of a qualitatively new era (cf. Chapter 2 below), following the tumultuous collapse of communism in Eastern Europe in 1989 and the disintegration of the Soviet Union two years hence.

However, the *earliest* beginnings of the end of the Cold War can be traced back much earlier. One could probably go as far back as the late 1970s, certainly no later than the early 1980s, when, as Richard J. Krickus (1987) put it, both superpowers were "in crisis" as a direct result of the mutual confrontation policy that necessitated their cutthroat nuclear arms race. Both superpowers, Krickus concludes, had to save themselves from the "crisis" of the mid-1980s by reversing the Cold War gears. Alternatively, one could agree with Richard Thornton (1985) that mid-1984 was the decisive crisis point in Soviet strategy, forcing the hand of Mikhail Gorbachev when he ascended to the post of general secretary of the Soviet Communist Party the following year. Since the Cuban Missile Crisis of 1962, two assumptions had underlined the Soviet bid to achieve military superiority over the United States. The first was that military superiority was a necessary and sufficient condition to alter the existing geopolitical balance to advantage. Second, the Soviets had assumed that the cost of attaining that condition could be borne without inflicting undue hardship upon the Soviet people. By mid-1984, however, it was clear to Moscow that both these assumptions had turned out to be false, as I shall explain below.

In the first place, after the successful U.S. anti-ballistic missile (ABM) test above Kwajalein Island in the Pacific, held on June 10, 1984 (Edwin Black 1984), it became devastatingly clear to the Soviets that, by employing current technology to combine a highly sensitive long-wavelength infrared sensor with an on-board optical homing device and solid-state minicomputer, the United States could design a nonnuclear ABM system capable of intercepting incoming ballistic missiles outside the earth's atmosphere at altitudes between 60 and 100 miles. This lesson raised the unhappy prospect that Moscow's twenty-year investment in offensive ballistic missile technology would soon be rendered obsolete and irrelevant (Thornton).

Second, in 1983–1984 Moscow suffered a double shock of agricultural failures and the precipitous decline of world petroleum prices. This double loss, which severely strained the Soviet economy, put Moscow's defense buildup in jeopardy. The severity of the strains can be seen from the fact that Soviet borrowings from Europe and Japan almost tripled in 1984, to nearly $3 billion (Michael Smith 1985). Thus, for the first time since the Soviet missile buildup began in 1962, Moscow came to grips with the stark reality that the strategy could not be pursued without wrecking the Soviet economy. Within three weeks of the Kwajalein test, on June 29, 1984, Moscow decided to return to the nuclear arms–reduction bargaining table in Geneva, from which they had walked away the previous November. Thus, Gorbachev's strategic rethinking, which was responsible for the general thaw with the United States—and, more specifically, for the eventual conclusion of the INF (Intermediate Range Force) reduction treaty of December 1987, as well as for the improved post-1987 Soviet attitude toward the United Nations (Hyland; Kozyrev; Bialer)—was all a product of this soul-searching imposed on the Soviet leadership in the aftermath of the mid-1984 crisis point.

Although I know of no serious attempt to define what the "end of the Cold War" really means in empirical terms, a parsimonious definition,[1] it seems to me, would have to include the following three desiderata:

1. The United States and the [former] Soviet Union no longer face each other off in a perpetual, ideologically motivated confrontation, in what used to be called the "bisuperpower conflict" (there is only one superpower left following Soviet collapse).

2. The two opposing alliance structures that underscored post–World War II world politics—as represented by the North Atlantic Treaty Organization (NATO) and the Warsaw Pact (WTO)—have ceased to be the vehicles for East-West conflict and have lost their own raison d'être. In fact, the WTO became extinct as of March 31, 1991. This demise would probably have happened even without the collapse of communism in Eastern Europe. With the conclusion of the Charter of Paris in November 1990, the thirty-four participants who were the original parties to the Helsinki Accord (minus East Germany, following the German unification) officially declared the end of the Cold War.

3. The international economic structure and the Third World are no longer the extended battlegrounds in the West's campaign against the communist world. To be more exact, these are no longer the domains from which the West endeavors to exclude the Eastern bloc. For confirmation of this change, beginning as early as late 1990, one need only look at two important developments: the extension of "observer" status to the Soviet Union by the General Agreement on Tariffs and Trade (GATT),[2] and the U.S.–Soviet alignment on the same side over the Gulf crisis of 1990–1991, in respect of both the Security Council votes on sanctions and, eventually, in the council's vote on using force against the recalcitrant Iraq. Like Moscow, Beijing also joined the United States in denouncing the acts of Saddam Hussein's Iraq, an incontrovertibly anti-West and anti-Israel Third World state that would have automatically won Chinese backing during the Cold War.

■ KEY ATTRIBUTES OF
THE NEW WORLD ORDER

The new world order following the end of the Cold War distinguishes itself in three key respects. First, a multipolar world will replace the bipolarity that dominated the world system for over four decades. Second, the post–Cold War world will witness the transition from nuclear to conventional deterrence. The third, and final, characteristic of the new world order is the rising importance of economic security to rival, even eclipse, military security (Hsiung 1991a). A few words of elaboration are in order for each of these pregnant points, which are at times counterintuitive.

☐ *Multipolarity*

Nuclear bipolarity since the late 1940s has served to guarantee what John Lewis Gaddis (1986) calls Europe's "long peace." In post–Cold War Europe, the continent sees the return of a fluid balance among six major powers. Measured by the size of their respective military forces alone, they are: the [former] Soviet Union, France, [united] Germany, Great Britain, Poland, and Hungary. In contrast to the nuclear bipolar system, however, the post–Cold War multipolarity bodes ill for the stability of the world system, for reasons I shall explain.

Multipolarity necessarily means an increase in the number of dyads and alliance permutations. It also means more uneven distribution of power across the system, making balance of power more difficult. In game-theoretic language, defections by states will be harder to detect as the number of players in the game expands; and the costs of sanctions against defections will also go up. These in turn will make deterrence correspondingly more difficult. In the real world, the multipolar system of 1816 through 1946 was one that was visited by numerous major wars, including the two world wars (Mearsheimer 1990, p. 154). Unlike other continents, Europe, with the largest group of developed nations, is the only one that is not going to see "time's cycle" (i.e., a return of the past). The post-bipolar "instability" may not take the same forms here as elsewhere (Jervis 1992, 46–55). But, for the moment, one can safely say that cohesions within NATO will be harder to maintain. In 1991, for example, dissensions surfaced in the course of the Yugoslav civil war over whether or not NATO ought to recognize the independence of the breakaway republics of Croatia and Slovenia. The assertiveness of (now united) Germany, which stood firm on the issue until other NATO members relented by early January 1992, is a case in point. Resurgent hypernationalism and ethnic disputes are other sources of conflict in Eastern Europe.

☐ *Decline in the Salience of Nuclear Deterrence*

In the Cold War era, the balance of terror made conquest difficult and expansion futile. The futility of expansion was only one, albeit an important, factor accounting for the robust deterrence that assured stability in the (nuclear) bipolar world. Other reasons for robust deterrence included the futility of nuclear overkill and the fear that a reverse proxy war might escalate into a nuclear conflagration embroiling the superpowers themselves (Hsiung 1992; Jervis 1985, pp. 193ff). As conventional deterrence returns, the world will have to brace itself for greater instability emanating from the inherent power imbalance. As there is no equivalent of an overkill restraint on conventional weapons, the unchecked races in conventional armaments will create endless imbalances, affecting systemic stability.

Proliferation of biochemical and other weapons of massive destruction will further complicate the situation. Deterrence, which has to depend on threat making, will be more difficult, as threat making will not work well in conditions of power imbalance. If directed against the inferior party, the threats will heighten that party's resolve to redress the balance. (Following the second Moroccan crisis in 1911, Germany decided to catch up with Great Britain militarily, in response to Lloyd George's unyielding stance [Langer 1952, p. 758].) If, conversely, threats are directed against the superior party, they will only encourage it to strike first before the balance is reversed. (Thus, Germany decided to strike first in 1914 to arrest the incipient erosion of the superiority enjoyed by the Dual Alliance of Germany and Austro-Hungary, vis-à-vis the military might of the Triple Entente, paving the way for World War I [Sarbrosky 1989].)

Empirically, the nineteenth century was a typical period of conventional deterrence. If Alan Alexandroff's study (1981, p. 67) is any indication, conventional deterrence had only a 37 percent chance of success.

In the "nonnuclear," multipolar world emerging from the ashes of bipolarity, the world's stability is most likely to be threatened by local bullies, some armed with weapons of massive destruction, such as Saddam Hussein's Iraq.

☐ *Rise of Geoeconomics*

Because of both the end of the Cold War and the dire internal problems underscoring the disintegration of the (former) Soviet Union, the military threat once ominously posed by the "evil empire" has fast receded. (A residual threat, though, is posed by the uncertain control over the nuclear armaments inherited from the former Soviet authority by the components of the successor commonwealth, such as surfaced in the feuds between Ukraine and Russia.)

In the postnuclear world, nations will rely for their security on their own means of defense (as opposed to the nuclear umbrella extended by a superpower). In other words, national weapons of states will replace extended nuclear deterrence. Consequently, the requirements for world leadership, or hegemony, will be different. During the Cold War era, U.S. hegemony was in large measure founded on that crucial public good—i.e., the nuclear deterrence umbrella—that Washington was able to provide to its allies and followers. More than ever before, however, the hegemon will now find its leadership dependent on its ability to provide stable international monetary, financial, and trading conditions in the new world order. The United States can no longer lead just from its nuclear predominance, and it will be at a disadvantage as it is forced by the new circumstances to compete, in the economic domain, with such economic superpowers as Japan and Germany (Makin 1989, pp. 10–18). In terms of international relations theory, geoeconomics will replace geopolitics in the global strategic-balance-of-power game, as economic security intrudes into our consciousness (Dell 1987).

■ EFFECTS ON ASIA PACIFIC

Given the critical changes in the post–Cold War world, as noted above, one logical question for our interest is: How will all this change affect Asia Pacific in terms of its international relations? The question, in turn, subsumes three interrelated but separate subquestions, namely: (1) How will the global changes manifest themselves at the Asia Pacific regional level? (2) Is there anything on the Asia Pacific horizon that deviates from the global patterns? and, finally, (3) How will all these new circumstances affect the relations among members of the Asia Pacific region? The ensuing chapters in the volume will, each in its own way, attempt to provide some answers, more particularly to the third subquestion. In the remainder of this chapter, I shall attempt to tackle the other two subquestions.

□ *Global Changes and Asia Pacific*

Let us first examine how the global changes outlined above will manifest themselves at the Asia Pacific regional level.

The rise of multipolarity on the global level is to be repeated on the Asia Pacific regional level. Here, the game will be played out by four major powers: the United States, China, Japan, and the successor state to the Soviet Union. Of the four, only Japan is not a nuclear power, although it has the wherewithal to become one should domestic politics so direct. Outside the four major powers, the region's alignment patterns will probably revolve around two other clusters: (1) the so-called Asian NIEs (newly industrializing economies)—i.e., South Korea, Taiwan, Hong Kong, and Singapore; and (2) the Association of Southeast Asian Nations (ASEAN), which consists of Thailand, Malaysia, Singapore, Indonesia, the Philippines, and Brunei. Neither cluster is an alliance. The common concern about stability in Indochina since the Vietnam War has been a contributing factor to the relative cohesion of the ASEAN as a loose policy-coordinating network. The post–Cold War changes, including the truce in Cambodia, may or may not affect the vigil that has underscored the ASEAN consensus. One interesting development was the signing by Vietnam, along with Laos, of a treaty of amity and cooperation with ASEAN members on July 2, 1992.

As for the Asian NIEs, Hong Kong will revert to Chinese sovereignty in 1997, pursuant to the Sino-British treaty of 1984. The remaining NIEs—South Korea, Taiwan, and Singapore—will probably find their respective futures better served by the nascent Asia Pacific Economic Cooperation (APEC) forum than by going alone (see Chapter 10). Barring unforeseen circumstances, they will most likely be drawn into the Japanese economic orbit, with some possible variations, as described below.

In the first place, after U.S. withdrawal from Subic Bay in the Philippines after 1992, Singapore will be drawn closer to the United States as it agrees to serve as a naval tending and resupply station for the U.S. Seventh Fleet (Conboy 1992, p. 8). Second, if unification should come to the Korean peninsula and to the two Chinese nations separated since 1949 by the Taiwan Strait, the strategic fault lines of alignment in the area will look very different from now.

Nevertheless, to the extent that nuclear capability will count less as an index of power in the new age, the power ratio among the four major actors in the region will be redefined. In the postnuclear world, Japan's present 250,000–strong conventional forces, which exist under the euphemism of "self-defense forces" to circumvent the country's constitutional outlawry of an armed force, will figure much more prominently on the international scales of power. It is in this context that one has to view the recent Diet approval of PKO (peacekeeping operations), authorizing the dispatch of Japanese forces to join UN missions. Invoking traumatic memories of the past, the prospect of sending Japanese forces abroad brought strong reactions in China, Korea, and Taiwan, among other places, immediately after the Diet vote in mid-June 1992. Japan's defense budget, at $32.9 billion in 1991, was more than four times China's $7.5 billion (International Institute of Strategic Studies 1991, p. 150; p. 165). By 1990 Japan's defense budget was already the world's third largest, after the United States's $292 billion and the Soviet Union's official $117 billion (Cropsey 1991, p. 5).

Earlier, we noted that a probable wrinkle to the postnuclear multipolar order is the local-bully syndrome exemplified by Saddam Hussein's Iraq. In Asia Pacific, that problem may find an incarnation in the last remaining Stalinist regime, North Korea, which is known to have nuclear aspirations. In a very real sense, Pyongyang's bid to acquire a nuclear capability is a vestige of the Cold War. But a nuclear North Korea will offer powerful incentives for South Korea to go nuclear, with repercussions extending even to Japan. That will no doubt complicate the regional balance in Northeast Asia. The final, though reluctant, consent by Pyongyang to open its nuclear sites to inspections by the International Atomic Energy Agency (IAEA) in early 1992 signified the end, though after a delay, of the Cold War in the Korean Peninsula.[3]

A speck on the horizon, though, is the reported Japanese importation of plutonium, an element indispensable for nuclear energy generation but also the stuff atomic bombs are made of. Only eight kilograms (or 17.6 pounds) of reprocessed plutonium are needed to make a Nagasaki-grade bomb. The first shipment of thirty tons of reprocessed plutonium arrived in Japan in January 1993. By the year 2000, if the country's energy planners have their way, Japan will have accumulated at least ninety tons of the material (*Economist* April 18, 1992, p. 32). It remains to be seen to what use the Japanese will put their imported plutonium. But in the post–Cold War era, whether Japan will become a nuclear weapons state is immaterial for its status as an economic superpower.

As military confrontation at the global level phases out, calculations regarding the power configuration of states will increasingly have to weigh in each nation's economic prowess. This observation takes us to the third, and last, characteristic of the new world order noted above: the rise of geoeconomics, wherein economic security will likely outweigh military security.

Future competition in Asia Pacific, as elsewhere, will be primarily in the economic sphere. More than ever, a country's claim to being a major power will be based on its economic might. In order to assess the future of geoeconomic interests in this region, we have to place it in the larger context of the global political economy.

As a result of the rising importance of economic security and the potential of regional protectionism, the world by the year 2000 is likely to face a multiplication of economic power centers. Western Europe, North America, and Asia Pacific are each likely to become a mammoth free trade superbloc unto itself (Garten 1989). From this assumption, we will proceed to make a few general propositions regarding the macropolitical situation likely to emerge in the coming century.

First, by virtue of its phenomenal economic success and rapid growth rates, which are expected to continue well into the twenty-first century, Asia Pacific will stand out as the most crucial region for the United States in comparison with other groupings of nations. By 2000, according to the *Asian Wall Street Journal*, the Asia Pacific region's combined GNP of $13 trillion will be double that of the integrated European Community (EC). If that figure seems overly upbeat, a more sober U.S. government estimate puts the combined GNP of Northeast Asia (comprising just Japan, China, Taiwan, and South Korea) at $8.5 trillion by the year 2010 (Rand 1989). This figure tops the estimated $7.9 trillion for the United States or the estimate of comparable size for Western Europe by the same year.

Two indices will factor into any comparative forecasts for the future. One is Asia Pacific's aggregate population, which at 1.7 billion (1991) is almost three times the combined total of North America's (279 million) and Western Europe's (345 million). The Western rim of the Pacific, from Japan in the north to Australia in the south, contains about 40 percent of the world's population. The other, and more important, index is Asia Pacific's sustained high economic growth rate for the last decade, which has averaged over 6 percent annually, as compared with North America's 2.7 percent and Western Europe's 2.3 percent during the same period (International Financial Statistics 1990). Even in the face of the slow growth rates of the world's major economic powers in the early 1990s, the Asian NIEs (South Korea, Taiwan, Hong Kong, and Singapore), plus Thailand and Malaysia, were expected to show annual growth of 7 percent or higher, according to the Organization for Economic Development and Co-operation (OECD).[4] Between 1960 and 1982, the ratio of Asia Pacific gross domestic product (GDP) to U.S. GDP grew from 18 percent to 53.2 percent (Linder 1986, p. 11). By 2000, the whole Pacific region will account for 50 percent of the world's gross national product (GNP), with the western Pacific alone posting a 25 percent share of world GNP. Available statistics also show that the economies in the Asia Pacific basin will continue to grow faster than those of the United States or Western Europe (Linder 1986, p. 13; Drysdale 1986, p. 11f). Looking to the twenty-first century, many expect the world's ecopolitical gravity to shift to Asia Pacific, and one of the reasons is that this is the only region that can provide a counterbalance to Western Europe.

Second, as the European Community is poised to move into a fully integrated "single market," the United States is to confront a condition of uncertainty utterly unparalleled in history (U.S. Department of State 1988). The stakes are high. The EC has 345 million people and a combined GNP of over $5.9 trillion. The EC's trade with the United States is second, as a region, only to U.S. trade with Asia Pacific (Statistical Abstract 1990).[5] Despite the EC's assurances that market integration will not result in "Fortress Europe," there is a risk, nonetheless, that intra-European deals will be made and a Eurocentric regime inaugurated at the expense of outside trading partners. For one thing, there is more intraregional trade within the EC than in any other region. The trend may only expand after the consummation of the EC single-market initiative. If so, the United States will be impelled by circumstances to move even closer to Asia Pacific in meeting its economic security needs (more on this point in Chapter 12).

Third, the economic might of Asia Pacific will have a peculiar significance for world politics in the next century, as the successor state to the former Soviet Union recedes from the position as the world's third-largest economic power, which the USSR had occupied. This retreat would happen even if the Soviet Union had not come apart and the Cold War had not ended (Commission on Integrated Long-Term Strategy 1988, p. 20). The United States, however, is likely to face an unusual situation in which the fading military threat of a longtime adversary (the USSR) will be replaced by the potent economic threat of a longtime client and partner (Japan).

As economic security becomes more important than military security in the new era, the Japanese threat will be even more acute. Many fear that Japan will pose as the primary threat to the United States in the region. This threat will heighten as the Japanese lead in technologies and economic expansion continues to grow. The increase in Japanese influence in the region means a relative decline in U.S. influence (Huntington 1991, p. 10). Not surprisingly, the United States is already obsessed with Japan "for the same reasons that it was obsessed with the Soviet Union" before.[6]

These fears may or may not be justified, but they typify the centrality of economic security concerns in the post–Cold War world. The geoeconomic preoccupation will shape much of international relations in Asia Pacific as elsewhere. For instance, the Gulf crisis of 1990–1991 taught the Japanese a crucial lesson about economic security. It drove home the vulnerability of Japan's economy resulting from its dependency on extraregional supplies of vital resources. Access to these supplies could be in jeopardy at any flare-up of a crisis in a far-off place. Japan, therefore, learned to appreciate, even more than before, the value of a closer-to-home sourcing of strategic resources. Thus, while other industrial nations still stuck to their post-Tiananmen sanctions, Japan began quietly in the fall of 1990—i.e., during the course of the Gulf crisis—to switch gears and upgrade its relations with China.[7]

☐ *Any Deviations from the Global Pattern?*

The above discussion shows that the global patterns characteristic of the post–Cold War world order hold true for Asia Pacific, by and large. Our next question is whether there is anything that marks the region off as distinct from other areas. For one thing, Asia Pacific, in the 1990s, is the only region in the world where not just one but a group of communist regimes has survived the death of communism in Eastern Europe and the Soviet Union. Besides in China, Communist regimes exist in North Korea and Indochina. Furthermore, the residual Communists in the former Communist-ruled Mongolia reconstituted themselves as the Mongolian People's Revolutionary Party (MPRP) and still retain control, having won 95 percent of the seats in Parliament in the June 28, 1992, election. This situation stands in stark contrast to the lone existence of Cuba in Latin America.

One other possible variation from the global norm seems to be in the area of nuclear proliferation. On closer examination, however, the area's only open challenge to the worldwide nuclear nonproliferation regime is North Korea's attempt to acquire nuclear weapons. That exception alone does not make Asia Pacific much different from either South Asia or the Middle East. In the former, India and Pakistan vie with each other in a conscious nuclear arms race. (In July 1992, New Delhi made it known that India would not become party to the Nonproliferation Treaty [NPT] before 1995, when the pact is up for review and renewal, and even after that would ratify only with severe conditions.)[8] In the Middle East, Saddam Hussein is trying to develop Iraq into a nuclear-armed power in competition with Israel. One other wrinkle on the proliferation score is China's reported assistance to Syria and Algeria in their respective bids to develop nuclear armaments. Beijing has persistently denied these allegations. But, even if the reports are true, the instances simply add to the massive evidence of what Jennifer Scarlott (1991, p. 691ff) calls the "weakness of the nonproliferation regime."

The lack of any effective enforcement of the nonproliferation regime allowed significant transfers of nuclear-bomb material and technology in past decades. The United States assisted France with its nuclear program; the United States, Canada, and Great Britain assisted India; Germany, Great Britain, the United States, and Israel assisted South Africa; France and the United States assisted Israel; France, West Germany, and the United States assisted Iran; and the Soviet Union assisted Libya, Syria, and Cuba (Scarlott 1991, p. 690). As John Mearsheimer (1990, p. 228) suggests, a consequence of the withdrawal of the superpower nuclear umbrella in the post–Cold War era is likely to be regional nuclear proliferation. The race to acquire nuclear weapons by North Korea, Syria, and Libya, not to mention Iraq and others, may well be indications of this phenomenon. One heartening turn of events, nevertheless, is China's acceptance of the Nonproliferation Treaty at the close of 1991.[9] This move will allow inspections by the IAEA for the safeguarding of both material and technology. It is an indication that China's leaders have come to the realization that nonproliferation is in China's interest in the postnuclear world. For in the new era, security in Asia Pacific, as in other areas, will not depend on nuclear deterrence, at least not to the same extent as before.

On another score, Asia Pacific has been spared the sort of ethnonational strifes that has plagued post–Cold War Europe. True, there are memories of multicommunal schisms in Malaysia, insurrections in the Philippines, and ethnic fights in Sri Lanka and (former) Burma. But there has not been any large-scale conflict approximating the civil war in Yugoslavia or the ethnic disputes in post-Soviet republics and bicommunal Cyprus. If the post–Cold War order is going to bring greater instability to the Asia Pacific region, it will probably take the form of tensions *across* national boundaries rather than within them. Although Asia Pacific has been spared the kind of hypernationalism that has surfaced in post–Cold War Europe, the region has seen an occasional rise in nationalist sentiments, such as in South Korea, Japan, Taiwan, Vietnam, the Philippines, and even New Zealand. With few exceptions, these upsurges of nationalism were largely anti–United States in nature. In Japan, the former Soviet Union has been the target of part of the resurgent Japanese nationalism when the issue is the disputed northern islands. At other times, when trade is the focus, the target may shift to the United States. The most virulent anti–U.S. sentiments probably surged in street riots in such places as Kwangju and Seoul, South Korea; but these instances took place before 1991 and were quite unrelated to the Cold War issue. The important thing, it remains true, is that there has been no significant flare-up of conflicts fueled by Asian nationalism to date.

■ SECURITY IN POST–COLD WAR ASIA PACIFIC

This discussion of the new world order as it bears on Asia Pacific would not be complete if it said nothing specifically about the region's security in terms of the traditional interests of national defense (as opposed to geoeconomic interests). There is no doubt that, for the half-century since the end of the Pacific War in 1945, regionwide security in Asia Pacific has been largely dependent on the hegemonic role played by the United States. U.S. security policy in this region, as in the rest of the world, was based on two desiderata: (1) Cold War commitment to containing Soviet expansionism, and (2) U.S. self-reliance on its own preponderant power (Bosworth 1992, p. 113). One might add a qualification that, for lack of a better term, may be called "Eurocentricity" (Harris 1991, p. 2), in that Washington tended to see Asian issues basically in light of their European consequences as part of the bipolar ideological conflict in the world.

By now, both the Cold War commitment and the assumed sufficiency of U.S. preponderance are in doubt. The attribute of Eurocentricity is also in question. In view of our discussions above about the paramountcy of economic interests and the weight of Asia Pacific's economic dynamism, one may reasonably expect that the United States will henceforth have to consider Asia Pacific's security in its own right, in terms of its strategic value to U.S. interests, without regard to Europe or even at Europe's expense.

Furthermore, there is a distinct geopolitical transformation in the Eurasian land mass requiring some serious rethinking of the United States' global strategic design. In contrast to the state of affairs prevailing at the close of World War II, when the Eurasian heartland was strong and its peripheries weak, the situation today is simply reversed: the heartland power (i.e., the former Soviet Union) is in the throes of crisis, and the Eurasian peripheries are generally strong (Scalapino 1991). Nowhere is this strength more evident than in the outreaches of the western Pacific Rim. We shall reserve the concluding chapter as the place for doing a bit of "horizon-gazing" into the next century. Among other things, we shall then speculate on what is likely to be a sensible U.S. security strategy befitting the new era. At this juncture, however, we shall do no more than take a brief glance at the region's security landscape. This we will do by briefly assessing what has happened to the post-1945 "security theaters," now that the Cold War has ended and the Eurasian heartland power is undergoing the crisis of dismemberment.

□ State of the Traditional Security Theaters

Before the dawn of the new age, four security theaters were usually identified (Morley 1986, p. 11), as follows:

1. The Sea of Okhotsk—where Japan, supported by the United States, was in dispute with the Soviet Union over the ownership of four islands to the north of Hokkaido;
2. The Korean Peninsula—where North Korea, backed by the Soviets and the mainland Chinese, was locked with a U.S.-backed South Korea in a struggle for survival and for the control of the peninsula;
3. The Taiwan Strait—where mainland China's bid to reunify with Taiwan was surrounded by uncertainty; and
4. The Sino-Soviet border—where China, Outer Mongolia, and the Soviet Union had heavy forces deployed in a potentially confrontational posture.

Until 1991, these were the four potential flash points where a serious armed conflict could erupt in any crisis. But as the global and regional security map has drastically changed, the nature of the problems surrounding the four security theaters has changed accordingly.

Of the four security theaters named above, the first one, the Sea of Okhotsk, has lost much of its previous strategic value as a haven for anchoring 30 percent of the Soviet submarine-launched ballistic missile (SLBM) force. This force would have been an important part of the Soviet second-strike capability should a nuclear war break out with the United States at the height of the Cold War. To the Soviets in the 1980s, the Okhotsk SLBM force was second in importance only to the Soviet SLBM forces shielded under the Barents Sea and the adjacent Arctic waters (Jacobson 1982, Chapter 3). But as the age of nuclear deterrence recedes to the background, the relevance of the Sea of Okhotsk to Russia is largely limited to the latter's relations with Japan, more specifically with regard to the four disputed islands. As an economic superpower, Japan commands tremendous resources and is in a strong position to deal with the disputes without involving any external power. Thus, in the new international milieu, the Okhotsk seems no longer a trouble spot threatening the region's security as before.

Another potential trouble spot, the Sino-Soviet border, was first mollified by the Sino-Soviet normalization of May 1989, then rendered moribund by the Soviet collapse after 1991. That leaves us only the Korean Peninsula and the Taiwan Strait remaining as potential sore points.

Two important developments on the Korean Peninsula unfolded in the course of 1991: (1) North Korea agreed to accept IAEA inspections of its nuclear plants; and (2) the two Koreas concluded a historic agreement of mutual nonaggression on December 12, 1991. These developments seem to have greatly reduced the security liability of the Korean Peninsula for the immediate future.

The last remaining spot on our list of potential security theaters is, therefore, the Taiwan Strait, to which we shall now turn. For the first time, the interests of mainland China and Taiwan began to move toward convergence after 1987. At the time, Taiwan, under the late President Chiang Ching-kuo, was facing severe pressure from Washington to reduce its reliance on the U.S. market and to democratize. In order to support both moves, Chiang decided to explore overtures with mainland China across the Taiwan Strait in search of alternative markets. The first step was to open the floodgates for visits to relatives on the mainland by the surviving veterans of the Nationalist military personnel who had evacuated with the Kuomintang (KMT) to Taiwan in 1949 (Hsiung 1991b, p. 376). This move, begun in late 1987, was received and reciprocated by Beijing with great enthusiasm. Later, the right to visit the mainland was extended to other constituents in Taiwan and, by 1992, even to faculty and university presidents in the state-run sector of the higher education system, plus some lower echelons of government bureaucracy, up to the subcabinet levels. One thing led to another. By the end of 1991, three million people from Taiwan had visited the mainland, including many on business trips. Indirect trade (via Hong Kong) had topped $5.8 billion (Fang Sheng 1992). In the first half of 1992, this trade increased by 34 percent over the same period of the previous year, to a total of $3.4 billion.[10] Taiwan investments in 2,000-some projects on the mainland in 1990 aggregated $1.6 billion (Silk 1990; N. T. Wang 1991). Mainland China became Taiwan's fifth-largest trade market, whereas Taiwan was the mainland's sixth-largest trading partner (Fang Sheng 1992, p. 30).

In early 1991, a National Unification Commission (NUC) under the direct supervision of the president sprang into being in Taipei. To help implement its policy directives, a new cabinet-level action arm known as the Mainland Affairs Council was created. In addition, a semiofficial Straits Exchange Foundation (SEF) was set up to run errands for the council on a contractual basis. It sent its first delegation on an exploratory mission to Beijing, where it met with officials in the Taiwan Relations Office under the State Council in April–May 1991. The SEF has since developed into a conduit for routine liaisons with the mainland. More important, a "historic" National Unification Program was adopted, after much debate, by the NUC in March 1991 as the ultimate directive guiding Taiwan's approach to its relations with the mainland (Hsiung 1992). On May 1, 1991, the Nationalist government in Taipei officially ended its hostility toward the Communist regime on the mainland by ending the so-called period of Mobilization for the Suppression of Communist Rebellion after more than forty years.

Taiwan did condition its further opening to the mainland on Beijing's pursuing internal democratization, renouncing the use of force in dealing with Taiwan on unification, and agreeing not to isolate Taiwan diplomatically. Although it remains to be seen where all these developments will lead, one thing is clear: Contacts between the two sides across the Taiwan

Strait are no longer illegal. Besides, exchanges are now institutionalized and coordinated at the operating level between the SEF and the Association for Relations Across the Taiwan Straits inaugurated on the mainland in 1991. The latter serves as a counterpart to Taiwan's SEF, coordinating all routine liaisons from Beijing's end.

This cursory account of the developments since 1987 is enough to illustrate the drastic transformation of relations across the Taiwan Strait. It is questionable whether the Taiwan Strait should remain on the list of potential trouble spots posing security threats for the Asia Pacific region.

All the above events demonstrate the extent to which the end of the Cold War has affected Asia Pacific in terms of regional security.

☐ *Territorial Disputes*

Earlier we said that future conflicts in Asia Pacific will probably not follow the ethnic and ethnonational lines that have characterized turmoils engulfing Yugoslavia and the post-Soviet republics. Instead, we believe future conflicts in this region will be *across* national boundaries, not within them. Now that we have eliminated one by one the four so-called security theaters, the only instances of instability will most likely be territorial disputes. We can think of three broad areas where these can happen:

1. Russian-Japanese disputes over the four northern islands off Hokkaido and at the fringe of the Sea of Okhotsk;
2. Sino-Russian boundary disputes, particularly over the vast tracts of land lying north of the Amur River and east of the Ussouri River, totaling 600,000 square miles (or twelve times the size of New York state), which Manchu China lost under duress to czarist Russians per the Tientsin Treaty of 1858; and
3. Offshore islands in the Yellow Sea (the Diaoyutai/Senkaku Island), with China and Japan as the contending claimants, and in the South China Sea, over the Paracels and Spratlys. At least seven parties, including China, Vietnam, Malaysia, Indonesia, Brunei, the Philippines, and Taiwan, have laid claims to the latter islands, which are rich in oil and other resources (Harris 1991, p. 17). I will return to this question in Chapter 4.

One related issue is the fate of the geostrategic straits and channels in Southeast Asia, where Malaysia and the Indonesia archipelago intersect (see Map 1.1). Only a few of the myriad channels through the Indonesia archipelago are wide and deep enough to permit the safe passage of submerged submarines. Control over these channels could be used to monitor or interdict the passage of warships or merchant vessels moving between the western Pacific and the Indian Ocean. The channels are: (1) the Sunda

Strait, with a governing depth of 120 feet and a minimum width of twelve nautical miles; (2) the Lombok Straits, with a depth of 600 feet and a width of eleven nautical miles; (3) the Ombai-Wetar Straits, with a depth of 600 feet and a width of twelve nautical miles; and (4) the Straits of Malacca, with a depth of 75 feet and a minimum width of eight nautical miles.[11] During the Cold War era, control of these straits in friendly hands was essential to thwarting Soviet antisubmarine warfare (ASW) measures and maintaining effective U.S. ASW systems (Garver 1983, p. 89f). Until 1992, the United States was determined, at all costs, to retain its Subic Bay and Clark Field bases in the Philippines largely for the sake of control over these choke points. In the new era, it is unlikely that the Russians will pose similar threats in these waters, although the Pacific Fleet inherited from the former Soviet navy remains the largest of the Russian fleets. It goes without saying that it is in U.S. interests that these channels not fall into unfriendly hands, whomever they may be, in the future. The loss of U.S. bases in the Philippines, nonetheless, will mean that U.S. surveillance over the strategic straits will weaken. But it also signifies the advent of the new era.

Under a joint border committee, Malaysia and Indonesia have exchanged intelligence on some maritime security issues. Similar intelligence-sharing arrangements are known to exist with Singapore (Richard Stubbs 1992, p. 404). Presumably, the three ASEAN nations will be the guardians of the strategic channels just mentioned if the U.S. military presence should dwindle in western Pacific after 1992. The recent revival of the Five Power Defense Arrangement (FPDA), which ties the nonregional countries of Australia, Great Britain, and New Zealand into the defense of Singapore and Malaysia, will provide an additional framework for security cooperation. Greater coordination is expected for the future in the areas of defense policy, military training, and armament procurement among ASEAN countries (Stubbs, p. 405f). It is likely that a result of the end of the Cold War, as it affects Asia Pacific, is that the ASEAN will increasingly assume common defense functions for its members, quite contrary to its primary focus on trade cooperation thus far. Again, for states and regional organizations (such as ASEAN) to assume a greater share of the defense burden is a natural outgrowth of the demise of nuclear bipolarity, which necessarily removed the fortuitous benefits of the nuclear umbrella such as a superpower was able to provide.

■ CONCLUSION

We have seen how the major global effects stemming from the end of the Cold War will likewise appear on the Asia Pacific regional scene in the new era. These include the characteristics of the new era: multipolarity, the receding salience of nuclear deterrence, and the rising importance

Map 1.1   Strategic Straits in the Southeast Asian Region

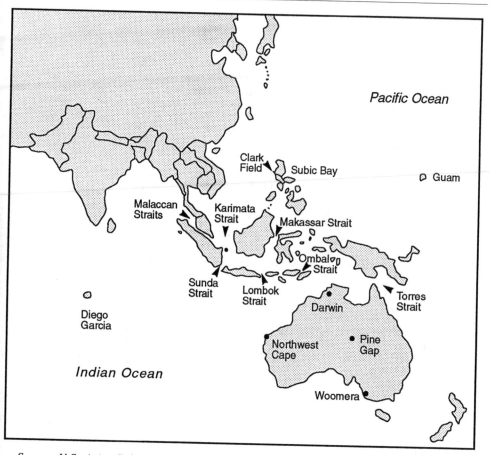

Source: U.S.–Asian Relations, ed., James C. Hsiung. New York: Praeger, 1983; p. 90. An imprint of Greenwood Publishing Group, Inc. Westport, CT. Reprinted with permission.

of economic security (as distinct from military security). Whatever deviations are discernible at the moment are mainly variations of the essentially similar patterns, such as in how postbipolar instability manifests itself. Instead of ethnic and ethnonational strifes, such as have infested post–Cold War Europe, the new instability in Asia Pacific will take the form of territorial disputes, or conflicts across, rather than within, national boundaries. But it bears reiterating that future security concerns, here as elsewhere, will be largely of a geoeconomic sort. So fundamental has been the transformation of the structure of international relations that all nations in the Pacific Basin, as elsewhere, will have to rethink their security strategy accordingly.

■ NOTES

1. I am relying on my own formulation in Hsiung 1991a.
2. The United States, in a shift of approach to aid to Moscow, called on the International Monetary Fund to ease demands for harsh reform and not to delay aid agreement once Moscow commits itself to economic changes. See *New York Times*, June 19, 1992, p. 1.
3. North Korea agreed to these inspections in early 1992. See *New York Times*, January 7, 1992.
4. As reported by the Reuters in a dispatch from Paris, dated June 25, 1992. See *Qiao Bao* (The China Press) (New York), June 26, 1992, p. 1.
5. U.S. trade with Asia Pacific (Japan, South Korea, Taiwan, Hong Kong, and Singapore) is the largest share of U.S. global trade. It totaled $229.9 billion in 1988, which was $35.4 billion higher than U.S. trade with Western Europe (including OECD), or $47.1 billion over U.S. trade with EEC the same year. Figures compiled from *Statistical Abstract* 1990, p. 808f, Table 1406.
6. Interview with Samuel Huntington, *New York Times*, December 9, 1991. 1991.
7. "Japan to Mend China Ties While World Eyes the Gulf," *Japan Times Weekly*, September 24–30, 1991, p. 1.
8. Associated Press dispatch from New Delhi, dated June 30, 1992.
9. *Renmin Ribao* [People's Daily] (Overseas Edition), December 30, 1991, p. 1.
10. According to statistics released by the trade office, Ministry of Economic Affairs (Taipei), reported in a dispatch from Taipei, carried by the *Qiao Bao* (The China Press) (New York), August 27, 1992, p. 2.
11. Michael Richardson, "Missile Maneuvers," *Far Eastern Economic Review*, April 30, 1982, pp. 32–33; cited in John Garver 1983, p. 89.

■ REFERENCES

Alexandroff, Allan. 1981. *The Logic of Diplomacy*. Beverly Hills, CA: Sage Publications.
Bialer, Seweryn, and Michael Mandelbaum. 1988. *Gorbachev's Russia and American Foreign Policy*. Boulder, CO: Westview Press.
Black, Edwin. 1984. "Why the Soviets Sought the Talks," *Washington Times*, August 2, 1984, p. 1c.

Bosworth, Stephen. 1992. "The U.S. and Asia," 71 *Foreign Affairs* 1 (Winter 1991–1992).

Chan, Steve, and Cal Clark. 1992. The *Evolving Pacific Community*. Boulder, CO: Lynne Rienner Publishers.

Commission on Integrated Long-Term Strategy. 1988. *Discriminate Deterrence*. Washington, D.C.: Government Printing Office.

Conboy, Kenneth J. 1992. "The U.S.–Singapore Relationship: A Model for Southeast Asia," Asian Studies Center, *Backgrounder* 120 (March 12, 1992). Washington, D.C.: Heritage Foundation.

Cropsey, Seth. 1991. "The Washington-Tokyo Defense Relationship: Where Now?" *Backgrounder* 116 (September 20, 1991). Washington, D.C.: Heritage Foundation.

Dell, Edmund. 1987. *Politics of Economic Interdependence*. New York: St. Martin's Press.

Drysdale, Peter. 1986. "The Pacific Basin and Its Economic Vitality." In *The Pacific Basin*, ed. James W. Morley. New York: Academy of Political Science.

Fang Sheng. 1992. "Prospects for Mainland-Taiwan Relations," *Beijing Review*, April 27–May 3, 1992, pp. 30–32.

Gaddis, John Lewis. 1986. "The Long Peace: Elements of Stability in the Postwar International System," 10 *International Security* 4:99–142.

Garten, Jeffrey E. 1989. "Trading Blocs and the Evolving World Economy," *Current History* (January 1989).

Garver, John. 1983. "The Reagan Administration's Southeast Asian Policy." In *U.S.–Asian Relations: The National Security Paradox*, ed. James C. Hsiung. New York: Praeger.

Harris, Stuart. 1991. "The Political and Strategic Framework in Northeast Asia." In *The End of the Cold War in Northeast Asia*, eds. Stuart Harris and James Cotton. Boulder, CO: Lynne Rienner Publishers.

Hsiung, James. 1991a. "The Post–Cold War World Order and the Gulf Crisis," 18 *Asian Affairs* 1:31–42 (Spring 1991).

Hsiung, James. 1991b. "The Political Economy of Taiwan's Democratization." In *Distribution of Power and Rewards*, eds. James C. Hsiung and Chung-ying Cheng. Lanham, MD: University Press of America.

Hsiung, James. 1992. "China in the Twenty-First Century Global Balance: Challenge and Policy Response." In *The Evolving Pacific Community*, eds. Steve Chan and Cal Clark. Boulder, CO: Lynne Rienner Publishers.

Huntington, Samuel P. 1991. "America's Changing Strategic Interests," 33 *Survival* 1:3–17.

Hyland, William. 1990. *The Cold War Is Over*. New York: Knopf.

International Financial Statistics Yearbook: 1991. Washington, D.C.: International Monetary Fund.

International Institute of Strategic Studies. 1991. *The Military Balance: 1991–1992*. London: IISS.

Jacobsen, C. G. 1982. *The Nuclear Era: Its History; Its Implications*. Cambridge, MA: Oelgeschlage, Gunn and Hain.

Jervis, Robert, Richard Ned Lebow, and Janice Gross Stein. 1985. *Psychology and Deterrence*. Baltimore, MD: Johns Hopkins University Press.

Jervis, Robert. 1992. "The Future of World Politics: Will It Resemble the Past?" 16 *International Security* 3:39–73 (Winter 1991–1992).

Kozyrev, Andrei V. 1990. "The New Soviet Attitude Toward the U.N.," 13 *Washington Quarterly*, 3:41–53 (Summer 1990).

Krickus, Richard J. 1987. *The Superpowers in Crisis: Implications of Domestic Discord*. New York: Pergamon-Brassey's.

Langer, William. 1952. *An Encyclopedia of World History.* Boston: Houghton Mifflin.

Linder, Staffan. 1986. *The Pacific Century: Economic and Political Consequences of Asian-Pacific Dynamism.* Stanford, CA: Stanford University Press.

Makin, John. 1989. "American Economic and Military Leadership . . ." In *Sharing World Leadership? A New Era for America and Japan,* eds. John H. Makin and Donald C. Hellmann. Washington, D.C.: American Enterprise Institute.

Mearsheimer, John. 1990. "Back to the Future," 15 *International Security,* 1:6–56.

Morley, James W. 1986. *Security Interdependence in the Asia Pacific Region.* Lexington, MA: D.C. Heath.

Rand. 1989. *Long-Term Economic and Military Trends: 1950–2010.* Santa Monica, CA: Rand.

Sarbrosky, Alan Ned. 1989. "From Bosnia to Sarajevo." In *Choices in World Politics,* eds. Bruce Russet, Harvey Starr, and Richard Stoll. New York: W. H. Freeman.

Scalapino, Robert. 1991. "The U.S. and Asia: Future Prospects," 70 *Foreign Affairs* 5:19–40 (Winter 1991–1992).

Scarlott, Jennifer. 1991. "Nuclear Proliferation After the Cold War," *World Political Journal* (Fall 1991), pp. 687–710.

Silk, Mitchell A. 1990. "Silent Partners: Taiwan Businessmen Are Bullish in China," *China Business Review* (September–October 1990), pp. 32–41.

Smith, Michael. 1985. "Soviet Bloc Returns to Capital Markets," *Journal of Commerce,* January 18, 1985.

Statistical Abstract. 1990. *The Statistical Abstract of the United States,* 11th ed. Washington, D.C.: U.S. Department of Commerce.

Stubbs, Richard. 1992. "Subregional Security Cooperation in ASEAN: Military and Economic Imperatives and Political Obstacles," 32 *Asian Survey* 5:307–410 (May 1992).

Tabata, Masanori. 1992. "Ground Self-Defense Force: Planners Study Major Restructuring," *Japan Times Weekly* (international edition), June 24–30, 1991, pp. 1 and 4.

Thornton, Richard C. 1985. *Is Detente Inevitable?* Washington, D.C.: Washington Institute for Values in Public Policy.

U.S. Department of State. 1988. "The European Community's Program to Complete a Single Market by 1992" (pamphlet). Washington, D.C.: Department of State, Bureau of European and Canadian Affairs.

Wang, N. T. 1991. "Taiwan's Economic Relations with Mainland China," 18 *Asian Affairs* 2:99–120 (Summer 1991).

■ 2

Russia and Japan in the Post–Cold War Era
Peter Berton

Before I can meaningfully discuss the post–Cold War relationship between Russia and Japan, I must address two interrelated subjects. First, I will briefly touch upon the strategic equation in the Asia Pacific region before the advent of Mikhail Gorbachev. Second, I will inquire into the concept of "the end of the Cold War," particularly as it relates to the Asia Pacific. I can then deal with the Gorbachev phenomenon: the transition from the inherited Cold War, the evolution of his new political thinking and glasnost, and the end of the Cold War. At the same time, I will attempt to analyze how each stage affected Japan and Soviet relations with Japan. I shall then delve into the relationship between Japan and Boris Yeltsin's new Russia and discuss the impact of the Cold War on Japan's defense policy. Finally, I will analyze the political and international security implications for both Russia and Japan.

■ THE STRATEGIC EQUATION IN THE ASIA PACIFIC REGION BEFORE GORBACHEV

The legacy of Leonid Brezhnev's rule (1964–1982) is that he successfully built up the Soviet armed forces, particularly the strategic nuclear component, to relative parity with the United States. This policy was, no doubt, a reaction to the Cuban Missile Crisis of 1962, when the Soviet Union found itself staring at a U.S. ultimatum in a condition of definite strategic inferiority. The Sino-Soviet dispute also contributed to the massive increase of Soviet ground forces in the Far East from some thirteen or fourteen divisions to over fifty. Henry Kissinger's secret trip to Beijing in mid-1971, leading to a Sino–U.S. rapprochement, further stimulated the growth of Soviet armed forces in the Asia Pacific region, including the steady increase in the size and quality of the Soviet Pacific Fleet.

Of course, one could argue that Richard Nixon and Kissinger embraced a détente relationship with the Soviet Union and announced an equidistant treatment of Moscow and Beijing. This policy included negotiating a Strategic Arms Limitation Treaty (SALT) with the Soviets and a withdrawal from Vietnam. But détente did not mean self-restraint for the Soviet leadership. Instead of using the détente to cut down on wasteful military spending, Brezhnev and company pursued their military buildup and took advantage of the post-Vietnam syndrome in the United States in the mid-1970s to engage in aggressive adventures in the Third World. These policies, along with the invasion of Afghanistan in the waning days of 1979, led to the formation of an informal anti-Soviet coalition that included not only the United States and its NATO allies, plus Japan and other Asian allies, but also China.

The continuous buildup of the Soviet Pacific Fleet, the stationing of long-range bombers and intermediate-range missiles near Japanese territory, and the militarization of the disputed northern islands gradually created public support in Japan for its self-defense forces and for an alliance with the United States. This sentiment, in turn, strengthened the pro-defense forces in the Japanese establishment, and Japan began to play a more active military role. For example, in 1980 the Japanese navy (literally the maritime self-defense force) joined in RIMPAC naval exercises sponsored by the U.S. Pacific Command, which brought together the navies of several U.S. allies. The Japanese defense establishment also developed a quite sophisticated electronic intelligence-gathering capability, which was demonstrated in the aftermath of the Soviets' shooting down of a Korean airliner with many Japanese passengers aboard. In short, by the mid-1980s the Japanese self-defense forces were a significant complementary component in the U.S.-led anti-Soviet coalition.

■ THE END OF THE COLD WAR:
WHEN, WHERE, AND HOW

I will argue that it is unclear when and how the Cold War ended and whether it ended simultaneously in all regions.

The end of the Cold War connotes several dramatic events that occurred before, and some international developments that have arisen after, the end of that era. The first of these dramatic events was the inauguration of Gorbachev's new political thinking in Soviet foreign policy, which was an important ingredient in his policy of perestroika. This reorientation took place shortly after he had assumed power in March 1985. The revolutions in Eastern Europe in late 1989, which led to the dissolution of the War-saw Pact and Comecon and the unification of Germany on Western terms, certainly qualify as another epoch-making event. The failed coup d'état in Moscow in mid-August 1991, resulting in the destruction of the Communist Party apparatus, guaranteed that there would be no Soviet attempt to reverse these strategic setbacks and restore the status quo ante. The dissolution of the Soviet Union in late December 1991, with Russia emerging as the successor state (inheriting the permanent membership with veto powers in the UN Security Council), was perhaps most symbolic of the end of the Cold War.

Almost all the constituent Soviet republics (except the Baltic states and Georgia) banded together in a Commonwealth (Sodruzhestvo) of Independent States on the territory of the former USSR. In theory, the commonwealth was supposed to inherit all Soviet armed forces, including their gigantic nuclear arsenal. In reality, however, we saw the fragmentation of this gigantic military machine. There is a chance, however, that strategic nuclear weapons will continue to remain under single Russian control. The collapse of the Soviet Union has for all practical purposes ended the nuclear confrontation between the two superpowers. Although the weapons of mass destruction are still largely in place, Presidents George Bush and Yeltsin reached an agreement in 1992 to reduce them drastically, albeit over a relatively long period of time.

The question is, when in this sequence of events did the Cold War really end? Did it happen when President Gorbachev and Foreign Minister Eduard Shevardnadze announced it? Or when both superpowers—the Soviet Union and the United States—agreed that it had ended? Or when NATO officially declared the end of the Soviet threat? I would argue that it is impossible to date precisely the end of the Cold War because of the fact that these momentous events took place largely in Europe and were perceived differently by the leaderships in different countries. More important from the standpoint of the topic of this chapter, Japan lagged behind all other Western powers in coming to grips with these developments and recognizing the new reality.

Although the leadership of the new Russia is proclaiming the end of Cold War relationships everywhere, including those with Japan, it is difficult to pinpoint when, or whether, the Japanese leadership perceived that the Cold War had ended in the Asia Pacific region. To determine what is at stake as the Cold War winds down, perhaps we should briefly look at Japan's policy at the beginning of the Cold War. Because Japan was occupied by the United States (technically it was an Allied occupation) after World War II and Japan was not a sovereign state when the Cold War broke out in the 1947–1948 period, we should first examine U.S. policy toward Japan.

The collapse of the Grand Coalition of World War II and the onset of the Cold War had a profound effect on U.S. policy toward Japan. In the immediate post–World War II period, the United States began to treat Japan as an enemy that had to be defanged and controlled. In fact, preparations were underway to dismantle some of the remaining industrial plants and ship them as reparations to the victims of Japan's aggression. But as the confrontation with the Soviet Union grew, U.S. policy toward Japan changed 180 degrees: Japan was increasingly seen in Washington as a potential ally in the emerging anticommunist coalition. Thus, Japanese industry was not to be dismantled but strengthened instead. The United States also insisted that the Japanese rearm (first a police reserve and then self-defense forces) to strengthen the U.S.-led alliance system in Asia, in spite of the original plans to keep Japan thoroughly disarmed under the so-called Peace Constitution.[1] The outbreak of the Korean War in June 1950, of course, hastened U.S. policy on Japanese rearmament.

The Japanese conservative leadership went along with these ideas in order to speed an end to the occupation and become a sovereign state once again. But there was a good deal of opposition to Japan's rearmament not only from the public and the leftist parties but also from inside the conservative establishment. Under the Yoshida doctrine (named after long-serving Prime Minister Shigeru Yoshida), Japan would concentrate on rebuilding its economy, leaving its defense (including the nuclear deterrent) to the United States. Given the antimilitary and pacifist sentiments among the Japanese public, the restrictions imposed by the Peace Constitution, and the opposition of the leftist political parties, the Japanese government maintained a fine line in defense matters between what the United States demanded and what was politically possible. In the 1960s, the Japanese government proclaimed the three nonnuclear principles (not to manufacture, acquire, or allow the stationing of nuclear weapons), for which Prime Minister Eisaku Sato received the Nobel Peace Prize. In the mid-1970s, dovish Prime Minister Takeo Miki imposed a limit on defense spending of 1 percent of GNP. All along, the Japanese have scrupulously tried to distinguish between defensive and offensive weapons. Thus, the origins of Japan's participation in the Cold War and its gradual evolution as a military partner of the United States are important factors in assessing its response to the international developments that one associates with the ending of the Cold War.

As mentioned above, Japan lagged behind all the other Western powers in recognizing these new realities. I will try to explain why Japan was the odd man out as I try to assess the impact of all these events on Japanese relations with Russia, more broadly on its relations with the United States, and on Japan's defense policy. Likewise, I will look at Soviet policy toward Japan in the final months of the USSR's existence and the new Russia's complex relationship with this neighboring economic power, an ally of the United States that was clearly on the opposite side during the long Cold War. Soviet/Russian relations with Japan will be considered within the context of the former nation's broader policy toward the Asia Pacific region.[2]

■ GORBACHEV'S NEW POLICIES: JAPAN'S RESPONSE AND SOVIET PERCEPTIONS OF JAPAN

Long before the 1989 revolutions in Eastern Europe, the Soviet leadership became aware that the country and its empire (both internal and external) were in deep economic trouble, if not in a crisis situation. General Secretary of the Communist Party of the Soviet Union (CPSU) Yuri Andropov's moves to reform and rejuvenate the Soviet system in 1982–1983 were clear proof of economic and social malaise. Of course, when Mikhail Gorbachev became general secretary in March 1985, his calls for perestroika were even clearer proof of a deep crisis in the Soviet system. First Soviet economic growth had slowed down; negative economic growth followed, leading in later years to the disintegration of the Soviet economic system.

One of the most far-reaching elements in Gorbachev's perestroika was his new political thinking (note the word political). Foremost in it was the repudiation of Brezhnev's policies striving for absolute security based on an *offensive* posture. Instead, Gorbachev advocated deep mutual arms cuts and a military doctrine of reasonable sufficiency, based on a *defensive* posture.

The 1980s saw Japan's sudden emergence as a major financial power and the largest creditor nation in the world. This transformation came on top of Japan's long record of remarkable economic growth, industrial achievements, and technological sophistication. How did Gorbachev's perestroika affect Soviet policy toward Asia as a whole and Japan in particular? How did this rising power respond to the problems of the Soviet superpower in decline?[3]

Just as Gorbachev wanted to fix the Soviet system rather than radically transform it, in the beginning of his tenure he probably wanted to improve relations with Japan rather than resolve the lingering territorial dispute that was the stumbling block to a rapprochement between the two neighbors. In August–September 1945, the Red Army occupied the Kurile Islands and some adjoining islands near Hokkaido. This maneuver was sanctioned by President Franklin D. Roosevelt and Prime Minister Winston Churchill at their meeting with Joseph Stalin at Yalta in February 1945. Japan subsequently relinquished all right and title to the Kurile Islands at the San Francisco Peace Conference in 1951. The problem is that the Japanese government does not consider the two southernmost islands, Kunashiri and Etorofu, nor Shikotan and the Habomai group of islets as belonging to the Kurile chain. In 1956 the Soviet Union promised to return

Shikotan and the Habomais upon conclusion of a peace treaty in which the Japanese would relinquish their claim to Kunashiri and Etorofu. This the Japanese were not prepared to do; moreover, in 1960 the Soviets unilaterally withdrew even their offer to return Shikotan and the Habomais.[4]

Generally speaking, during the six and a half years between Gorbachev's assumption of power in March 1985 and the August 1991 aborted coup, negotiations between Japan and the Soviet Union were getting nowhere. Foreign Minister Shevardnadze targeted Japan as one of the first Western countries he would visit in January 1986 and implied recognition of the territorial issue. In some ways this was progress, because for a quarter-century before that, Foreign Minister Andrei Gromyko had never even acknowledged the existence of a territorial dispute.[5] But that was as far as it went: Gorbachev's projected visit to Japan in 1987 was postponed, and Shevardnadze did not again visit Tokyo until almost three years later (despite an agreement to hold annual foreign ministerial talks).

How did Japan respond to Gorbachev's bold new policies and foreign policy initiatives? As I have written elsewhere,[6] Japan was the only major Western power that did not respond positively, and the Japanese public lagged behind the people of Western Europe and the United States in perceiving the significance of reforms in the Soviet Union and the changing nature of Soviet foreign policy. The Japanese continued to perceive a greater Soviet threat than citizens of any of the other Western allies. Thus, in 1986, a year after the advent of Gorbachev, the Japanese (together with their U.S. counterparts) topped the West Europeans, especially the West Germans, in a five-nation Soviet-threat-perception poll.[7] In fact, the Japanese perception of the Soviet threat was a tiny fraction *higher* in 1986 than in 1983, 1984, or 1985.

These Japanese attitudes toward the Soviet Union did not change with the announcement of the Intermediate-range Nuclear Force (INF) accord between the Soviet Union and the United States in late 1987. Thus, in December 1987, in a similar five-nation survey, the Japanese were the most skeptical about the decrease in East-West tensions. The Japanese were also last among all polled countries in believing that the Soviets had become a trustworthy country.[8] Perhaps this skepticism is why it took Gorbachev six years after his assumption of the top position in the Soviet hierarchy to visit Japan in April 1991, the first Soviet or Russian head of state to do so.

Another poll, commissioned by the Japanese prime minister's office and conducted for over a decade, began by asking questions on how the respondents felt toward a number of countries: (a) friendly, (b) more or less friendly, (c) more or less unfriendly, or (d) unfriendly. The latest available data are for October 1991 (published in March 1992).[9] Although the number of nations in the "friendly" category showed a steady increase, punctuated by a near 50 percent jump from 1987 to 1988, the main breakthrough came in October 1990, when the numbers almost doubled compared to 1989 and tripled compared to 1985. On the other hand, the number of "unfriendlies" remained roughly the same from 1985 through 1989, and then dropped only by a little over 10 percent in 1990 and 1991.

Next, let us take a look at Japanese public opinion polls on attitudes toward different foreign countries. How does the Soviet Union compare in popularity (or unpopularity) with other countries? Here, again, let us take the prime minister's office polls, which provide continuous comparative coverage since 1960.[10] Until a few years ago, these polls showed the Soviet Union as the most disliked country (except for Communist China during the Cultural Revolution). Now this dubious honor belongs to North Korea, which used to be the runner-up. The Soviet invasion of Afghanistan in December 1979 and the shooting down of the Korean airliner in September 1983 raised the negative opinion of the Soviets to almost 60 percent (in a multiple-choice questionnaire).[11] Gorbachev's reforms brought this negative rating steadily down to the low forties. After Gorbachev let the Eastern European countries shed their communist systems, the negative rating further declined to the mid-thirties, bottoming out at 28.5 percent in November 1990. By way of comparison, North Korea's negative rating is almost 50 percent, South Korea's around 20, China's between 10 and 20, and the United States' between 5 and 10 percent.

Why were the Japanese the most suspicious among the Western allies about Gorbachev's domestic reforms and his new foreign policies? The officials of the Japanese Foreign Ministry, especially those charged with Soviet affairs, have for a long time had the reputation of being the most hardline anticommunists in the Japanese government. Moreover, the Japanese have long felt an animosity toward their northern neighbors. Russia was long a potential enemy, starting with raids on Japanese settlements in the north in the early nineteenth century. Rivalry over Korea and later over Manchuria in the last decade of the nineteenth century led directly to the Russo-Japanese War of 1904–1905. After the Russian revolution, anti-Russian feelings were reinforced by anticommunist sentiment as the Bolsheviks created the Third International, whose Japanese arm—the Japanese Communist Party—conspired to overthrow the imperial system. Then there was the Soviet declaration of war on Japan a week before Japan's surrender in August 1945, seen by the Japanese as a stab in the back in view of the existence of a neutrality pact between the two countries. Over half a million Japanese (military and civilian) were captured by the Red Army in Manchuria and North Korea in August 1945, sent to Siberia, and were held in forced-labor camps for several years, in contravention of international treaties that obligate the combatants to return their prisoners of war promptly. In the post–World War II period, especially in the 1970s and 1980s, the Japanese felt that the Soviet Union posed a military threat to the security of their country. Finally, and probably most important, the

Soviets continued to occupy four Japanese islands and until very recently even refused to acknowledge the existence of a territorial dispute.

Compared with these rather negative images of the Soviet Union in Japan, Soviet respondents paint a totally different picture of Japan and its people. Some years ago, a startling 88 percent of Soviet citizens expressed "good feelings" toward Japan; 98 percent characterized Japan as "economically developed" (compared to only 35 percent of the Japanese viewing the Soviet Union this way); 96.5 percent wanted to increase economic and trade relations (including joint ventures) with Japan; and 99 percent wanted an improvement of relations with Japan.[12] A joint Japanese-Soviet poll found 77 percent of the Soviet respondents feeling "very friendly" and "friendly" toward its neighbor (compared to only 25 percent of the Japanese) and only 9.5 percent "not friendly" and "antipathetic" (the Japanese figure about the Soviet Union and its people was 67 percent). Not only are these figures grossly asymmetrical, but the images of the people projected most startling contrasts. The Soviet's considered the Japanese "diligent," "neat," "creative," "cultural," "kind," and "patient" (only 2.2 percent rated the Japanese as "insincere"). On the Japanese side, the Soviets were "closed," "dark and cold," "self-centered," and "secretive," although some responded with "patient," "open-minded," and "serious."[13]

■ GORBACHEV'S POLICY TOWARD ASIA

Given the fact that Gorbachev badly needed to create a favorable international environment in order to reduce military spending and tinker with the economy, it is understandable that he targeted the United States as his first foreign policy priority. Nonetheless, by July 1986 he also turned his attention to Asia. In a well-publicized visit to Vladivostok, the headquarters of the Soviet Pacific Fleet, he outlined his plans for the Asia Pacific region and his policy toward the major Asian powers.[14]

In his Vladivostok speech, Gorbachev singled out China for a good deal of comment. He stressed the importance of Soviet relations with China, noted improvement in that regard, and offered the hope that the border between the two countries would become "a zone of peace and friendship." He pointed out the complementary nature of the Soviet and Chinese economies and called for the expansion of economic ties. In the most important Soviet concession in the entire speech, Gorbachev accepted the Chinese formula for delineating the Sino-Soviet border in the Amur River basin.

Gorbachev then paid homage to Japan for having "turned into a power of front-ranking significance," and he called for "deeply intensified cooperation on a healthy and realistic basis . . . in an atmosphere of calm *unburdened by the problems of the past*" (emphasis added). This was a clear hint that the Japanese should forget about their territorial demands. Gorbachev also offered to cooperate in space research, one of very few areas where the Soviet Union was technologically ahead of Japan.

One of Gorbachev's major proposals at Vladivostok was to apply the Helsinki process to Asia. The Helsinki agreement effectively froze the post–World War II territorial status quo in Europe. This proposal, as many of his other proposals, was basically self-serving; it would have frozen the territorial status quo, much to the dismay of China and Japan, who had territorial disputes with the Soviet Union and with each other. Moreover, the other numerous territorial conflicts in the Asia Pacific region would remain unresolved. Counting the Helsinki proposal in the politico-diplomatic sphere, Gorbachev seems to have had a fourfold strategy vis-à-vis the Asia Pacific region as a whole. In the military-strategic sphere, Gorbachev wanted to maintain the Soviet position in the region while attempting to weaken the position of the United States and its allies, primarily Japan and South Korea. Third, in the nuclear weapons arena, he tried to encourage the forces working for the establishment of nuclear-free zones, especially in Southeast Asia, Australasia, and Japan. Such antinuclear movements had the potential to destabilize relations between the United States and its allies, in the process weakening the position of the U.S. Navy. Finally, his fourth proposal dealt with economic matters. Here he was trying to develop Siberia and the Soviet Far East by integrating them with the dynamic economies of the Asia Pacific region. Of course, at that time both the United States and Japan were opposed to the admission of the Soviet Union to the Pacific Economic Cooperation Conference (PECC).

A little over two years after the Vladivostok speech, in September 1988, Gorbachev delivered another major address on the Asia Pacific region in the Siberian city of Krasnoyarsk.[15] This time he paid more attention to Japan than to China and specifically brought up relations with South Korea. As in the Vladivostok speech, Gorbachev ended with concrete proposals, many of which were carryovers from Vladivostok. These included reduction of nuclear weapons (he did not specifically call for the establishment of nuclear-free zones) and a freeze followed by reduction in naval and air forces, coupled with a restriction on their activity in areas where the seaboards of the USSR, China, Japan, and North and South Korea were in proximity to one another—an obvious attempt to limit the activity of the U.S. Seventh Fleet. Gorbachev proposed some "negotiating mechanism" (starting with discussions among the Soviet Union, China, and the United States, as permanent members of the UN Security Council) to discuss Soviet or other proposals relating to the security of the Asia Pacific region. Whereas in Vladivostok Gorbachev called for the United States to abandon its bases in the Philippines and promised an appropriate Soviet response, in Krasnoyarsk he offered to exchange the U.S. bases in the Philippines for Soviet bases in Vietnam, a strikingly asymmetrical proposal.

On the whole, both of these policy speeches were quite one-sided and contained much Soviet rhetoric (propaganda might be a more appropriate term) addressed to world opinion rather than to the leaders of the United States, Japan, and other Asia Pacific powers. Nonetheless, the speeches signaled the eventual Soviet withdrawal from Afghanistan. Also, Gorbachev offered concrete concessions to China on the territorial issue, albeit none to Japan.

Evaluating in another publication[16] the record of Gorbachev's diplomacy in the Asia Pacific region during the 1985–1991 period (leaving aside Soviet relations with the United States, which are of a global character), I gave him an "A" for dramatically improving relations with South Korea, a "B" for achieving a breakthrough in normalizing relations with China, a "C" for modestly improving relations with the members of ASEAN (Association of Southeast Asian Nations) and Australasia, and a "D" for his inability to come to some sort of an understanding with Japan, unquestionably the most important neighbor in that region.

■ SOVIET-JAPANESE RELATIONS, 1988–1991

As discussed earlier, Soviet-Japanese relations were in a state of suspended animation from mid-1986 to the end of 1988. During his second visit to Tokyo in December 1988, Shevardnadze and Japanese Foreign Minister Sousuke Uno agreed to set up a working group at the vice-ministerial level to settle the problems associated with the conclusion of a peace treaty. During the remaining three years of Gorbachev's tenure, there were eight such meetings. Yet no real breakthrough on the territorial question occurred, although some issues were clarified and the islands can be now visited by the Japanese without Soviet visas. Thus, it might be said that, preoccupied with more important issues (such as arms control negotiations with the United States), Gorbachev did not put enough energy nor attention into relations with Japan. I might also add in retrospect that Gorbachev in his early years in power could have made some concessions on the territorial issue when his policy of glasnost had not yet created a strong public opinion in the Soviet Union. But he missed the opportunity.

In discussing Japan's policy toward the Soviet Union, scholars have identified two basic approaches, known in Japanese as *iriguchi ron* (entrance theory) and *deguchi ron* (exit theory). The entrance theory calls for the solution of the territorial issue as a *prerequisite* for expanding ties with the Soviet Union; the exit theory calls for improving relations with the northern neighbor as a *means* of solving the territorial issue. Needless to say, whereas Japan stuck to the entrance theory, the Soviet Union clearly preferred the exit theory. Another way to conceptualize the two Japanese approaches toward the Soviet Union is to distinguish between *seikei bunri* (separation of politics from economics) and *seikei fukabun* (indivisibility of politics and economics), with Japan advocating the latter policy that the political (territorial) issues are inseparable from economic issues and that an increase in economic cooperation depends upon the solution of the territorial issue.

In trying to break the deadlock, Foreign Minister Sousuke Uno on a visit to Moscow in May 1989 advanced a new policy of "balanced expansion" (*kakudai kinko*), which on the surface looked like a policy somewhere between the entrance and exit theories. Uno proposed that, pending the conclusion of a peace treaty that would successfully resolve the territorial dispute, Japan and the Soviet Union should nevertheless proceed with negotiations over other matters, such as fishing rights, environmental protection, and visits by former Japanese inhabitants of the disputed islands to their ancestors' graves.[17] Although Japanese scholars like to describe this "expanded equilibrium" policy as falling between the entrance and exit theories, in reality it offers concessions on what, in the context of Sino-Soviet relations,[18] I have called "low politics" relations (distinguishing them from "high politics," which would definitely include territorial issues).

Gorbachev finally visited Japan in mid-April 1991, the first Soviet or Russian supreme leader to do so. He spent four days in Tokyo, holding almost constant meetings with Japanese Prime Minister Toshiki Kaifu.[19] His visit, however, did not lead to any breakthrough either on the territorial issue or on Japanese economic assistance to the Soviet Union. Moreover, Gorbachev made a couple of major diplomatic blunders, combining his visit to Japan with a stopover in South Korea and proposing a five-power conference with the participation of India. The Japanese would have preferred a special trip only to Japan, and they do not consider India a major player on the international scene. The general consensus of scholars and political observers was that the visit would have been a total failure if not for its symbolic value as an historic first.[20] Some fifteen agreements were signed during this visit, but none was very important and all could have been quietly signed by lower-level officials. Above all, Gorbachev did not make any of the spectacular proposals that we were led to believe was his diplomatic forte.

Partly because of the failure of the Gorbachev visit and partly because of the relative rise of Boris Yeltsin and the Russian Republic, the Japanese Foreign Ministry began to practice a two-track diplomacy at the Soviet Union (Gorbachev) and the Russian Republic (Yeltsin) levels. Significantly, this decision was made *before* the August 1991 coup, and contacts on both levels intensified after the aborted coup.

Japan is not geared to respond quickly to foreign crises. Just as in its response to the Gulf crisis, the Japanese government temporized when it heard about the coup against Gorbachev. It looked to the United States and

Western Europe for guidance, but in spite of U.S. "guidance" it hesitated to act. In the end, when it was clear that the coup had failed, Japan made all the right gestures, albeit too little and too late.

Between the time of the aborted coup in August 1991 and Gorbachev's resignation at the end of December, the Japanese Foreign Ministry continued its two-track diplomacy. At the end of September, this approach was officially codified in the five principles of Japan's Soviet policy, the first two promising to "step up aid for *Soviet* reform" and to "strengthen cooperation with the *Russian* Federation" [emphasis added].[21] The diplomatic pattern saw largely *Russian* visitors to Tokyo and Japanese visits to Moscow, where contacts were made with both the *Soviet* and *Russian* leaders. Prominent Soviet leaders did not or could not come to Japan, but additional meetings with the Japanese were held at the United Nations headquarters in New York as part of the annual meetings of the UN General Assembly.

■ THE NEW RELATIONSHIP BETWEEN JAPAN AND RUSSIA

Even before the demise of the Soviet Union, Russian leaders stressed to the Japanese the centrality of Russia in the solution of the territorial dispute. The islands belonged administratively to the Russian Federation, and its officials dropped hints that they would be more flexible than Gorbachev. At the same time, they were careful to note that the islands could not be transferred to Japan without a popular referendum. The Soviet leaders were more interested in Japan's economic aid, although they too made vague references to the territorial issue. By early October 1991, Japan finally agreed to match the contributions of the European Community (EC) and the United States to the relief and stability of the Soviet Union at the $2.5 billion level.[22] With the exception of some humanitarian aid, however, most of the Japanese "assistance" was earmarked to insure Japanese firms doing business with Russia.

How did Russian President Yeltsin feel about the territorial dispute with Japan? Actually, he visited Japan in January 1990, ahead of Gorbachev, and presented a five-stage plan for the solution of the Soviet-Japanese territorial dispute that would take fifteen to twenty years. First, the Soviet Union would acknowledge the existence of the territorial dispute with Japan. (Gorbachev acknowledged it only in April 1991 during *his* visit to Japan.) Second, the Soviets would establish a free economic zone on the four islands and, third, would demilitarize the islands. Fourth, the two countries would sign a peace treaty, and in the fifth and final stage, the question of the ownership of the islands would be left to the next generation of Soviets and Japanese.[23] The fifth point, postponing the solution of the territorial issue, was probably taken from Deng Xiaoping's "Senkaku Island Formula": When China and Japan were negotiating a peace treaty in the late 1970s, Deng suggested that the final settlement of their territorial dispute over the Diaoyutai-Senkaku island be postponed until the next generation.

To prepare the residents of the disputed islands (initially those on the smaller islands of Shikotan and the Habomais promised to Japan in 1956), Yeltsin in late September 1991 sent his deputy foreign minister, Georgy Kunadze, and two Russian People's Deputies to Sakhalin and the islands. Their mission was to explain Russia's obligations under international law, at the same time reassuring the residents that their interests would not be neglected. The head of the Sakhalin administration (which had jurisdiction over the Kurile Islands), former economics professor Valentin Fyodorov, did his best to undermine the visit and to stir up local opposition. He even stooped to making ethnic slurs about the Georgian background of the minister, declaring that a person with a name such as Kunadze had "absolutely no moral or ethical right to decide the fate of Russian territory."[24]

Yeltsin did not want to repudiate a loyal supporter; in fact he appointed Fyodorov "governor" shortly after the visit. This was an astute step, as conservative People's Deputies in the Russian parliament took up the cause of the Kurile islanders. Two such deputies traveled to Sakhalin and the disputed islands, supported Fyodorov's position, and reassured the residents that no territorial concessions were going to be made.[25] Yeltsin's Vice President, General Aleksandr Rutskoi (who has been openly attacking and undermining Yeltsin's economic policies), joined the defenders of the Kurile Islands, complicating the already complex situation.

By the end of December 1991, the Soviet Union ceased to exist, and after the resignation of President Gorbachev, Japan officially recognized Russia not only as a sovereign state but also as the successor state to the Union of Soviet Socialist Republics. Japanese diplomacy is thus back to a single track, but now with Russia instead of the Soviet Union and Yeltsin instead of Gorbachev.

In one of his first acts as the foreign minister of Russia without having a Soviet foreign minister with authority over him, Andrei Kozyrev assured all the powers, including Japan, that Russia would honor all the treaties and agreements signed by the former Soviet Union. With respect to Japan, and in a significant departure from Gorbachev's position, Kozyrev specifically confirmed the legality of the 1956 Soviet-Japanese Joint Declaration. Needless to say, this reversal was a signal that Russia was officially ready to concede the validity of documents that explicitly mentioned the return to Japan of Shikotan and the Habomai islets upon the conclusion of a peace treaty. Kozyrev added, however, that this acknowledgment would not lead to an automatic and immediate concession of the islands; this outcome was subject to negotiations.[26]

Yeltsin briefly met with the new Japanese prime minister, Kiichi Miyazawa, in New York at the end of January 1992,[27] and the meetings of the vice-ministerial working group on the peace treaty resumed in February. The Japanese government was much impressed by a personal message from Yeltsin to Miyazawa, which ended with the statement that he considered Japan to be Russia's partner and potential ally, one that shares with Russia the same human values.[28] Miyazawa replied that he would like to build a "new age in Japan-Russia relations."[29]

While the peace treaty working group continued its negotiations, alternating between Tokyo and Moscow, the two foreign ministers were also exchanging visits. Kozyrev went to Tokyo for two days at the end of March, and Michio Watanabe traveled to Moscow in early May. Kozyrev's visit to Tokyo was the first by a Russian foreign minister fully in charge of relations with Japan, and the topics discussed ranged from the territorial issue and the peace treaty to economic matters and international security concerns. On another occasion, Kozyrev reassured the Japanese that Russia would no longer target Japan.

During Watanabe's visit to Moscow in early May 1992, the working group was charged to "exert utmost efforts" to come up with an acceptable draft of a peace treaty in time for Yeltsin's visit to Tokyo. For his part, Watanabe said that, should Russia acknowledge Japan's residual sovereignty over the disputed islands, the Japanese government would be quite flexible "about the time frame and the modality of their return." Practically, this meant that the Japanese would be prepared to sign a peace treaty on the basis of a Russian pledge to return first Shikotan and the Habomais and eventually the two larger islands, which would continue for a certain period to remain under Russian administration.[30]

A new, disturbing element in the Kurile equation is the growing Cossack movement in Russia. Although the newly organized Cossacks in the Don River area are genuine descendants of the Cossacks who were mercilessly persecuted by Stalin, the movement also attracts a bunch of adventurers who have no hereditary connection. In Sakhalin they are being supported by Fyodorov, who helped organize a national congress of all the Cossacks. One of the topics discussed at the congress was the problem of development and revival of the Kurile Islands, and the final resolution of the congress stressed opposition to the return of the islands to Japan.[31]

The second recent development complicating the quiet diplomacy between Russia and Japan to settle the territorial issue is the inauguration of an annual "Southern Kuriles Day,"[32] which took a leaf from the Japanese. (The Japanese parliament inaugurated "Northern Territories Day" in 1981.) There continues to be opposition to the return of the southern Kuriles to Japan, especially in the Russian Far East, and it is not restricted to the elements on the right. Perhaps the persistence of these feelings is the reason for a recent statement Kozyrev made on a trip to Kamchatka that "nobody intends to give away the southern Kuriles."[33]

Trade between the two countries was always more important for the Soviet Union than for Japan, which is one of the world's greatest trading nations. Bilateral trade peaked in 1989 at a little over $6 billion (1.3 percent of Japan's trade) compared to Japan's trade of some $30 billion with South Korea and close to $150 billion with the United States. Since 1989 Soviet-Japanese trade has fallen off because of economic difficulties and a shortage of foreign exchange in the Soviet Union. Trade volume dropped to $5.9 billion in 1990 and $5.4 billion in 1991.[34] More recently, Soviet firms could not pay their bills, one reason for Japan's $2.5 billion aid package, discussed above.

As I have written elsewhere,[35] proximity and complementarity are no longer relevant in this bilateral economic relationship, which is getting more and more asymmetrical. Furthermore, Japan has handsome investment opportunities in politically stable areas such as Western Europe and Southern California, not to mention the dynamic economies of South Korea, Taiwan, and the ASEAN countries. Thus, the development of Siberia has lost most of its attractiveness, even before the recent economic dislocations. The net effect of the dissolution of the Soviet Union is that Japan will have to provide credits and aid in the near term. Long-range economic relations will depend upon the stabilization of the Russian economy.

Meetings of high-ranking Russian and Japanese officials continued through the summer of 1992, but no breakthrough has occurred. Foreign Minister Watanabe's visit to Moscow in late August–early September was the last official meeting prior to President Yeltsin's scheduled trip to Japan in mid-September, and it probably reinforced the perception in Moscow that the Japanese were pushing their agenda without regard for the political realities in Russia.[36] On September 9, four days before his scheduled departure for Tokyo, Yeltsin abruptly canceled his visit to Japan and Korea. The Korean visit was rescheduled, but the trip to Japan was not. Significantly, Yeltsin visited China in December and India in January 1993.

Given the political developments in Russia in August and early September, it seems clear that Yeltsin was torn between his desire to go to Japan and move Russo-Japanese relations forward, with all accompanying economic benefits, and his political instincts, which cautioned against the trip—making even the smallest territorial concessions to Japan could destabilize his position at home. By refusing to budge on the residual sovereignty issue for all four islands, the Japanese tipped the scale in favor of cancellation. In retrospect, Yeltsin should have made his decision earlier so as not to insult his Japanese hosts. The abrupt cancellation was portrayed in the Japanese media as a snub of the emperor, whose cooks must have prepared everything for the banquet at the Imperial Palace. In public opinion polls taken in Japan a couple of weeks after Yeltsin's cancellation, unfavorable attitudes toward Russia shot up 50 percent to the 1988 levels,[37] erasing all the positive images arising from the end of the

Cold War, the disintegration of the Soviet Union, and the emergence of a new Russian neighbor.

In early October, Yeltsin began to talk about rescheduling his visit to Japan and brought up again the possible return of the two smaller islands to Japan. Gorbachev's April 1991 visit did nothing to considerably improve Soviet-Japanese relations. Yeltsin's September 1992 nonvisit set Russo-Japanese relations back. If Yeltsin erred on the tactical issue of timing, the Japanese should shoulder the responsibility for lack of strategic considerations.

■ THE END OF THE COLD WAR AND JAPAN'S DEFENSE POLICY

Perhaps the greatest impact of the dissolution of the Soviet Union and the diminution, if not disappearance, of the Soviet threat is bound to be in the area of Japan's defense and the country's alliance with the United States. During the 1980s, defense outlays and international economic aid were the only areas of the national budget that were steadily rising. In the case of defense, the annual increases were around 6 percent per annum. The 1992 fiscal year budget (which begins on April 1, 1992) only allocates 455 billion yen, or a 3.8 percent increase, for defense.[38] The dollar figure, of course, depends on the yen/dollar rate of exchange, which constantly fluctuates (with swings of up to twenty percent in the early 1990s). But in rough terms the Japanese defense budget is around $35 billion, which makes it the third-largest in the world, although a distant third after the United States and the former Soviet Union. (It may well be that in time Japan's defense budget will surpass that of Russia and become the world's second largest.) Although the Japanese defense budget broke through the self-imposed limit of 1 percent of the GNP in the mid-1980s, because of the growth of the Japanese economy the proposed 1992 defense budget represents only 0.941 percent.

The Japanese Defense Agency each summer publishes an annual white paper on security matters. Since 1980 the publication has made references to "a potential threat" from the Soviet Union. The original draft of the 1990 edition contained this phrase, but it was dropped at the insistence of Prime Minister Kaifu, who wanted to make a political point. Perhaps this gesture was made in anticipation of Foreign Minister Shevardnadze's forthcoming visit to Tokyo. Shevardnadze came to Japan for the third time in September 1990 to prepare for Gorbachev's visit. On this occasion, he and his Japanese counterpart issued a joint statement on the situation in the Persian Gulf, for the first time broadening the scope of Soviet-Japanese interactions to include security matters.

The 1991 Defense of Japan white paper, which was issued in late July before the Soviet coup d'état, again did not mention "the Soviet threat" but implicitly argued that the end of the Cold War did little to bring a significant relaxation of tensions in the area around Japan.

International Situation

The military situation includes uncertain elements in Asia. The Soviet Union is facing crises. The military and political situation in Asia and the Pacific is much more complicated than in Europe.
The military situation in the Far East remains severe despite *the end of the cold war,* as the Soviet Union has reduced its forces quantitatively in the region but boosted them qualitatively [emphasis added].

Asian Military Situation

The military situation in the region remains severe despite Soviet President Mikhail Gorbachev's pledge during his April visit to Japan to reduce Soviet forces in the northern territories.[39]

At the end of November 1991, well after the failure of the August coup d'état and the gradual softening of Soviet foreign policy, a report prepared for a government-sponsored think tank in Tokyo by a Japanese defense-establishment analyst described in detail the Soviet military assets in the area and urged a cautious attitude. The Soviet threat was analyzed in terms of intent, capabilities, and the strategic environment. The author conceded that, at least for the present, the Soviet Union did not have an aggressive *intent* either on the European front or on the Far Eastern front. But as far as *capabilities* were concerned, the situation in the Far East was seen as different from that of Europe. Here Soviet capabilities were being substantively upgraded, and this trend was likely to continue. The reduction of military assets was largely restricted to obsolete or near-obsolete equipment. Moreover, one could notice a significant modernization of the remaining military assets. One reason for these developments was that reductions were limited by the decision to maintain the Sea of Okhotsk sanctuary for Soviet SSBNs.

As for the *strategic environment,* it had not changed in the Far East, in contrast to that of Central Europe. Training and maneuvers in the Sea of Okhotsk sanctuary were brisk, and one could not escape the conclusion that the structure behind the Soviet potential threat to Japan had not changed. The author further speculated that only the removal of the Soviet SSBNs to the Arctic Ocean, away from Japan, would create a strategic environment less threatening to Japan.

Around the same time, Gen. Colin Powell, the chairman of the U.S. Joint Chiefs of Staff, made a visit to Tokyo and met with his Japanese counterpart, Admiral Makoto Sakuma. This top Japanese officer in the self-defense forces said that the Soviet units stationed in the Far East were still a threat to Japan despite overall reductions in the Soviet military. He and General Powell agreed that a modernized Soviet military remains a potential threat to East Asia.[40]

Has there been a change in the Japanese perception of the Soviet/Russian threat since the disintegration of the Soviet Union in December 1991? Certainly, this event has given the opportunity for some Japanese opposition parties to argue for cuts in the defense budget, but it is still the Liberal Democratic Party (LDP) that calls the shots. As discussed in the first part of this chapter, the Japanese public's perception of the Soviet/Russian threat has not changed drastically enough to force the ruling party to reexamine its defense priorities, aside from limiting the increase in the defense budget to 3.8 percent. Moreover, if the Japanese were to initiate drastic cuts in defense spending, they would have to consider possible U.S. objections.

The Japanese defense establishment, likewise, has not drastically revised its estimates of Soviet capabilities in the area. A senior Japanese defense analyst writing in *The Journal of National Defense* in June 1992 pointed out that in the Asia Pacific region there are several unresolved problems carried over from the period of the Cold War and that there remain important causes of regional conflict. Among the legacies of the Cold War he cites the northern territories problem and the division of the Korean Peninsula.[41]

The 1992 defense white paper issued in August 1992[42] toned down the appraisal of the situation around Japan, noting that the military situation was "unstable" rather than "severe," as characterized in the 1991 white paper. Of course, instability is also a cause for concern, but it is not as troublesome as deliberate Russian policies directed against Japan. The prognosis, thus, is for a cautious wait-and-see attitude.

■ CONCLUSIONS: POLITICAL AND INTERNATIONAL SECURITY CONSEQUENCES FOR JAPAN AND RUSSIA

The Cold War started shortly after the end of World War II as an accumulation of policies, statements, and actions initiated primarily, though not exclusively, by the Soviet Union. This conflict—which saw serious crises, prolonged confrontation, and phony détentes—lasted over forty years, and it is also appropriate to call this period, as some analysts do, "The Long Peace." Everyone now talks about *the end of the Cold War,* but there is no agreement on precisely when or how it ended. There are different perceptions in different countries; I argue that Japan was the last country among the Western powers to evaluate favorably Gorbachev's perestroika and new political thinking. As a result, Japan lagged behind Western Europe and the United States in perceiving increased trustworthiness on the part of the Soviet Union and a lessened Soviet threat.

The collapse of the Warsaw Pact effectively removed the threat of a Soviet-led invasion of Western Europe on the central front; there is nothing comparable in the Soviet Far East. One can even argue that the Russian war machine in Northeast Asia is leaner but meaner, with the Pacific Fleet now concentrated in the Seas of Japan and Okhotsk rather than being dispersed over a large area of the Pacific Ocean. At the same time, although no rational military planner would impute hostile *intent* to the Russians, their job also calls for coping with *capabilities.*

What is the effect on Japan of the collapse of the Soviet empire, the disintegration of the Soviet Union, and the discrediting of communism, socialism, and central economic planning, beyond the narrow focus on Japan's relations with its northern neighbor? In terms of domestic politics, these developments greatly strengthen the LDP and the government and vindicate its privatization policy (national railroads, communications, etc.). Though the LDP is somewhat in disarray because of continuously breaking news of bribery scandals, the weakness of Japanese opposition parties allowed it to register important gains in the House of Councillors (the "Upper House") elections that took place in late July 1992.

The opposition parties, traditionally seduced by Marxism and socialism, are obviously much more affected by the fall of the USSR. The main opposition group, the Japan Socialist Party (JSP), in contrast to the West German Socialist Party or the British Labor Party, has never repudiated its devotion to doctrinaire Marxism. In 1960 the party's right-wing moderates seceded to form the Democratic Socialist Party (DSP). After the exodus of the moderates, the remaining JSP leadership was split between left and right, the left-wing curiously following policies *to the left* of the Japan Communist Party (JCP). In recent years, the leadership was in the hands of right-wing "moderates" who used to frequent Beijing, Moscow, and especially Pyongyang. In response to the dramatic developments in Eastern Europe and the Soviet Union, the JSP for some reason changed its *English* name to the Social Democratic Party of Japan but retained its Japanese name (Nihon Shakai To). The socialists also have their own share of bribery scandals, although on a much smaller scale than the business-oriented and more powerful LDP.

The three remaining opposition parties (the Buddhist-affiliated Komeito, or Clean Government Party, the Democratic Socialists, and the Communists) have in recent elections lost parliamentary seats to the JSP. The Democratic Socialists are truly a party of the center: They have supported the self-defense forces and the security alliance with the United States, and on certain issues they vote with the government party, such as the recent important vote on sending the Japanese self-defense forces abroad for United Nations peacekeeping operations. But as often happens (as, for example, with the British Social Democrats), the centrist parties get squeezed from both the left and the right. The Komeito is probably less affected than the others by the collapse of communism and central planning, although this party also espouses socialism, albeit "humanitarian."[43] This party will probably be more weakened by the excommunication of its parent Soka Gakkai organization by Buddhist authorities.

We now come to the Japan Communist Party. Some fifteen years ago, the JCP dropped all references to dictatorship of the proletariat and Marxism-Leninism (calling it now "scientific socialism"). Over the years, it also opposed Soviet (and Chinese) expansionism and interférence in the affairs of other communist parties (including the JCP) and could note with satisfaction the collapse of the Soviet empire. In the fall of 1988, it launched a strident critique (on pure Marxist grounds) of Gorbachev's perestroika[44] and now could say "we told you so." But the party has yet to feel the full backlash of the Japanese electorate. In the February 1990 elections to the powerful House of Representatives (only two months after the total rejection of communism in one Eastern European country after another), the JCP polled over five million votes, losing only 200,000 votes compared to the previous election in 1986. In a more recent gubernatorial election in Osaka in November 1991, the party amazingly garnered almost a quarter of the vote. As I wrote in a recently published book,[45] the JCP may well become the last remaining nonruling Communist Party in the world.

I have followed Japan's policy toward the Soviet Union/Russia during the recent period of momentous change in Eastern Europe and in the Soviet Union itself. The Japanese have been the most cautious of all the Western powers in their approach, partly because of the inability of the Japanese system to react quickly and partly because of the long-lasting territorial dispute with Moscow and the resultant anti-Sovietism. There is also the U.S. angle: Japan was a partner, if not an equal ally, in the anti-Soviet coalition. The Japanese government now has to adjust its Russian policy, taking into account U.S. policy toward Russia and other dimensions of the Japan–U.S. relationship, such as continuous friction in economic matters. During the Cold War era, when Japan's bases and military cooperation were vital to the U.S. position in the western Pacific, the Pentagon could be counted upon to counteract anti-Japanese policies emanating from the economic agencies of the U.S. government, such as the Department of the Treasury, the Department of Agriculture, and the Office of the Trade Representative. Now the pro-Japanese leverage by the Pentagon would be much weaker.

If the Japanese and the United States have long perceived the Soviet Union as a *military* threat to their security, they increasingly see each other as their greatest *economic* threat. Some years ago, the prestigious *Nihon Keizai Shimbun,* the Japanese counterpart of *The Wall Street Journal,* tried to assess both military and economic threats. In this poll, conducted in

Japan and the United States well before Gorbachev's policies began to change the Western perception of the Soviet threat, each saw the greatest economic threat emanating from the other. This perception was held by surprisingly similar numbers of over 70 percent, a remarkable trans-Pacific mirror image.[46]

If the United States is Japan's greatest economic threat, what do the Japanese people think about post–Cold War relations with the United States and the future of the Japan–U.S. alliance? After the disintegration of the Soviet empire in Eastern Europe, the United States Information Agency began commissioning periodic polls on the subject. The interviewees were asked to choose between two policy options:

1. The Cold War has ended and the security alliance with the U.S. is no longer needed to ensure continued peace and prosperity in Asia and the Pacific; or
2. Tensions remain despite improved East-West relations. The Japan–U.S. security alliance is still essential for continued peace and prosperity in Asia and the Pacific.

The results are fairly consistent (the latest poll was taken in May 1992), with roughly two-thirds of the respondents choosing the second statement, 11 to 16 percent feeling that the alliance with the United States has outlived its usefulness, and the rest in the "don't know" category.[47]

As for the question of how Japan should deal with world problems, 1 percent want a partnership with Western Europe alone, a quarter would like to see Japan as a leader in Asia, and about half of the Japanese want a global partnership either with the United States alone or with the United States and Western Europe. At the same time, almost 60 percent think Japan's foreign policy is too closely tied to that of the United States, and about a quarter think Japan has an independent policy and simply shares many policy goals with the United States.[48]

As the Cold War is relegated to history books and the Soviet Union is split into a dozen quarrelling republics, the international security system has become unipolar. The nuclear terror is gone, but we still worry about the tens of thousands of nuclear weapons on the territory of the former Soviet Union. We also have new concerns about the potential sale of latest model fighter planes, missiles, and nuclear technology to the Third World and China. There is also fear that Russian nuclear scientists and technicians might find lucrative job opportunities in Iran, Libya, and other dangerous terrorist states.

Although the international *security* system has become unipolar, the international *economic* system has become decidedly multipolar, with the relative weight of the United States gradually reduced. Furthermore, analysts are now writing about the decline of geo*politics* and the emerging importance of geo*economics*. In this new world, Russia is a middle power (although in the long term a potential superpower) and Japan is a superpower. But Japan's position is paradoxical. On the one hand, its relative weight in this new economic system is greatly enhanced. On the other hand, the end of the Cold War has weakened its position in the international security system. On balance, Japan's rise in the geoeconomic world is bound to lead to greater friction with the United States. The creation of a single North American Free Trade Agreement (NAFTA) is also of considerable concern for the Japanese. Given the undeniable fact that the U.S. market is of utmost importance for Japan, Japan is likely to be worse off in the post–Cold War era.

Having lost its empire, Russia is obviously much weaker in the post–Cold War period. It was said that the eagle of the Romanov dynasty had two heads to look west and east. Where is the new Russia facing in the 1990s? Foreign Minister Kozyrev is reported to have said that "We have an unprecedented opportunity to be Asians in Asia and Europeans in Europe."[49] That may be wishful thinking, as few, if any, Chinese, Koreans, or Japanese consider the Russians to be Asians. (In 1941 Stalin also talked about "Us, Asians" to Japanese Foreign Minister Yosuke Matsuoka—but then Stalin *was* an Asian.)

But although the bulk of Russia's population and industry remains in Europe and its trade with Europe is three times the size of its trade with Asian countries, the Asia Pacific region has assumed an added importance for the country. Vladimir Lukin, a prominent Russian specialist on the Asia Pacific region and the current ambassador to Washington, in a recent contribution to the journal *Foreign Policy* wrote that "[a]side from Europe, relations with countries of the Asian-Pacific region continue to be of critical significance to Russia." He also felt that because the Russian Far East remains largely underdeveloped and underpopulated, "Russia is additionally sensitive to security concerns emanating from the Asian-Pacific region."[50] Another prominent Russian scholar stresses the importance of the Asia Pacific region and Russia's relations with Japan and the United States:

> In terms of economic interests, sources of capital investments and market opportunities, the importance of the Asia Pacific region goes far beyond the interests of the Russian Far East. The future of Russia's economic reforms, the accesses to global markets, technologies and investment, as well as the security of the country, depend not only upon stable and friendly relations with the U.S. and Japan, but also on the stability of these two powers' long term relationship.[51]

A high-ranking Russian diplomat agrees with this evaluation: "Due to the logic of circumstances, relations with Japan should become one of the priorities of the foreign policy of sovereign Russia."[52] In other words, relations with Japan transcend the Asia Pacific region and assume critical importance for the future of Russia. To be sure, in the past the Soviet Union could not join the various organizations in the Asia Pacific (such as PECC) without the concurrence of Japan and the United States. Good relations with Japan were a prerequisite for the economic integration of the Soviet Union in the region. Although Russia is now a member of PECC and is treated quite differently than was the Soviet Union, Japan is still the key to the economic future of Russia in the Asia Pacific.

The Russian scholar cited above goes on to comment on the discontinuity between the foreign and defense policies of the former Soviet Union and Russia in the Asia Pacific region: "The continuation of the role the former Soviet Union played in the region is neither possible nor desirable. It is also a problem of entirely new strategic thinking and new priorities both in Russian foreign policy and defense posture."[53]

Ambassador Lukin rather optimistically sees Russia's new role "as the most important pillar of equilibrium, in concord with other leading powers that have vital stakes in Eurasian stability, rather than to disturb the equilibrium." In the Far East, Lukin says, Russia, "by maintaining constructive relations with China, Japan, and other states in the region, . . . can become an important balancer, preventing any one of them from dominating others without itself posing a threat to the region."[54] He assumes that the Bush-Yeltsin declaration in June 1992 has created a new partnership between the two erstwhile antagonists, which will have a positive impact on Russia's relations with Japan and South Korea: "We expect to develop friendly, mutually useful relations with such U.S. allies as Japan and the Republic of Korea. We see those countries as allies of our partner, and hope that they see us as a partner of their ally."[55]

Although this may be an unduly optimistic assessment of the role Russia can realistically play in the Asia Pacific region, we need to consider Russia's new strategic thinking and new priorities in the region. Much will depend not only on the policies of the other powers in Asia Pacific vis-à-vis Russia but also on the political evolution and economic development of the Russian Far East. In mid-August 1990 the leaders of the Yakut Autonomous Soviet Republic, the Khabarovsk and Primorskii (Maritime) territories, and the Jewish Autonomous, Amur, Kamchatka, Magadan, and Sakhalin regions formed the Far Eastern Association to promote social and economic cooperation. In May 1991 a regional forum was held in Khabarovsk to organize a People's Movement for the Formation of a Far Eastern Republic. The idea was to raise the constitutional status of the area to give it better control over its natural resources and a stronger voice vis-à-vis Moscow.[56] So far, centrifugal forces have not led to an independent far eastern republic, but much depends on the degree to which Moscow will grant autonomous status to the area, so far from the Russian capital and Europe and so close to China, Korea, and Japan. But irrespective of Moscow's relations with the Far East, the latter three countries are bound to exert a strong pull, at least economically.

In the national security dimension, future relations between Russia on the one hand and Japan and the United States on the other will to a large extent be determined by Russian decisions regarding the future of its strategic submarine nuclear force in the Sea of Okhotsk sanctuary. If the submarines remain, the attendant need to devise a protective shield for them will cause much of the present tension to remain. But if the submarines are moved elsewhere (such as to the Arctic Ocean) and some security regime is found for the Sea of Okhotsk, then we have a different situation with profound implications for the U.S. Pacific Fleet and especially for the overall defense strategy of Japan.

Thus, in the *economic* sphere future developments in the Asia Pacific depend in large measure on Japan (and the United States), but in the *security* sphere it is Russia, weakened though it is, that will play the dominant role in determining the strategic balance in the post–Cold War era.

■ NOTES

I wish to thank the Center for International Studies, School of International Relations, University of Southern California for their support; the School of International Relations for a travel grant; and Minoru Koide and Elizabeth Knowlton of the University of Southern California for research and editorial assistance, respectively. I am very grateful to Paul Langer and Michael Blaker, who have read the manuscript and offered very helpful suggestions. In addition, I am indebted to Michael Blaker, Ronald Hinckley, Toshihiko Ikura, James Marshall, Shigeki Nishimura, and Yakov Zinberg for providing me with research materials. I would also like to thank the compilers and editors of the *SUPAR Report* put out by the Center for the Soviet Union in the Pacific and Asian Region, University of Hawaii (Patricia Polansky, John Stephan, and Robert Valliant) for making this outstanding research tool available. As is customary to add, final responsibility is mine.

1. The text of Article 9 of the Japanese Constitution reads:

Aspiring sincerely to an international peace based on justice and order, the Japanese people forever renounce war as a sovereign right of the nation and the threat or use of force as means of settling international disputes.

In order to accomplish the aim of the preceding paragraph, land, sea, and air forces, as well as other war potential, will never be maintained. The right of belligerency of the state will not be recognized.

2. This chapter logically follows two of my most recent 1992 publications, and the reader might profitably be referred to:

Peter Berton, "The Impact of the 1989 Revolutions on Soviet-Japanese Relations," Chapter 8 in Young C. Kim and Gaston J. Sigur (eds.), *Asia and the Decline of Communism* (New Brunswick, NJ and London: Transaction Publishers, 1992), pp. 133–153; and *idem.*, "Gorbachev's Policy in the Asia Pacific Region with Particular Reference to Soviet Relations with Japan," *Osaka Gakuin Daigaku Kokusaigaku Ronso—International Studies,* Vol. 2, No. 2 (March 1992), pp. 195–234.

3. See also Gilbert Rozman, *Japan's Response to the Gorbachev Era, 1985–1991: A Rising Superpower Views a Declining One* (Princeton: Princeton University Press, 1992).

4. For a detailed account of the Soviet-Japanese territorial dispute, see Peter Berton, "The Japanese-Russian Territorial Dilemma: Historical Background, Disputes, Issues, Questions, Solution Scenarios—A Thousand Scenarios for the Thousand Islands Dispute," white paper prepared for the Strengthening Democratic Institutions Project at the Kennedy School of Government, Harvard University, July 17, 1992.

5. Peter Berton, "Soviet-Japanese Relations: Perceptions, Goals, Interactions," *Asian Survey*, Vol. XXVI, No. 12 (December 1986), pp. 1259–1283.

6. See the section on "Gorbachev's Reforms and Opening to the West: The Impact on Japan and Japanese Public Opinion," in my chapter "The Impact of the 1989 Revolutions on Soviet-Japanese Relations" in Kim and Sigur, *Asia and the Decline of Communism.*

7. See Table 8.1 in *ibid.*, p. 135.

8. See Tables 8.2 and 8.3 in *ibid.*, pp. 136–137.

9. *Gaiko ni kansuru Yoron Chosa* [Public Opinion Survey on Diplomacy], conducted annually in October and published in pamphlet form by the Prime Minister's Office (Tokyo: Naikaku Sori Daijin Kambo Koho Shitsu [Public Information Office, Prime Minister's Secretariat]) in March or April of the following year.

10. For charts showing nations liked and disliked by the Japanese during the 1960s and 1970s, see Peter Berton, Paul F. Langer, and George O. Totten (translators, contributors, and editors); and Nobori Shomu and Akamatsu Katsumro, *The Russian Impact on Japan: Literature and Social Thought: Two essays* (Los Angeles: University of Southern California Press, 1981). Supplemented by *Jiji Yoron Chosa Tokuho* [Jiji Public Opinion Survey: Special Report] (Tokyo: Jiji Tsushin Sha, three times a month). Updated through October 1992.

11. The respondents have to name three countries they like and three countries they dislike.

12. Joint Soviet-Japanese poll conducted by telephone in February 1988 in both countries (250 localities in Japan and in Moscow, Leningrad, Kiev, Khabarovsk, and Vladivostok). *Tokyo Shimbun,* March 6, 1988, p. 1.

13. Joint Soviet-Japanese poll conducted in March 1988 by the *Yomiuri Shimbun* and the Soviet Institute of Sociology. *Yomiuri Shimbun,* May 25, 1988, pp. 1, 14, and 15.

14. Mikhail Gorbachev's Vladivostok speech on July 28, 1986, *FBIS,* July 29, 1986, pp. R1–R20. See also *Security in the Asia Pacific Region: The Soviet Approach—Documents and Materials* (Moscow: Novosti Press Agency Publishing House, 1988), pp. 16–28.

15. Mikhail Gorbachev's Krasnoyarsk speech, *Pravda,* September 18, 1988, 2nd edition, pp. 1–3: translated in *FBIS,* September 20, 1988, pp. 29–41.

16. Berton, "Gorbachev's Policy in the Asia Pacific Region," p. 214.

17. Peggy Levine Falkenheim, "Moscow and Tokyo: Slow Thaw in Northeast Asia," *World Policy Journal* (Winter 1990–1991), pp. 159–179.

18. Peter Berton, "A Turn in Sino-Soviet Relations?" Chapter 2 in James C. Hsiung (ed.), *Beyond China's Independent Foreign Policy: Challenge for the U.S. and Its Asian Allies* (New York: Praeger, 1985), pp. 24–54.

19. Shinjukai (comp.), *Go Daitoryo Rai-Nichi to Kongo no Nisso Kankei* [President Gorbachev's Visit to Japan and Future Japanese-Soviet Relations] (Tokyo: Compiler, July 1991); Hiroshi Kimura, "Gorbachev's Japan Policy: The Northern Territories Issue," *Asian Survey*, Vol. XXXI, No. 9 (September 1991), pp. 798–815; and Tsuyoshi Hasegawa, "Gorbachev's Visit to Japan and Soviet-

Japanese Relations," *Acta Slavica Iaponica* (Slavic Research Center, Hokkaido University), Tomus X (1992), pp. 65–92.

20. For more details, see the section "Gorbachev's Visit to Japan, April 1991," in Berton, "Gorbachev's Policy in the Asia Pacific Region," pp. 226–229.

21. Tokyo, Kyodo, September 24, 1991 in FBIS-EAS-91–185 (September 24, 1991), p. 6.

22. More specifically, $500 million was earmarked for humanitarian aid (food and medicine), $200 million for project loan, and the remaining $1.8 billion for insurance. *Yomiuri Shimbun,* October 9, 1991.

23. "Yeltsin Hastens Isle Solution: Offers To Settle Territorial Dispute Ahead of Schedule," *Daily Yomiuri,* October 1991, p. 1.

24. "Attitude in Sakhalin 'Seething,'" Moscow Russian Television Network, October 8, 1991 in FBIS-SOV-91–203, International Affairs, October 21, 1991, p. 18.

25. Moscow Interfax, October 10, 1991 in FBIS-SOV-91–198 (October 11, 1991), p. 59.

26. "Russia Recognizes Legality of 1956 Joint Declaration," *Daily Yomiuri,* December 29, 1991.

27. *Japan Times,* February 2, 1992, p. 1.

28. *Yomiuri Shimbun,* February 29, 1992, p. 1.

29. *Yomiuri Shimbun,* March 18, 1992.

30. John-Thor Dahlburg, "Russia, Japan Set Target Date for Drafting World War II Peace Pact," *Los Angeles Times,* May 5, 1992, p. A39.

31. "Sovet Soiuza Kazakov Rossii" [Council of the Cossack Union of Russia], *Kommercheskii vestnik* [Commercial Bulletin] (Yuzhno-Sakhalinsk), No. 9 (February 1992).

32. "Den' Iuzhnykh Kuril" [Southern Kuriles Day], *Gubernskie vedomosti,* June 12, 1992, p. 2.

33. *Argumenty i fakty* [Arguments and Facts] (Moscow), No. 72 (1992), p. 4.

34. "1991 Nen no Nisso Boeki" [Japan-Soviet Trade in 1991], *Soren Too Keizai Sokuho* [Soviet and East European Economic Bulletin], No. 881 (March 15, 1992).

35. Berton, "The Impact of the 1989 Revolutions on Soviet-Japanese Relations." See also Shinichiro Tabata, "The Japanese-Soviet Economic Future," *Acta Slavica Iaponica,* Tomus IX (1991), pp. 189–205.

36. For a detailed account of Russo-Japanese relations through September 1992, see Tsuyoshi Hasegawa, "Russo-Japanese Relations in the Post-Perestroika Period," chapter in Ramesh Thakur and Carlyle Thayer, eds., *Regional Conflicts in the Asia Pacific Region* (Boulder, CO: Westview Press, forthcoming in 1993). For a critique of Japanese policy in the territorial dispute with Russia, see Professor Hasegawa's "'Hoppo Ryodo shokogun' ni ochiitta Nihon" [Japan that Is Afflicted with the "Northern Territories Syndrome"], *Chuo Koron* [Central Review], No. 9 (September 1992), pp. 86–97.

37. *Jiji Yoron Chosa Tokuho,* October 1, 1992.

38. *Yomiuri Shimbun,* December 28 and 29, 1991.

39. *Yomiuri Shimbun,* July 27, 1991.

40. Kyodo, November 18, 1991, in FBIS-EAS-91–222 (November 18, 1991), p. 1.

41. Shigekatsu Kondo, "Reisen-go no Ajia Taiheiyo Chiiki no Anzen Hosho wo ika ni Kakuho suru ka" [How Can We Assure the Security of the Asia Pacific Region in the Post–Cold War Era], *Shin Boei Ronshu—The Journal of National Defense,* Vol. 20, No. 1 (June 1992), p. 64.

42. *Yomiuri Shimbun,* August 8, 1992.

43. See "The Komeito: Party of 'Buddhist Democracy,'" in Ronald J. Hrebenar, *The Japanese Party System,* 2nd revised ed. (Boulder, CO: Westview Press, 1992).

44. See Peter Berton, "The Japanese Communist Party's View of Gorbachev's Perestroika," *Acta Slavica Iaponica* (Slavic Research Center, Hokkaido University, Sapporo, Japan), Tomus VII (1989), pp. 121–144. See also some of my other writings on the JCP: "Japan: Euro-Nippo-Communism," Chapter XV in Vernon V. Aspaturian, et al. (eds.), *Eurocommunism Between East and West* (Bloomington: Indiana University Press, 1980), pp. 326–362; "The Soviet and Japanese Communist Parties: Policies, Tactics, Negotiating Behavior," *Studies in Comparative Communism,* Vol. XV, No. 3 (August 1982), pp. 266–287; and "Japanese Eurocommunists: Running in Place," *Problems of Communism,* Vol. XXXV, No. 4 (July–August 1986), pp. 1–30.

45. Peter Berton, "The Japanese Communist Party: The 'Lovable' Party," in Hrebenar, *The Japanese Party System,* pp. 116–147.

46. *Kawaru—2010 Nen no Sekai to Nihon* [Change: The World in the Year 2010 and Japan] (Tokyo: Nihon Keizai Shimbun Sha, 1986), pp. 267–270.

47. "'Global Partnership:' Views of the Japanese Public," *Opinion Research Memorandum* (Washington, D.C.: United States Information Agency, Office of Research, August 6, 1992), p. 13.

48. *Ibid.,* pp. 13–14.

49. John-Thor Dahlburg, "Look Eastward, Russia: The New Asian Interest," *Los Angeles Times,* October 27, 1992, pp. H1 and H5.

50. Vladimir P. Lukin, "Our Security Predicament," *Foreign Policy* (Fall 1992), p. 59.

51. Vladimir I. Ivanov, "'Northern Territories' and U.S.-Japan-Russia Relations in the 1990s," first draft of a paper prepared for the Program on U.S.–Japan Relations, Center for International Affairs, Harvard University, May 1992, p. 22.

52. V. I. Saplin, "Russian-Japanese Relations: Between the Past and the Future," unpublished paper presented at a seminar at Princeton University, April 1992.

53. Ivanov, "'Northern Territories' and U.S.-Japan-Russia Relations," p. 22.

54. Lukin, "Our Security Predicament," p. 67.

55. *Ibid.,* p. 71.

56. The Far Eastern Republic [Dal'nevostochnaia Respublika (or DVR)] is a reference to the Far Eastern Republic that was proclaimed during the Siberian Intervention (1918–1922) to deal with the occupying powers, especially Japan. When the foreign occupation ended, the Far Eastern Republic incorporated itself into the Bolshevik state (later known as the USSR) and ceased to exist.

See the "Agreement on the Basic Principles of Economic and Social Cooperation Between the Yakut ASSR, Maritime Territory, Khabarovsk Territory, the Jewish Autonomous, Amur, Kamchatka, Magadan, and Sakhalin Regions of the Far Eastern Area of the RSFSR," *Far Eastern Affairs,* No. 1, 1991, pp. 13–15.

For current activities, see the Section on "Regionalism" in SUPAR Report, No. 11 (July 1991), pp. 122–123.

∎ 3

Japan: Searching Once Again
Bernard K. Gordon

In international politics, much more so than in domestic affairs, Japan is a nation that doesn't know what to do with itself. Of course, like any other major industrialized nation, it has its internal problems. It has its homeless and its unemployed (though both issues are more masked in Japan than elsewhere), and it has its worries for the future. For example, there is a widening "class gap" in Japan; its rural areas haven't seen the prosperity of the cities; it doesn't know what to do about its farmers, as more and more of its people produce the world's most sophisticated products; and there has been some very troubling financial speculation. But overall, Japan today is an astoundingly wealthy nation, and its people increasingly share in that wealth. They travel everywhere; they often wear the world's most fashionable clothing and drive its most expensive cars; and in general they enjoy the "good life." The life-style of many Japanese would lead most U.S. and European onlookers to conclude that "Japan has made it."

No doubt the average Japanese, even those who drive a fancy car and travel abroad, would not agree. They would say, "I work longer hours than you; I don't have a house, and if I do, it's much smaller than yours." And the unaverage Japanese—the few who think about, work in, and in their writings tell other Japanese what and how to think about world affairs—have another concern. To them, the question is, "Now that Japan and the Japanese are rich, what do we do now?" In the words of the Peggy Lee song, "Is that all there is?" They dare not say yes, because they believe that somehow, there must be more for Japan than just being rich. They suspect that as a very large nation—with 124 million people, whose per capita income is the highest among major nations, and with the world's second-largest gross national product (almost $3 trillion, compared with the United States's almost $5 trillion)—Japan should play some kind of a "role" in the world.

But what kind of role? That, literally, is the question posed to the Japanese every day. They know they are widely seen as a cash cow for every worthwhile (or other) cause, from poverty in Bangladesh to a new nuclear super-collider in Texas. But they are stung by the view that Japan and the Japanese are only an "economic animal." Even now, many recall that in the 1960s, France's President Charles DeGaulle kept a Japanese prime minister waiting with the comment: "Is the transistor salesman here?" Yet even as the Japanese resist the view that all they can do in world affairs is make money for themselves and contribute some of it to others, they fear going beyond that. Their thoughts of playing a political role are filled with memories of their past excursions into world politics, and what they recall is more bad than good. Indeed, the main factor that shapes Japanese thinking about again taking on a foreign policy role is fear of rekindling the past. It is reinforced by two others: smugness about the present and uncertainty about the future.

■ FEAR OF REKINDLING JAPAN'S PAST

Japan's fear of resuming a major role in world politics stems mainly from its World War II experience. Many of its cities and almost all of its factories and harbors were destroyed by bombing and fires in which hundreds of thousands of its civilians were killed. It all culminated in the instant deaths of hundreds of thousands more in the atomic bombings at Hiroshima and Nagasaki, and nuclear after-effects caused slow deaths to additional thousands. Equally horrific were the war's consequences for Japan's armed forces: those of its young men and boys sent to the Pacific islands seldom returned at all, and many of those who fought in China and on the Asian mainland came home only years later. When they did, it was to a Japan occupied and run by foreigners—the first time that had ever happened—and to a nation hungry, cold, and poor. It remained that way until 1949 or 1950. Japan's condition was summed up by Gen. Douglas MacArthur, the nation's effective ruler during the U.S. occupation. When he arrived at the end of the war he described to Washington the circumstances he faced and asked for what he needed to govern: "Send me either bullets or butter."

Washington, of course, sent butter, and to this day almost all Japanese respect and even revere MacArthur. They remain thankful for the compassion and generosity of the United States of those years—even as they are becoming increasingly ambivalent about the United States of this era. That subject will come up again later in this chapter, but what must be stressed now is that when today's Japanese think of again playing a "role" in the world, they recall what their past policies brought them: at home, patriotic hysteria, military dictatorship, and a war that accomplished only destruction and death; abroad, a legacy of distrust and suspicion; not only from the United States as a result of the attack without warning on Pearl Harbor but also from the Asian peoples whose lands they invaded and whom they then governed with much brutality.

These are heavy burdens for a Japanese people who pride themselves on cultural sensitivity and scrupulous honesty. The memories are sharpest for the older generation, but Japan's young people also have had driven into them the view that war is hell and that Japan, for whatever reason, should do nothing that could lead to it again. Nothing dominates Japanese thinking about a future foreign policy role more than these memories of the past, and the problem is compounded because Japan's responsibility for the Pacific War, and for the often terrible behavior of those who acted in its name, still remains largely unacknowledged officially.

■ PRIDE AND ARROGANCE

If fear of rekindling the past is the first factor that shapes Japan's foreign policy thinking today, the second is Japan's smugness about its modern accomplishments. All Japanese, young and old, know that their nation not only has recovered from the war but quite literally has risen from its ashes to become an economic and industrial giant. They are aware that their country *alone* accounts for 16 percent of the world's gross national product, and they also know that much of what Japan produces is made nowhere else. Moreover, they know that in Europe and the United States, and of course in the developing countries, many seek to "learn from Japan"—to borrow its methods in engineering, education, industrial management, and much else. When Harvard professor Ezra Vogel published his *Japan as Number One* in 1978, it became an instant best-seller in Japan—far more successful there than anywhere else.

Of course the Japanese are flattered by this attention, but more is involved. There are deep and widely held Japanese views that their nation and people are special, quite unique, and probably superior to most or all others. The evidence that they not only have caught up to but may actually have bested the West (and especially the United States), in the one area where it excelled—industry, wealth, and the good life—has for many Japanese reinforced the view that their way is the best way. The result has been self-confidence for most, smugness for many, and arrogance for some who are quite prominent.

The sharpest and best-known illustration of that arrogance is in the writings of Diet member Shintaro Ishihara. In his book *The Japan that Can Say No* (initially coauthored with Sony founder Akio Morita), he argued that without Japan and its computer chips, the United States can do nothing. Ishihara even suggested, in an era when the USSR was still a "rival" to the United States in world politics, that Japan held the "balance" between them and could tip it by providing chips to the Russians! Ishihara's is an extreme and still clearly a minority view, but it is common in today's Japan to believe that the United States, and especially its economy, are in decline. This belief was reinforced when President Bush visited Japan in early 1992 and brought with him the heads of the "big three" U.S. car companies. They were there to insist that Japan buy more U.S.-made cars, but the Japanese view was that U.S. producers could not succeed on their own in Japan and needed the president to help them.

The image of a sick United States was graphically reinforced when President Bush himself took ill at a state banquet in Tokyo. On television all over Japan were pictures of the president of the United States, unconscious on the floor where he had collapsed, being comforted and consoled by the prime minister of Japan. It symbolized a nation that is weak and tired, an image daily compounded by the picture of the United States regularly portrayed by Japan's media. In this view, the key elements of U.S. decay are an educational system that does not prepare its children to compete effectively; an industrial sector that is itself wasteful and self-indulgent; and a society racked by urban violence and racial conflict. The contrast with peaceful, safe, and homogenous Japan is barely concealed and recalls the German word *schadenfreude:* to take pleasure in somebody else's suffering.

Of course, some Japanese caution against this view. Shin Kanemaru, the former vice president and behind-the-scenes "godfather" of the ruling Liberal Democratic Party (and the man who largely determined who would be Japan's prime minister) is a good example. In 1992 he warned the LDP never to forget that "America can live without Japan, but Japan cannot live without America." Nevertheless, the image of a Japan ascendant and a United States in decline is a powerful one. It strengthens the view that in world affairs Japan's way is best and that its great wealth is the proof of its wise policies. The result is a growing conviction that if there must be a world role for Japan, it should be as "contributor" to the efforts of others rather than as a direct actor. By "contributor," the Japanese mean literally just that: to pay for what Japan wants and for what important others say must be done in world affairs. This view was highlighted by two developments of the early 1990s: relations with the United States during the 1990–1991 Gulf War and relations with the former Soviet Union just afterward.

In the Gulf War, Japan went through an agonizing debate about how to respond to Iraq's invasion and attempted incorporation of Kuwait. The United States, with the endorsement of the UN Security Council, insisted on Iraq's withdrawal and ultimately used massive military force to achieve it. Great Britain, France, Saudi Arabia, and a few others also used their forces, but in Japan there was only a great quandary. Its prime minister sought in vain for parliamentary approval to send at least some Japanese military units that could participate in actual combat, but Japan provided only minesweepers and doctors. It did respond to U.S. insistence that it at least help pay the financial costs of the war ($10 billion was ultimately provided), but even that good effort became a point of upset. The reason was that the value of the U.S. dollar declined after Japan agreed to pay the yen equivalent of almost $13 billion. Its contribution therefore amounted to fewer dollars than initially agreed to, and Diet members wanted to hold to the original yen figure. In the end they appropriated more, but with bad feelings. When it was all over, the commonly heard view in Japan was that the United States had "made money on the war," and the episode left a sour aftertaste in several other respects as well.

First, the very fact that Washington so strongly insisted that Japan help pay for the war reinforced growing Japanese doubts about the United States' "superpower" status. It also allowed U.S. armed forces to be pictured as mercenaries: troops for hire. For people such as Ishihara, this perception underlined the Japanese view of the United States as a place where one buys or rents what one wants—but not more than that. Moreover, because Japan was able to limit its role to sending only money, many Japanese now believed their country had fully and properly discharged its responsibility in defeating Iraq's aggression. And if this method were acceptable in the Gulf War, why not elsewhere? In other words, when other foreign policy issues become troublesome, why not simply pay what's needed to get what Japan wants?

The clearest manifestation of this approach is in Japan's dealings with Russia, the main successor to the former Soviet Union. Russia controls the Northern Territories, four small islands north of Hokkaido occupied by the USSR at the end of World War II and held under Moscow's authority ever since. Japan has called for their return since the 1950s, and the issue has again come to a head because the Soviet collapse has brought new and sometimes frightening issues to world politics. The former Soviet nuclear arsenal is still in existence, and its former republics now demand their own place in the sun. But they are almost all desperately poor; they cannot agree about who owns what, including who controls Soviet strategic nuclear weapons; and the result is enormous potential for chaos and danger.

To avoid that, the major Western nations have begun to provide massive economic assistance to the Commonwealth of Independent States (CIS) that has succeeded most of the former Soviet republics. Without such help, U.S. and European leaders fear, terrible turmoil will break out in Eastern Europe, with dangerous implications for many. One worry is a return to hard-line dictatorship in Moscow and the other republics, and with that a return to aggressive and even expansionist foreign policies. Another worry is that unless economic conditions improve in the former Soviet Union, there will be a massive emigration to Western Europe. And lurking behind all this is the worry that thousands of nuclear weapons and missiles formerly controlled by Moscow will come into the hands of who knows what?

The result of all these concerns is that in the winter of 1991–1992 there were large Western European and U.S. food shipments to Moscow and St. Petersburg (Leningrad). In addition, hundreds of millions of dollars were authorized to stabilize the former Soviet economies, and the West approved their membership in the International Monetary Fund (IMF). But Japan has largely stood aside from all this collective effort. It has stated it will "cooperate" with Western efforts to help but will provide no substantial funds until Moscow agrees to return the northern territories. In a word, Japan's policy is one of blackmail. As world leaders elsewhere conclude that there is great need to prevent total chaos from the Soviet collapse— and plead with their legislatures for the money to avoid it—Japan has insisted first on resolution of a narrow and altogether bilateral issue.

In this respect Japan's policy is reminiscent of Iraq's when the Shah of Iran was overthrown. At that point, with Iran in turmoil, Iraq's Saddam Hussein tore up his recently signed border agreement with Iran and attacked his neighbor. In this case, Japan is not attacking Russia, but it is exploiting Moscow's sudden weakness and internal unrest. Tokyo has chosen this moment to insist, more firmly than ever before, that the northern territories be returned. It seems oblivious to the need both to build good long-term ties with Moscow and to the prospect that, like Iraq, it too will be seen as a state anxious to exploit its neighbor's troubles. Such a policy can only bolster the already negative image of Japan among so many nations with which it deals. Even now, it is widely seen as a nation wholly self-centered and insensitive to the needs of others, whether on issues of trade, economic policy, or security. By linking aid to Russia with its insistence on first returning the northern territories, Japan is likely to add to that reputation.

■ UNCERTAINTY ABOUT THE FUTURE

Part of the reason for this behavior is that Japan is genuinely uncertain about what foreign policy role it should play and even more deeply about where its interests lie. During the Cold War years, especially when Japan was very weak, there were easy answers to such questions: Japan needed security, and it needed to recover economically. In security terms, its overwhelming concern was the Soviet Union—feared not only because of its communism but also because of its long territorial ambitions and presence in Siberia and the Far East.[1] The Soviet image as a powerful, influential, and threatening state was further enhanced in those early Cold War years by Moscow's seemingly close ties to China and even North Korea.

Japan recognized that it needed military protection from all this, and its leaders also knew that for its economic recovery three other factors were essential: foreign markets for Japan's products; minimal spending for defense (and therefore minimal foreign worries); and, finally, a big brother —one who could speak for Japan in the many places where it was still distrusted or simply not known. In all these respects the United States was Japan's savior, and it is worth recalling the roles the superpower played. First, the United States assured Japan's security against any threat not only with its bases in and near Japan but ultimately with its nuclear umbrella. Second, the enormous and open U.S. market provided the economic opportunity from which Japan could rebuild and then expand its export capacity. Third, Washington shepherded and ushered Tokyo into world councils of political and economic importance, including the UN, the OECD, and most important, the General Agreement on Tariffs and Trade (GATT).

The result was that Japan became a tight formal ally of the United States. In most matters, it almost literally hitched its wagon to the United States' lead, and it adopted, as the bedrock of its foreign policy, the view that its U.S. connection was the foundation of its economic well-being and physical security. Of course, there were always some questions and doubts about this close alignment. For example, a persistent question involving overall foreign policy was whether Japan should be more of an "Asian" nation or whether it should be globally active and involved. In military policy, the question quickly arose whether Japan should accept U.S. insistence that it rebuild its defense forces, despite Tokyo's "no war" constitution. Likewise, should Japan house U.S. nuclear warheads on its territory despite its commitment to avoid any entanglement with such weapons? Should Japan follow the United States's lead toward China in regarding Beijing as the principal threat to Asian security and (until 1971) seeking to isolate it from the world community? Finally, should Japan support the U.S. war in Vietnam?

There were also economic questions dating from the mid-1960s. In those years, as Japan began to record a small trade surplus with the United States, it was faced with growing pressure to limit its exports to the U.S. market. Textiles were first, followed by steel, then televisions, finally cars, machine tools, and much else. Then, as the U.S. trade deficit grew, Japan was asked to increase its imports from the United States. At first the issues were mainly agricultural: Washington wanted Japan to buy more foreign oranges, then beef and rice. Later this shifted to cars and computer chips, and eventually to intangible, or "service," products: finance, banking, investment, insurance, and construction. In these and other fields— even legal services are now included—the United States has long held that

Japan's market is largely closed. Only partly in jest, some Japanese now answer that because the United States produces too many lawyers, it wants to ship the surplus to Tokyo.

These and myriad other issues increasingly nettled the relationship as Japan grew up after the war, and Tokyo finessed them all. On the China issue, it reminded Washington that China was, after all, its neighbor: true, Japan didn't like China's communism, but there were after all historical and cultural ties; and besides that, there was money to be made. So Japan would have to insist that, in dealing with China, "politics and economics are separate." It would therefore do business with China, lend it much money, and at the same time quietly maintain "unofficial" ties with Taiwan. Likewise, in its direct or bilateral economic relations with the United States, Japan adapted. It entered into a series of "voluntary" export-restraint agreements with its ally that began with textiles, were extended to steel, and continue to this day in connection with cars. The goal was to keep the United States quiet—to avoid upsetting the security relationship on which Japan's safety depended.

But even as Japan adapted and at U.S. insistence made many changes in its economic and trade policies, most Japanese have forgotten a fundamental point: Most or all of the changes Japan made were also economically rational from the perspective of *Japan's* development. The adjustments helped smooth the process by which its economy steadily moved "up the economic ladder" to high value-added goods such as electronics and cars and left to others those products—such as textiles and later steel—where Japan's higher wages were making it no longer competitive. But these rational and beneficial steps were seldom portrayed that way in Japan. Instead they were pictured as the result of *"gai-atsu,"* the need to respond to pressure from outsiders, usually and most notably from the United States.

The tendency for Japan to blame the United States for what Japan needed to do anyway has become a familiar pattern in relations between the two nations and continues to trouble their relationship today. When individuals behave in that way—blaming others for what they know should and must be done—their behavior is considered childish. Among states it is similarly a mark of immaturity or, more accurately, political irresponsibility. In Japan's case it is the result of a political leadership unwilling to level with its people, a fundamental failing in a democratic society. But whatever the cause, the result has been pernicious. It has led the Japanese to view the United States as a nagging shrew: always demanding, always insisting, never satisfied, and always wanting to force Japan to do something it doesn't want to do or that is "alien" to its culture.

Sometimes this behavior has near-comic manifestations, as in the case of those Japanese who argue that to eat foreign rice—or to allow foreign lawyers to practice in Japan—will destroy Japan's traditions and its culture.[2] But the effects are also always tragic, because they have brought a corrosive cancer to Japan's relations with the United States. The result is that the nation that was Japan's political and military protector and whose open economy provided the rich and enormous market that was absolutely essential to Japan's recovery and growth has now become instead a burden to be tolerated. That view has shaped the vocabulary, and therefore the political context, in which Japan's foreign policy dialogue is now conducted. It is reflected in the fact that what the Japanese increasingly believe the United States and others seek from Japan is a "contribution" to international affairs. The word itself figures prominently in almost every discussion of Japan's foreign policy—although, as Shinichi Kitaoka wrote recently, "contributions" have no place in diplomacy. In foreign policy, he writes, a nation should be acting to protect its own interests; "policy measures must not be portrayed as charitable acts."[3]

Yet that is precisely how potential foreign policy actions are portrayed every day in Japan—as gifts to those who are needy, or to placate others who are important. Of course, there are some specialists who argue against this view. They recognize not only that Japan has greatly benefited from the open economy and relatively peaceful world of the postwar era but also that the United States has been its key. They therefore urge that it is in Japan's own interest to work closely with the United States to maintain the present world structure. But this is very much a minority view, and what dominates the foreign policy debate is the notion that Japan's task is to make an "international contribution."

The result is that the Japanese people have a highly distorted view of what they should do in world affairs. Rather than being told that their nation has interests to protect and should therefore cooperate with others who share those interests, they have been led to believe that when Japan cooperates with other nations, it is mainly to help *the others*. Not surprisingly, therefore, Japan's foreign policy debate has centered on finding the least onerous way to make such contributions, and no issue better symbolizes this orientation than the subject of Japan's role in military and security affairs. The issue comes up in several contexts—first in connection with overall security in Asia, second with regard to military cooperation with the United States, and most recently on whether and how Japan should participate in "peacekeeping" operations under UN auspices.

■ JAPAN'S ARTICLE 9 AND THE PKO

Issues of defense and a military role have confounded Japan's politics for many years, but it was the Gulf crisis of 1990–1991 that brought them to a head. When the United States led a UN effort to force Iraq out of Kuwait, part of its concern was to assure continued commercial access to

Middle Eastern oil. Washington hoped that Japan's uniquely heavy dependence on that oil would persuade Tokyo to participate in the UN effort, but, as mentioned before, Japan's leaders were unable to gain support for any kind of direct military role. Germany also did not participate militarily, and Bonn and Tokyo both suffered heavy U.S. criticism as a result. The people and leaders of Japan, however, were mainly aware of criticism aimed at them, and many Japanese agreed: They concluded that their nation had been called upon and found wanting. Even now the Gulf crisis is seen as one of the true watersheds in Japan's postwar foreign policy.

The ostensible core of the problem was a prevailing view that Japan's postwar constitution forbids it to send military forces abroad. Some believe it forbids the maintenance of *any* military forces. The issue is Article 9, which says that

> the Japanese people forever renounce war as a sovereign right of the nation and the threat or use of force as a means of settling international disputes. . . . In order to accomplish the aim of the preceding paragraph, land, sea, and air forces, as well as other war potential, will never be maintained.

There are roughly four views in Japan about what those words mean. The first—the "strict constructionist" view—holds that Article 9 means Japan simply cannot possess, and certainly cannot use, armed forces. A second group believes Article 9 *does* allow defensive military forces— after all, every nation must be able to defend itself—but that Japan should be like Switzerland: a lightly armed state able to protect itself but not able to act militarily abroad. A third group brings a more political perspective to the constitution. It includes many "conservatives" and a number of Japan's "defense intellectuals." This group argues that the intention of Article 9 is conveyed in its first sentence, by which Japan renounced force as a means of "settling international disputes." In the view of this third group, the purpose of Article 9 is not to renounce the use of force in general, merely to renounce what Japan did *in World War II*: making war to achieve *solely Japanese* national goals. Thus, the constitution not only allows defense forces but makes it perfectly legal to use them in international operations—especially under UN auspices. There is a fourth group of so-called "right-wingers," probably a very small minority. They would like to scrap the constitution and Article 9 altogether, return to the good old days when Japan was like everybody else, and rebuild sizable military forces.

Article 9, however, is only the ostensible cause of the problem, because in fact Japan *has* maintained military units since the 1950s. They are called ground, sea, and air self-defense forces (SDFs) and they now number roughly 250,000 people. Moreover, although Japan rarely spends more

than 1 percent of its GNP directly on defense (this is *not* a legal require-
ment but stems from a 1960s policy decision), Japan's GNP is so big that
its military budget is among the largest in the world. At $16 billion today,
it is about the same as Germany's and not much smaller than that of
France or Great Britain ($18 billion and $19.5 billion, respectively).
Japan's defense spending is also much larger than any other nation in
Asia—double India's, and triple China's.[4]

Such sums also mean superb equipment and high readiness, as I observed during a "scramble" at a Japanese air base on the northern main island of Hokkaido. As sirens announced "enemy" aircraft approaching and
senior officers checked their stopwatches, impressive young pilots raced
from their barracks and had the world's most advanced fighter-bombers in
the air well under the one- and five-minute deadlines.

It is just such élan and discipline, of course, along with Japan's World
War II history, that is said to worry not only Japan's neighbors but many
Japanese as well. Overwhelmingly, most Japanese do not want to see a return to the military spirit that characterized much of society early in this
century. Even less do they want a revival of the military control of both
domestic affairs and foreign policy that reigned between 1930 and 1945.
Likewise, many Asian leaders—especially in China, Korea, the Philippines, and sometimes Singapore—have cautioned Japan against any
thought of a return to those days.[5] Consequently, when the Persian Gulf
disappointment led Japan's leaders to seek clear authority to participate in
future peacekeeping operations, they were hobbled by this combination of
foreign and domestic worries about the "revival of militarism." Those worries shaped the two-year campaign to pass a peacekeeping (PKO) bill. The
PKO law was enacted in June 1992, but the process further underlined the
unreality that often affects Japan's approach to foreign policy.[6]

The debate was heavily shaped by the objections of Japan's Socialist
Party, although it has not been in office since a brief interlude in 1955 and
has no hope of coming to power today.[7] The Socialists were joined by the
Communist Party, which is even more stridently antimilitarist and has
even less prospect of taking power. Two "centrist" parties that often cooperate with the ruling Liberal Democratic Party also raised major objections to the PKO bill, and there were LDP dissenters as well. The arguments of all rested on four main points: prohibitions in Article 9; the
danger of a militarist revival; the need to assure Asian nations that Japan
will not again seek to dominate them; and Japan's allegedly special obligation—as the only victim of atomic bombing—to renounce force.

Although the centrist parties ultimately voted for the bill, they exacted
as the price of their support limitations on Japan's peacekeeping role to assure that it will be minimal at best, perhaps farcically so. For example, the
bill's opponents initially demanded that in deference to Article 9, no

regular SDF units could serve in a peacekeeping operation. They must instead be "new" units, meaning that Japan would require *two* armed forces—one for home and one for abroad. Others believed it would be acceptable for SDF units to serve but thought each soldier should first take a "leave of absence" from the SDF. Even more strange was the widely supported proposal that no Japanese PKO member *could be armed*—or sent anyplace where there was a prospect of actual combat! Apparently others would have already enforced a "peace"—Japanese soldiers would merely ensure things stayed that way. It was actually proposed at one point in the debate that if there *were* a prospect of violence breaking out, Japan's troops would immediately leave the scene.

After two years of debate that ended in mid-1992, the bill's final form—compared to the "elephant that gave birth to a mouse"—reflects many of these concerns. For example, no more than 2,000 Japanese troops can be sent overseas in a PKO force, and even those troops can perform only noncombat functions that are strictly defined. They can supervise the disarming or withdrawal of troops; monitor compliance with cease-fire arrangements; patrol buffer zones; collect, maintain, dispose of, or check on the movement of weapons; assist in cease-fire-line demarcation; and help in prisoner exchange. They can, in other words, do anything but fight. Just to make sure no PKO soldier becomes involved in the actual use of force, the law says that *only in "unavoidable situations [can] individual members use small arms to protect themselves."*[8]

Even so, the PKO law means that for the first time since 1945 Japan can send troops abroad, and Japan's leaders congratulated themselves that the nation can now make what all called its "international contribution." That phrase and concept entered the foreign policy dialogue in the PKO debate, and when the law was passed it was discussed precisely in those terms. A good example came in a newspaper report on public reactions to the bill's imminent passage. The views of four "average citizens" in downtown Osaka were reported, and without exception each described the PKO in terms of Japan's "international contribution." Two excerpts give the flavor: "I support the fact that Japan is making an international contribution," and "there are better ways for Japan to make an international contribution." Still absent, in other words, was the understanding that as a beneficiary of world order, Japan has a responsibility to help maintain it.

■ FINDING JAPAN'S PLACE: THE NEXT STAGE

The PKO episode reflects both a negative and a more encouraging lesson about Japan as it confronts the post–Cold War period. The negative one is that it illustrates once again the unreality that still colors much of Japan's foreign policy debate. On the positive side, the debate also reflected the understanding that significant change is taking place in Japan's foreign policy environment. The key elements in that change are relations with the United States, and with what is loosely called "Asia."

There are also important specific issues with regard to China and Russia, but the largest factor is Japan's U.S. connection. Relations with Washington are still seen as fundamental to Japan's security and well-being, but it is widely understood that the U.S. relationship is under stress. That awareness has prompted a reexamination of two issues: Japan's role in Asia, and its place in the global economy.

The two are very tightly linked, largely because Japan is truly a giant in today's world. That point should be stressed, because Japan is still too often regarded as something of an anomaly—a wealthy, industrious, but nevertheless relatively small group of islands off the East Asian coast. Nothing could be more misleading. In terms of population alone, Japan's 124 million people make it one of the world's half-dozen largest nations, more than double the size of Great Britain, Germany, or France. Moreover, although there is general awareness at home and abroad that Japan is a major economic power, the sheer scale of its industry and economy also needs to be recalled. As I mentioned at the beginning of this chapter, its GNP is roughly $3 trillion. That is *triple* Germany's, almost *four times* the size of France's or Great Britain's and two-thirds that of the United States—whose population is twice as large as Japan's. Indeed, because Japan's GNP growth far exceeds that of any other industrialized nation (4.5 percent from 1985 to 1989), its GNP is likely to *equal* the U.S. GNP in the coming generation.[9]

It is precisely that economic gigantism that brings Japan most of its foreign policy troubles today—as its trade surplus with the United States demonstrates. Economists usually do not regard such bilateral trade "deficits" as being of major economic significance, but the issue has nevertheless soured every other aspect of Japan's relations with the United States. The reason is that trade deficits are politically explosive, especially when they are large and continuing, and that is the case between the United States and Japan. In 1991 the U.S. merchandise trade deficit with Japan stood at $44.4 billion. That was much smaller than the record $56 billion deficit reached in 1987—and also represents a steadily *declining portion of their overall trade*—but it was nonetheless larger than with any other trading partner. That fact has mesmerized U.S. attention and led the nation—even while the USSR was intact—to regard Japan as the greater threat to its security. It has also increasingly led the Japanese to express their doubts and worries (and more recently their recriminations) about the United States.

One result has been the rise of what the Japanese call *kenbei*, or dislike of the United States. Another has been a growing sense that if Japan wants to retain close ties to the United States, it must somehow change its economic practices. Mr. Akio Morita, chairman and joint founder of the Sony Corporation, has made headlines with that view. In 1991 he called on Japanese industrialists to abandon the principle that has shaped their business strategy throughout the postwar era: to make and sell good products at low prices. That, he said, had produced an obsession with "market share," and the result is rising anti-Japanese sentiment and threats of retaliation everywhere, especially from the United States. Consequently, Morita urged businessmen to concentrate less on market share and more on their profits and improving the life of the average Japanese. In the same vein, during the 1992 U.S. presidential campaign, the U.S. ambassador, Michael Armacost, urged Japan's industrial leaders to cut their trade surplus with his nation. Otherwise, he warned, Japan would become a campaign issue and that would be good for neither country.

A third consequence of Japan's growing worries about the United States is the revival of the "return to Asia" theme in its foreign policy thinking. That is an old issue and can be traced to prewar days. In the 1920s and 1930s, Japan saw itself as "the light of Asia," and dressed up its World War II goals with the "Greater East Asia Co-Prosperity Sphere" label. In a new guise, and without that era's intended aim of overt political and economic dominance, the same "return to Asia" theme is being resurrected today—and not only in Japan. It is reflected in the fact that Tokyo has become the largest foreign aid grantor to the developing East Asian nations, especially those in ASEAN—the Association of Southeast Asian Nations.

Even more important, Japan has become by far the largest investor in the East Asian region. Its investments in ASEAN, Taiwan, Korea, and Hong Kong are now at more than $60 billion—an amount at least double the U.S. investment.[10] Perhaps most important, Japan increasingly is becoming the major trading partner for the East Asian economies. This new role can be quickly seen by comparing Japanese and U.S. trade in Asia. Tables 3.1 and 3.2 make that comparison: Table 3.1 shows Japanese and U.S. exports to seven East Asian nations, Table 3.2 their imports from the same nations. The nations included are Taiwan, Korea, and five major ASEAN members.

Table 3.1 shows that in 1991, without exception, Japan exported more to each of those economies than did the United States. As a point of reference, I have also included U.S. and Japanese exports to the same markets in 1982, almost ten years earlier. In that year, the United States was the larger exporter to Korea and the Philippines, and in Taiwan it was at about the same level as Japan. But no more: In 1991 the United States sold $12.7 billion to Taiwan; Japan's exports were $18.3 billion. In Korea, where the United States was the larger exporter in 1982, it is now the smaller by almost $5 billion. Even in the Philippines, so long a traditional U.S. market, the United States now sells less than Japan ($2.27 billion versus $2.66 billion).

Table 3.1 U.S. and Japanese Exports to Asia, 1989–1991 (billions of $)

To	From	1982	1989	1990	1991	1982–1991 percent change	1989–1991 percent change
Taiwan	USA	4.6	11.0	11.1	12.7	179	176	15	15
	Japan	4.8	15.4	15.4	18.3	282	281	18	18
Korea	USA	6.0	13.2	14.1	15.2	155	153	15	15
	Japan	5.3	16.5	17.4	20.0	277	277	21	21
Thailand	USA	1.1	2.3	3.0	3.8	230	245	65	65
	Japan	2.0	6.8	9.1	9.4	372	370	38	38
Malaysia	USA	2.2	2.9	3.4	3.9	79	77	36	34
	Japan	3.1	4.1	5.5	7.6	146	145	85	85
Philippines	USA	1.9	2.2	2.5	2.3	22	21	3	4
	Japan	1.7	2.4	2.5	2.7	58	59	12	12
Indonesia	USA	2.4	1.3	2.0	1.9	-22	-21	51	46
	Japan	4.3	3.3	5.0	5.6	31	30	70	70
Singapore	USA	3.6	7.3	8.0	8.8	142	144	20	20
	Japan	5.0	9.2	10.7	12.2	144	144	32	33

Table 3.2 compares Japanese and U.S. *imports* from those same economies from 1989 to 1991. It shows that the United States is often the larger importer. The exception is Indonesia—a special case because of its oil and gas exports to Japan. But even as an importer, Japan is in several cases closing the gap. In Taiwan, for example, where the United States is a far larger customer ($23 billion vs. $9.5 billion), U.S. imports declined by 5 percent in 1991, whereas Japan's rose by 6 percent. In Korea, which has experienced an overall decline in competitiveness, both U.S. and Japanese imports declined, but the former's decline was 14 percent, the latter's only 5 percent. In Thailand, the most rapidly growing of the world's economies and one in which the United States previously was well ahead of Japan as an importer, U.S. imports grew by 39 percent, Japan's by 47 percent. Only in Singapore has the United States continued to do very well, but even there Japan's 1989–1991 increase was 16 percent, compared to 11 percent for the United States.

Japan's financial role in Asia is related to these trade patterns. Its overall investment began to rise in the late 1970s, and in the 1980s Japan moved ahead of the United States as the major investor in most of the region. This arrangement took on a whole new meaning after 1985, when the United States—in the so-called Plaza Accords—insisted on a rise in value of the yen in relation to the U.S. dollar. At first, that was a disturbing prospect to Japan's industry: It meant that Japanese goods, unless produced at

Table 3.2   U.S. and Japanese Imports from Asia, 1989–1991 (billions of $)

From	To	1989	1990	1991	1989–1991 percent change	
Taiwan	USA	24.2	22.5	23.0	-5	-5
	Japan	9.0	8.5	9.5	6	6
Korea	USA	19.6	18.3	16.8	-14	-14
	Japan	13.0	11.7	12.3	-5	-5
Thailand	USA	4.4	5.3	6.1	39	39
	Japan	3.6	4.2	5.3	47	47
Malaysia	USA	4.7	5.3	6.1	29	30
	Japan	5.1	5.4	6.5	27	27
Philippines	USA	3.1	3.4	3.5	13	13
	Japan	2.1	2.2	2.4	14	14
Indonesia	USA	3.5	3.3	3.2	-8	-9
	Japan	11.0	12.7	12.8	16	16
Singapore	USA	9.0	9.8	10.0	11	11
	Japan	3.0	3.6	3.4	16	13

Sources, Tables 3.1 and 3.2: IMF, *Direction of Trade Statistics,* various years; U.S. Department of Commerce, *U.S. Merchandise Trade: December 1991 FT–900 Supplement;* and Japan Tariff Association *1991 Annual,* pp. 32–33.

lower cost, might become uncompetitive in their export markets. But Japan's industrialists rose to the challenge, partly by increasing efficiency at home but also by transferring much production to "offshore" locations in Thailand, Malaysia, and Singapore. For those countries, as well as for Taiwan and Hong Kong, this approach has had two important consequences. The first is that these Asian NICs (newly industrializing countries) have greatly increased their own role as exporters, though often as producers for Japanese companies. The second result is that they have also sharply increased their exports to Japan itself.

The combined result of all these developments is that Japan is again facing the question of whether to act as Asia's acknowledged "leader." Many Japanese welcome that prospect or regard it simply as inevitable or "natural." A popular Japanese belief is that Asia's postwar economic development has followed a V-shaped "flying geese" pattern, with Japan at its head. Japan's growth led the way, and just behind it are the already industrialized economies of Taiwan, Korea, and Singapore. Behind them are the fast-growing economies of Thailand and Malaysia, and in the next rank are Indonesia and the Philippines. Ultimately they will be followed by Indochina's still-"socialist" economies. There is also a growing view—not only in Japan—that Asia's economies should link their currencies to the yen. The result would be a so-called "yen bloc."

Proposals along these lines have been endorsed by Malaysia's prime minister, who has worked very hard to build close relations with Japan and distanced himself from the United States. He has openly called for the establishment of an East Asia Economic Group (now Caucus) that would include Japan *but not the United States.* That idea has infuriated the latter nation, which in 1989 helped establish a much broader group known as APEC (Asia Pacific Economic Cooperation). APEC includes not only the United States, Japan, Australia, New Zealand, and Canada but *all* the East Asian and Pacific economies except Indochina. The United States has made it entirely clear—especially to Japan—that it wants to hear no more of Malaysia's EAEG concept, and Tokyo is in a quandary. The situation brings to a head, and possibly to a choice, two deep strands that have long affected Japan's policy thinking: Is Japan an essentially Asian nation, or is it instead a Western industrialized nation that happens to be in Asia?

That question will continue to trouble Japan. To a non-Japanese the answer might be obvious—that Japan's future as an economically very advanced nation is with others like itself—but the choice is not so clear to many Japanese. It becomes more difficult as doubts rise in Japan about the economic, political, and even military strength of the United States and as the latter behaves in ways that seem to the Japanese at best insensitive, at worst downright hostile and discriminatory. Many already believe that U.S. talk of "global partnership" with Japan is just that: that the United States does not and perhaps cannot treat Japan the same way it does European nations.[11] In this view, Japan's fifty years of cooperation with the United States have been the exception; its Asian identity is the rule. As evidence that in the final analysis the United States will go its own way, Japan can point to the U.S. initiative in building a regional free trade area in the Western Hemisphere.

That proposal, known as NAFTA (North American Free Trade Agreement), has put a cold chill into much Japanese leadership thinking. NAFTA started with only a U.S.–Canada agreement, but the United States moved quickly to include Mexico. Several South American nations, beginning with Chile, have also expressed their desire to join, and many Japanese worry about the implications. To them, U.S. insistence on building NAFTA underlines the country's historical and cultural ties: It shows that U.S. policy is shaped far more by its Western Hemisphere geography than by its asserted Pacific identity. Thus, the Japanese worry that with Europe already integrated economically in the EC and with the United States about to launch what they fear will be a similar trade-restricting "bloc" in the Americas, Japan will be not only left out but economically damaged. To avoid that outcome, increasingly important voices urge Japan to do as the United States is doing: find its destiny in East Asia, in something such as Malaysia's proposed East Asia Economic Group.[12]

Japan will seek to finesse this issue, and already some in Asia have accused it of being two-faced on the matter—of trying to placate Asians and at the same time please the United States. The Japanese are very torn by this dilemma because it could lead to more tension with Washington—particularly if Tokyo is seen as dragging its feet in the APEC context. That prospect puts Japan in the position it most wants to avoid—having to choose between the United States and Asia. It also poses to Japan the largest question of all for its foreign policy: Can it act as a truly major nation with global interests and responsibilities, or is it still "little Japan," concerned mainly by its sense of uniqueness and belief that it has been victimized and convinced it is too little "understood"?

The evidence so far is not encouraging. Although many Japanese fully understand and urge on their people the need for what former Prime Minister Nakasone called "internationalization," the actual substance of Japan's foreign policy rarely reflects that quality. It reflects instead a single-minded political emphasis on solely *Japanese* concerns that is strongly and strangely inconsistent with Japan's economic status as a nation of the very first rank. Relations with China and the former Soviet Union illustrate this ambivalence, as does one final issue: Japan's role in the United Nations. In each of these cases, the common thread is the legacy of World War II and Japan's continuing inability to come to grips finally with its meaning and consequences.

China presents the deepest of all ambivalencies to Japan. Tokyo has made massive efforts to promote good ties with China, many of them quite unselfish. Every year, for example, Japan provides hundreds of scholarships to Chinese students and professionals for study in Japan. Specialized training in medicine and engineering are among the most sought-after fields. Japan has also extended very large loans to China and is its largest foreign investor. The result is that trade has flourished: In 1991 their total trade was almost $23 billion, and in 1992 it was expected to exceed $25 billion. These are higher levels than U.S.–China trade and mean that from China's perspective (aside from its special relationship with Hong Kong), Japan is China's leading trade partner. In this case, moreover, it is *Japan* that has the trade deficit.[13]

Tokyo has also been quite indulgent vis-à-vis China's politics. At the time of the brutal crackdown on student protest at Tiananmen Square in 1989, Japan's reaction was muted, and it was quick to mend and gloss over what little disturbance did occur. Japan has generally looked the other way regarding China's suppression of civil liberties and experiences no parallel to the regular most-favored nation debates in the United States. Few if any Japanese, in other words, argue that trade with China should be restricted until Beijing ends its denial of civil liberties. Even so, their relations are on tenterhooks, in part because China continues to remind Japan of its past—and official Japan wants no reminders.

The issue that has most clearly brought this situation to a head is a long-discussed plan for Japan's emperor to make a state visit to Beijing. China's leadership clearly wants that, arguing that it is time to put the relationship on a new footing, and many foreign policy professionals in

Japan also favor a visit. But there is also deep Japanese opposition, apparently at levels in the ruling Liberal Democratic Party that were long able to exercise a veto. The principal reason is a concern that if the emperor visits China, Beijing will use the occasion to greatly publicize Japan's aggression and trumped-up invasion in the 1930s; its massacres of thousands of Chinese civilians; its policies of forced-labor and prostitution; and much else. Worst of all, it is feared, the emperor will be expected to make a clear and unambiguous formal apology on behalf of Japan and all Japanese.[14]

That is a severe sticking point, because unlike Germany—whose president has made a clear and forthright statement accepting the German people's responsibility for the war and Nazi atrocities—nothing of that sort has yet come from Japan's leadership. Prominent Asian leaders such as former Singapore Prime Minister Lee Kwan Yew have repeatedly urged Japan to take the step, arguing that it will be best for Japan and everyone else to put the past firmly and clearly behind them. But there is as yet no evidence that Japan's leadership is willing to do so. (Note: The emporer did visit China, in October 1992; he did not make apologies.)

The probable reasons are all troubling, and just two will be mentioned. One is reflected in the well-known pattern by which the Ministry of Education closely monitors Japan's schoolbooks—*and orders them rewritten* —if they too fully discuss Japan's World War II record or even its earlier takeover of Korea. As this practice shows, and as the PKO debate also demonstrated, Japan's leaders are not yet willing to tell their people the truth about foreign policy—not about today's conditions nor about yesterday's. The second reason is just as troubling—the likelihood that Japan's official ambiguity and even deceit regarding its wartime history has a contemporary political purpose. I call this the "no fault" explanation: that Japan's leaders want to erase much of the war record because they also want to erase its political consequences.

The best-known illustration of this effort is Japan's steadily increasing pressure to retrieve the northern territories—the four islands occupied by the USSR at the end of the war. Today's campaign directed toward Moscow is very reminiscent of Japan's effort directed toward the United States in the 1960s. Then the goal was the "reversion" of Okinawa from U.S. occupation: Washington was told insistently that the two nations could not build a solid postwar partnership until the wartime era was brought to a final end, which required the end of all U.S. control. In the current case, as I mentioned earlier, Tokyo has refused to grant substantial aid to Russia without an agreement on return of the islands. Japan has further escalated the pressure by asking that the other major nations add their voice, and from the United States at least, the Japanese have won that assurance.[15]

One final aspect of this effort to remove as far as possible the remaining disturbing outcomes of the World War II should be mentioned. This is Japan's desire to take a permanent seat on the UN Security Council— where the victorious wartime allies now sit. That goal, announced by

Prime Minister Kiich Miyazawa at the UN in 1991, raises troubling implications. The clearest stems from Japan's view, which began to be expressed more widely just before the Miyazawa speech, that the UN should
remove from its charter references to Japan (and Germany) as "former
enemy states." How, after all, could a nation so designated also serve as a
permanent member of the Security Council? Likewise, how could Japan's
new "peacekeeping" force be expected to serve on UN-endorsed military
operations when it could not be assured that Japan's voice would be heard
on the Security Council?

The reality, of course, is that Russian occupation of the northern islands and the UN charter's references to Japan as an "enemy state" are
factual and undeniable consequences of World War II. The Pacific War in
turn was a factual consequence of Japanese behavior in Asia, most obviously its simultaneous undeclared attacks on Pearl Harbor and British and
Dutch locations on December 7, 1941. But that day is not much taught
about in Japanese schools, and when it is briefly mentioned it is likely to
be discussed as an attack on "Shinju Wan," rather than by the name known
to the rest of the world: *Pearl Harbor.* It is as if U.S. schoolbooks were to
write of atom bombs dropped on "Broad Island" and "Long Point"—the
English translations of Hiroshima and Nagasaki.

The continuing pattern of obfuscation and euphemisms that so deeply
colors Japan's discussion of past and present foreign policy issues cannot
be dismissed. Despite the presence of many Japanese who do discuss and
are aware of the realities, Japanese official behavior suggests a leadership
that insists on refusing to present those realities to its own people. Its people, in turn, have only a very distorted and extremely vague appreciation
of the world political environment that affects Japan and in which it must
shape its policies.

That remains a deeply troubling aspect of Japanese foreign policymaking today, especially for a nation that both regards itself and wants
others to regard it as a genuine democracy. The reality, however, is that
there is no true debate about foreign policy in Japan, not of the sort found
in the other major industrialized nations regarded as democratic. Part of
the reason is the admittedly different nature of politics in Japan, for it is a
society in which the population looks with more acceptance to the policy
guidance of its leaders. But another reason is that in international politics,
Japan is a nation that doesn't know what to do with itself. That remains
its condition today.

■ NOTES

1. Russia is widely regarded in Japan as a long-standing rival, and knowledgeable Japanese never forget the "Nomohan Incident" of 1939, in which Japan's

army suffered a crushing and humiliating defeat by large Soviet tank forces on the China-Mongolia border.

2. For an example, see the article on "Foreign Lawyers in Japan," by Professor Toru Yano, in *Japan Times,* May 5, 1992.

3. As Kitaoka puts it, "the term *contribution* . . . has emerged as the key word used to encapsulate the relationship between Japan and the world" (Kitaoka Shinichi, "Opting for a Global Alliance," in *Japan Echo,* Vol. XIX, Special Issue, 1992). This is an abridged translation of "Nichi-Bei no chikyu teki domei wasa kano ka," in *This Is Yomiuri,* December 1991.

4. These figures are drawn from the International Institute for Strategic Studies, *The Military Balance, 1991–92* (London, 1991, p. 212). Japan's "1 percent" limit relates to its direct military spending. It does not include much else that is closely related, including that which is spent to facilitate and house the U.S. presence. When all that is included, Japan's defense spending comes close to 2 percent of its GNP.

5. Although these reminders are probably also used as a bargaining stick—to beat on Japanese heads in the context of their current relations—Koreans, Chinese, and others all have good reason to be deeply resentful about Japan's past behavior. An occasional reminder may help guard against too much Japanese arrogance today.

6. For a devastating critique of Japan's approach to the Gulf crisis and its response in the PKO bill, see Shiina Motoo, "Japan's Choice in the Gulf: Participation or Isolation," *Japan Echo,* Volume XVIII, No. 1, Spring 1991. This is a translation of his article "Kokuren gaiko ka Nichi-Bei domei ka," in *Chuo Koron,* November, 1990. Shiina is a member of the Diet.

7. Japan's Socialist Party now refers to itself, *in English only,* as the Social Democratic Party, or "JSDP," but it has not changed its name in Japanese. It should *not* be confused with the Democratic Socialist Party (DSP), which has long since split from the Socialists, and often cooperates with the governing Liberal Democratic Party (LDP).

8. From the English-language report of the PKO Law's main points in *The Japan Times,* June 17, 1992. My emphasis.

9. A convenient and annually revised source of statistical data on Japan is in *Japan: An International Comparison,* published each year in Tokyo by the Japan Institute for Social and Economic Affairs. For very current indicators on society, trade, and the economy, the biweekly publications of the *Japan Economic Institute* (Washington, D.C.) are very useful.

10. Japanese investments in China, at about $4 billion, are much smaller: only 1 percent of Japan's total (*Financial Times,* July 15, 1992). Data for the remainder of Asia are from a compilation prepared for MITI (Ministry of International Trade and Industry) by Sanwa Research Institute, May 1992, p. 43 (mimeo). A less detailed report, indicating lower levels of Japanese investment, is in *The Far Eastern Economic Review,* March 19, 1992, p. 41.

11. This view is taken even by Professor Masamichi Inoki, a leader of Japan's "defense intellectuals" and one who has argued most strongly to maintain the closest of ties with the United States: "The United States will never treat Japan with the kind of respect it accords France until the Japanese are able to tell the Americans what they don't care to hear." See "Reviewing the Structure of Japan-U.S. Relations," a dialogue between Inoki and Professor Ronald Dore, in *Japan Echo,* Special Issue, 1992, p. 41. This is a translation of the original in *Sekai,* May 1991, pp. 146–157.

12. A prominent example of support for the EAEG notion is Yotaro Kobayashi, head of Fuji Xerox. There are also reports that the EAEG idea not did come

initially from the Malaysian prime minister but was a *Japanese* response to the U.S. NAFTA initiative—specifically Mr. Saburo Okita, a prominent economist and former foreign minister. This idea would be consistent with Okita's lifelong advocacy of Asian regional economic cooperation and his frequent reference to the "flying geese" image in Asian development. As a young man just before Pearl Harbor, Okita served on a study group associated with the Greater East Asia Co-Prosperity Sphere, though it should be stressed its sponsor was Prince Konoye—a prominent nobleman not favorable to Japan's war plans.

13. In 1991, Japan's exports to China were $8.6 billion, whereas it imported $14.2 billion (*Financial Times,* July 15, 1992).

14. In August 1992, after intensive intra-LDP negotiations, Tokyo finally announced that yes, the emperor would go to China. Prime Minister Miyazawa had to pay a steep price: It was agreed that he and several other cabinet ministers would pay "non-official" visits to the Yasakuni Shrine. That shrine is where many of Japan's war dead are entombed, including a number who were tried and executed as war criminals in World War II. Japan's conservatives and "rightists" regard visits to the Yasakuni Shrine as deeply symbolic of the view that Japan was no more guilty of war crimes than any of the other combatants. By the same token, many Japanese (and foreigners) recognize visits by Japanese leaders to the shrine as symbolic of the view that Japan refuses to acknowledge war guilt.

15. Prime Minister Miyazawa made the "no islands, no money" linkage even more explicit in an address to the National Press Club in Washington on July 3, 1992: "Let me be clear, however, that neither Japan nor Russia can hope to press ahead without solving the Northern Territories question. . . . The government and people of Japan highly appreciate the U.S. government's firm support for Japan's position on this issue" (text in *Japan Times,* July 4, 1992).

■ 4

China in the Postnuclear World
James C. Hsiung

The terms "post–Cold War era" and "new world order" have been used as if they were interchangeable. Strictly speaking, a fine differentiation should be made. There is, admittedly, general agreement on the meaning of the "post–Cold War era"—i.e., the period after the end of the Cold War, as defined in Chapter 1. There is, however, no consensus on what constitutes the "new world order," to which different nations may attach different meanings. President George Bush trumpeted his version of the new world order in the wake of Operation Desert Storm in 1991. In the Bush formulation (Donnelly 1992, p. 249f), it is synonymous with a world ripe for the promotion of political openness and human rights under the leadership of the West (read: the United States). The Chinese not only took exception to this view, but also took pains to enunciate their opposing views on what the new world order is or ought to be.

■ CHINA'S RESPONSE TO THE NEW WORLD ORDER

Contrary to expectations, the Chinese did not see anything new in the new world order trumpeted by President Bush. In a nutshell, the world remains one of "turbulence" and "has not become a more peaceful and tranquil place," lamented Foreign Minister Qian Qichen (1990a). Instead of one Cold War, Beijing claimed, the world now has two—namely, the struggle between capitalism and the remaining communist countries, and the growing frictions within the Western alliance.[1] The official *Renmin Ribao* (People's Daily) published a lengthy report on July 30, 1991, summarizing the views expressed at a symposium held in Beijing at the prestigious Chinese Institute for International Studies on the "Inauguration of a New World

Order." The report outlined the goals Washington purportedly sought to achieve through its brand of the new world order:

1. To make the United States the world's leader by dint of its being now the sole, and unchallengeable, superpower;
2. To keep members of the Western alliance in line as the United States' partners;
3. To promote U.S. values and ideologies, sell the U.S. economic and political system as the model for the world, and convert the entire world to capitalism; and
4. To put in place an international security structure, to be backed up by U.S. military might, sparing no force and violence in the defense of U.S. strategic interests around the world.[2]

It is obvious that Beijing sees sinister designs in the U.S.-touted new world order, especially in its professed aim of promoting political openness and human rights (Sutter 1991). The Chinese also view George Bush's design for a "unipolar" world as unfeasible (Wang Ling 1991, p. 4) if it should be a disguise for Washington's attempt to assert its monopolistic leadership after the retreat of Soviet power. In the first place, the United States does not have the "strength at home" to support the attainment of the unipolar goal. Second, allies may not be willing to support U.S. pretensions. President François Mitterand of France, for example, publicly stated that the new world order must not impose peace under U.S. domination. Third, the attempt to impose U.S. values on others is bound to provoke wholesale resistance from the rest of the world, asserts *Beijing Review*.[3]

Beijing launched a campaign to promote a counterversion of what the new world order should be, which consists of the following tenets: (1) that in the new world order all countries, big and small, should be equal, and no one power should dictate the affairs of others; (2) that the "unipolar" (read: U.S.) monopoly of power should be checked and countered by a collegial sharing of power among countries, with the United Nations playing a leading role; and (3) the new world order should likewise contain a "new economic world order" in which the developed nations help the developing nations in their path to development (Sutter, p. 4; Wang Ling, pp. 1ff).

Some of these tenets are revived from the five principles of peaceful coexistence (PCX) postulated in the 1950s (Hsiung 1972, Chapter 2; Wang Kangtai 1991, p. 6). Deng Xiaoping, China's ultimate leader, had first suggested the substitution of PCX for the politics of hegemony as early as 1988.[4] In 1991 China began its campaign in the non-Western world to seek endorsements for the revived PCX tenets as the governing principles of the new world order.[5] Purportedly speaking for the Third World, the Chinese flaunted the idea of a "right to subsistence" for the people in the developing countries. This right had been openly endorsed by the UN General Assembly in its Declaration on the Right to Development, adopted with the overwhelming support of the developing nations in 1986 (Li Hong 1992, p. 12).

Chinese leaders were also consciously engaged in an effort to rally support in the non-Western world for China's own views on what the new world order ought to be. In their speeches before the United Nations and other forums and in joint statements with other governments, they reiterated the same themes.[6] During his visit to six African countries in January 1991, for instance, Foreign Minister Qian Qichen struck a responsive chord when he stressed that the new world order should not be dictated by a unipolar power; that the West's foreign aid should not have any political strings attached to it; and that Third World nations should have the freedom to find their own ways to democratization.[7]

☐ *The Rationale for the Chinese Stance*

Chinese resentment of the West for what their country had gone through at the hands of "imperialists" of all colors since the mid-nineteenth century may have provided the fuel for the newly enunciated Chinese position on the new world order. But there clearly also is a geostrategic twist to it, as China is smarting under the shift from the Cold War alignment, in which China was a beneficiary of the U.S.–Soviet rivalry. In the new era, China's status has apparently suffered.

China's Stakes in the Old Order

For a number of reasons, the People's Republic of China (PRC) derived much benefit from the old order characterized by bisuperpower conflict during the Cold War and hence had stakes in it. First, the bipolar nuclear deadlock made the Chinese nuclear capability extra impressive, conferring a special, exalted status on the PRC. For one thing, nuclear China was immune from nuclear blackmail by either superpower and enjoyed the envy of the likes of India and Egypt.

Second, as long as the U.S.–Soviet stalemate persisted in the Cold War, the entry on the world stage of a nuclear-armed China changed nuclear deterrence from a dyadic to a triadic game. The multipolar deterrence scene brought with it many heretofore unknown problems—e.g., the dangers of nuclear gang-up, "nuclear anonymity," and "catalytic war" (Rosecrance 1972, p. 136).[8] Because of these potential dangers, each of the two superpowers would want to win the PRC over in its running feud with the other superpower. Hence, the so-called "swing factor" (Pollock 1984, p. 174) gave China a special, otherwise undeserved importance in the tangle of bipolar conflict: The side that China should "swing" to in the superpower rivalry would gain at the expense of the opposing side. Both Washington and Moscow eventually came to grips with the unique role China played in relation to the U.S.–Soviet rivalry. It eventually transformed their respective foreign policy and their mutual relations. President Richard Nixon thus began his "grand design" in reshaping U.S. foreign policy, starting in 1972 by reversing U.S. nonrecognition of China (Schurmann, Chapter 5) and duly making China an equal player in what eventually became known as the "strategic triangle."

Finally, both superpowers became aware of what in the scholarly world was known as the "victor's inheritance" dilemma (Rosecrance, p. 136f). In other words, in the unlikely event of a nuclear exchange between the two superpowers, no matter who should win, both would have lost vis-à-vis China, the bystander, whose nuclear arsenal would have remained intact. The nuclear exchange between the two superpowers, in that event, would have brought irreparable damage of their own making to themselves. Hence, the deadly logic of this "victor's inheritance" problem provided a powerful incentive for the United States and the Soviet Union to endeavor not to get into a nuclear conflagration. The multiple deterrence context thus paved the way for stability within the nuclear strategic triad and, in effect, magnified the power status of China as a world-class player.

All three of these factors decidedly accounted for the PRC's special prominence, making it a celebrated case of what Georg Simmel would call *tertius gaudens* [the laughing third] in the strategic Cold War triangle (Hsiung 1985, p. 116; p. 122).

China in the New Era

However, all three elements that catapulted the PRC to the forefront of world politics in the last two decades were rendered inoperative by the end of the Cold War. When states such as Germany and Japan are thrust forward by their industrial prowess to play in the game of economic superpowers, their importance skyrocketing with the ascendancy of geoeconomics, the PRC finds itself no longer enjoying the same stature as before. One of the key characteristics of the post–Cold War era, as discussed in Chapter 1, is the receding salience of nuclear deterrence. Although the existing nuclear states may still cling to their nuclear weapons and nuclear proliferation may very well continue in the new era, the fact remains that nuclear weapons have lost much of their importance. Hence, the new age might as well be called "postnuclear," and China has to adjust itself to the changed circumstances. With its geopolitical stock having declined, China may have to invest more, not less, in conventional armaments as well as in anti-ballistic missile defense. In this sense, the end of the Cold War, paradoxically, has brought no "peace dividend." Instead, China finds itself worse off in the new circumstances, as it has to worry about its economic statecraft to a degree unknown before.

Hence, the PRC's negative reactions to the ascent of the United States as the unchallenged unipolar power after the retreat of Soviet power are inseparable from Chinese assessments of what appear to be unmistakable losses in their country's geopolitical standing in the new world order. The low esteem in which Beijing is now held, with or without Tiananmen, is not just limited to China. The stigma is worn by socialism and by all remaining socialist regimes, now that the mother of Leninism has vanished from the surface of the earth. China's top strategic thinkers have had to dissociate the demise of the Soviet Union from the shortcomings of socialism, instead pinning the blame for the Soviet downfall on an "external cause"—namely, the West's "strategy of peaceful evolution carried out . . . over the years" by the United States and its allies (Chai 1992, p. 6).

Under the West's strategy of peaceful evolution, according to this view, subversion from within was staged by Western agents against the Soviet Union and other socialist regimes through creation of internal opposition, using the calls of human rights, freedom, and democracy as rallying points (Chai, pp. 6–7). Hence, the Chinese have two objections to the new world order flaunted by Washington. The first is its detriment to China's importance, as the Cold War triangle diminished, upsetting the old "world equilibrium" (Jiang 1992, p. 10). The second reason is the Chinese fear that the same strategy of "peaceful evolution" might be pulled on China by the West.

■ NEW CHINESE POLICY INITIATIVE

In addition to promoting a peaceful-coexistence version of the new world order, China embarked upon a post–Cold War foreign policy initiative that is distinct in two ways. One is its inherent, conscious effort at purging ideology from foreign policy, in that national interest will replace socialist "moralism."[9] In other words, the PRC will no longer sacrifice its own interests for the sake of advancing socialism in the Third World. The other distinct feature is what emerges as a schematic pattern of realignment efforts. These are aimed at bolstering China's foreign relations and, in some instances, even at making diplomatic breakthroughs, such as in the normalization of relations with Vietnam and Israel.

This post–Cold War foreign policy initiative coincides with Beijing's endeavor to break its diplomatic isolation after Tiananmen. A first giant step toward the latter goal was the visit by Prime Minister Toshiki Kaifu of Japan in August 1991. The prime ministers of Great Britain and Italy followed a couple of months later. Beijing also mounted what appeared to be a systematic, purposeful campaign of crisscross missions abroad by China's top leaders. The following is only a partial list up to July 1992: (1) Foreign Minister Qian Qichen's tour of Botswana, Zimbabwe, Angola, Zambia, Mozambique, and Lesotho in July 1989; (2) Prime Minister Li Peng's visits to Pakistan, Nepal, and Bangladesh in November 1989; (3) President Yang Shàngkun's May 1990 excursion to Latin America, the first by a Chinese head of state, during which he lobbied for increased trade and support for PRC membership in the General Agreement on Tariffs and Trade (GATT); (4) President Yang's missions to Pakistan and Iran in October 1991 and to Singapore and Malaysia in January 1992; (5) Premier Li Peng's visit to Singapore and Indonesia in the summer of 1991, followed by his December visit to India; (6) Foreign Minister Qian's tour of six African countries—Mali, Guinea, Ghana, Senegal, Côte d'Ivoire, and Namibia in mid-January 1992; (7) the late-January 1992 visits by Premier Li Peng to Italy, Switzerland, New York (where he attended an important UN Security Council meeting), Malta, Portugal, and Spain; (8) Foreign Minister Qian's mission to Western Europe in March 1992; (9) Deputy Premier Zhu Rongji's mid-February 1992 visit to Australia; (10) a visit to Japan by General Secretary Jiang Zemin of the Chinese Communist Party in April 1992, when he extended a personal invitation for the emperor to pay a state visit to China later in the year; (11) Foreign Minister Qian's sally to Australia and New Zealand in mid-June 1992; (12) a May 28–June 5 visit to Japan by Wan Li, head of the National People's Congress; and (13) President Yang Shangkun's state visits to Morocco, Tunisia, and Côte d'Ivoire in July 1992.[10]

☐ China in Asia Pacific

On the surface, it appears as though the PRC were copying the "omnidirectional" (or "be nice to everybody") foreign policy of Japan in the early 1970s (Emmerson 1981, p. 29). This impression is sustained by a cursory reading of China's stepped-up contacts with so many countries, including (but not limited to) the two Koreas, Japan, the ASEAN nations, and Vietnam. China's relations with the last-mentioned country were normalized in November 1991, after a twelve-year rupture following the 1979 open war. Diplomatic relations with South Korea were established on August 24, 1992. A closer examination, however, reveals a distinct pattern and a rationale.

There is no doubt that the PRC is spinning an extensive web extending to all corners of the region and, for that matter, beyond to points such as Israel and Africa. At the center of this web of realignment spun by Beijing is the fulcrum of two triads. The first, the strategic triad, comprises China, Japan, and the United States. The other triad, the minor of the two, consists of China and the two Koreas. Next to these, the ASEAN constitutes an additional strategically important tier in China's diplomatic and security realignment bid. In the post–Cold War era, Indochina is open to unprecedented Chinese influence. We shall discuss them separately below.

The First Triad

That the PRC is adept at playing triadic international relations is amply shown in its impressive performance in the erstwhile U.S.–Soviet–PRC triad of the 1980s. In that earlier game, China was the weakest of the three players, in a 3:2:1 ratio of power distribution (then defined in military terms alone). Yet China was able to gain handsomely as a *tertius gaudens,* reaping benefits disproportionate to its power. In that game, China's leverage came from the deadlocked relationship between the other two players in the triad, especially during the years after the Soviet invasion of Afghanistan, 1980–1985, which allowed the Chinese to play one against the other (Hsiung 1985, Chapter 7). In hindsight, though, one should also give credit to Beijing's diplomatic adroitness in exploiting the U.S.–Soviet strife as an important factor for China's success.

In the post–Cold War period, that earlier U.S.–Soviet–PRC strategic triad has been replaced by an emergent U.S.–Japan–PRC triad. The salience of Japan will become increasingly pronounced as certain conditions crystalize: e.g., the continued retreat of Soviet influence from the region, the rising paramountcy of economic interests, and the persistent impasse in U.S.–Japan relations. From the Chinese perspective, there is reason to assume that future U.S.–Japan conflict will be the centerpiece of international relations in Asia Pacific (Chen 1990; Ding and Chen 1992, p. 23). Under the circumstances, the Chinese also believe, China will be in a position to play an arbitrating role between Tokyo and Washington.[11]

In order to do so, China must not be left out in the scramble for economic power and, just as important, must keep in good relations with both wings of the new triad (Hua Di, 57ff). Chinese response in this respect consists of both a domestic and a foreign policy aspect. Domestically, China is committed to quickening the momentum of the post-1978 economic reforms, which were only superficially sidetracked by the Tiananmen episode. Beijing has pledged to double, by the year 2000, the nation's 1990 GNP of ca. $400 billion and to make China a "basically modernized (*xiaokang*) country" by the middle of the twenty-first century (*Renmin Ribao* 1991a; 1991b). In its foreign policy agenda, China has two distinct goals regarding the Asia Pacific region for the 1990s: (1) to maintain and upgrade Chinese relations with Japan; and (2) to improve relations with all parties in the region (a strategy known as *zhoubian* diplomacy) while riding out the post-1989 low tides in Sino–U.S. relations. Both goals are intermediate to the larger strategic objective of positioning China for the twenty-first century, so that it can be a useful player in world politics.

Thus viewed, the different pieces of the jigsaw puzzle of the seemingly hit-or-miss Chinese realignment patterns will come together. China's promotion of closer ties with Japan and other countries, important in itself, will also boost Chinese diplomatic capital with which to deal with Washington and other major powers on the larger scene. In the language of the triadic game, future improvement on the Sino–U.S. tangent will be helped by what happens on the Sino-Japan tangent—because this is still a ménage à trois game (Hsiung 1985, p. 115), and it is to Beijing's advantage to keep it that way. Although China's relations with the United States remain as low and as bumpy as they have been since Tiananmen, China can rebuild it's own diplomatic strength under the present circumstances through improved ties with the other actors, especially Japan (Jiang 1992). Thus, by appearance, the new Chinese foreign policy is "omnidirectional." What is not so apparent is the rationale behind it.

The Second Triad

Although it is only newly emergent, the second triad, involving the PRC and the two Koreas, is taking on new significance for the Chinese, for four reasons. The first and most immediate reason is Beijing's interest in developing the Tumen River economic zone, which borders on North Korea. The project straddles the area where China, North Korea, and Russia converge, creating a duty-free shipping and processing zone covering 4,000 square miles. With the participation of the United Nations Development Program (UNDP), the Tumen project, which requires a $3 billion investment and twenty years to complete, aims at creating a northeast Asian trading center that would rival Rotterdam as the world's busiest port. As a gift of the end of the Cold War, cooperation among the six neighboring nations is now possible: China, Russia, Mongolia, the two Koreas, and Japan. The six began negotiations in 1992 on cooperation in the project (Kristof, p. 18; Li, p. 5). In order to assure the project's success, China needs the goodwill of North Korea over, among other things, Chinese navigation of the Tumen River.

Second, for its internal development, China also needs a tranquil international environment along its borders.[12] In addition, China needs and welcomes South Korea's business and investment. In this regard, the end of the Cold War freed Beijing from its past fears of Pyongyang's possible objections to Chinese liaison with South Korea. Intensified Chinese contacts with the South Koreans, at both the private and official levels, came into the open after the 1990 Asian Games held in Beijing, which the South Koreans attended (Kim, 1991). Beijing keeps alert to South Korea's relations with Japan, lest it should become an economic satellite of the latter. Equally, it is keen on North Korea's role in the stability of the peninsula. Two important outcomes came on the heels of President Kim Il Sung's October 1991 visit to China, when he was given an exceptionally warm reception (*Asian Bulletin* 1991). These were North Korea's acceptance of IAEA inspections of its nuclear sites (until withdrawn in March 1993, ostensibly in protest to the nontermination of joint U.S.–South Korean military exercises), and the conclusion of a historic agreement on mutual nonaggression between the two Koreas on December 12, 1991. The agreement terminated four decades of armed hostility in the Korean peninsula, further symbolizing the end of the Cold War (Tao 1992).

For the first event, North Korea's acceptance of external inspections, Western commentators may credit the withdrawal of U.S. missiles from

South Korea, which Pyongyang had demanded as a condition. But one must not forget that the other North Korean condition—i.e., that the annual joint U.S.–South Korean military exercises be terminated—was not yet met when Pyongyang announced its decision regarding inspections. Thus, the Chinese may have had a lot more to do with the shift in Pyongyang's stance than meets the eye. By coincidence (or not), Beijing also announced in the same month its own consent to accept International Atomic Energy Agency (IAEA) inspections. The cutoff of Soviet supplies of offensive weapons to North Korea, possibly at the urging of the South Koreans (*Asian Bulletin* 1991), with whom Moscow has since 1990 maintained regular contacts, may have given a further boost to China's influence in Pyongyang.

The third reason for Chinese interest in the peninsula has to do with the relations between the two Koreas per se. Although they support the Korean aspirations for national unification, the Chinese are concerned about the disparities in the relative strengths of the two parties: North Korea's $47.9 billion GDP (1990) and 23.3 million population is no match for South Korea's $239.77 billion GDP (1990) and 44.3 million population (Institute of International Strategic Studies 1991, p. 167; p. 169). To Beijing, the German model of unification, in which the former (Communist) East Germany was simply annexed and engorged by West Germany, would not be acceptable in the Korean situation. The Chinese hope to be able to play a constructive role in assuring a smooth transition, so that when Korean unification does come its form will be acceptable to China. For the latter, the test of acceptability lies in whether the model will be constructive to the PRC's own unification bid with Taiwan and whether it will assure ultimate stability in Northeast Asia (Cotton 1991; Gong 1991).

The fourth and final reason for China's interest in the Korean Peninsula is its own stake in Sino-Japanese relations. In simple language, stability in the peninsula is vital to Japan's security, in particular to its business interests in South Korea. To the extent it can be a regional stabilizer, China's bargaining power vis-à-vis the Japanese will increase. Next to China's market and resources, which Japan covets, the possibility of this stabilizing role will be a decisive factor that will dominate Tokyo's calculations about future Japan-China relations. A secure Sino-Japanese tangent will in turn help stabilize relations in the Sino–U.S. tangent. Not only that, China's ability to mediate in the event of U.S.–Japan adversity will be all the greater when it has healthy relations on both flanks. In the language of the three-person game, China will then be in a pivotal role (Hsiung 1985, p. 176f) if deadlock should develop on the U.S.–Japan tangent. On the strength of that alone, China will then be a heavyweight player on both the regional and global scales.

This is why, in the near to intermediate term, Japan is so crucial to China. Most writings on the subject focus mainly on Japan's vital importance to China's internal economic development. What is revealed here is that the Chinese attach much more than just economic importance to their relationship with Japan. They know that before they can mend fences with the United States, relations on the Sino-Japanese tangent must be secure (Ji 1991; Jiang 1991). I might add in this connection that, because Japan is also crucial to Taiwan's economy, there is an additional, though somewhat hidden, triangle comprising Beijing, Tokyo, and Taipei. But, as the Beijing-Taipei tangle will be touched upon below, I shall not belabor the point here.

The ASEAN Tier

In the world beyond the end of the Cold War, the ASEAN will be both more important in its own right and more disposed to establish closer ties with China. It will be more important because of the economic vitality of its members. To give one indicator, the combined GNP of ASEAN's five members (minus Brunei) was $238 billion in 1989, or 70 percent of China's $337 billion GNP for the same year (INS 1990). Other indicators of strength are ASEAN's growth rates, which averaged between 5.4 percent (Indonesia) and 7.2 percent (Thailand) in the decade of the 1980s, as compared with China's 7.3 percent from 1985 through 1990. During the Cold War period, the Soviet threat skewed ASEAN to the side of the United States, thanks to the security umbrella the latter was able to provide (Brown 1991). By contrast, the post–Cold War era, in which ASEAN nations will have more freedom to act independently, offers the prospect of a more "normal" relationship with China.

Since the summer of 1990, China has established diplomatic relations with Singapore and restored normal relations with Indonesia. Both are significant feats: Singapore, which had prided itself on maintaining close ties with Taipei concurrently with its working relationship with Beijing, had always been reluctant to extend diplomatic recognition to the PRC. And Indonesia had deliberately kept the PRC at a distance since the abortive 1965 Communist coup, for which Jakarta blamed Chinese influence and covert aid to the PKI (the Indonesia Communist Party). All this changed. Premier Li Peng's visits to these two countries and to Thailand in 1990 were followed by President Yang Shangkun's mission to Singapore and Malaysia in January 1990. As one writer (Xie Xide 1991, p. 176) put it, China and the ASEAN nations had "entered a new age, marked by all-rounded development of both political and economic relations." One indication of what this new development signifies for regional peace is the settlement of Cambodia's twelve-year civil war, which was made possible by the collaborative brokering of China and the ASEAN nations through the medium of the United Nations.

ASEAN is clearly prominent on China's coalition-making map. If the strategic goal of the realignment initiative is to enhance China's diplomatic capital, having ASEAN in its orbit will add to China's bargaining power within the Sino–Japan–U.S. strategic triad, to say the least.

☐ *The Indochina Frontier*

Until the Soviet withdrawal, Beijing's Indochina policy was to seek the reduction of Soviet influence through the "Balkanization" of the region (Ross 1991, p.1171). Its strategy was to impose such high costs on its adversaries that they were compelled to abandon their objectives and to conciliate. In addition to its deliberate campaign to isolate Hanoi, Beijing even sought to fortify Mynmar and Thailand, on Vietnam's flanks, through arms sales (Buszynski 1992, p. 837; Gill 1991, esp. p. 536). The retreat of Soviet influence made it possible for Sino-Vietnamese relations to be "normalized," giving the Chinese enough leverage to be able to broker (along with the United States and other Security Council members) a tenuous peace in Cambodia. Apparently in an attempt to break its continuing isolation, Vietnam (along with Laos) signed a treaty of amity and cooperation with ASEAN in July 1992, less than eight months following Hanoi's normalization of relations with China. The withdrawal of Soviet influence from Indochina and the post-Tiananmen sanctions against China gave Hanoi and Beijing strong incentives to mend fences after the brief hot war of early 1979. But the defiant Vietnamese claim to the Paracel Islands, lying off the Vietnamese coast but in the South China Sea, remains an insurmountable hurdle to substantive, good relations with China. An instinctive Chinese reaction apparently is to play "balance of power," with the goal of containing what the Chinese used to call Vietnam's "regional hegemony." One sign of this balancing game is China's belated effort at building closer relations, including even inchoate military ties, with India. Reports were circulating in late 1992 that the first visit by a Chinese warship to India was scheduled in the next few months. The visit was agreed to during the first-ever trip to China by an Indian defense minister in July (FEER 1992). China's overtures to ASEAN nations, especially Indonesia but also Thailand, may also have the goal of enhancing Chinese influence in Indochina in mind. The bottom line is that if China can be perceived as the one outside power to wield decisive sway in Indochina, at a time when Washington under the Clinton administration seeks to normalize relations in the area, it would enhance Chinese leverage enormously in dealing with the United States.

The "Greater China" Scenario

Another part of the PRC's geoeconomic strategy is its "Greater China" bid. I am borrowing the term "Greater China" from other writers (e.g., Christopher Howe, 1990, p. 689) to refer to a scenario of economic integration among the three Chinese economies: mainland, Hong Kong, and Taiwan. The scheduled reversion of Hong Kong to Chinese sovereignty in 1997 will add a vibrant economy with a $62 billion GNP (1990) to the PRC, whose $400 billion GNP (1988) economy is weighed down by its huge (1.1 billion) population and an antiquated (communist) system. Moreover, under its treaty with Great Britain, China is committed to respecting (i.e., preserving) Hong Kong's present socioeconomic system for fifty years. Barring unforeseen circumstances, one would expect the former colony's economic vitality to stimulate the coastal Chinese provinces' economies to new heights. This annexation may turn out to be the catalyst needed to galvanize the whole Chinese economy into closer integration with the global economy. With Hong Kong in tow, then, mainland China will be in a unique position to woo Taiwan—its GNP at $160.7 billion—into an economic "conglomerate" (Fang Sheng 1991), even if reunification falls short. This conglomeration will mean the bunching together of three economies with a composite GNP of well over $622.7 billion, which exceeds by 30 percent the combined GNP of the current four Asian newly industrializing economies (NIEs)—namely, South Korea, Taiwan, Hong Kong, and Singapore—and is more than twice the combined GNP of the ASEAN nations. In the postnuclear age, when economic security reigns supreme, the PRC's geoeconomic interests will provide a more powerful impetus for its Greater China scenario than what nationalism alone can. The drive for reunification with Taiwan, after Hong Kong's return, will be for the large part the most enduring guarantee why the Greater China scenario—and, for that matter, the Dengist economic reforms begun in 1978—will continue beyond the life of Deng Xiaoping himself.[13]

□ *The Defense Posture*

Earlier, we noted the two aspects of China's response to the rise of the new age after the end of the Cold War: Beijing's diplomatic realignments abroad and its deepening economic reforms at home. In addition to pursuing these two aspects, one would expect the Chinese to so reorient their defense posture as to meet the challenge of the postnuclear era. China may find itself impelled by the new circumstances to increase its defense spending on conventional armaments and ballistic missile defense. But on this score, we are getting mixed signals. On the one hand, there is no solid evidence to suggest that the PRC is investing disproportionately more in defense than before. But on the other hand, the PLA (People's Liberation Armed Forces) has been steadily pressing on with the modernization of its air and naval capabilities.

PRC Defense Expenditures

Let us first look at the PRC's defense spendings. Available statistics provided in the annual issues of the *Military Balance*, published by the prestigious London-based International Institute of Strategic Studies, indicate no significant increase in the PRC's defense expenditures between 1988 ($5.8 billion) and 1990 ($6.1 billion). Allowing for inflation, these figures almost remained constant. Reports from Taipei, however, alleged some hefty 12 to 15.5 percent annual increases (!) in the PRC's defense outlays for the three years 1990–1992.[14] But closer examination reveals that the figures were given in *renminbi* and were not inflation-adjusted: 29 billion yuan (1990); 32 billion yuan (1991); and 37 billion yuan (1992). If converted into U.S. dollars after inflation, these figures would come out, respectively, as $6.1 billion for 1990 (at the ratio of 4.7 yuan to the dollar for the year), $6.2 billion for 1991 (at 5.2 yuan/dollar), and $6.4 billion for 1992 (at 5.8 yuan/dollar). The increases, at 0.01–0.02 percent annually, were far below the rates reported in Taipei. The Taipei reports also had alleged that Beijing was purchasing an aircraft carrier from the Ukraine. The report was officially denied by Wang Zhaoguo, head of the PRC's Taiwan Relations Office in Beijing during a meeting with a visiting delegation from Taipei.[15]

Other unconfirmed reports alleged PRC purchases of 8 MIG–31 fighter planes, 72 SU–27 fighters, and 440 T–72–M tanks from Russia.[16] However, other than the tanks, the purchases, if confirmed, probably are related to the continuing PRC investment in modernizing its air force and navy in anticipation of future showdowns in disputes regarding the Paracel and Spratly islands in the South China Sea. This concern seems to be at the heart of China's current defense planning.

The Paracels are located about 200 miles equidistant from the coast of Vietnam east of Danang and south of China's Hainan Island. The Chinese claimed this island chain as early as the fifteenth century; Vietnam dates its claim to 1802 A.D. (Conboy, p. 6). The Spratly archipelago stretches 620 miles south of China's coast nearly to Brunei. It is the object of contention by seven claimants: China, Vietnam, Taiwan, the Philippines, Malaysia, Indonesia, and Brunei. The Chinese and the Vietnamese have fought twice, in 1973 and again in 1988, over these contested islands. China is known to be readying itself for possible future projection of power in these troubled waters (*ibid.*).

PLA Air and Naval Modernization

Since the mid-1980s, the Chinese, although shrinking defense spendings in other aspects (e.g., demobilizing over one million personnel from active duty), have shifted priorities to upgrading their air and naval power. They have since acquired new long-range bombers, in-flight refueling technology, a marine corps, and longer-range naval capabilities, including resupply. For the first time in 1986, long-range naval air force bombers conducted exercises in the Pacific. The following year, part of the East China Sea Fleet exercised right into the disputed areas of the South China Sea. By the end of 1987, a new type of frigate with modern weapons came into service (Gelber, p. 666). In 1988 the PRC navy began to assert its control over the Spratly Islands, encountering the Vietnamese naval forces in several small but decisive battles, which the Chinese won (Conboy, p. 6).

In October 1989 the PRC air force commander announced the acquisition of new radar systems permitting all-weather operations. The PRC navy, in September of the same year, began a long Pacific cruise. As one analyst puts it, the PLA has been mapping not just its own territory but also those contested offshore islands and neighbors with whom China is in dispute (Segal 1988). The *Military Balance* (IISS, p. 149) reports that the Chinese navy in 1991 completed the modernization of a second Luda destroyer and now has at least four helicopter-equipped ships. It further reports that China has abandoned the construction of more Xia SSBNs (nuclear-fueled ballistic missile submarines) and is planning the development of a larger and more modern ballistic missile submarine.

Our interpretation of the above seemingly incongruent data is twofold: (1) The PRC is cost-conscious (with a GNP of $400 billion, it has been carrying an annual foreign debt burden of $41 billion to $45 billion since 1989 and had a national budget deficit of $15 billion in 1991) and has been apparently shifting its limited resources to the modernization of its air and naval power; and (2) China seems to be reorienting its military strategy in keeping with the dictate of the postnuclear age. Its abandonment of the construction of more Xia-class nuclear-fueled submarines in favor of developing (conventional) ballistic missile submarines seems to confirm this point. In other words, the Chinese navy clearly anticipates conventional, rather than nuclear, firepower to be central in future naval battles.

In order to establish the suspected link between Chinese naval planning and the locale of future operations, it is important to note the Chinese acquisition of aerial refueling technology. Until recently, the range of Chinese fighter-bombers was only a few hundred miles; their longest-range bomber could barely make a return trip from the Spratlys. With the introduction of the B–6 Badger bomber as an aerial tanker, the range of Chinese fighter-bombers is greatly expanded. U.S. analysts believe that in future operations against any of the other contenders to the Spratly Islands, 620 miles away from the China coast, the PRC will have "total air superiority" (Chanda 1992, p. 3). A related development is the promulgation of a new Chinese law, called the Territorial Waters Law, in February 1992, which legally places not only the Paracels and the Spratlys but also the Tiaoyutai (or, in Japanese, Senkaku) Islands well within Chinese territorial waters. As such, the law states, China has "the right to adopt all necessary measures to prevent . . . the harmful passage of vessels through its territorial waters" (*ibid.*).

One can only guess that the law was passed in time for the subsequent seven-nation conference convened by Indonesia in early July 1992, to discuss how to resolve the competing claims to the Paracel and Spratly Islands. One indication that the law, as well as the air/naval modernization drive, was designed to stiffen the spines of PRC negotiators at the meeting is that, just as the conference was going on, a Chinese foreign ministry spokesman told a press conference in Beijing on July 2, 1992, that although China had indisputable rights to these offshore islands, its position was that the disputes should be shelved, without prejudice, in favor of joint development by all the contestant powers in consortium.[17]

An alternative explanation for the Chinese law is that it was timed to lend sanctity to an oil exploration contract China signed on May 8, 1992, with Crestone Energy Corp., a U.S. company based in Denver.[18] If the law would give China the right to use naval force to assert its claims to an area also claimed by Vietnam, that would not take anything away from our speculation that the Chinese defense posture is in keeping with the strategic shift from nuclear to conventional defense in the postnuclear era.

One other challenge to this categorization is China's May 21 underground testing of a nuclear weapon with a force of one megaton of TNT. We do not claim to have privileged information regarding this event and its timing, but our reaction is that it was probably the consummation of a big project that had been conceived long before and simply was not scratched after the arrival of the postnuclear era. There can be two reasons why the project was continued despite the change of time. First, even with the end of the Cold War, China knows that it is targeted by both the ex-Soviets and U.S. SIOP (Single Integrated Operations Plan). So until the elimination of these nuclear threats to their security, the Chinese may have decided not to take any chances (Zhai, p. 170). Second, judging by the unlikelihood that the former Soviet Union will abandon its nuclear arsenal before it regains world-class economic strength, it is possible that wielding a sizable nuclear arsenal still confers an unusual power status in the hard reality of world politics in the new era (*ibid.*). Hence, China may want to send the world a reminder that, despite the declining value of nuclear weapons, it is still a nuclear state to be reckoned with.

Thus viewed, the recent nuclear test does not necessarily mean that China is proceeding against the dictate of the postnuclear age in its defense program.

One other thing to consider is that in the Asia Pacific regional rivalry, Indonesia, Malaysia, and Thailand, among others, are all expanding their conventional naval forces (Fisher 1991, p. 4). China has no choice but to do likewise, which means that it will have to do the kinds of updating of its conventional air and naval forces mentioned earlier. Therefore, there is no Chinese departure from what the postnuclear era dictates.

■ CONCLUSION

The above discussion has been premised, broadly, on the three defining characteristics of the post–Cold War world as set forth in Chapter 1. It is apparent that the Chinese defense posture acknowledges the second of the three characteristics, i.e., the declining importance of nuclear weapons. We have seen that the PRC is apprehensive that the breakup of the old bipolarity system will result in "unipolar" U.S. dominance, wherein Washington imposes its will and values on other nations. As noted, one Chinese objection is to the U.S. view of human rights, which does not include the rights of distributive justice, e.g., the right of subsistence for the people in developing nations.

Reacting to the declining importance of nuclear weaponry, Beijing has shed its previous objection to NPT, and it may have been instrumental in getting the North Koreans to agree to external inspections of their nuclear sites. Moreover, China's leaders seem to have come to grips with the linkage between the postnuclear norm of the new era and the next defining norm—namely, the rise of economic security in competition with military security. They seem to recognize that China's future role in world politics will no longer be based on its membership in the nuclear club; Beijing's defense planning demonstrates a clear shift to conventional arms. They also seem to recognize that, in the area of economic security, China's ability to play a regional (or global) role will depend largely upon its own economic capability and diplomatic resourcefulness.

Thus, domestically, China is determined to redouble its efforts in making economic reforms, despite the momentary uncertainty caused by Tiananmen. On the diplomatic front, it has embarked upon an initiative aimed at building a network of realigned relationships radiating from the immediate Asia Pacific environs to other areas. China now has formal diplomatic ties with all nations in Asia Pacific through the Middle East. Diplomatic relations with South Korea, the last exception, were established on August 24, 1992. An earlier barrier to PRC–South Korea normalization had been North Korea's objection. The switch was a tangible result of the breakup of the Soviet Union, China's longtime rival for influence in North Korea. On the global scale, China maintains diplomatic ties with 140 countries (Qian 1991). It bears noting that in Asia Pacific China now maintains diplomatic ties with more countries than does the United States.

Yet this new Chinese coalition-making drive has a different twist from past campaigns. For one thing, it is not ideologically conceived. China is on record as no longer willing to sacrifice its own national interests just to advance the socialist cause in the Third World. Rather, the new initiative is based on a special concern shared with like-minded nations, such as India, that the remaining superpower should not foist its own values on others. For over three decades since 1959, China and India had been at loggerheads; but in the new world order they became united by this common conviction. During his tour of Africa in 1991, Foreign Minister Qian Qichen found common cause with his hosts on the theme that Third World nations should have the freedom to find their own way to democracy instead of being dictated to by any external power, even an aid donor. In return, his hosts—for example, Côte d'Ivoire's foreign minister—thanked China for never dictating to the Third World.[19]

In some quarters, the new Chinese realignment initiative is characterized as a response to Beijing's diplomatic isolation after Tiananmen. It is argued that only Third World states are receptive to a Chinese outreach attempt.[20] But this explanation is not entirely convincing if one considers the new, openly stated pragmatic Chinese stance toward the Third World. True, in its reaction to the U.S. version of the new world order, Beijing insisted that a true new world order must also offer a "new economic world order." It is plain that the Chinese initiative should be seen in the light of the country's alleged common cause with the Third World. But Deng Xiaoping has insisted that China will not try to lead the Third World as the remaining major communist regime.[21]

Admittedly, one realistic reason for Beijing's spinning of a new network of upgraded relations is its conscious effort to reduce its dependence on the U.S. market by spreading out Chinese trading ties with new partners in other parts of the world.[22] After all, one source of friction with Washington since the late 1980s has been the Chinese trade surplus with the United States to the tune of $10 billion to $15 billion a year. But this alone cannot fully explain the broad sweep Beijing has taken in its diplomatic endeavors.

China's realignment efforts within the Asia Pacific region are decidedly born of the new era with a view to its economic security. The Asia Pacific aspect of Beijing's response to the challenge of the new era is known as its *zhoubian* diplomacy (Jiang 1991; Qian 1990b). This epithet means, in loose translation, a good-neighbor diplomacy toward countries in China's immediate "circumference." Thus, we have seen China's special attention to northeast Asia (Japan and the Korean Peninsula), the ASEAN, and the Greater China scenario. To assure security in the international environs surrounding China, we have seen a persistent effort at modernizing the Chinese air and naval power. This effort is actually the "stick" accompanying the "carrot" of *zhoubian* diplomacy.

The rationale for the *zhoubian* diplomacy is best revealed in statements made by China's leaders during their recent missions to surrounding countries. A consensus on what the new world order should be was reached, for example, with India during Premier Li Peng's visit to that country in December 1991. Both nations agreed that, in their preferred new world order, no country should decide on values for others. It is instructive that, during his visit to Singapore and Malaysia in mid-January 1992, President Yang Shangkun, in agreement with his hosts, called special attention to the imperative of *regional economic cooperation*. Noteworthy is Yang's emphasis on the indispensability of regional stability to China's economic development at home and his emphatic wish that no

88 *James C. Hsiung*

major conflict will ever again visit upon Asia Pacific.[23] This theme of a tranquil international environment echoes similar pronouncements by other Chinese leaders such as party Secretary-General Jiang Zemin (1991) and Foreign Minister Qian Qichen (1990a).

The bottom line is, therefore, that the geoeconomic dictate has entered into the consciousness of China's top leadership and that it has provided the momentum of China's new diplomacy of coalition making. Of special relevance to our interest is the Chinese awareness that China owes it to itself to work, in concert with others such as Japan, for the regional economic prosperity of Asia Pacific in the 1990s and beyond (Ji 1991).

To reiterate, the new Chinese foreign policy is conceived in the critical changes wrought by the coming of a postnuclear, geoeconomic age on the heels of the demise of the Cold War. That policy is, in turn, prompted by a desire to safeguard China from the fate that befell most other communist systems and, hopefully, to lead a revamped Chinese nation onto the new terrain of world politics beyond the 1990s.

In sizing up the new age, analysts such as Robert Jervis (1992, p. 61) usually forecast a higher, not lower, incidence of conflict in the post–Cold War world arising from resurgent nationalistic sentiments, ethnic disputes, and regional rivalries, as well as the disappearance of restraints imposed by the erstwhile bisuperpower confrontation. Such does not seem to be in the cards for Asia Pacific—at least not nearly to the same extent as in, say, Europe or the Middle East. The realignment strategy in China's new foreign policy, to be sure, seems to confirm this prognostication for the region in the new era.

■ NOTES

1. *New York Times,* April 21, 1992, p. 1.
2. *Renmin Ribao* [People's Daily] (overseas ed.), July 30, 1991, p. 6.
3. "New World Order—According to George Bush," *Beijing Review,* October 28–November 3, 1991, p. 13f.
4. *Chung-kung wen-ti tsu-liao yen-chiu* [Problems of Chinese Communism Weekly] (Taipei), No. 481 (August 19, 1991), p. 15.
5. Premier Li Peng's statement made during his visit in India, December 12, *People's Daily* (overseas ed.), December 13, 1991, p. 1. Also, President Yang Shangkun's news conference in Singapore, *People's Daily,* January 10, 1992, p. 1; his speech in Malaysia, January 11, 1992, carried in the *World Journal* (New York), January 12, 1992; and "Building a Just and an Equitable Politico-Economic New World Order," *People's Daily* (overseas ed.), July 30, 1991, p. 6. See also Foreign Minister Qian's visit to Africa in January 1992, cited in note 19.
6. See for example Premier Li's speech before the UN Security Council, January 31, 1992; 35 *Beijing Review* 7:12–14. See also instances listed in n. 5 above.
7. Reuters reports carried in the *Qiao bao* (The China Press) (New York), January 18, 1992, p. 1.
8. Nuclear "catalytic war" refers to the outbreak of a nuclear exchange in a group of nuclear-weapons states, A, B, and C, when State C erroneously unleashes

retaliatory nuclear firepower against B after having been hit by nuclear weapons actually fired off from State A but disguised as an attack from State B. For as long as the identity of the initial nuclear attack on State C (from A) were to remain undiscovered before C retaliated, it would be an "anonymous" war—hence "nuclear anonymity." In this phenomenon, an "anonymous" war (waged by A against C in disguised form) triggers off a "catalytic war" between C and B after C, not knowing the true identity of its attacker, erroneously fires back on the innocent B. This can happen only in a multiple, as opposed to bilateral, nuclear deterrence situation. It is exacerbated by the urgency with which a decision to retaliate has to be made so as to ward off a presumed second wave of attack; it therefore cannot wait until the investigation on the true identity of the attacker is completed.

9. This is the essence of a secret "red-heading" document issued by Beijing recently. See the *Chao-liu* [Currents] monthly (Hong Kong), November 1991; the gist is reproduced in *Chung-kung wen-ti tsu-liao yan-chiu* [Problems of Chinese Communism Weekly] (Taipei), No. 496 (December 20, 1991), p. 60.

10. Based on my own tallies from various sources.

11. "Post–Gulf War Strategic Pattern," *Beijing Review*, November 25–December 1, 1991, pp. 11–13; Chen 1990, p. 5; Tao 1984, p. 2; Yuan 1984, pp. 2–5; Howe 1990, p. 680. See also Lin Xiaoguang, "Japan Seeks Greater Role in the World," *Beijing Review*, February 3–16, 1992, p. 10f.

12. The "tranquil international environment" theme here was developed in Foreign Minister Qian's report to the Standing Committee of the National People's Congress, in *People's Daily* (overseas ed.), December 26, 1991, p. 4.

13. For the momentum of support for the PRC economic reforms, see Nicholas Kristof's report "Support for Move to Freer Markets Is Growing in China," *New York Times*, June 28, 1992, p. 1. See also his report "Foreign Investments Pouring to China," *New York Times*, June 15, 1992, p. D–1. For an official view on the status of the marketization reforms, see "The New Stage of the Chinese Reforms and Opening-Up," *People's Daily* (overseas ed.), June 9, 1992, p. 1. After a visit to observe the economic reforms on the mainland, Chao Yao-tung, Taiwan's former economic minister and currently an advisor to President Lee Teng-hui, made an important report upon return to Taiwan. He noted (1) that the mainland Chinese economic reforms exceeded his wildest possible conjecture; (2) that the reforms had passed the point of no return; and (3) that it would be to Taiwan's and the mainland's advantage to join hands and work together in the interest of creating a "greater China." *Central Daily News* (Taipei), June 10, 1992, p. 1.

14. *Central Daily News* (Taipei), June 19, 1992, p. 1.

15. *The China Times* (Taipei), July 6, 1992, p. 3. Foreign Minister Qian Qichen confirmed, at a news conference in Beijing on March 23, 1992, that China's defense budget for the year was $7.3 billion, or $6 per capita, as compared with the United States' $1,100 per capita defense spendings and Japan's $300 per capita, *Qiao Bao* (The China Press), March 24, 1993, p. 2.

16. *The China Times* (Taipei), June 21, 1992, p. 1.

17. Dispatch from Beijing, carried by the *Central Daily News* (Taipei), July 4, 1992, p. 1.

18. Nicholas Kristof, "China Signs U.S. Oil Deal for Disputed Waters," *New York Times*, June 18, 1992, p. 8.

19. Reuters dispatch carried in the *Qiao Bao* (The China Press) (New York), January 18, 1992.

20. *New York Times*, January 15, 1992, p. 7.

21. Deng Xiaoping, China's senior leader, responded to the collapse of communism in Eastern Europe and the Soviet Union with a cryptic 24-character advisory, the last four characters of which (*juebu dangtou*) means "never [attempt to]

lead [any others]." See discussion in *Kuo-shih ping-lun* (National Affairs Review] (Hong Kong), No. 1 (January 1992), p. 4.
    22. Dispatch by New China News Agency, dated January 4, 1992, as carried in *Qiao Bao* (The China Press) (New York), January 15, 1992, p. 2.
    23. *People's Daily* (overseas ed..), January 10, 1992; *The China Times* (Taipei), January 10, 1992, citing wire service reports from Singapore.

■ REFERENCES

Asian Bulletin. 1991. "Results of Talks Hailed as Historic Breakthrough," 16 *Asian Bulletin* (Taipei) 12:25–29 (December 1991).
Bernstein, Carl. 1992. "The Holy Alliance: How Reagan and the Pope Conspired to Assist Poland's Solidarity Movement and Hasten the Demise of Communism," *Time,* February 24, 1992.
Brown, Frederick. 1991. "Security Issues in Southeast Asia." In Frank Macciarola and Robert Oxnam, eds., *The China Challenge: American Policies in East Asia* (see below).
Buszynski, Leszek. 1992. "Southeast Asia in the Post–Cold War Era: Regionalism and Security," 32 *Asian Survey* 9:830–847.
Chai Chengwen. 1992. "The Disintegration of the Soviet Union and Its Implications," *International Strategic Studies* 1 (1992). Beijing: Beijing Institute for International Strategic Studies.
Chanda, Nayan. 1992. "China Posted Newest Threat to Contested Islands," *Asian Wall Street Journal Weekly,* March 23, 1992.
Chen, Luzhi. 1990. "Taipingyang qu jingji hezuo de tedian [The Characteristics of Economic Cooperation in the Pacific Region]," in *Guoji wenti yanjiu* [Study of International Problems], No. 2 (February 1992). Beijing.
Conboy, Kenneth. 1992. "Conflict Potential in Southeast Asia." Washington, D.C.: Heritage Foundation. No. 365, Heritage Lecture Series.
Cotton, James. 1991. "Conflict and Accommodation in the Two Koreas." In *The End of the Cold War in Northeast Asia*, eds. Stuart Harris and James Cotton. Boulder, CO: Lynne Rienner Publishers.
Ding Shichuan and Chen Wei. 1992. "Trend of Development of Japan–U.S. Relations Fifty Years after the Pacific War," *International Strategic Studies,* No. 1 (March 1992). Beijing: Beijing Institute for International Strategic Studies.
Donnelly, Jack. 1992. "Human Rights in the New World Order," A *World Policy Journal* 2 (Spring): 249–278. New York: World Policy Institute.
Emmerson, John. 1981. "Japan and U.S. Foreign Policy: Old Ally and New Environs." In James C. Hsiung, *Asia and U.S. Foreign Policy* (see below).
Fang Sheng. 1991. "Economic Cooperation Between Mainland, Taiwan, and Hong Kong," *Beijing Review,* November 25–December 1, 1991.
Fisher, Richard. 1991. "Why Asia Is Not Ready for Arms Control." Washington, D.C.: Heritage Foundation. Asia Studies Center *Backgrounder.*
Gelber, Henry G. 1990. "China's New Economic and Strategic Uncertainties and the Security Prospects," 30 *Asian Survey* 7 (July 1990), pp. 646–668. Berkeley, CA: University of California Press.
Gill, R. Bates. 1991. "China Looks to Thailand: Exporting Arms and Exporting Influence," 31 *Asian Survey* 6:526–539.
Gong, Gerrit. 1991. "China and the Dynamics of Unification in Northeast Asia." In Frank J. Macciarola and Robert Oxnam, eds., *The China Challenge: American Policies in East Asia.*

Harding, Harry, ed. 1984. *China's Foreign Relations in the 1980s.* New Haven, CT: Yale University Press.

Howe, Christopher. 1990. "China, Japan, and International Independence," *China Quarterly* [London], 124:662–693.

Hsiung, James C. 1972. *Law and Policy in China's Foreign Relations.* New York: Columbia University Press.

Hsiung, James C. 1983. *Asia and U.S. Foreign Policy,* ed. with Winberg Chai. New York: Praeger.

Hsiung, James C. 1985. *Beyond China's Independent Foreign Policy.* New York: Praeger Publishers.

Hua Di. 1990. "A Comprehensive Economic Security Understanding of a Future PRC–U.S.–Japan Triangular Relationship." In James Radvaanyi, ed., *The Pacific in the 1990s.* Lanham, MD: University Press of America.

IFS 1990. *International Financial Statistics.*

Institute of International Strategic Studies. 1991. *The Military Balance: 1991– 1992.* London: IISS.

Jervis, Robert. 1992, "The Future of World Politics: Will It Resemble the Past?" 16 *International Security* 3:39–73 (Winter 1991–1992).

Ji Chongwei. 1991. "Asian Pacific Regional Economic Development and Sino-Japanese Economic Cooperation," *Renmin Ribao* [People's Daily] (overseas ed.), November 15, 1991.

Jiang Zemin. 1991. "China's Relations with Surrounding Countries Are Sound," *People's Daily* (overseas ed.), December 27, 1991.

Jiang Zemin. 1992. "World Situation and Sino-Japanese Relations," *Beijing Review,* April 20–26, 1992.

Kim, Hakjong. 1991. "China's Korea Policy Since the Tiananmen Square Incident." In Frank J. Macciarola and Robert Oxnam, eds., *The China Challenge: American Policies in East Asia.*

Kristof, Nicholas. 1992. "In Corner of Asia, Hope for New Trading Center," *New York Times,* February 10, 1992, p. 18.

Li, Haobao. 1992. "Tumen River Delta: Far East's Future Rotterdam," *Beijing Review,* April 20–26, 1992.

Li Hong. 1992. "Developing Countries Fight for the Right to Subsistence," 35 *Beijing Review* 8:12–13.

Macciarola, Frank J. and Robert Oxnam. 1991. *The China Challenge: American Policies in East Asia.* New York: The Academy of Political Science.

Pollock, Jonathan. 1984. "China and the Global Strategic Balance." In Harry Harding, ed., *China's Foreign Relations in the 1980s.*

Pollack, Jonathan. 1990. "The Sino-Japanese Relationship and East Asian Security," *China Quarterly* 124:714–729.

Qian Qichen. 1990a. "The Current International Situation and Sino–U.S. Relations," speech before Council on Foreign Relations. New York City, October 4, 1990.

Qian Qichen. 1990b. "The Asian Situation and China's Relations with Its Surrounding Countries," speech at the Asia Society, New York, October 2, 1990.

Qian Qichen. 1991. "Independent Foreign Policy: Endeavoring for the Future," *People's Daily* (overseas ed.), December 16, 1991.

Renmin Ribao. 1991a. "Proposal of the CCP Central Committee on the Formulation of the Ten-Year Plan for National Economic and Social Development; and the Eighth Five-Year Plan." Full text in *People's Daily,* January 29, 1991.

Renmin Ribao. 1991b. "Strive for the Realization of the Strategic Goals of the Second Step," *People's Daily* (overseas ed.), January 31, 1991.

Rosecrance, Richard. 1972. "Deterrence in Dyadic and Multipolar Environments." In Richard Rosecrance, ed., *The Future of the International Strategic System.* San Francisco: Chandler.

Ross, Robert. 1991. "China and the Cambodia Peace Process," 31 *Asian Survey* 12:1170–1185.

Schurmann, Franz. 1987. *The Foreign Policies of Richard M. Nixon.* Berkeley, CA: Institute of International Studies, University of California.

Segal, Gerald. 1988. "As China Grows Strong," *International Affairs* (Spring 1988), pp. 217–231.

Sutter, Robert. 1991. "China's View of the 'New World Order': Possible Implications for Sino–U.S. Relations," Congressional Research Service Report, 91–665F, September 11, 1991. Washington, D.C.

Tai Ming Cheung. 1992 "Smoke Signals," *Far Eastern Economic Review,* November 12, 1992, pp. 29–30.

Tao Bingwen. 1992. "The Historic Twist to the Korean Peninsula," 11 *Guoji wenti yanjiu* [International Studies] 2 (1992). Beijing: Beijing Institute for International Studies.

Wang Kangtai. 1991. "The Five Principles of Peaceful Coexistence are the Foundation of a New World Order," *Guoji zhanwang* [International Outlook] 14 (July 23, 1991). Shanghai: Institute for International Studies.

Wang Ling. 1991. "America's New World Order and the New International Order: Preliminary Thoughts," *Guoji zhanwang* [International Outlook] 15 (August 8, 1991). Shanghai: Institute for International Studies.

Xie, Xide. 1991. "A Chinese Educator's View of China–U.S. Relations," in Frank J. Macciarola and Robert Oxnam, eds., *The China Challenge: American Policies in East Asia.*

Yuan, Yuzhou. 1984. "The Fluctuating Stability of Asia Pacific," *Shijie zhishi* [World Knowledge] 9:2–5. Beijing.

Zhai, Zhihai. 1992. "The Future of Nuclear Weapons: A Chinese Perspective." In Patrick Garrity and Steven A. Maaranen, eds., *Nuclear Weapons in a Changing World.* New York: Plenum Press.

■ 5

Philippine and South Korean International Relations in Post–Cold War Asia Pacific

Albert F. Celoza & Martin H. Sours

The formal dissolution of the USSR represents in concrete form the conclusion of what was generally accepted as the Cold War—that is, a period following World War II in which international relations at the global level were defined by superpower rivalry between the United States and the USSR. The multiplicity of issues associated with that era are now under review by a host of scholars; within the context of regional analysis, a key topic has been alliance structuring and maintenance and the development of client-state relations.

In the Asia Pacific region, the two explicit long-term client states of the United States were the Philippines and the Republic of Korea (South Korea). Fundamentally, these two countries were traditional client states because they were unequally associated with the United States by virtue of traditional military action. The Philippines were formally colonized by the United States after the Spanish-American War and subsequent counter-revolutionary suppression of the independence movement. South Korea did not feature in U.S. hegemonic regional relations until after World War II, but like the Philippines it was the object of direct military action by the United States (and its allies under the flag of the United Nations) and therefore became similarly linked in military/political terms to that superpower.

Although much has been made in the literature concerning the market access/political alignment relationship of Japan and the United States during the Cold War, that relationship was clearly different from, and therefore should not be compared with, the direct client-state framework of

Philippine and South Korean relations with the United States. Most significant, the permanent stationing of substantial U.S. military forces anchored these two countries directly to the international alliance system of the United States during this period.

Now the passing of the bipolar Cold War period and the emergence of a multipolar international order poses a new set of challenges to these two states. For purposes of this analysis, we will focus on four key aspects: the comparative historical framework(s) that allowed client-state relations to dominate Philippine and South Korean interaction with the United States; the symbiotic relationship of domestic authoritarian rule in these two states and U.S. foreign policy congruence; the emergence of indigenous democratization and the concurrent loosening of foreign policy bonds with the United States; and the political economy implications of this shift, as global international relations become more economy-centered in general.

Overall U.S. involvement in Asia, the wellspring from which the particular relationships with Korea and the Philippines emerged, has its roots in a combination of idealistic and mystical notions of "the Far East" and practical business and trade economic interests. U.S. clipper ships and missionaries together were involved in "the China trade," but as late imperialists, the United States operationalized its interests early on by "indirect" approaches to Asia through the Northeast Asian Great Circle route from the U.S. West Coast to Japan (and ultimately to Korea) until victory in the Spanish-American War ensured direct entry into Southeast Asia. For the United States, then, both realism and idealism coexisted in its foreign policy goals toward Asia, but as it lacked a clear focus on one or the other, the two contradictory approaches tended over time to inconsistently clash. For example, the U.S. commercial treaty with the Korean kingdom in 1882 was the first Korean agreement with a Western power, yet the U.S. government also executed the Taft-Katsura Agreement in 1905, giving Japan a free hand to colonize Korea in return for Japan's recognition of the U.S. colonial position in the Philippines.

The World War II "summit conferences" of Cairo, Yalta, and Potsdam were presented to the U.S. public as cementing logical chain of agreements to create an idealistic world in which independent states would live in peace, prosperity, and harmony. Yet the postwar bipolar world compromised this vision so thoroughly that the containment policy that followed created a popular U.S. worldview in which all states became part of a worldwide struggle against communism. U.S. "allies" such as the Philippines and South Korea were portrayed as virtuous states in a global struggle, justifying military commitments and the use of force. Against this backdrop of "sentimental imperialism,"[1] developments in the Philippines and South Korea can be discussed in more detail.

■ HISTORICAL FRAMEWORK

☐ *Philippines*

The group of islands that would be named the Philippines was conquered by Spain in the sixteenth century. The Spanish conquistadors were looking for an alternative route to Asia and a stake in the lucrative spice trade. They were also in search of land, riches, and converts to Christianity, all for the glory of Spain. The fragmented nature of Philippine geography and society made the conquest possible. The Filipinos did not have a central government and were divided into various ethnolinguistic groups. Thus, one group collaborated with the Spaniards to subjugate another. In addition, the Spaniards used the Filipino ruling class to quell the masses. They also established an extractive colonial system that used Filipino forced labor and tribute (of cash and kind) to sustain the colonial government and its commercial enterprise. The government had the monopoly of trade—the galleon trade—with China and Mexico. Because of the union of church and state, the Catholic hierarchy was influential in the islands. The friar was the sole authority in town; frequently he was the only Spaniard and thus the agent of the colonial government.

During the eighteenth century, economic changes connected the Philippines to world trade. The galleon trade declined, requiring another activity to make the colonial enterprise profitable. Cash crops were introduced: Tobacco, sugar, abaca, opium, and others were planted, processed, sold, and exported under government monopoly. The production of the staple crop, rice, declined, as earning cash took priority. Ports that were closed to other Europeans were opened. British and U.S. economic involvement increased, as did the role of Chinese merchants, who played middlemen. The Spaniards retained their political authority, but their legitimacy began to be questioned. Socioeconomic change created a class of Filipino landed elites who availed themselves of European education, imbibed liberal ideas, and subsequently demanded reform in the colonies. These mestizos (half-native and half-Chinese or half-Spanish) of the landed class began to perceive themselves as separate from the colonial masters and identified with their native land. The confluence of these factors ushered in Philippine nationalism. Ironically, the writings of the Spanish-educated reformers inspired the colony against Spanish rule.

In 1898, war brought the United States to the Philippines. The U.S. navy defeated the Spanish fleet, and after a "mock battle" to save the honor of Spain, U.S. soldiers occupied Manila. At this time, the Filipino revolutionaries were already in control of other parts of the country and had established the Philippine Republic, the first independent republic in Asia. However, through the Treaty of Paris of December 1898, the Philippines, together with Guam and Puerto Rico, were acquired by the United States from Spain. The Filipinos fought for their independence but were defeated by the might of U.S. arms. Thus, the Philippines became a U.S. colony, and their political and economic systems were subordinated to the United States. As in the previous colonial regime, the Philippines were ruled by a governor-general from the *metropole* mandated to implement its laws and politics. What was different under the United States, however, was the greater degree to which the Filipinos were allowed to participate in the bureaucracy and in the legislative and judicial branches of government. Filipinization policy was adopted in order to guide the Filipinos toward their promised independence. It was also designed to appease Filipino nationalists and reformers and co-opt them to U.S. rule. Though democratization was promised, its fruits were mostly enjoyed by the elites. In 1935 the Philippines began a commonwealth government, a transition period toward independence. Selfish U.S. economic considerations, rather than benevolent ones, heavily influenced this decision: The Depression increased the burden of colonial governance, and the threat of cheap labor, sugar, and other imports from the Philippines induced U.S. interest groups to support Philippine independence. Filipino elites, who publicly were championing independence, privately were apprehensive of a system in which their market ties with the United States could potentially be threatened.

The Philippines were granted independence on July 4, 1946, after a period of limited self-rule disturbed only by the Japanese occupation during World War II. The Philippines thus graduated from a colony to a neocolony. Its political and economic policies became appendages of U.S. interests. Its exports were tied to U.S. markets, and U.S. corporations and nationals were granted parity (equal) rights under the Philippine constitution in the exploitation of natural resources. The structure of Philippine government, as well as its institutions and practices, were patterned after the U.S. bureaucracy. The Philippines' cardinal foreign policy stand, explicitly pronounced by the first president of the republic, was to follow the lead of the United States. In terms of defense and security U.S. influence was also pervasive. The Philippines signed a military agreement allowing the use of naval and air force bases for a period of ninety-nine years. Internally and in its foreign relations, it was staunchly anticommunist and received help from the United States in quelling local·insurgencies and communist movements. Through the Joint U.S. Military Advisory Group and other agencies, the United States influenced the conduct of national defense. The Philippines, thus, perceived the outside world from the United States' view.

☐ South Korea

The foundations of the South Korean state were laid under Japanese colonial rule (1910–1945), universally recognized as a harsh and uncompromising political regime. The Japanese administration is generally known for its policies of total suppression of the distinct Korean cultural tradition, including the ban on the Korean language in schools, and forcible conscription of Koreans in the development of other parts of the Japanese empire.

One far-reaching result of the Japanese experience was the political fragmentation of Korean elites. Although it is generally recognized that anti-Japanese Korean nationalists followed both communist and noncommunist traditions, the overall impact of the Japanese on the society was much more widespread and destructive. At the turn of the century (the period of U.S. colonial suppression of the Philippine independence movement) some Koreans identified with Japanese rule as a way to modernize their country. The traditional court of the declining Yi dynasty had failed to provide a forum for effective Korean national modernization, and the upper 20 percent of the society, which did not live on the land and engage in peasant agriculture, drifted away into various occupational groups, including basic manufacturing, trading, transportation, and other entrepreneurial economic activities. Some enthusiastically supported the Japanese, others simply acquiesced. Lower classes within this group were co-opted into local police and military forces.

In order to implement infrastructural development projects to exploit the natural resources of the area for the benefit of Japan, new corporate structures were needed in colonial Korea. To accomplish that end and facilitate a modest capital flow from Japan to Korea, a limited financial market and some joint stock companies did develop. However, their purpose was to ration capital and maintain managerial control over the enterprises, not generate a market-driven return to stockholders. Many wealthy Korean landholders collaborated with Japanese corporate and imperial actors to dominate the business community and assure that businesses acted in the interest of the Japanese government.

Taken together, these two trends produced a profound contradiction within colonial Korea. On the one hand, political, intellectual, and student elites were fractured and divided along lines of political action and orientation to Japanese colonialism, all the way from complete collaboration (sometimes in the name of "progress" as well as expediency) to radical opposition under the framework of Asian communism. These shades of political opinion also operated within Korea and among exiles, creating the basis for factionalism and suspicion within the political culture in general. At the same time, the foundations of the business system were laid within a context of central control, in which power was exerted through business activity, from 1910 to 1945, the very years when the foundations for modern business everywhere in the world were laid. Thus we can see that dependency as well as a desire and drive for independence, coexisted in the formation of the modern Korean state during the colonial period. It is too simple to say the aggressive Japanese colonialism carried the seeds of its own destruction, for the complex strains of this period created multiple "Koreas" within an overall colonial framework.

■ POSTWAR AUTHORITARIAN RULE
AND U.S. RELATIONS

□ *Philippines*

The post–World War II Philippines was faced with the immense challenge of reconstruction. It had to accede to U.S. impositions in order to receive economic aid. Independence did not bring absolute control of internal and external affairs; these were compromised by the new nation's economic condition. In addition to struggling with reconstruction, the government was troubled by the Hukbalahap, or Huk, rebellion, which was fueled by social injustices in the rural areas and festered internally by massive graft and corruption. To help cope with the crisis situation, the United States used Ramon Magsaysay, Philippine secretary of defense, as a conduit for its intervention. His candidacy and presidential tenure were bolstered by CIA support. However, his reign as a charismatic leader was cut short by a fatal plane crash, ending expected reforms in Philippine politics. In its foreign relations, the Philippines aligned itself with the "free world" through the Southeast Asia Treaty Organization (SEATO), whose goal was to defend the member countries against and contain communism in Asia. Ironically, the organization included only two Southeast Asian countries, the Philippines and Thailand, both clients of the United States.

In 1965 Ferdinand Marcos was elected Philippine president. Prior to his election, he vehemently opposed Philippine involvement in the Vietnam War. He immediately changed his position as president and thereafter received considerable public support and military aid from the United States. Marcos was plagued by demands from nationalists for a drastic sociopolitical overhaul of Philippine society. A constitutional convention was called to revamp the Philippines' basic law, which was a product of its colonial past. Denouncing Marcos's government and its alliance with U.S. imperialism, student and labor demonstrations became a prominent scene in Manila. Marcos ensured his reelection in 1969 through massive fraud and bribery, which emptied public coffers. Because he could not legally run for a third term, Marcos imposed martial law in 1972, inaugurating the authoritarian period in the Philippines' political history. In spite of U.S. commitment to human rights and the democratic process, it supported Marcos's authoritarian move. After all, martial law did not affect U.S. investments in the Philippines and continued to guarantee the use of military bases. Marcos, therefore, remained a strong ally of the United States. He followed the U.S. example of opening diplomatic relations with the People's Republic of China and increased contacts with the communist world. At the same time, Marcos continued to project an anticommunist image to both international and domestic constituencies. In his martial law proclamation, Marcos portrayed the insurgency movement and its alleged foreign supporters as posing dangerous threats to the security of the state. He contended that the subversives could only be suppressed through drastic measures under an emergency government. (This communist insurgency, however, increased its strength and support under the Marcos regime.) Marcos also wanted to project his image as a leader of the Third World. The Philippine foreign ministry thus expanded the scope of its foreign policy attention and cultivated multilateral ties to address Marcos's domestic and international agenda.

U.S. bases remained the centerpiece of Philippine foreign policy. The United States needed them for its worldwide containment policy and as a means of power projection (especially during the Cold War period under Reagan). The strategic value of the bases was not lost to Marcos. He bargained with U.S. leaders from Nixon to Reagan, using their desire to maintain a presence in Asia Pacific to his benefit.

To show his legitimacy, Marcos manipulated legal and constitutional mechanisms. He intervened in the constitutional convention to guarantee the continuation of his rule. To show that he had the mandate of the people, he called several orchestrated referendums indicating almost 100 percent support. He favored friends and dealt harshly with enemies. The regime incarcerated journalists, students, political opponents, and dissenters. Human rights violations ranged from threats to outright assassinations. Marcos, however, was selective in his abuses. He sought to co-opt his opponents first with rewards before using heavy-handed techniques.

Marcos benefited his friends by giving their businesses special access to government loans and loan guarantees, monopoly decrees (e.g., sugar and coconut), and contracts. In the name of security, opposition industries were confiscated and turned over to crony enterprises. During the martial law period, the military became a prominent interest group and participant in the Philippines. Marcos courted them by increasing their salaries, benefits, and influence in running the country. Thus, he turned to U.S. aid and foreign loans to finance government overspending, which required increased financial resources. The appetite of the Marcos family for wealth accumulation was so uncontrolled that even foreign cash infusions were insufficient to sustain economic growth. The Marcos family increased its wealth while the Philippines suffered a decrease in growth and lowered living standards.

Marcos's gesture of lifting martial law in 1981 coincided with the inauguration of Ronald Reagan to the White House (as well as the papal visit to the Philippines). His move was appreciated by the supportive Republican administration, which was less concerned with human rights than with maintaining the rights to retain the military bases. Marcos's domestic constituents, however, became increasingly unhappy. The communist insurgency increased in strength, and independent businessmen and the church started to vocally complain about the decline in the quality of life, fairness, and equity under authoritarian rule.

The assassination of prominent opposition leader Benigno Aquino in 1983 triggered protest from the populace. There were strong accusations of Marcos-military complicity in the murder. Marcos's image as a strongman was weakened by his inept response to the people's outcry. Rumors of his illness also contributed to fears of instability, disorder, and violent power struggles in the event of his death. As the communist New People's Army continued to gain influence, these uncertainties in political succession became a threat to Philippine stability and U.S. interests. Economic conditions and law and order further deteriorated, creating an unfavorable environment for business and investment. The United States then began to pressure the Marcos government to institute reforms to strengthen it against the insurgency and establish its credibility with its own people. A parade of high Reagan administration officials visited Manila to address these issues with Marcos himself. Before a U.S. television audience (on the David Brinkley show), Marcos called a snap election to once and for all show the United States that he had the mandate of his people. The opposition was fractured and divided, but at the last minute it was forced by Cardinal Jaime Sin, the archbishop of Manila, to unite under Corazon Aquino, Benigno's widow. The election was closely covered by the U.S. media and an official delegation from the U.S. government. Marcos claimed victory, but massive fraud and cheating was committed during the counting of votes. President Reagan was reluctant to disavow Marcos, but professional military and diplomatic officials were ready to break U.S. ties with the dictatorship. Military defectors backed by thousands of civilians rebelled against Marcos in the famed People Power Revolution of February 1986. Marcos was forced to leave the Philippines under U.S. protection, with an invitation to live on U.S. soil. To its very end, his rule and dramatic departure symbolized dependency on the United States.

☐ South Korea

The division of Korea at the end of World War II and the Korean War that followed continue to be sources of endless debate. The key foreign policy element is the fact that official U.S. governmental action set the "temporary" border between "north" and "south" Korea. It is generally recognized (except among radicalized South Korean political elements) that the action was done in haste primarily to limit the southward expansion of Soviet influence in the wake of the collapse of Japan after the two atomic bombs were dropped to end World War II. Yet the symbolic tone was set—the United States was "in charge" in South Korea. The overthrow of the government of Syngman Rhee in April 1960 led to a further conservative drift in U.S.–Korean relations, in that Park Chung Hee, an anticommunist military man, took control of the South Korean government in May 1961.

The Park goal of industrialization seemed impossible at the time, but the regime established the most complete form of government-driven developmental state within the context of U.S. regional security concerns. The first "five year plan," a socialist-sounding slogan, was announced by the newly formed Economic Planning Board (EPB) in January 1962, and in 1965 diplomatic relations with Japan, Korea's formal colonial master, were normalized. At the same time, the permanent stationing of U.S. ground forces, backed up by U.S. air power within the country and naval exercises offshore, institutionalized the dependent position of Korea within the U.S. global security network, designed to contain communism anywhere and everywhere in the world.

The differentiation in the treatment of domestic politics, which were completely constrained, and economic and business development, which was encouraged, has been attributed by some to a conscious policy orientation by Park, possibly even an obsession with securing self-sufficiency from the United States in the long-standing tradition of Korean autonomy.[2] A more realistic analysis from our perspective recognizes and accepts the traditional role of Korea as being dependent on its "big brother," historically China but now the United States, and utilizing centralized authority and top-down support to foster economic development and growth. This framework led to the development of the *chaebol,* the Korean multinational corporations that emerged during the Park era as the true *Korean* international actors while South Korea as a state (i.e., as the Republic of Korea) was allied politically and diplomatically with the United States.[3] An emerging literature on *chaebols* exists,[4] but for our purposes we want to focus upon the independent foreign policy implications of the *chaebols'* worldwide activity.

Shielded by the presence of U.S. military troops on South Korean soil, the *chaebols* became the international outreach organization of the South Korean *state* even though they were "private" corporations. This contradiction points up the dilemma for Asian states during the period of U.S. hegemony in the western Pacific. Allies of the United States, particularly client states such as South Korea, could not have independent "foreign" policies. Yet they could utilize what may genuinely be called "state" enterprises to conduct an outreach process that went beyond the narrow confines of traditional bipolar Cold War relationships. In a real sense, the Korean *chaebols* conducted the foreign policy of the South Korean *state* while the *government* maintained a traditional and conservative pro-U.S. and anticommunist position in generalized international affairs.

The assassination of Park Chung Hee in December 1979 led to the illegal seizure of power by Chun Doo Hwan, the second of the national-military-authoritarian leaders in the evolution of South Korea. Chun's emergence was particularly controversial because the U.S. government did not intervene to preserve the constitutional succession of presidential power after Park's murder. Some radicalized elements within the Korean polity have subsequently adopted the position that the U.S. government has always been selective and manipulative in its treatment of Korea, intervening when that course of action suited U.S. governmental aims but refraining from action that could have insured a more democratic transition at times such as the Park assassination, opting instead for nonintervention to preserve an authoritarian puppet.

Chun's legacy is particularly confused, in that his initial policy statements and actions implied an anti-U.S. tone (no more deference to "big brother," a clear reference in context to the United States, not China, the historic "big brother"). He also came to power claiming to represent traditional Korean values, attacking the wealth and lifestyles of urban elites and *chaebol* leaders and their families. After consolidating his power, he reverted to the more traditional Park pattern of concentrating on personal political power and allowing the *chaebol*s to maintain their dominant position within the Korean economy. His hold on power was secured with an early summit meeting with President Reagan, which, in the conventional sense, confirmed Chun as the leader of a U.S. client state. Yet his entire term of office was marred by growing opposition sentiment inside Korea that Chun's own seizure of power was the last mature act of the South Korean state as truly dependent regime within the bipolar Cold War.

■ DEMOCRATIZATION AND ANTI-AMERICANISM

☐ *Philippines*

Corazon Aquino assumed the presidency and began dismantling the authoritarian system built by the Marcos family and his friends. She established an agency to sequester Marcos's ill-gotten wealth, abolished monopolistic industries, offered peace to Communist rebels, and strengthened links with the United States in view of the Philippines' needs for economic recovery and democratization. However, the Aquino administration's attitude toward the United States was mixed. The Reagan administration reluctantly accepted her in place of Marcos, but in some ways her ascent to power was also influenced by the United States. One continuing question was Aquino's position regarding the bases. Her favored reply was that she wanted to "keep her options open." In 1988 her government finalized the renewal of the military agreement until its expiration in 1991. Negotiations were carried out with much bargaining and nationalist grandstanding. U.S. budget cuts and the reevaluation of its defense policy in view of the changing international climate also affected the discussions. The nationalist anti-military bases group in the Philippines, now free to express its opinion, was able to articulate its opposition. Particularly significant were

Philippine government officials and members of the Philippine congress, especially senators, who expressed their intention not to renew the agreement. They feared that the continued presence of U.S. bases would invite nuclear attack or retaliation by other nuclear powers in case of a war. More important, the bases were a symbol and a continuing reminder of unequal relations and U.S. domination. Nationalists felt that Filipinos had not been treated fairly or with respect and dignity as a sovereign nation in their relations with the United States, especially regarding the bases. In the words of Foreign Secretary Raul Manglapus, it was essential to slay the father image of the United States for the Philippines to finally establish its very own identity.

Before the 1991 deadline, U.S. and Philippine negotiators hammered out a pact that would grant the United States ten more years of military base rights, sometimes referred to as a period of phaseout or phasedown. The agreement did not garner the two-thirds vote in the Philippine Senate required for ratification. Aquino suggested the possibility of bringing the matter before a referendum, but this idea was set aside. In 1991 the eruption of Mount Pinatubo destroyed Clark Air Force Base and caused heavy damage to the Subic Bay naval base, destroying the future value of these bases. The confluence of several factors—natural calamity and elite anti-U.S. sentiments—decided the issue for the Filipinos. On the U.S. side, changes in the domestic economy, budget constraints, and the examination of U.S. defense policy and requirements in the light of the end of the Cold War were the deciding factors. With mounting budget deficits, spending scarce resources on the Philippine bases was not justified. An international relations policy that was no longer obsessed with superpower conflicts made the continued use of the bases of questionable importance. Both President Aquino and Secretary Manglapus tried to find a way to resuscitate some form of agreement with the U.S. government, but rejection by the Philippine Senate once and for all settled the issue.

Democratization in the Philippines was carried out with pride during the first years of the Aquino administration. The People Power Revolution restored the Filipinos' positive feelings about themselves. They were proud that they had carried out a nonviolent revolution against a dictatorship and also proud that the drama of thousands of citizens protesting in the city streets was being replayed all over Eastern Europe. (These Eastern European protests also led to the overthrow of their authoritarian regimes.) The euphoria over democracy, however, raised expectations for a miraculous transformation of the impoverished islands. Miracles were expected from President Aquino, who was practically anointed saint of the Filipino people.

Democratization had its successes, limitations, and failures. Aquino was able to establish a philosophy and framework for government through the 1987 constitution (sometimes called the Cory Constitution, as its approval was based on her popularity). The document was nationalist in its political and economic policies, antiauthoritarian, pro–human rights and pro–social justice. In foreign relations it declared that the state "shall pursue an independent foreign policy. In its relations with other states the paramount consideration shall be national sovereignty, territorial integrity, national interest, and the right to self-determination" (Article II, Section 7). The following section declared the Philippines free from nuclear weapons. (This provision put in question military bases at Subic and Clark, as the U.S. military could not, for security reasons, confirm nor deny the existence of nuclear facilities.) In its transitory provisions (Article XVII, Section 25), it made explicit that 1991 would be the expiration date of the military agreement and required that its renewal be in the form of a treaty, duly confirmed by the Philippine Senate or, when the congress so mandated, ratified by a majority vote in a national referendum. The document also was to be recognized as a binding treaty by the United States. This provision made it difficult to approve an agreement, as it was required to be in treaty form. Should the Philippine congress relinquish its responsibility of deciding the fate of the bases, it would be able to wash its hands in the matter and let the issue be put to rest by a majority of Filipino voters.

The constitution had provisions regarding social justice, human rights, education, and agrarian and natural resources reform as well as urban land reform and housing. In Article XII (National Economy and Patrimony), it asserted preeminence of national goals, called for the protection of Filipino enterprises against unfair foreign competition and trade practices, reserved the enjoyment of natural resources exclusively for Filipino citizens, promoted the preferential use of Filipino labor and goods and the practice of professions by Filipino citizens, reserved at least 60 percent of ownership of investment and capital of corporations to locals, and stated that congress should encourage the "formation and operation of enterprises whose capital is wholly owned by Filipinos" (Article XII, Section 10). These provisions reflected the growing sense of nationhood and the desire of Philippine leaders to assert economic sovereignty in a competitive world.

The Aquino government had to assert itself as well in domestic politics. Six military coup attempts harassed Aquino and deflected her attention from democratization to regime survival. The sixth coup attempt almost dealt a fatal blow to her government; however, U.S. planes from Clark Air Force Base escorted Filipino air force planes against mutineers, and the coup was aborted. The contradiction between nationalism and self-determination on one hand and regime vulnerability and lingering U.S. dependency on the other was not lost to observers of Philippine–U.S. relations. In spite of internal dissension and conflicts, the Aquino government was able to establish a democratic framework through the constitution, reinstitute a pre–martial law congress and court system, and hold national and local elections. The democratizing legacy of Aquino was the first peaceful transition of presidential authority in the Philippines for many years.

☐ South Korea

The demonstrations that marked 1987 and led up to the popular vote for the presidency in December of that year showed some elements of continuity within the South Korean polity but mainly dramatized the shifts and changes toward a more open, pluralistic, and middle class–dominated national political process. The principal element of continuity was the eventual election as president of Roh Tae Woo, who was the hand-picked successor to Chun Doo Hwan and a military man. He won with about 38 percent of the popular vote. Yet the demands for direct elections that could not be manipulated showed the strength of change within the Korean political culture, which had moved away from traditional elitist direction from above. The two major opposition figures, Kim Dae Jung and Kim Young Sam, won about 55 percent of the total popular vote between them, but because they could not agree to maintain a single, formally unified opposition party, they split the opposition vote, giving Roh the election victory.

Yet after Roh was inaugurated on February 25, 1988, numerous signs of tensions in the transition to democracy persisted. The Olympic Games, staged in Seoul in the summer of 1988 after the Los Angeles spectacular four years earlier, did showcase the country and its advances but also resulted in tensions between the international press and the local citizens, charges of insensitivity on the part of Olympic participants, and other signs of discord between the society and a non-Korean global culture. Although treated as a passing phase of little significance in the international press, the societal tensions surrounding the Olympics indicated a continuing and fundamental difficulty within the Korean political culture associated with increasing internationalization of the society and economy.

The twin urban signs of this tension were (1) labor unrest in the form of demonstrations, job actions, and other efforts to change the historically paternalistic management approach (backed up by government authority); and (2) student unrest revolving around a student "agenda." The key elements within the student demonstrations were demands for demilitarization, better job prospects (especially for those from other than the "top" schools) and, most significant, rapprochement with North Korea under a foreign relations context of isolationism and anti-U.S. policy.

The reasons for this aggressive shift on the part of some Korean youth are complex. Clearly the rapid mobilization of the society has been destabilizing in general. Additionally, Korean urban youth of the 1980s developed an ideological culture that mirrored the 1960s generation in the United States—that is, a cult of difference. The strains of nativism were part of this differentiation process, which served to contrast the 1980s with the more passive and submissive era that immediately followed the Korean War (a period of true and total dependence on the United States). Also, Korean youth have continued to grow up in an extremely pressured environment, and for those who could not succeed in a traditional way the road of rebellion was a sort of perverse method of "standing up" in classic Confucian terms.

Regional differences within South Korea also played a role. In order to reduce this aspect of division a three-party alliance was fashioned by Kim Jong Pil that allowed his party to merge with the party headed by Kim Young Sam on January 22, 1990. By 1992, the result was the first election for South Korea's president in which all three candidates were civilians. Kim Young Sam, generally viewed as a regional outsider, was the candidate of the majority and ruling Democratic Liberal Party.[5]

General conventional scholarship suggests that the democratization process in South Korea will increasingly result in interest-group politics within the context of a maturing democratic system.[6] Independent of that evolutionary process, a multiplicity of attitudes from rural, urban, and youth constituencies all point to more "Koreanness" in the South Korean political process. In the wake of the 1992 Los Angeles riots, where Korean small businesses were particularly victimized, both popular and official governmental aid from South Korea flowed *to* the United States, and air travel from South Korea to the United States during the traditional "high season" that summer dropped, causing Korean air fares to fall. The emerging attitude of distinctiveness, even superiority, of Korea over the United States became the legacy of the Roh presidency, with its emphasis on an open political system.

■ POLITICAL ECONOMY AND FOREIGN RELATIONS

☐ *Philippines*

In May 1992 the Philippines elected a successor to Aquino. The multiplicity of presidential candidates and sponsoring political parties was reduced to seven coalitions after a number of aspirants dropped out or decided to run for vice president. The crowded field of presidential nominees included Fidel Ramos, Imelda Marcos, Eduardo Cojuangco, and Salvador Laurel, all of whom had been involved with the administration of the deposed Ferdinand Marcos. The others were staunch Marcos opponents: Jovito Salonga, Ramon Mitra, and Miriam Defensor Santiago. The tabulation of election returns was slow and tedious, as the ballot required voters to fully write out the names of their choices for president, vice president, twenty-four senators, and a member of the House of Representatives, as well as provincial and local officials. Prolonged brownouts and power failures also marred the process. Fidel Ramos, who was the anointed candidate of Aquino and her former defense secretary, as well as cousin of Marcos and his chief of the national constabulary (police), was elected with 23 percent of the votes. As one of the instigators of the People Power Revolution, he often spoke of translating the spirit of the revolution into government policy. As he was forming his government programs, however, what was becoming increasingly clear was the urgency of the economic agenda rather than a sense of populism. His supporters included military constitutionalists (those who favor civilian supremacy and an established constitution) and, most important Makati-based executives, who now play a prominent role in the cabinet and policymaking. The so-called "Council of Trent" composed of religious persons influential in the Aquino government is evidently being replaced by the Makati mafia, private sector—oriented men who perceive politics as a handmaiden for economic growth. Of urgent concern to Ramos is the continuing energy crisis and its negative developmental impact. He has also made law and order and crime eradication public priorities by proposing to reinstitute the death penalty. He is in conflict with the Catholic hierarchy and the Filipino bishops for advocating family planning programs to curb the population explosion, thereby increasing the gains of economic growth and reducing the burden to productive members of society. Aquino's successor has also proposed the repeal of the antisubversion act, amnesty for all antigovernment rebels, and legalization of the Communist Party of the Philippines. These measures might bring to a close domestic conflicts framed in the context of Cold War politics. Ramos has signed renegotiated debt agreements with foreign lenders as a sign of his policy of continuous dependence on international financial and economic systems. Selective debt repudiation as a policy had been explored by the previous administration, but free traders prevailed on this issue, and they continue to do so under Ramos. (Former Ambassador to the United States Emmanuel Pelaez was even appointed Philippine debt negotiator.) In terms of the United States, Ramos has spoken of the importance of trade relations, not foreign (U.S.) aid. (Decline in U.S. aid coincided with the nonrenewal of the bases agreement.) Though the military agreement was rejected by the Philippine Senate, Ramos still has the option of opening the possibility of continued U.S. access to Philippine military facilities. In his presidential platform, he stated that the nonratification of the Treaty of Friendship and Cooperation would have "serious economic and social effects" and "adverse implications for the international community" and favored gradual withdrawal of the bases.[7] Diplomatic and legal cracks might be opened to allow the pragmatic economic needs of the country to be met. Meanwhile, Japanese and Chinese (Hong Kong, Taiwan, and Singapore) investors have expressed interest in prospective projects in base lands to be vacated by the end of 1992. U.S.–Philippine security relations, therefore, have not been and will not be the sole preoccupation of the Ramos government in the 1990s. The continuing need for foreign investment has increased Asia Pacific regional participation in the Philippine economy.

Japan's role in the Philippines has progressively and continuously increased in the areas of foreign aid and capital and corporate presence and investment. This increased dependency on Japan is a reflection of that nation's preeminent role in the region and its crucial place in the new international political economy. During his regime, Marcos took advantage of the reopening of diplomatic ties with Japan and utilized its war reparations and aid to boost his image. (For example, the Pan Philippine-Japanese Friendship Highway was built through Japanese aid.) Relations with Japan also increased contacts and businesses for Marcos cronies. (Philippine Ambassador to Japan Roberto Benedicto, a Marcos crony, had a monopoly of contracts in shipping; business partners in local Philippine subsidiaries of Japanese companies were also Marcos friends.)

Japan distributed vast amounts of loans and aid without any consideration for the type or conduct of the government of its recipient. Aid money continued to flow under Marcos, who was not a target of Japanese criticism. Recently, however, with the continuing political and diplomatic significance of Japanese aid programs, Japan has started to scrutinize its projects and grantees (another indication of Japan's ascent as the principal regional/international power and its perception of crucial self-importance and influence). Like South Korea, the Philippines will find it difficult to avoid the rising influence of Japanese and Chinese capital in the region and its future political impact of national modernization.

□ *South Korea*

The twin themes of political and military dependence and economic independence through global trade and business ties form the central convergence of concepts necessary to the understanding of post–World War II South Korean international relations. The Park-Chun era witnessed a South Korean foreign policy that mirrored the bipolar world—strict anti-communism in tone and action, culminating with the dispatch of troops to the Vietnam War in support of U.S. policy there. The suggestion early in the Carter administration that U.S. ground troops be scaled back or even completely withdrawn was opposed by policy hard-liners in the U.S. and South Korea. The "Team Spirit" annual war games demonstrated the routinization of this relationship. Under the Reagan administration's forward maritime strategy, classified war games for U.S. forces projected to operate in the Sea of Japan were commonplace.

The increasing independence of the international political economy aspect of South Korean policy emerged more slowly during this period. It began with export-led growth, which matured into massive construction contracts in the Middle East during the petrodollar boom. This capital fueled an increasingly heavy reliance on advanced industry, yet a particular triangular trade relationship persisted. Despite official efforts to limit economic dependence on Japan, trade deficits with that country continued; however, trade surpluses with the United States were increasingly seen by observers as offsetting this imbalance.

At precisely the period of political transition in which the South Korean polity is moving toward a more independent political relationship with the United States, new structural issues have emerged in the Korean economy. Productivity and price competitiveness have been eroded as efficient low-cost producers in Southeast Asia and Eastern Europe enter the world economy. Inflation is always a potential problem, especially because the liberalization of Korean capital markets is difficult within the tradition of government regulation. The new Korean middle class, the key voting group that the ruling Democratic Liberal Party needs to remain in power, wants it all: more imports, more leisure and "quality of life," more "Koreanness," and low inflation—a difficult mix to deliver.

Key industries for the Korean international economy consist of both the old and the new. Textiles and footwear, for example, were the initial price-sensitive exports used to pull up the 1960s Korean economy. Now they are no longer competitive. Other low-end products have survived by copying trademarks and logos, a subject of international tension in the late 1980s and 1990s. Advanced products, such as specialty steel, electronics, and automobiles, now dominate the statistics of Korean business, and increasingly these complex goods have come to dominate the Korean economy in general. Concurrently, nativism in the form of "anti-luxury" campaigns, which often get translated into anti-foreign and anti-import attitudes, make a difficult mix for standard international business firms.

As the century draws to a close, Korean elites see a vision of an independent and unified Korea with commercial interests in north China and Siberia, and thus a political economy and nation-state that is truly independent.

■ **CONCLUSIONS**

Like most of its Southeast Asian island neighbors, the Philippines was a colonial creation. Western colonialism put together groups of islands with various languages and ethnicity into one political entity called the Philippines, named after King Philip II of Spain. Conversely, Korea had the opportunity of establishing its own identity and culture during the period of pre-Western hegemony. During the twentieth century, both states were subordinated to the world political economic system by dominant regional and international powers (the United States and Japan). Their economic and security interests became appendages of the national and international goals of the superordinate states. Neocolonial ties were justified by the policy of communist containment and the pursuit of economic growth. Mutuality of interest with hegemonic powers was concluded by local political elites who also benefited from close relationships. Both South Korea and the Philippines were taken over by authoritarian regimes having close and mutually beneficial ties with the United States. Korean industrialization was guided by its military regime, whereas Marcos's martial law paved the way for the Philippines' plunder and decline. In 1965 the Philippines was ahead of South Korea in terms of economic indicators and was considered a showcase of U.S. democracy in Asia. By 1985 South Korea had overtaken the Philippines as a newly industrializing country and had a vibrant, export-oriented economy. In 1986 the Philippines was to begin a democratization process under Corazon Aquino, and in 1987 popular elections in Korea brought Roh Tae Woo to the presidency. Both countries continued to be plagued by domestic disturbances and dissension, but the Philippines still gropes in the economic field while South Korea continues its increased economic influence in the Asia Pacific region. There is a continued rise of nationalism and assertion of self-determination expressed in the government policies and national goals of both countries, most noticeably the prominence placed on economic development.

Thus, Philippine and South Korean international relations in the post–Cold War Asia Pacific will focus on economic as well as security factors. These two countries will attempt to pursue multidirectional and multilateral relationships and veer away from dependent bilateral ties with regional hegemonic powers. They will balance political reform, stability, democratization, and economic growth and competitiveness. As the century draws to a close, Korean elites envision a unified Korea with commercial interests in northern China and Siberia, and thus a political economy and nation-state that are truly independent. The 1987 Philippine constitutional framers envisioned a state that would "promote a just and dynamic social order that will ensure the prosperity and independence of the nation and free the people from poverty through policies that provide adequate social services, promote full employment, a rising standard of living, and an improved quality of life for all," capped by the "promotion of social justice in all phases of national development" and the promotion of "dignity for every human person and guarantees [of] full respect for human rights" (Article II, Sections 9–11). Ironically, this quest for national sovereignty and true independence is coming as the world in general is becoming more interdependent, and progressive leaders in these societies are calling for more internationalism rather than less, setting up yet another set of contradictions for these two countries.

■ NOTES

1. For an expanded analysis see James Thomson, Peter Stanley, and John C. Perry, *Sentimental Imperialists* (New York: Harper & Row, 1981).

2. See Ezra F. Vogel, *The Four Little Dragons* (Cambridge: Harvard University Press, 1991), Chapter 3.

3. The Republic of Korea did pursue a parallel "Third World" diplomacy during this period, particularly with key radicalized Arab states such as Libya.

4. See, for example, Richard Steers, Yoo Keun Shin, and Gerardo Ungson, *The Chaebol* (New York: Harper & Row, 1989), and Kae Chung and Hak Chong Lee, *Korean Managerial Dynamics* (New York: Praeger, 1989).

5. For some details on Kim Young Sam, see "Korea's Kim Young Sam Finally Stands Good Chance of Becoming President," *Wall Street Journal,* July 6, 1992, p. 8.

6. Ahn Byung-Joon, "Korea's International Environment." In Thomas W. Robinson, ed., *Democracy and Development in East Asia* (Washington, D.C.: AEI Press, 1991).

7. *1992 and Beyond: Forces and Issues in Philippine Elections* (Manila: Philippine Center for Investigative Journalism and the Ateneo Center for Social Policy and Public Affairs, 1992), p. 230.

■ 6

Taiwan in Post–Cold War Asia Pacific
Cal Clark

The breakup of the Soviet Union ushered in what is called the post–Cold War period, which has perhaps three fundamental defining characteristics: (1) the division of the world into competing capitalist and socialist blocs has ended; (2) as political-military competition among the Great Powers has faded, there has been a corresponding increase in concerns about economic competition among previous allies; and (3) a tremendous wave of democratization has occurred during the 1980s and early 1990s.

Taiwan, or, as it calls itself, the Republic of China (ROC), has been strongly affected by all three of these post–Cold War features. Taiwan's participation in Cold War diplomacy is strange and paradoxical to say the least. On the one hand, the continuing rivalry and mutually incompatible sovereignty claims between the ROC and the People's Republic of China (PRC) that governs the Chinese mainland is one of the few remnants of the Cold War, now that even North and South Korea are able to reach some agreement. On the other hand, despite the refusal of the two governments even to talk to each other officially, China and Taiwan are becoming closely tied by a rapidly expanding network of economic and cultural ties; and informal contacts and bargaining are clearly proceeding apace *sub rose.* Moreover, the United States dramatically changed the nature of the Cold War equation across the Taiwan Strait as early as the Shanghai Communique of twenty years ago, when Richard Nixon and Henry Kissinger recruited the PRC as a Great Power ally against the Soviet Union.

Taiwan's position in terms of external economic tensions has also moved into the post–Cold War era, albeit with a paradoxical twist. With its extremely rapid economic growth, the country was first touted as a show-place of capitalism by the ROC's patron, the United States. However, by the early 1980s Taiwan's export drive had created escalating tensions with the United States, as the small island became the second-largest contribu-tor to the burgeoning U.S. trade deficit. Conversely, Taiwan's economic success and growing prosperity has priced it out of its old low-cost, labor-intensive niche in the international political economy. As a consequence, many of the ROC's small businessmen are moving their operations to de-veloping areas further down the international product cycle, in particular the Chinese mainland. They have also made a significant contribution to the current wave of PRC exports to the United States, which have strained Sino–U.S. economic relations (in 1991, the mainland moved past Taiwan into second place in terms of trade surplus with the United States).

Finally, political liberalization has been quite dramatic since the late 1980s, but again the internal political dynamics on the island seem quite ironic in view of Cold War stereotypes. Through the 1970s, the national-level government and leadership of the ruling Nationalist, or Kuomintang (KMT), party were almost exclusively composed of "Mainlanders" (i.e., the 15 percent of the population who fled to Taiwan with Chiang Kai-shek in 1949), who justified their rule with the Cold War rhetoric that they con-stituted the legitimate, anticommunist government of all China. Significant liberalization began under the leadership of Chiang's son, Chiang Ching-kuo, in the 1970s and 1980s, and these reforms accelerated after 1986, bringing Taiwan to the verge of a democratic polity. "Islanders," or those whose roots on Taiwan predated the KMT (typified by President Lee Teng-hui, who succeeded to the leadership of the government and the party after Chiang Ching-kuo's death in 1988), consequently have become much more powerful. The logic of ethnic rivalry stands Cold War rela-tionships on their head. Many old stalwart KMT Mainlanders are the ones most interested in reunification with the PRC, whereas the Islander-domi-nated opposition Democratic Progressive Party is raising the spectre of Taiwan independence and provoking PRC demands for its old enemy, the Kuomintang, to crack down on the domestic critics of this once anticom-munist paragon.

This chapter, therefore, discusses each of these three facets of Tai-wan's somewhat paradoxical position in the post–Cold War political econ-omy of the Pacific Basin. The first section considers the dynamics and consequences of Taiwan's "economic miracle," because it affected both domestic political development and the crosscutting relations that have de-veloped across the Taiwan Strait. The second reviews political change on the island and its implications for what Clark and Chan (1991) have called "ROC-PRC (non) Relations." Finally, the complex and contradictory rela-tionship between Beijing and Taipei is explored.

◼ THE CONSEQUENCES OF RAPID ECONOMIC GROWTH FOR TAIWAN'S POST–COLD WAR POSITION

Taiwan is often cited as an "economic miracle," and the data reviewed below give substantial support to such praise. However, the dynamics and consequences of the ROC's rapid development are rather ironic in terms of its initial Cold War position as an anticommunist client of the United States supported as an alternative to the Communist regime in the PRC. Despite the fact that the United States pushed Taiwan to open its economy and adopt liberal free market policies, the ROC's resulting superlative export performance brought it into increasing conflict with its patron in the 1980s. Moreover, economic success gradually priced Taiwan out of the low-cost labor niche in the global economy, which ultimately stimulated substantial "capital flight" to the epitome of communism and the ROC's arch enemy—the People's Republic of China.

Taiwan's record in the economic realm since the early 1950s has been phenomenal by almost any standard, as indicated by the data in Table 6.1. For the last thirty-five years, real (i.e., inflation-adjusted) GNP growth has averaged approximately 9 percent, one of the highest rates in the world, demonstrating sustained development. Income per capita rose fiftyfold, from $200 in 1952 to $1,500 in 1978 to $6,000 in 1988 to an estimated $10,000 at the end of 1992 (a substantial part of this growth since the mid-1980s resulted from a 40 percent appreciation of the New Taiwan (NT) dollar, but even this consideration suggests that before then the island's GNP per capita had been grossly understated in U.S. dollars). Concomitantly, the economy was transformed from a predominantly agricultural to a predominantly industrial one. The export-led nature of the ROC's development after the early 1960s is also quite clear. Exports have constituted almost half of GNP and been overwhelmingly industrial in composition since the early 1970s, in stark contrast to the 1950s, when sugar and rice constituted about three-quarters of the island's foreign sales. This surge in exports was accompanied by a dramatic change in the nation's balance of trade to the current huge (and, for U.S. trade, politically embarrassing) surplus. By the late 1980s the ROC ranked a close second in the world, behind Japan, with foreign reserves in the $70–$80 billion range (it momentarily moved into first place after Japan paid off its Gulf War pledge in 1991). Furthermore, once growth began to accelerate in the 1960s, savings and investment rates became extremely high, averaging about 30 percent of GDP during the 1970s and 1980s, allowing massive capital accumulation without much foreign borrowing or deficit spending by the government. Thus, the phasing out of U.S. aid in the 1960s had no deleterious impact upon the economy (Chan and Clark 1992; Clark 1989; Galenson

1979; Gold 1986; Haggard 1990; Ho 1978; Kuo 1983; Kuo et al., 1981; Li 1988; Lin 1973; Myers 1984; Wade 1990; Winckler and Greenhalgh 1988; Wu 1985).

The land reform of the 1950s was quickly followed by an import substitution industrialization program based on strong protectionist controls (Lin 1973; Ranis 1979). Import substitution produced a spurt of light industrial growth, but by the early 1960s the domestic market was becoming saturated. The ROC then made the fateful decision to radically change its economic strategy to liberalize trade and emphasize labor-intensive export industries (Galenson 1979; Gold 1986; Haggard 1990; Ho 1978; Kuo 1983; Lin 1973; Wade 1990). More was involved here than simple economic liberalization and provision of incentives or exports, though. First, Taiwan continued to provide considerable protection to its domestic industries (Wade 1990). Second, in addition to actively soliciting foreign capital in certain key export sectors (e.g., electronics), the government maintained a highly regulated environment in order to ensure that multinational corporations (MNCs) contributed to the national development project (Haggard and Cheng 1987; Huang 1989). Finally, the government proved extremely adept at negotiating with trade partners, in particular the United States, as protectionist pressures grew in the industrialized nations (Chan 1987; Yoffie 1983).

This new strategy proved extremely successful. Sparked by a real export surge of over 20 percent annually, GNP grew at a rate of 11 percent per year between 1963 and 1973, and the period from the early 1960s to the early 1970s saw major improvements in most of the economic and social indicators in Table 6.1. By the mid-1970s, however, rising labor costs and growing international protectionism were beginning to undermine Taiwan's position. Thus began to emerge new strategies of promoting first capital-intensive heavy industry in the 1970s and then high technology production in the 1980s. The heavy industry drive was centered on state corporations (e.g., China Steel, whose success is indicated by its central role in the ROC's abortive negotiations to become a large minority owner of McDonnell-Douglas). These high tech industries involved a new solicitation of foreign capital (note the rebound of MNC's share of Taiwan's total investment in the 1980s after its precipitous drop in the 1970s in Table 6.1), an upgrading of some small indigenous businesses, and some state backing in the R&D field (Chan and Clark 1992; Gold 1986; Haggard 1990; Lam and Lee 1992; Wade 1990; Wu 1985).

Unfortunately, Taiwan's trade success increasingly exacerbated trade relations with its chief economic partner (and quasi-political patron), the United States. In fact, Taiwan became one of the first countries to feel the thrust of the United States' much more aggressive trade policies in the mid-1980s. The spiraling U.S. trade deficits and almost overnight transformation

Table 6.1   Indicators of Development Level, Taiwan

	1952	1958	1962	1968	1973	1978	1988
Population (millions)	8.1	10.0	11.5	13.7	15.6	17.1	19.9
GNP per capita (thousands NT $)	2.0	4.3	6.5	12.1	26.6	58.3	173.1
GNP per capita (U.S. $)	153	173	162	302	696	1,575	6,055
Manufacturing (% NDP)	10.8	15.5	16.9	24.0	36.2	34.1	35.1
Agriculture (% NDP)	36.0	31.1	29.4	22.1	14.1	11.3	6.1
Agriculture (% employment)	56.1	51.1	49.7	40.8	30.5	24.9	13.7
Savings (% GNP)	9.2	9.9	12.4	22.1	34.6	34.9	34.9
Investment (% GNP)	15.3	16.6	17.8	25.1	29.1	28.2	24.0
U.S. Aid (% investment)	45.5	37.3	20.2	0.6	0.0	0.0	0.0
Foreign Investment (% investment)	0.5	0.8	1.5	8.4	7.9	2.8	4.2
Exports (% GDP)	8.5	8.6	11.3	18.6	41.6	47.4	50.5
% Industrial Exports	8.1	14.0	50.5	68.4	84.6	89.2	94.5
Trade Balance (millions U.S. $)	-71	-70	-86	-114	691	1,660	10,929
% Exports to U.S.	3.5	6.2	24.4	35.3	37.4	39.5	38.7
State % Industrial Production	56.6	50.0	46.2	31.1	21.1	21.5	18.1
State % Investment	55.7	62.6	46.8	36.6	34.7	45.0	34.6
Gov't Spending (% GDP)	—	23.8	20.0	19.5	19.5	22.9	24.0
Unemployment (%)	4.6	4.0	4.3	1.8	1.3	1.7	1.7
Income Ratio[1]	20.47[2]	—	—	5.28	4.49[3]	4.18	4.69[4]
Daily Caloric Intake	2,078	2,359	2,317	2,545	2,754	2,822	3,017
Food (% of household spending)	55.6	51.7	50.1	44.8	41.3	39.8	30.1[4]
Health Personnel (thousands)	—	10.8	12.7	12.5	20.4	36.2	83.0
Communicable Diseases (per 100,000)	14.1	22.7	8.3	6.3	1.3	0.5	1.2
% Students Reaching Jr. High	34.9	51.1	53.8	74.2	83.7	94.1	99.1
Real Expenditure per Primary Student (1981 NT $)	3,296	2,784	3,501	4,781	7,861	13,002	20,224

*One year later (1953) or earlier (1972 & 1987).
1. Ratio of the income of the richest fifth of the population to that of the poorest fifth.
2. 1953 data
3. 1972 data
4. 1987 data
Source: Taiwan Statistical Data Book, 1989. Taipei: Council for Economic Planning and Development, 1989.

from the world's largest creditor to largest debtor made the Reagan administration forgo its commitment to "free trade" for a much greater emphasis on "fair trade" and "aggressive reciprocity" (Destler 1986; Pearson 1989), although its attempts to use economic power to offset its declining performance were not as strident as might have been expected (Clark 1993; Goldstein 1988; Milner 1988).

Taiwan could certainly qualify as a target of aggressive reciprocity on several grounds of varying legitimacy. First, its trade surplus with the United States, which had never been great enough to be a matter of political controversy before, skyrocketed in the mid-1980s, as demonstrated by the data in Table 6.2. Clearly, Taiwan was a major beneficiary of the U.S. recovery and expansion that began in 1983 as the ROC's exports jumped from $9 billion in 1982 to $15 billion in 1984 to $24 billion in 1987. Just as clearly, increased Taiwan–U.S. trade was almost entirely a one-way street, as the ROC's trade surplus quadrupled from $4 billion to $16 billion, making Taiwan the second-largest contributor to the U.S. trade deficit, after Japan.

Table 6.2   Taiwan's Trade with the United States in the 1980s

	Total Trade with U.S. (in billion $)			U.S. Share of ROC Trade (in percent)	
	Exports	Imports	Balance[1]	Exports	Imports
1980	6.8	4.7	2.1	34.1	23.7
1981	8.2	4.8	3.4	36.1	22.5
1982	8.8	4.6	4.2	39.4	24.1
1983	11.3	4.6	6.7	45.1	22.9
1984	14.9	5.0	9.8	48.8	23.0
1985	14.8	4.7	10.0	48.1	23.6
1986	19.0	5.4	13.6	47.7	22.4
1987	23.7	7.6	16.0	44.1	21.8
1988	23.4	13.0	10.4	38.7	26.2
1989	24.0	12.0	12.0	36.2	23.0
1990	21.7	12.6	9.1	32.8	23.6
1991	22.3	14.1	8.2	31.2	24.1
January–May 1991	8.2	5.8	2.4	33.6	27.1
January–May 1992	9.4	6.3	3.1	28.3	22.1

1. Trade balance may not precisely equal the difference between exports and imports because of rounding.
Sources: Monthly Statistics of Exports and Imports, Taiwan Area, The Republic of China, August 1990. Taipei: Department of Statistics, Ministry of Finance, 1990, pp. 13, 58.
Monthly Statistics of Exports and Imports, Taiwan Area, The Republic of China, May 1992. Taipei: Department of Statistics, Ministry of Finance, 1992, pp. 13, 64.
Taiwan Statistical Data Book, 1989. Taipei: Council for Economic Planning and Development, 1989, p. 215.

In addition to running a considerable imbalance in U.S.–Taiwan trade, the ROC retained both tariff and nontariff barriers to imports in a wide array of disparate sectors (e.g., agriculture and electronics products) even after any justification for "infant industry protection" had long since passed. Furthermore, the NT dollar had changed little in its relationship to the value of the U.S. dollar despite the ROC's blossoming trade surpluses during the first half of the 1980s. In the early 1980s, Taiwan was also widely seen, with much justification, as the "pirate capital" of the world. Finally, Taiwan's dependence upon the U.S. market and upon implicit U.S. diplomatic support would seemingly have made it quite vulnerable to U.S. pressures.

The United States began putting more pressure on Taiwan in the mid-1980s, and by 1985 Taiwan began to make major concessions in the hope of placating its patron. For example, substantial tariff cuts became a highly publicized annual event; serious negotiations were begun on "intellectual property rights"; and government procurement missions scurried to the United States with million-dollar contracts, mostly for agricultural and energy goods (Chang 1984; Hsiung 1986).

U.S. pressures and Taiwanese concessions reached a peak in 1987–1988, when the escalating trade surplus noted above was combined with a presidential election year in the United States. Taiwan responded with several important concessions. First, the ROC appreciated its currency almost 40 percent against the U.S. dollar and moved the NT dollar to a floating exchange rate determined by market forces. Second, in 1987 Taiwan opened its markets to U.S. liquor and tobacco products in what had previously been a state monopoly. Third, in the late summer of 1988 the government reversed itself on a major agricultural dispute—major in domestic salience if not in the economic impact of the "turkey parts" that were its subject. Finally, Taiwan made important concessions in response to U.S. demands for liberalization of the service sector (Copper 1989; Li 1988; Seymour 1989). Consequently, Taiwan's trade surplus dropped to the $10–$12 billion range in 1988–1989 and to $8–$9 billion in 1990–1991. This drop probably explains why trade conflicts between the U.S. and the ROC eased in the early 1990s.

However, the combination of a U.S. recession, President Bush's falling popularity in the 1992 presidential campaign, and a growing tendency to blame foreigners for U.S. economic shortcomings made the Bush administration more aggressive on the trade front. Consequently, frictions rose again. The United States put pressure on Taiwan in the ongoing intellectual property rights negotiations by placing the ROC on the "Special 301" list. Taiwan quickly passed a new intellectual property rights law that met with mixed reviews on the island (Liu 1992). In addition, despite a significant appreciation of the NT dollars against the U.S. dollar in 1992, the United States pressured Taiwan for further appreciation. Still, with the

U.S. deficit with Taiwan having fallen by a half after 1987, trade disputes will probably fade after the 1992 U.S. elections.

Although the economic dynamics of Taiwan's rapid growth have strained relations with its Cold War ally and patron, they have had a second, ironic result of forging growing contacts and ties with its Cold War ideological rival for the "soul" of China—the PRC. Taiwan's growing prosperity and full employment meant that real wages began to rise consistently after the late 1960s. This trend put increasing pressures on small-scale businessmen whose labor-intensive assembly operations (e.g., textiles, shoes, and low tech electronics) could only be competitive internationally if workers earned low wages. Given their very limited ability for large-scale investments in new technology or R&D activities, many of these businessmen clearly had to do something differently. Some were able to upgrade their firms into more high tech production (Lam and Lee 1992).

Many, however, decided to save their firms by moving "offshore" to poorer nations with plentiful labor forces, where they could resurrect their previous ventures in low-cost, labor-intensive production. At first, Southeast Asia was a favored target for such capital flight, but by the late 1980s the People's Republic of China provided a new base of operation that was very attractive because of its cultural similarity and geographic proximity to Taiwan. The availability of the PRC reflected major political changes in both countries. On the one hand, Deng Xiaoping's economic reforms in China attempted to rebuild the destruction left by the Cultural Revolution by using the market mechanism to encourage entrepreneurship and to attract foreign capital (Chang 1988; Harding 1987). On the other, the ROC government bowed to growing popular pressure to allow at least indirect links with the Chinese mainland, beginning with the decision in late 1987 that ROC citizens would be allowed to "visit relatives" on the mainland (Wu 1990).

As a result, a tremendous growth in trade and investment across the Taiwan Strait occurred in the late 1980s and early 1990s, as illustrated by the data in Table 6.3. In fact, by the early 1990s there even appeared to be something of a movement toward economic integration between Taiwan and southern coastal China, especially Fujian province, which many Taiwanese Islanders (i.e., those who dominate the small-business sector) regard as their homeland. Thus, trade and especially investment across the Taiwan Strait reflect a complementarity between the two economies. China needs investment and entrepreneurial know-how; Taiwan's businessmen in labor-intensive assembly activities need an economic environment akin to Taiwan's in the 1960s and 1970s.

Thus, ironically from an ideological standpoint, Taiwanese capitalists showed little concern with the Tiananmen Square tragedy and played a major role in fueling Communist China's export drive of 1990–1991, which resulted in the PRC's moving past Taiwan into second place for the

Table 6.3   ROC Trade with and Investment in the PRC
(in million U.S. $)

	Total Exports	Total Imports	Cumulative Foreign Investment
1979	21	56	—
1980	242	79	—
1984	426	128	—
1987	1,227	289	100
1988	2,239	478	520
1989	2,897	587	1,000
1990	3,278	765	2,200

Source: Reprinted with permission from Chu-yuan Cheng, "Trade and Investment Across the Taiwan Strait: Economic Consequences and Prospects," *Strategic Studies Series.* Montclair, CA: Claremont Institute, 1992, pp. 11–12.

largest trade surplus with the United States in the latter year. These economic ties are escalating so fast that many political leaders in Taiwan are now worried that the PRC may be able to manipulate rich businessmen, who are gaining substantial political clout in Taiwan because of the democratization reforms. Thus, for example, ROC law still only allows trade and investment with the Chinese mainland to be conducted "indirectly" through third countries such as Hong Kong, although the distinction between direct and indirect economic interactions is becoming fairly fuzzy (Cheng 1992; Hickey 1991; Kuo 1991; Wu 1991).

■ DEMOCRATIZATION AND THE REVERSAL OF THE COLD WAR STEREOTYPES IN TAIWAN'S DOMESTIC POLICY

For much of the postwar era, the ROC's domestic political arrangements seemed to epitomize the Cold War division of the world and the United States' willingness to consider anticommunist allies as part of the "free world" no matter what limits on freedom their regimes enforced. In fact, the suspension of important democratic elements in the 1947 constitution of the Republic of China were explicitly justified by Cold War logic—that is, that the Taipei regime was actually the legitimate government of all China. More recently, however, a dramatic transformation toward democracy has occurred in Taiwan that has rearranged the country's political spectrum. As with economic relations, the results have been extremely ironic in terms of the old Cold War cleavages. The Chinese Communist Party (CCP) now denounces the major opposition party for criticizing the "fascist" Kuomintang; moreover, many "conservative" Kuomintang leaders now seem the most eager in Taiwan to move toward rapprochement and reunification with the PRC.

When Chiang Kai-shek's Nationalist government evacuated to Taiwan in 1949, it created a clearly authoritarian regime. The Nationalist government justified its preventing the majority of Islanders from selecting the "national" leadership on the grounds that it was still the legitimate government of all China. Thus, the members of the national parliament (the Legislative Yuan) and the electoral college (the National Assembly, which selects the powerful president) who had been elected from mainland constituencies in the late 1940s, were allowed to keep their seats until the "Communist bandits" were driven out. This policy allowed the Mainlander minority (about 15 percent of the population) to dominate the government. Moreover, relations between the Mainlanders and Islanders were severely strained. After Taiwan reverted from Japanese to Chinese control at the end of World War II, the island fell under the brutal rule of a military administrator. The Islanders ultimately provoked a spontaneous uprising on February 28, 1947, which was put down with massive reprisals and killing (Lai, et al. 1991).

Despite these dictatorial aspects of early KMT rule on Taiwan, the regime took several important steps that were ultimately to transform the polity. First, radical land reform opened the way to economic and political mobility in the countryside. Second, the regime's commitment to industrialization and economic development meant that technocrats with liberal perspectives had to be incorporated into the top circles of power. Third, the government allowed elections and limited democracy at the local level, which forced the massive recruitment of Islanders into the lower and middle tiers of the KMT party (because without KMT backing Islanders had a very hard time winning at the polls). Fourth, the economic liberalization of the 1960s primarily benefited Islander entrepreneurs, who gradually became rich and powerful enough to influence political officials. Finally, rapid economic growth itself created a substantial educated middle class that increasingly questioned the traditional way of conducting politics (Clark 1989; Gold 1986; Hsiung 1981; Tien 1989; Winckler and Greenhalgh 1988).

The pressure from below for political liberalization from the growing business community and middle class was then matched by significant liberalization from above once Chiang Ching-kuo, Chiang Kai-shek's son, became premier (and subsequently president after the elder Chiang's death) in the early 1970s. Chiang Ching-kuo cracked down on corruption, brought more well-educated technocrats and Islanders into the leadership circle, and exerted a far more populist appeal than had his austere father. As a result, a gradual but cumulative liberalization occurred over about a fifteen-year period in terms of freedom of speech, latitude for political opposition, and so forth (Clough 1978; Copper 1988; Hsiung 1981).

This cumulative movement toward political liberalization picked up considerable speed after 1986. The first step was the open formation of an opposition party—which was technically illegal under the martial law provisions that had been in force since the late 1940s (opposition figures could and did run as independents and, after the late 1970s, had at least semiformal party organizations). In the fall of 1986, the opposition proclaimed the formation of the Democratic Progressive Party (DPP). After a brief interim of KMT threats, Chiang declared that martial law would be ended and that new parties could be formed as long as they supported the constitution and renounced communism and Taiwan independence. The December elections, therefore, marked the first time that the KMT faced an actual opposition party. The ruling party won handily with its normal 70 percent of the vote, but the DPP received a respectable 20 percent (Copper 1988; Myers 1987; Sutter 1988).

The next step was the formal abolition of martial law in the summer of 1987. Although this move had little direct impact on Taiwan's politics, it marked a symbolic break with the past and opened the way for many of the recent reforms to be institutionalized (e.g., the legalization of new political parties). It also helped create a more open, even raucous style of politics. Street demonstrations that had been unthinkable before 1986 became a common occurrence, and debates in the Legislative Yuan became quite strident, with the regular breaking of microphones and swinging of fists. Furthermore, the balance of power within the KMT appeared to be moving in a more liberal direction. Chiang Ching-kuo's sudden death in January 1988 threw this trend into some question. However, the new president, liberal Islander technocrat Lee Teng-hui, was able to consolidate power, move younger and more liberal leaders into top positions, and push through innovative domestic and foreign policies. In the 1989 elections, for example, the DPP gained about 10 percent and the KMT lost about 10 percent, reducing the ruling party's majority to a still comfortable 58–30 percent but suggesting that real two-party competition might be in the offing (Cheng 1989; Cheng and Haggard 1991; Copper 1988; Domes 1989; Gold 1989; Hsaio 1991; Lasater 1990; Ling and Myers 1990; Myers 1987; Tien 1989).

Even though the KMT won strong majorities in essentially open elections, however, the government remained nondemocratic in the very basic sense that the opposition was structurally prevented from taking power *even if it received majority support*—"senior legislators" elected from the mainland in the late 1940s continued to hold majorities in the National Assembly and Legislative Yuan. At the beginning of the 1990s, however, these last impediments to democratization were removed. President Lee repealed the "Temporary Provisions," which curtailed many of the democratic guarantees in the constitution, and a ruling by the ROC's Supreme Court forced all "senior legislators" to retire at the end of 1991 (Cheng and Haggard 1991). Democratization in the political realm was accompanied by the upsurge of a politically tinged nativist "Taiwanese popular culture," indicating the growing clout of the Islander majority (Bosco 1992). The first elections in which a winning party could literally take all were held in December 1991 for the National Assembly that would rewrite the ROC constitution. The DPP pushed a radical and confrontational policy line and was seemingly punished by the voters as the Kuomintang majority at the polls jumped back up to its pre-1989 level, 71 to 24 percent (Kristof 1991).

The dynamics of competition between the KMT and DPP in the late 1980s and early 1990s produced a seemingly strange alignment of political positions—strange at least to anyone not familiar with the idiosyncrasies of Taiwan's domestic policies. The ruling Kuomintang had evolved from a primarily military regime into one in which first economic technocrats and then "electoral politicians" came to occupy a major role (Domes 1981). With the growing power of Islanders under President Lee Teng-hui and with the promotion of liberal KMT leaders by electoral dynamics, many of the "old guard" Mainlanders, ironically including those associated with the security sector, began to see reunification with the PRC as one possibility for escaping the box of their declining status. In addition, many (but certainly not all) of the technocrats continued to favor state leadership of the economy, especially as it was exercised through mostly Mainlander-dominated state corporations. Thus, important elements in the supposedly staunchly anticommunist KMT were seen as favoring either rapprochement with the hated Communist foes and/or statistic economic policies that some conservatives elsewhere consider well down the communist "road to serfdom" (Hayek 1944).

For their part, the positions of the opposition Democratic Progressive Party had confusing (in terms of Cold War logic) elements as well. In the 1980s, the opposition to the KMT contained both "moderates," whose primary goal was promoting democratization and the interests of Islander businessmen, and "radicals," who wanted to declare Taiwan "independent" from China (which, in their view, would ensure majority rule and send KMT "Mainlander carpetbaggers" packing). Thus, the opposition to the supposedly rightist Kuomintang contained criticism of government interference in the economy and appealed to fears that KMT Mainlanders might "sell out" to their old enemies in the CCP rather than accept a democratic verdict by the people of Taiwan (Kau 1991; Moody 1991; Tien 1989).

This standing on its head of the old Cold War ideological logic culminated in the 1991 election campaign for the National Assembly. The DPP had been frustrated by the fact that the ruling Nationalists had "stolen their issues" in terms of democratization and other reform measures, seemingly consigning the DPP to the position of a permanent minority party. Thus, under pressure from its radical (New Tide) faction, the DPP openly called for Taiwan Separatism as its major campaign theme—which, incidentally, violated ROC law. This stimulated the PRC to threaten retaliation if Taiwan did declare independence and to chastise its old enemy for not suppressing the "treasonous" DPP. Finally, the "anti-mainstream" faction of older Mainlanders in the KMT began to push for "reunification" more strongly, and many both inside and outside Taiwan feared that the country might be torn apart by an "independence-unification" battle (Kau 1991). The KMT's landslide victory, then, suggested that the people preferred the status quo. Still, the domestic political equation had departed from the Cold War communist vs. anticommunist battle to such a tremendous degree that it was clearly time to consign the old formula for viewing Chinese politics to the "dustbin of history." The more recent election of December 1992 showed no exceptions, as both supporters of unification with the mainland and those of a runaway independent Taiwan scored clear victories in the national legislature.

■ ROC-PRC (NON) RELATIONS: MOVING BEYOND THE COLD WAR CLEAVAGE?

For most of the postwar era, the unremitting hostility between the PRC and the ROC and their mutually incompatible claims to be the sole legitimate government of China epitomized the Cold War division in Asia. During the 1950s and 1960s, the United States staunchly supported Taiwan as a Cold War client against the communist camp. At the beginning of the 1970s, however, President Richard Nixon and Henry Kissinger created a rapprochement with the PRC in order to manipulate the "strategic" triangle among the United States, USSR, and China that was formalized in the 1972 Shanghai Communique. This development was accompanied by a tremendous deterioration in Taiwan's diplomatic status as it was replaced in the United Nations by the PRC and lost its diplomatic recognition from all but a score or so of nations. Since then the United States has tried to maintain good relations with both sides of the Taiwan Strait, a delicate balancing act at best given the enmity between the ROC and PRC.

Maintaining good relations with both sides was made especially difficult by the fact that both Beijing and Taipei adhered to a Chinese "Hallstein doctrine" of refusing to recognize any country that had diplomatic relations with its rival. Moreover, since the Shanghai Communique the United States has maintained (with varying degrees of explicitness) that Taiwan is part of China. This position has been tempered, however, by what Hickey (1988) calls the United States' "two-point policy" about Taiwan: (1) that the Taiwan problem should be solved peacefully, and (2) that the Chinese people should solve it themselves without outside interference.

Consequently, even after its rapprochement with the PRC in 1972, the United States retained formal diplomatic ties (and a mutual security treaty) with the ROC, at the same time establishing what might be termed quasi-diplomatic relations with the People's Republic that differed from formal ones in name only. In turn, when the United States switched its diplomatic recognition to the PRC in 1979, it maintained informal links to Taiwan "privately" through the American Institute in Taiwan (AIT), which represented the United States, and the Coordination Council for North American Affairs (CCNAA), which represented Taiwan. These were in reality embassies and consulates, but their official disassociation with their respective governments proved sufficient to save face in Beijing, Taipei, and Washington. In addition, the United States passed the Taiwan Relations Act (TRA) in 1979 which, in essence, pledged that it would continue to treat Taiwan as a sovereign entity and would even sell it "defensive" weaponry to protect its sovereignty (Chiu 1979; Clough 1978; Lasater 1984).

Although both the PRC and ROC considered each other military threats and engaged in rival military modernization programs (Gregor and Chang 1984; Lasater 1984 and 1989; Sutter 1988; Snyder, et al. 1980), by the 1980s open warfare between them seemed fairly unlikely; their competition primarily moved into the political realm, which inevitably involved the legitimacy of the two regimes, especially the one on Taiwan. Throughout most of the 1980s, the Chinese conducted a "peace offensive," offering Taiwan autonomy and peace (along the lines of Hong Kong's "one country, two systems" solution) if only it would recognize China's sovereignty; and the leaders of the Chinese Communist Party reserved threats of military action only for such heinous actions as declaration of "Taiwan Independence," development of nuclear weapons, or establishment as a protectorate of the Soviet Union. Taiwan for its part saw such offers as only the pretext for unconditional surrender and responded with a steadfast adherence to its policy of the "three nos"—no contacts, no negotiations, no compromises (Kau 1988; Lasater 1984 and 1989).

In the late 1980s, though, Taiwan began, at least informally, to initiate a more "flexible diplomacy" in an attempt to improve its international position vis-à-vis China. Heralding its new outlook in cabinet-level official Wei Yung's position paper suggesting that "dual recognition" of the two Chinese governments might be feasible, Taiwan used its economic power to try to gain entrance into international bodies (most recently, its drive for membership in the General Agreement on Tariffs and Trade) and to win wider recognition, either formal or informal, of Taiwan as a sovereign entity. In particular, it stressed the establishment and upgrading of foreign commercial offices and, in the case of the United States, contacts with Congressmen and subnational officials (e.g., the opening of state trade offices in Taipei), for which the national administration could not be "held responsible" by the PRC (Ho 1990).

In short, Taiwan tried to improve its diplomatic status by rejoining international organizations under names less challenging to the People's

Republic than "Republic of China" and by finding ways to establish better relations with countries that grant diplomatic recognition to the PRC but not the ROC. In the last few years, Taiwan has had some success in this area because of a combination of factors: (1) its growing economic clout; (2) the diplomatic adroitness of its policy initiatives; (3) China's international "image problem" after the Tiananmen tragedy; and (4) the fact that the growing indirect interactions between Taiwan and China are undermining the PRC's ability to threaten retaliation against other nations that deal with the ROC. Thus, although "flexible diplomacy" has yet to score any dramatic breakthroughs, it has seemingly solidified and upgraded Taiwan's international status to a considerable extent, as evidenced by the fairly strong verbal response from Beijing. Yet the PRC did countenance some diplomatic upgrading by Taiwan. For example, both now participate in the Asian Development Bank, and in November 1991, the PRC, Taiwan, and Hong Kong were simultaneously granted membership in the Asia Pacific Economic Cooperation, or APEC (Wang 1990).

Flexible diplomacy proved most spectacular, though, in the changing "nonofficial" relations between Taiwan and China. Up through the mid-1980s, there were almost no direct contacts between the citizens of the two countries, although much "indirect" trade, primarily conducted through Hong Kong, was permitted and some residents of Taiwan were able to make short surreptitious visits to China (Chinese authorities would not stamp their passports). President Chiang Ching-kuo of Taiwan then announced in late 1987 that people would be allowed to "visit relatives" on the mainland for humanitarian purposes, and over the next few years the Taiwanese government greatly expanded the scope of legal contacts. The island's residents and businessmen happily stretched the legal limits quite a bit.

The monthly number of visitors flowing across the Taiwan Strait rose to over 10,000; indirect trade and investment jumped to several billion dollars annually; direct mail was instituted, and millions of pieces of correspondence have since been exchanged; cultural contacts were encouraged; Taiwan's mass media began to cover China directly; Finance Minister Shirley Kuo made a precedent-shattering visit to Beijing in the spring of 1989 to attend an Asian Development Bank meeting there; and by 1990 prominent politicians from Taiwan were making "unofficial" visits to the mainland. Clearly, a "China fever" had broken out on Taiwan that even the tragedy of Tiananmen Square (which was well covered by Taiwan television) could only dampen temporarily (*Free China Review* 1991).

The two regimes may even be groping toward at least semiofficial dealings with each other, although blusters and threats continue, especially from the PRC side. For example, the Red Cross organizations of the two countries reached an agreement to repatriate illegal aliens from the mainland to Taiwan via Quemoy in the fall of 1990. Much more important, the

ROC created an ostensibly private Straits Exchange Foundation in October 1990 to handle relations with the PRC on an "unofficial basis"; its members are now making regular trips to China. For its part, the PRC established a parallel Association for Relations Across the Taiwan Straits (ARATS) in December 1991 (Cheng 1992; Clark and Chan 1991; Kao 1991; Wu 1990).

However, all is not entirely rosy. The PRC makes periodic threats against Taiwan, including the use of military force if the Kuomintang authorities will not resolve the "unfinished Chinese civil war" on what Beijing considers a reasonable basis (which Taipei considers surrender). Perhaps the most severe threats from Beijing came during the fall of 1991 in response to the increasingly open calls for Taiwan independence by the DPP. This disharmony evidently stimulated the United States to take a slightly more active role in maintaining stability in the Taiwan Strait. For example, in late 1991 former Ambassador to China and future Assistant Secretary of Defense James Lilley and several other officials concerned with Taiwan made what seemed to be semiofficial warnings to the PRC not to make good some of their more bellicose threats toward the island (Yu 1991)—which, in any case, flew in the face of their general attempts to win friends throughout the Asia Pacific (Hsiung 1992a). In part, Beijing's thrusts represent the frustrations of the aging CCP leadership; in part, they represent a probably realistic assessment that democratization and economic development on Taiwan are increasingly precluding reunification on terms acceptable to the PRC.

The relations between the Republic of China on Taiwan and the People's Republic of China, therefore, are a complex amalgam of leftover Cold War hostilities and emergent post–Cold War linkages. The harsh legacy of the Cold War is most evident in the stark refusal of the two sides even to talk officially with each other because of their mutually incompatible sovereignty claims. For most of the 1980s, the PRC seemed the most flexible with its "peace offensive," whereas Taiwan played ostrich with the "three nos." Since the late 1980s, however, it is Beijing that simply recites "one country, two systems" in ritualistic response to Taiwan's more flexible diplomacy and its attempts to find a basis for interaction (e.g., officially ending the Chinese civil war in terms of ROC law and suggesting slogans, such as "one country, two governments," or "one country, two areas"). These rhetorical points and counterpoints suggest some narrowing of differences. However, the deadlock will probably not be broken until the older leaders on both sides of the Taiwan Strait are replaced by a more pragmatic successor generation. In particular, as Hsiung (1992a & 1992b) implies, the fulfillment of Deng Xiaoping's economic *and* political reforms is probably necessary before more fruitful relations can be achieved.

The stalemate between aging leaderships in at least a modified Cold War rivalry, however, should not blind us to the fact that much different post–Cold War relations are evolving, independent of and perhaps despite the wishes of the orthodox CCP and KMT old guards. To some extent Taiwan and southern coastal China have become integrated to a significant extent (Clark and Chan 1991). A complementary economy with increasingly tight linkages is being established; despite the problems caused by Tiananmen Square, tourism, news coverage, and family communications are creating a significant cultural network; and last (and far from least), some leaders in both the PRC and ROC are reacting to each other in practical, nonideological ways. This change can be seen in the attempts of provincial leaders in China to woo Taiwanese businessmen without any concern about problems of "sovereignty," as well as in the attempts of many businessmen, legislators, and even government officials in Taiwan to adopt bolder policies promoting the island's "China fever." It would be foolish to predict voluntary reunification in the near or even not-so-near future, especially given the growing democratization and "Taiwanization" within the ROC. Still, relations across the Taiwan Strait have moved much further toward a more productive post–Cold War state than a reading of official statements and propaganda might lead one to believe.

■ IMPLICATIONS

The emerging post–Cold War order is marked by three salient elements: (1) the end of the diplomatic/military confrontation between the socialist and capitalist worlds; (2) growing economic competition and tension among developed and newly industrializing economies (NIEs) who were former Cold War allies; and (3) a wave of democratization. For most of the postwar era, Taiwan represented the epitome of the Cold War. It was the anticommunist alternative to the communist regime in Beijing, which in turn, hoped to eradicate it; it was a strongly dependent client state of the leader of the anticommunist world, the United States; its economic miracle was considered a showpiece of capitalism; and its authoritarian regime was justified by its contribution to the "free world's" battle against communism.

Times have certainly changed. In all three of these areas, Taiwan's position has been essentially turned on its head, with the partial exception of its continuing rivalry with the PRC. Although presently muted, since the early 1980s, controversy and conflict have marked (and probably will mark in the future) trade relations with the United States because the "new model" in the showcase of capitalism is simply outcompeting the old standard-bearer. Taiwan has joined the new wave of democratization in the Second and Third Worlds, and the Kuomintang must be credited with one of the most stable and successful transitions from one-party authoritarianism to pluralistic politics. Yet the political forces and coalitions that now mark the ROC's polity bear little relation to the Cold War cleavage between leftists and anticommunists. Finally, despite the continuing (non) relations with Beijing, many positive linkages between the island and the mainland have sprouted over the last decade—the antithesis of Cold War confrontation. In sum, many of the changes in Taiwan's position in the Asia Pacific seem strange and ironic in terms of Cold War stereotypes. What they demonstrate, however, is that Taiwan has moved a very long way from being the epitome of the Cold War to being the epitome of the new post–Cold War order.

■ REFERENCES

Balassa, Bela. 1981. *The Newly Industrializing Countries in the World Economy.* New York: Pergamon.

Bosco, Joseph. "The Emergence of a Taiwanese Popular Culture," *American Journal of Chinese Studies.* Forthcoming.

Chan, Steve. 1987. "The Mouse that Roared: Taiwan's Management of Trade Relations with the U.S.," *Comparative Political Studies* 20:251–292.

Chan, Steve and Cal Clark. 1992. *Flexibility, Foresight, and Fortune in Taiwan's Development: Navigating Between Scylla and Charybdis.* London: Routledge.

Chang, David Wen-wei. 1988. *China Under Deng Xiaoping: Political and Economic Reform.* New York: St. Martin's.

Chang, Paris H. 1984. "Taiwan in 1983: Setting the Stage for Power Transition," *Asian Survey* 21:122–126.

Cheng, Chu-yuan. 1992. "Trade and Investment Across the Taiwan Strait: Economic Consequences and Prospects," *Strategic Studies Series.* Montclair, CA: The Claremont Institute.

Cheng, Tun-jen. 1989. "Democratizing the Quasi-Leninist Regime in Taiwan," *World Politics* 41:477–499.

Cheng, Tun-jen and Stephan Haggard, eds. 1991. *Political Change in Taiwan.* Boulder, CO: Lynne Rienner Publishers.

Chiu, Hungdah, ed. 1979. *China and the Taiwan Issue.* New York: Praeger.

Clark, Cal. 1989. *Taiwan's Development: Implications for Contending Political Economy Paradigms.* New York: Greenwood.

Clark, Cal. 1993. "The Limits on America as a 'Predatory Hegemon': The Case of U.S. Trade with Taiwan." In *Competitiveness, Technonationalism, and Threats to the World Trading Order,* ed. William P. Avery and David P. Rapkin. Boulder, CO: Lynne Rienner Publishers.

Clark, Cal and Steve Chan. 1991. "ROC-PRC (Non)Relations: Groping Toward the German Model?" *Issues and Studies* 27:56–71.

Clough, Ralph N. 1978. *Island China.* Cambridge: Harvard University Press.

Copper, John F. 1988. *A Quiet Revolution: Political Development in the Republic of China.* Washington, D.C.: Ethics and Public Policy Center.

Copper, John F. 1989. "Taiwan: A Nation in Transition." *Current History* 88:173–176, 198–199.

Cumings, Bruce. 1984. "The Origins and Development of the Northeast Asian Political Economy: Industrial Sectors, Product Cycles, and Political Consequences," *International Organization* 38:1–40.

Destler, I. M. 1986. *American Trade Politics: System Under Stress.* New York: Twentieth Century Fund.

Domes, Jurgen. 1981. "Political Differentiation in Taiwan: Group Formation Within the Ruling Party and Opposition Circles, 1979–80," *Asian Survey* 21:1011–1028.

Domes, Jurgen. 1989. "The 13th Party Congress of the Kuomintang: Towards Political Competition?" *China Quarterly* 118:345–359.

Fei, John C. H. 1991. "A Historical Perspective on Economic Modernization in the ROC." In *Two Societies in Opposition: The Republic of China and the People's Republic of China After Forty Years,* ed. Ramon Myers. Stanford: Hoover Institution Press, pp. 97–110.

Fei, John C. H., Gustav Ranis, and Shirley W. Y. Kuo. 1979. *Growth with Equity: The Taiwan Case.* New York: Oxford University Press.

Free China Review. 1991. "Taiwan-Mainland Relations," 41:4–51.

Galenson, Walter, ed. 1979. *Economic Growth and Structural Change in Taiwan: The Postwar Experience of the Republic of China.* Ithaca: Cornell University Press.

Gallin, Bernard. 1966. *Hsin Hsing, Taiwan: A Chinese Village in Change.* Berkeley: University of California Press.

Gilder, George. 1981. *Wealth and Poverty.* New York: Basic Books.

Gold, Thomas B. 1986. *State and Society in the Taiwan Miracle.* Armonk, NY: M. E. Sharpe.

Gold, Thomas B. 1989. "Taiwan in 1988: The Transition to a Post-Chiang World." In *China Brief, 1989,* ed. Anthony J. Kane. Boulder, CO: Westview Press, pp. 87–108.

Goldstein, Judith. 1988. "Ideas, Institutions, and American Trade Policy," *International Organization* 42:179–217.

Gregor, A. James and Maria Hsia Chang. 1984. *The Iron Triangle: U.S. Security Policy for Northeast Asia.* Stanford: Hoover Institution Press.

Haggard, Stephan. 1990. *Pathways from the Periphery: The Politics of Growth in the Newly Industrializing Countries.* Ithaca: Cornell University Press.

Haggard, Stephan and Tun-jen Cheng. 1987. "State and Foreign Capital in the East Asian NICs." In *The Political Economy of the New Asian Industrialism,* ed. Frederic C. Deyo. Ithaca: Cornell University Press, pp. 84–135.

Harding, Harry. 1987. *China's Second Revolution: Reform After Mao.* Washington, D.C.: Brookings Institution.

Hayek, Frederich A. von. 1944. *The Road to Serfdom.* Chicago: University of Chicago Press.

Hickey, Dennis Van Vranken. 1988. "America's Two-Point Policy and the Future of Taiwan," *Asian Survey* 28:881–896.

Hickey, Dennis Van Vranken. 1991. "Will Inter-China Trade Change Taiwan or the Mainland?" *Orbis* 35:517–531.

Ho, Samuel P.S. 1978. *Economic Development in Taiwan, 1860–1970.* New Haven: Yale University Press.

Ho, S. Y. 1990. "The Republic of China's Policy Toward the United States, 1979–1989." In *The Foreign Policy of the Republic of China on Taiwan: An Unorthodox Approach,* ed. Y. S. Wang. New York: Praeger. pp. 29–44.

Hsiao, Hsin-huang Michael. 1991. "The Changing State-Society Relations in the ROC: Economic Change, the Transformation of Class Structure, and the Rise of Social Movements." In *Two Societies in Opposition: The Republic of China and the People's Republic of China After 40 Years,* ed. Ramon H. Myers. Stanford: Hoover Institution Press, pp. 127–140.

Hsiung, James C., ed. 1981. *Contemporary Republic of China: The Taiwan Experience, 1950–1980.* New York: Praeger.

Hsiung, James C. 1986. "Taiwan in 1985: Scandals and Setbacks," *Asian Survey* 26: 93–101.

Hsiung, James C. 1992a. "China and Asia Pacific in the Post–Nuclear World." Presented at the annual meeting of the International Studies Association, Atlanta.
Hsiung, James C. 1992b. "China in the Twenty-first Century Global Balance: Challenge and Policy Response." In *The Evolving Pacific Basin in the Global Political Economy: Domestic and International Linkages,* ed. Cal Clark and Steve Chan. Boulder, CO: Lynne Rienner Publishers.
Huang, Chi. 1989. "The State and Foreign Investment: The Cases of Taiwan and Singapore," *Comparative Political Studies* 22:93–121.
Kao, Lang. 1991. "A New Relationship Across the Taiwan Strait," *Issues and Studies* 27:44–68.
Kau, Michael. 1988. "Beijing's Campaign for Unification." In *Taiwan in a Time of Transition,* ed. Harvey Feldman, Michael Y. M. Kau, and Ilpyong J. Kim. New York: Paragon House, pp. 175–200.
Kau, Michael Ying-mao. 1991. "Conceptualizing Political Conflict in Taiwan." Presented at the conference on Permutations Across the Taiwan Strait, Texas A&M University.
Kristof, Nicholas D. 1991. "Nationalists Win 71 percent of Taiwan Vote," *New York Times,* December 22, p. 5.
Kuo, Cheng-Tian. 1991. "Disunited Fronts at the Front." Presented at the conference on Permutations Across the Taiwan Strait, Texas A&M University.
Kuo, Shirley W. Y. 1983. *The Taiwan Economy in Transition.* Boulder, CO: Westview Press.
Kuo, Shirley W. Y., Gustav Ranis, and John C. H. Fei. 1981. *The Taiwan Success Story: Rapid Growth with Improved Distribution in the Republic of China.* Boulder, CO: Westview Press.
Lai, Tse-han, Ramon H. Myers, and Wou Wei. 1991. *A Tragic Beginning: The Taiwan Uprising of February 28, 1947.* Stanford: Stanford University Press.
Lam, Danny Kin-Kong and Ian Lee. 1992. "Guerrilla Capitalism and the Limits of Statist Theory." In *The Evolving Pacific Basin in the Global Political Economy: Domestic and International Linkages,* ed. Cal Clark and Steve Chan. Boulder, CO: Westview Press.
Lasater, Martin L. 1984. *The Taiwan Issue in Sino-American Strategic Relations.* Boulder, CO: Westview Press.
Lasater, Martin L. 1989. *Policy in Evolution: The U.S. Role in China's Unification.* Boulder, CO: Westview Press.
Lasater, Martin, L. 1990. *A Step Toward Democracy: The December 1989 Elections in Taiwan, Republic of China.* Washington, D.C.: American Enterprise Institute.
Li, K. T. 1988. *The Evolution of Policy Behind Taiwan's Developmental Success.* New Haven: Yale University Press.
Lin, Ching-yuan. 1973. *Industrialization in Taiwan, 1946–72: Trade and Import-Substitution Policies for Developing Countries.* New York: Praeger.
Ling, Ts'ai and Ramon H. Myers. 1990. "Winds of Democracy: The 1989 Taiwan Elections," *Asian Survey* 30:360–379.
Liu, Philip. 1992. "Tougher Laws Make Better Software," *Free China Review* 42:42–45.
Milner, Helen V. 1988. *Resisting Protectionism: Global Industries and the Politics of International Trade.* Princeton: Princeton University Press.
Moody, Peter R., Jr. 1991. "The Democratization of Taiwan and the Reunification of China," *Journal of East Asian Affairs* 5:144–184.
Myers, Ramon H. 1984. "The Economic Transformation of the Republic of China on Taiwan," *China Quarterly* 99:500–528.

Myers, Ramon H. 1987. "Political Theory and the Recent Political Developments in the Republic of China," *Asian Survey* 27:1003–1022.
Olson, Mancur. 1982. *The Rise and Decline of Nations: Economic Growth, Stagflation, and Social Rigidities.* New Haven: Yale University Press.
Pearson, Charles S. 1989. *Free Trade/Fair Trade? The Reagan Record.* Lanham, MD: University Press of America.
Ranis, Gustav. 1979. "Industrial Development." In *Economic Growth and Structural Change in Taiwan: The Postwar Experience of the Republic of China,* ed. Walter Galenson. Ithaca: Cornell University Press, pp. 206–262.
Seymour, James D. 1989. "Taiwan in 1988: No More Bandits," *Asian Survey* 29:54–63.
Snyder, Edwin K., A. James Gregor, and Maria Hsia Chang. 1980. *The Taiwan Relations Act and the Defense of the Republic of China.* Berkeley: Institute of International Studies, University of California, Berkeley.
Sutter, Robert G. 1988. *Taiwan: Entering the 21st Century.* Lanham, MD: University Press of America.
Tien, Hung-mao. 1989. *The Great Transition: Political and Social Change in the Republic of China.* Stanford: Hoover Institution Press.
Wade, Robert. 1990. *Governing the Market: Economic Theory and the Role of Government in East Asian Industrialization.* Princeton: Princeton University Press.
Wang, Yu San, ed. 1990. *The Foreign Policy of the Republic of China on Taiwan: An Unorthodox Approach.* New York: Praeger.
Winckler, Edwin A. and Susan Greenhalgh, eds. 1988. *Contending Approaches to the Political Economy of Taiwan.* Armonk, NY: M. E. Sharpe.
Wu, An-chia. 1990. "Taipei's Mainland Policy in the 1990s: Institutionalization of Bilateral Relations." Presented at the annual meeting of the American Association for Chinese Studies, California State University, Fullerton.
Wu, Yu-shan. 1991. "The Political Economy of Taiwan-Mainland Economic Relations." Presented at the conference on Permutations Across the Taiwan Strait, Texas A&M University.
Wu, Yuan-li. 1985. *Becoming an Industrialized Nation: ROC's Development on Taiwan.* New York: Praeger.
Yang, Martin M. C. 1970. *Socioeconomic Results of Land Reform in Taiwan.* Honolulu: East-West Center Press.
Yoffie, David B. 1983. *Power and Protectionism: Strategies of the Newly Industrializing Countries.* New York: Columbia University Press.
Yu, Susan. 1991. "Lilley Says Beijing Threats Unrealistic." *Free China Journal,* December 10, p. 1.

■ 7

Southeast Asia
After the Cold War
Bernard K. Gordon

The end of the Cold War as it applies to Southeast Asia is unlike the topics of most other chapters in this book. The reason is that Southeast Asia is not a nation or an issue. It is mainly a geographic expression, and not a very old one at that. It was invented during World War II to help British and U.S. officers plan their military operations in Japanese-held territory. As a phrase used to describe political, military, or economic issues, "Southeast Asia" has almost no history.

Nevertheless, it has now gained wide acceptance, and today it is used as a label to indicate a number of nations in the Pacific region. Even so, not everybody agrees on what is included. Some would say that if geography is the criterion, Hong Kong and perhaps Taiwan are part of Southeast Asia. It could also be argued that Australia and perhaps even New Zealand should be included. But that would not be common usage. When governments or specialists discuss Southeast Asia today, they normally mean a region of two geographic sections: "insular" Southeast Asia and "mainland" Southeast Asia.

Insular Southeast Asia usually refers to Indonesia, the Philippines, much of Malaysia, and perhaps Singapore. A look at the map shows how large an expanse that covers. It is triangular, its top is in the northern Philippines, and it borders Taiwan. At its western base, the triangle stretches from the Indian Ocean (on the Indonesian island of Sumatra) across to New Guinea in the South Pacific. Mainland Southeast Asia is much more compact, and, as the label suggests, it is part of the Asian continent. It includes the Indochinese states (Vietnam, Cambodia, and Laos), Burma, Thailand, and what used to be called Malaya and is known now as West Malaysia.

In this chapter, I will deal with both the insular and mainland parts of Southeast Asia, partly because that is what the term usually means today but also because the nations involved *think* of themselves as part of a single Southeast Asia region. By that I mean that their political, business, and professional leaders consider their nations part of Southeast Asia and that those nations increasingly have important *interactions* with one another.

But those facts do not mean those nations or peoples are much alike. They include many different ethnic groups; they have different histories and colonial experiences; their postindependence political and economic systems have followed different models; and their foreign policies often have reflected strikingly different approaches to Asian and world affairs. The result is that there is no single meaning of the Cold War's end in Southeast Asia, though its leaders have begun to address its implications in regional terms. Like everyone else, they are especially concerned with the changed roles of the United States, Japan, Russia, and China. The policies of those large nations set the background conditions for Southeast Asia, and although more will be said about them later on, some main points involving each should be identified now.

The United States: For different reasons, almost all the nations in the region want the United States to stay "involved" in Southeast Asia. In *economic* terms, they all want U.S. investment, and those that already have a large U.S. market worry that the nation is becoming protectionist. In *military* terms, there is more divergence. Most Southeast Asian states want some kind of continued U.S. defense role, and a few actively welcome it. There is a growing concern that because the United States is no longer confronted by a large Soviet threat, it will disengage from Southeast Asia.

Japan: As with the United States, everybody wants Japan's investment and its markets. But there is more variety in attitudes toward Japan. Some fear that if U.S.–Japan disputes worsen and Tokyo replaces Moscow as the threat in U.S. eyes, Southeast Asians will suffer. The *economic* worry is that Washington will lose interest in the Pacific, move economically closer to Mexico and South America, and leave Asia to Japan. In *military* terms, many want the United States to stay because they do not want a larger Japanese role, and nobody wants to see major Japanese rearmament.

Russia: In the past, Moscow had four meanings for Southeast Asia. Some considered it their friend and supporter; for others it was a useful "balancer" against a solely U.S. military presence; for still others it was mainly a troublemaker; and for a few—just before its collapse—the USSR was a possible future market. Now it is none of those things; Moscow is seen as largely irrelevant, and not everybody agrees that is a good thing. The reason has to do with the last factor, China.

China: In Southeast Asian perceptions, China is the least-changed of all the large external post–Cold War factors. China was reforming its economy even before the end of the Cold War, thereby becoming an important economic competitor for Southeast Asia in two ways: as a magnet for Western investment and foreign aid and as a producer of lower-cost goods that Southeast Asians also sell to the world. Militarily, Southeast Asians worry that China will direct more attention to the Pacific as a result of the Soviet decline. Two signs are already evident: China's naval building program and its willingness to reassert political ambitions—as in a growing controversy over the contested Spratly Islands.

■ TWO SOUTHEAST ASIAS: ASEAN AND INDOCHINA

There is a risk in having set out the foregoing background conditions. It may imply a single Southeast Asian perception of world and Asian politics, and that is decidedly not so. Southeast Asia's foreign policies often have reflected strikingly different approaches to Asian and world affairs, and nothing illustrates that better than ASEAN, the Association of Southeast Asian Nations.

ASEAN was formed in 1967, and among the world's developing areas it is the only successful effort in "regional cooperation." ASEAN now includes Indonesia, the Philippines, Malaysia, Singapore, Thailand, and, most recently, Brunei. It is often called a "noncommunist" group because, aside from Indonesia, its original founders would have described themselves that way. Indonesia called itself "neutral" because it had also been a founder of the "nonaligned" group of nations, but by 1967 it was as thoroughly anticommunist as the others in ASEAN.[1] By that time, moreover, the Vietnam War was moving into its most intense phase, and that background is important to understand ASEAN.

What we usually call the Vietnam War was in reality the "second Indochina war." The word "Indochina" comes from colonial times, when the French ruled Vietnam, Cambodia, and Laos largely as a single unit called Indochina. When France sought to reimpose its authority after World War II, Vietnam's nationalist leaders—who were also communists—declared their independence. The result was the *first* Indochina war. France lost that conflict in 1954, and it led to Vietnam's division into a communist North and a strongly anticommunist South, as well as independence for Laos and Cambodia.

The North Vietnamese, however, did not accept the division, and in the early 1960s they launched the second Indochina war, what we generally call the Vietnam War. Hanoi's goal was to unify Vietnam under communism, and probably also to incorporate Laos and Cambodia, at least loosely, in a new "Indochina Federation." This goal existed because the Vietnamese saw themselves as the successors to France and also because they believed in the rightness of their communist cause.

The Vietnam War quickly took on implications beyond just Vietnam or Indochina. One reason for this consequence was that the fighting spilled over into Cambodia and Laos, both of which share borders with Thailand.[2] Another was that Vietnam had substantial Soviet support—political, economic, and military—and some help from China, too. That led Hanoi increasingly to be seen by its Southeast Asian neighbors as the capital of an expansionist state with a revolutionary communist ideology.

Those worries were intensified because the leaders and political elites of all those neighboring states were intensely antirevolutionary and often strongly traditionalist. Singapore's Prime Minister Lee Kwan Yew was a Socialist, but he was at the same time fiercely anticommunist. Consequently, all these leaders were anxious to build some kind of bulwark against communism and revolution in the region. This was the political impulse that led them to create ASEAN. Although they hoped the new group would also achieve economic and other forms of regional cooperation, their main bond was political, based on the shared conviction that the way to defeat the appeals of communism in Southeast Asia was through economic development, growing material prosperity, and political modernization.[3]

They were right: The ASEAN nations have for the most part progressed enormously in economic development, and several are now looked to as models by developing nations everywhere else. The greatest material advances have been made in Singapore, Malaysia, and Thailand, where average per capita incomes are now at roughly $12,000, $2,500 and $1,500, respectively, and where GNP growth rates are now regularly at 8–11 percent.[4] Those are growth rates achieved nowhere else in the world, and it is worth recalling what such economic growth means.

A 7 percent growth rate *doubles* a nation's GNP if sustained over ten years, which is what has happened among several of the ASEAN states. Even Indonesia, the largest and long the poorest of these nations, now has an annual GNP growth rate of at least 5 percent. Japan, by comparison, rarely exceeded 8 percent levels even at the height of its rapid growth in the 1960s and early 1970s and today is normally at 4–5 percent. Thus, by any economic measure the ASEAN nations (other than the Philippines) have made remarkable progress, and several of them seem poised to join the group known as the newly industrializing countries. Thailand, for example, traditionally exported mainly rice, timber, tapioca, and other agricultural commodities, but today 60 percent of its exports are manufactured goods, and it leads the world in economic growth.

The Indochinese countries, by contrast, are the world's poorest nations, and one of them—Cambodia—is in nearly total disarray. Some believe all of these problems stem from the Vietnam War, but the argument is generally not persuasive. It is true that in Cambodia, events of the 1960s and 1970s *do* explain today's potential for renewed Civil War, but those events were only indirectly connected to the Vietnam War. The main reality is that the Khmer Rouge—one of two communist groups that fought to control Cambodia in the 1970s—refuses to accept that the other communist faction won.[5]

In Vietnam it is even more difficult to show that its backwardness stems directly from its war with the United States. Of course, that war cost Vietnam dearly in people, property, and time, but it ended in 1975, and U.S. soldiers stopped fighting there in 1973. Since then, twenty years have passed, and the principal reason for Vietnam's economic underdevelopment today is that its leaders—like no others in the world except Cuba's Castro—continue to insist that Leninist communism is the correct political path for their people's economic improvement.

To be sure, there are other, external factors that have limited the ability of Vietnamese and Cambodians to start on the path to modern economic development (and, in Cambodia's case, even to stop the fighting). In Vietnam, for example, the United States, still smarting over its defeat in the Vietnam War, has insisted that Japan and other major aid-granting nations not provide much help. The United States also has effectively prevented international agencies such as the World Bank from aiding Vietnam. But Vietnam's own behavior—especially its invasion of Cambodia in late 1978—has been the main factor leading to its pariah status in the world community. Likewise, it has mainly been the Khmer Rouge—and China's dogged insistence on arming and supplying it—that has kept Cambodia in turmoil.

China's extremely cynical behavior in Cambodia stems from the centuries-old mutual enmity between China and Vietnam. Vietnam has always feared China, which ruled it for a thousand years, and China in turn is apprehensive about, and resentful toward, Vietnam. Their relations were worsened in late 1978 when Vietnam invaded Cambodia and ejected its Khmer Rouge government. The reason for this intervention was not that the Khmer Rouge had killed so many Cambodians, though that may have played a part. Instead, Hanoi was simply fed up with having an extremely radical Cambodian government on its borders—whose leaders it had helped bring to power in 1975 but who were now behaving like ungrateful upstarts. They were persecuting Cambodians friendly to Vietnam, demanding border revisions at Vietnam's expense, and, as a last straw, developing increasingly close ties with China.

Consequently, when Vietnam invaded Cambodia, its goal was to remove the Khmer Rouge from the capital of Phnom Penh and put in its place Cambodians who were less objectionable. To protect them, Vietnam then stationed hundreds of thousands of its troops in Cambodia. All this military activity led China to invade northern Vietnamese provinces. Beijing aimed to teach Vietnam a lesson, but the Vietnamese rebuffed the invasion and refused to heed the warning. They proceeded with their occupation of Cambodia and battled remaining Khmer Rouge forces into isolated redoubts.

The final stage in the conflict, which continues today, came when China began a long-term program to maintain the Khmer Rouge as a fighting force. Its ostensible reason is to help the Khmer Rouge at least share in Cambodia's governance and possibly even return to power, because Beijing regards the present Phnom Penh government as Vietnam's puppet. But the deeper reason is that China simply does not accept that the troublesome Vietnamese, by indirectly dominating Cambodia and Laos, might actually achieve their long-dreamed of hopes for an Indochina Federation.

I have recounted this episode in some detail because it is a reminder that the main political fact in Vietnam and Cambodia—and what sets Indochina apart from the ASEAN group—is that, like flies in amber, the Indochinese states have been frozen in a mold set long ago. Their postures reflect old hatreds reinforced by events that took place when the East-West conflict was the dominant fact of world politics. ASEAN is different: Its leaders have not forgotten their past, but they have become mainly forward-looking in their policies and beliefs. In response to evolving domestic and foreign conditions, they have already made major adjustments in their societies, and the newest change—the end of the Cold War—has reinforced their belief that even more adjustments may now be called for.

In that sense, there is not one Southeast Asia but two: an Indochina that is hardly able to deal with the present, to say nothing of the future; and an ASEAN group whose leaders are searching for ways to influence and even control their destiny, often with a deep conviction to avoid what they see as a repetition of the past—when outside powers largely shaped their region's affairs. But even as they want to shape their own future, there is one outside power—the United States—about which there are deep levels of ambivalence. No issue better describes the complexity of the post–Cold War era for Southeast Asia than the role the United States has played there.

■ ASEAN, THE UNITED STATES,
AND THE END OF THE COLD WAR

There is much worry, among the ASEAN nations especially, that the Cold War's end will bring a revival of U.S. isolationism. That is a very improbable development, mainly because of the sheer size of the United States and the scope of its foreign involvements. The United States is the world's largest economy, and its 250 million people make it also the largest industrialized nation (only China and India have more people). Moreover, the people of the United States increasingly recognize that events anywhere can affect their safety and well-being: Foreign trade, at 17 percent of the U.S. GNP, now plays the same role in the U.S. economy that it does in Japan's. Trade with Asia and the Pacific has become especially important in U.S. foreign economic ties, and the result is that the United States is the only nation whose people, economy, and political interests are strongly involved in *all* areas of the world. Finally, the United States's political and security concerns with Asia and the Pacific, which are even more deeply rooted than its trade and economic relations in the region, long precede the Cold War era. As every recent U.S. president has emphasized, the United States is a "Pacific power," and that will not change.

But these considerations are not deeply integrated into most Southeast Asian thinking. Many in the region believe it was mainly the Cold War—especially the United States's concern with communism—that brought it to the Pacific and Southeast Asia. U.S. rhetoric sometimes fed that view, leading Southeast Asians to believe the only thing that put them high on the United States' agenda was its desire to compete with the USSR and China. Indonesians are an example of those who should know better, and some do: They recall it was the United States that most strongly pressed the Netherlands to accept Indonesia's independence soon after World War II. Although it was not anxious to upset relations with Holland (because it was a NATO member and historically a very friendly ally), the United States nevertheless "brokered" Indonesia's independence from the Dutch, even while NATO was being formed. It did so because of its traditional opposition to colonialism and because it believed an Asia of independent nations was consistent with its own interests.

Washington's behavior was not so clear-cut in Indochina. In that case, the United States was strongly influenced by its need for French membership in NATO and by the outbreak of the Korean War in 1950. Paris exploited both concerns: It argued not only that victory in Indochina was vital to France's internal political stability but also that the Vietnam conflict was part of the global struggle against communism. The French stressed that Ho Chi Minh, the leader of the Vietnamese nationalists, was also a Communist with long and deep ties to Moscow—whose weapons were now killing GIs in Korea. The United States accepted that logic, and after 1950 it paid most of the costs of France's war in Indochina. Instead of playing the role it had in Indonesia, the United States allowed its global East-West concerns to override its opposition to Asian colonialism. Even more tragically, it stayed on in Indochina long after France's defeat and became South Vietnam's principal supporter.

It was in that period that Southeast Asians came to regard the U.S. presence as a permanent fixture. From the early 1960s to 1975 there was no higher issue on the United States' global agenda than the struggle in Southeast Asia, and when the Vietnam War ended three other factors kept Indochina a high U.S. priority. One was its bitterness at having been defeated by the Vietnamese—a point illustrated even today by the continuing emotional power of the MIA/POW issue. The second was Hanoi's invasion of Cambodia in 1978, proof to the United States of Vietnam's aggressiveness. The third was Vietnam's increasingly close ties to the USSR, symbolized not only by their 1978 Treaty of Friendship but also by Hanoi's decision to allow the Soviets use of Vietnam's naval facilities at Cam Ranh Bay. These had been developed by the United States during the Vietnam War and were only 600 miles from the United States's then-largest overseas naval base—at Subic Bay in the Philippines. Thus, in the late 1970s and 1980s, with the Soviet Union seemingly at the height of its military potency—and with its new leader, Gorbachev, talking of the USSR also as a "Pacific Power"—the U.S.-built facilities in Cam Ranh Bay were being converted into a Soviet naval base!

But today all this is gone. There is no more Soviet fleet—indeed, there is no more Soviet Union. Vietnam is poverty-stricken, and in any event it has withdrawn its forces from Cambodia. Cambodia itself is still the scene of conflict and possibly renewed war, but its travail seems to have few if any external implications. What this means for the rest of Southeast Asia—now that communism is gone—is that the United States, too, may go away. Others are only too aware that China, communist or not, is always present. And all look at Japan, sometimes apprehensively and sometimes with open arms. For all, however, the removal of the common thread of anticommunism could lead each to go its separate way. To understand why, it will be useful to look at the region's recent past, especially the record of several of ASEAN states.

■ THAILAND AND THE CAMBODIA CONFLICT

Thailand is a good place to begin for two reasons: first, because it has been heavily involved in much of the region's recent foreign policy experience; second, because—as the only Southeast Asian state never colonized—it has the longest and clearest foreign policy tradition. The Thais are very proud of that tradition; they believe they never lost their independence because of its wisdom. The reality is that their independence served the interests of Britain and France, the European rivals who carved up mainland Southeast Asia in the eighteenth and nineteenth centuries. The British were in Burma and Malaya (and Singapore), the French in Indochina.

Thailand was sandwiched between them, and its kings and advisors understood both the dangers and opportunities that position meant. They sought to maintain good relations with both and at the same time to keep the two European powers at a distance. Indeed, during the U.S. Civil War Thailand's king even offered elephants to President Lincoln. Today we would say the Thais "played each off against the other," but from the British and French perspectives it was just as well to have Thailand between them. The Thais knew that but were also powerless to prevent the Europeans from doing as they wished. Even now, Bangkok recalls that France took some Thai territory and added it to Cambodia.

From its balancing-act policy in that period, Thailand gained its foreign policy reputation as a "reed that bends in the wind" but is not broken. Its policy during World War II is a good example. There was a Thai embassy in Washington that called itself the representative of "democratic" Thai and which insisted Thailand was occupied by Japan. The reality is recalled in the film *Bridge Over the River Kwai* (the site is in Thailand): Thai officials did nothing to prevent Japan's free use of their territory and maintained cooperative ties with Tokyo. When Japan lost the war, Bangkok simply declared that those who had worked with Japan had not represented Thailand's "legal" government! The United States agreed, but Great Britain was livid. It regarded Thailand as one of the wartime "enemy states" and for a time resisted Thailand's application to join the United Nations.

The friendly relations Thailand built with the United States before and during World War II were strongly reinforced immediately afterward, and they became the cornerstone of Thai policy. When the United States created the Southeast Asia Treaty Organization (SEATO) in 1954, Thailand and the Philippines were the only truly Southeast Asian nations to join. The United States's aim in creating SEATO was to reassure Asians that it would stay in Southeast Asia despite France's defeat by the Vietnamese a few months earlier. Thailand, always looking for a protector when predators are in the neighborhood, was only too ready to join SEATO, and from then until the early 1970s it established an extremely close relationship with the United States.

Yet it was not long afterward that Thailand began to have some doubts about putting too many eggs in the one U.S. basket. In 1959 it began the process that ultimately led to the creation of ASEAN in 1967. The first step came in 1961, when Thailand, Malaya, and the Philippines created the Association of Southeast Asia (ASA). Until then, there had been hardly any contact among these states (a phone call from Bangkok to Manila in those days had first to go through the United States!). With that colonial-era separation in mind, the leaders of the three states hoped to speak to the major powers with one voice, and ASEAN has given them much of that. The Thai concern, however, has until recently been much less with the possible tangible benefits of regional cooperation than with its political and security advantages.[6]

ASEAN's role with regard to Vietnam's invasion of Cambodia illustrates the point: Thai policy became ASEAN policy, and "the political fortunes of ASEAN were made hostage to solidarity with Thailand."[7] Thailand's concern with Cambodia stems from its long-standing perception of Cambodia as a "buffer" state—against French expansion in the past and against Vietnam's in this era. That was a main reason Thailand supported U.S. policy so strongly in the Vietnam War, even to the point of sending some troops. But by the same token, the Thais felt deeply betrayed when

U.S. troops left South Vietnam in 1973 and horrified when Hanoi won total victory in 1975. With the images still fresh in their minds of U.S. diplomatic personnel leaving Saigon from the embassy roof, Bangkok reached out to Vietnam, hoping it would no longer be a threatening factor in the region.[8] Thailand even insisted the United States quickly vacate a military base previously used against North Vietnam. Washington's reaction was summed up when the U.S. ambassador carried off the flag: "The United States does not stay where it is not wanted."[9]

Against that background, Vietnam's invasion of Cambodia in December 1978 came as a shock to the Thais. Vietnam's Premier Pham Van Dong had come to Bangkok only weeks earlier and signed a joint statement on "the desirability of Southeast Asia being an area of peace, independence, freedom and neutrality." Now, with Vietnam's invasion of Cambodia and its replacement of the Khmer by Cambodians of its choosing, the Thai again reassessed their Vietnam policy. With impressive skill at the UN, they built an ASEAN-centered coalition designed to force Hanoi to rethink *its* assessment. Bangkok's goals were to focus world attention on Hanoi's behavior; persuade it to leave Cambodia; and accept an international settlement that would guarantee a neutral Cambodia.

The effort took twelve years and was uniquely complicated because Vietnam had at least rid Cambodia of the Khmer Rouge. Everyone knew of its "killing fields"; and Thailand and ASEAN were therefore opposing those who had ousted the worst butchers since Hitler. Even so, the UN effort largely succeeded: Vietnam is no longer in Cambodia; the government there is committed to neutrality; and in 1991 ASEAN and the UN arranged a settlement of the conflict (the "Paris Agreement") that led to the UN's largest peacekeeping operation. It may or may not finally work out, but much of its relative success stems from Thailand's ability to persuade others that its interest was also theirs.[10] The United States, for example, backed the effort partly because it was designed to punish and pressure Vietnam. Singapore backed it (and became ASEAN's sharpest spokesman on the issue) because, as a small state surrounded by bigger ones who are often jealous of its success, it wants to remind everyone that large and powerful nations must not invade their small neighbors. But Thailand also had to make a pact with more than one devil, and the issue troubles Southeast Asia's international politics today.

The main factor is China, the Khmer Rouge's spokesman as well as its principal supplier. China's help had to pass through Thai territory because no other coalition member borders Cambodia. In the process, however, the Thai military—which controlled the supply route—became China's agents, and that brought corruption in every sense of the word. As a result, although Thai foreign policy sought to end the Cambodian war, elements of the Thai military developed a self-interest in its perpetuation.

This paradox became very clear when the UN peacekeeping operation began in 1991. Though the Khmer Rouge had signed the Paris Agreement, it was soon erecting roadblocks to its implementation, and the question arose: how had the Khmer Rouge managed not only to sustain itself but to increase its political support? The answer was that it had become a trader in timber and gems—two of the region's most lucrative resources. Because those products have to reach hard-currency markets, it was also clear that Khmer Rouge timber and gems were getting to market through the connivance, and to the profit, of the Thai military.

Any country faces a problem when its armed forces conduct a separate foreign policy, and the problem is magnified in Thailand because of the present crisis over the political role of its military. Its generals have in effect controlled the country since 1932, and in the postwar era they have combined political power with dominance of the economy. This influence goes well beyond the timber and gem trade: The Thai military owns or controls two of the nation's four TV channels, half of its roughly 400 radio stations, the national airline (Thai Airways), the domestic and international telephone organizations, the major trucking company, the tobacco monopoly, and much else.[11] Many senior officers have become extremely wealthy as a result, and in 1992 a civilian coalition, perhaps backed by the king, seriously challenged their political and economic supremacy. It cannot be assumed the generals will willingly relinquish either the power or the money they enjoy, and the problem has foreign policy implications.[12]

In the past, Thailand's generals let the professionals attend to foreign policy, and the professionals acted mainly out of political considerations: They bent with the wind when necessary. But today, when foreign policy and economics are so intertwined, it may become more difficult to determine which is the prevailing wind. Thailand and others will face this dilemma as they shape policy toward Japan and the United States. As I have mentioned, many in ASEAN want to assure a continued U.S. presence, but in terms of trade and investment it is Japan that now looms larger. Reflecting that reality, several ASEAN voices now argue it is "natural" or "inevitable" for Japan to play an especially large role in Southeast Asia's affairs. Others worry exactly about that prospect, which is one reason why they urge the United States not to turn inward or become isolationist.

How Thailand will respond to such issues, especially when the military's authority is under such severe challenge, is far from clear. If the generals are to remain important, even Thailand's reformers concede it will be in the fields of foreign policy and national security. In that case, with communism no longer a threat, the "reed that bends in the wind" may face a new choice: between a United States always talking about human rights and business corruption and a Japan that rarely cares about such matters.

■ INDONESIA: SOUTHEAST ASIA'S GIANT

The largest single factor in Indonesian politics is the nation's size. Its many islands stretch across 3,000 miles, a diameter equal to that of the United States, and with almost 200 million people it is the world's fourth-largest nation. Indonesia is very much a multicultural state, but the insistence of its first president, Sukarno, on a single language, along with his commitment to religious tolerance, has made the building of a unified nation-state largely successful.[13] Important regional and cultural differences remain, and Javanese dominance is often complained about, but the days of genuinely threatening political separatism of the sort that afflicted Indonesia in its first decade are over. It is still relatively poor, partly as a result of 300 years of Dutch colonialism, but it has major natural resources, its economy is growing very rapidly, and it is a giant in every other way.

Indonesia's leaders and elites are acutely aware of their nation's size when they think about foreign policy. They openly regard it as Southeast Asia's "leading" state, and others in the region take it for granted that nothing can be done in foreign affairs that affects the region as a whole without Jakarta's support. That fact relegated ASA to being only an interesting development, because it did *not* include Indonesia, whereas ASEAN quickly became prominent because it did. A measure of Indonesia's prominence is its role among the world's developing nations; indeed, the Afro-Asian group, the precursor to the nonaligned movement, was established in Bandung, Indonesia, in 1955. That was the heyday not only of neutralism but also of U.S.–Soviet rivalry for nonaligned support. Sukarno was at his best in that milieu: Moscow and Washington vied for the loyalty of separate elements of Indonesia's armed forces, and Sukarno nurtured Indonesia's image as a nation to be wooed. He won approximately $1 billion in foreign aid from both Moscow and Washington.[14]

That era ended only ten years after Bandung, when the PKI—Indonesia's Communist Party—sought to take power in a September 1965 coup attempt about which there is still disagreement.[15] The coup led to the downfall of Sukarno and to the transformation of Indonesia's domestic politics and foreign policy. The army was the major beneficiary of the crisis, and it unleashed a nationwide orgy of killings ostensibly aimed at removing all "communist" influence. In fact, Indonesia's Chinese population mainly suffered, often for no reason other than that, as Chinese, they were owed money—which a dead man could not collect.

The events associated with "GESTAPU," the acronym for the coup, highlight two points of continuing political importance in Indonesia: the significance of its Chinese and of China and the role of the army. The army has long had high status in Indonesia because it is associated with what it calls the "struggle" for independence. This terminology overstates what happened: there *was* fighting, and Holland did not simply hand over power, as did Britain in Malaya and Singapore and the United States in the Philippines. But in the Dutch East Indies there was no real analogy to the long struggle that characterized France's refusal to leave Indochina or its defeat at Dienbienphu. Although Indonesia's army has burnished the image of its "generation of 1945" as those who fought for and won independence, the reality is that the United States persuaded a weak, tired, and by then anticolonial Holland to transfer power. Even today many Indonesians remain thankful for U.S. involvement.

In the 1950s, Indonesia's army did genuinely protect the state's integrity. It defeated several revolts against central authority, and its role both then and in the 1965 coup—either as intended victim or as eventual victor—provides the foundation for its power today. Since 1966 the army has dominated Indonesia and permeated its politics and economy far more deeply and with much more success and acceptance than has its counterpart in Thailand. Part of the reason is that the Indonesian army has combined its sometimes harsh authority with political and even intellectual sophistication. The other part of the reason is that in Indonesia the army is actually an army. As in Thailand, it, too, is much involved in business, and it, too, has shot down protestors. But part of the history of the army in Indonesia includes its combat role. In that mission it has performed well, whereas the Thai army not only has damaged some of the businesses it controls but also has lost skirmishes even to tiny Laos. It seems successful only at enriching its members and killing students.

If Indonesia's army was the main winner of the 1965 coup attempt, all those associated with China were losers. Indonesia's small but economically influential Chinese population was savaged, relations with China were broken, and communism suffered a setback from which it has never recovered. This backlash partly reflected long-standing Indonesian animosity toward its Chinese minority, but it also stemmed from evidence that Beijing had been the principal foreign supporter of Indonesia's then–very large Communist Party. The USSR sharply criticized what it called Beijing's anti-Leninist "adventurism," but the damage was done: The Indonesian army, whose leaders for years had been U.S.-trained, turned the nation's foreign policy strongly toward the West, even while insisting that Indonesia remained among the nonaligned.

That has been its orientation from the 1970s until now. Indonesia long desired to succeed to the chairmanship of the nonaligned movement it helped create and did so in 1992. But in practice, the main elements of Jakarta's foreign policy have centered on its key role in ASEAN, in particular its close association with the West and the United States. Yet Jakarta has been no mere stalking-horse for the United States. On Southeast Asian issues it has clearly put its own stamp on affairs; its role in settling the Cambodian conflict—Indonesia co-chaired the process that produced the Paris Agreement—illustrates that independence perfectly.

From the beginning of that conflict, Indonesia has always been more sympathetic to Vietnam than most others. There are three main reasons for this attitude, and the first stems from its self-perception as the child of an anticolonial war. Indonesians see a strong parallel between their own experience with the Dutch and that of the Vietnamese against the French. As a recent discussion of Indonesian-Vietnamese relations puts it: "Indonesia and Vietnam are the two countries in Southeast Asia that achieved their independence through revolution."[16]

Second, Indonesians know that when independence was declared, not everybody agreed they should inherit *all* of the Dutch East Indies. The Dutch (and some Indonesians) had less in mind, but Sukarno insisted on all Holland had ruled. Indonesia sees this, too, as an experience resembling Vietnam's in 1954, when the Geneva Conference did not award Hanoi all France had ruled. Hanoi's vision of an Indochina Federation dates from those days, and to Indonesians, Vietnam's view does not seem improper. As a result, Hanoi's invasion of Cambodia in 1978 evoked understanding and probably some sympathy in Indonesia.[17] The Khmer Rouge, like some outer-island Indonesians who have talked of independence from Jakarta, could be described as upstarts, ungrateful to the Vietnamese who actually defeated the French and the United States.

But probably the most important explanation for Indonesia's sympathy with Hanoi stems from Vietnam's opposition to China. Indonesia has always been suspicious of its Chinese minority and apprehensive about China's regional ambitions. That fear is common in Southeast Asia, where it has also been popular to link the two worries together—to see the region's Chinese as a "fifth column" for China itself. The argument has never been very persuasive (after all, the overseas Chinese *left* China to escape its miseries), and Indonesia's own PKI was not an especially Chinese movement. But Beijing's complicity in the coup gave new life to old fears in Indonesia. Important voices described Hanoi as the "cork in the bottle" against China's influence and saw its strong anti-China stance as serving Indonesia's interests, too. Thus, if Hanoi had to invade and control Cambodia to remove its China-supported Khmer Rouge, that was not altogether bad. As Indonesia's army chief of staff remarked in 1984, "Vietnam and the rest of Southeast Asia should forge closer ties to face the potential threat from a strong China."[18]

Accordingly, when dealing with Vietnam on the Cambodia issue, Indonesia skillfully exploited both its nonaligned background and its commonalities with Vietnam. To Hanoi, the combination made Jakarta more acceptable than any other ASEAN state, and these attributes continue to be assets today. Jakarta's role as the initial bridge to Hanoi is reflected in ASEAN's 1992 decision to accept Vietnam and Laos as full members, and that step also reflects Jakarta's long-term policy goals. Its aim is to make ASEAN the voice of Southeast Asia—a goal that has taken on even more meaning in the post–Cold War environment. For as close as Jakarta has been to the United States, it is not certain it wants an Asia where *only* the United States is powerful.

In these respects, Indonesia's careful and sophisticated foreign policy reflects the sometimes conflicting concerns of the region as a whole. Southeast Asians want to enlist the very valuable economic role of Japan, but they do not want a Japan that is again dominant. Likewise, most in the region regard China with much apprehension, but all recognize there is little they can do directly to affect Beijing's ambitions. Two good reflections of the concerns that China raises came in 1992. The first was its decision to escalate assertions of Chinese sovereignty over the Spratly Islands. Though uninhabitable, they are located over what may be an oil-producing ocean shelf, and both China and Vietnam—as well as three ASEAN members other than Indonesia—assert the Spratlys are theirs. Not surprisingly, Indonesia has taken the lead in trying to mute the conflict potential in this issue.

The second piece of unsettling Chinese business came with reports that Beijing would purchase a new aircraft carrier from Ukraine. If true, China will be the first East Asian state with that capacity, and it will further underline Southeast Asia's ambivalence about the United States' security role in the region. In the past, nobody has wanted the United States to leave, but at the same time all exhibited the NIMBY effect: "not in my backyard." Indonesia reflects the same ambivalence: During the long years of the Cold War, when the Soviets were a main security concern, Jakarta and everyone else wanted the U.S. Navy around—but just over the horizon.[19] Today Russia's presence does not cause the same concern as before, but Moscow's announced intention to maintain facilities at Cam Ranh Bay in Vietnam is not reassuring. It is one more reason why in the post–Cold War period Indonesia will maintain close ties with the United States and (at a slightly less warm temperature) with Japan, keeping a wary eye on everyone else. The skill and sophistication needed to deal with such complexity has characterized Jakarta's foreign policy even more than Thailand's. Less distinguished has been Indonesia's ethnic cousin, Malaysia.

■ MALAYSIA AND MAHATHIR

Mahathir bin Mohammed, Malaysia's prime minister, has put an extremely strong imprint on his nation's foreign policy and changed it substantially. Before he came to office in 1981, Malaysian diplomacy was strongly pro-Western and anticommunist. Its formative experience was the "emergency": the 1948–1960 Communist-inspired guerrilla war led largely by local Chinese and aimed at overthrowing the courtly and moderate leadership to whom Great Britain had handed independence.[20] This anticommunist background also inclined Malaysia to friendly relations with the United States, although they were never as close as Washington's ties with Thailand or Indonesia. One irritant was U.S. sales of surplus tin and rubber, which lowered the world price of two commodities traditionally exported by Malaysia. Nevertheless, during the Vietnam War, Kuala Lumpur drew on its guerrilla-war expertise to train U.S. soldiers, and the same anticommunist coloration led Malaysia to join with Thailand and the Philippines in creating ASA.

But there was a difference: Malaysia's leaders deeply wanted ethnically similar Indonesia to join such regional efforts, and this desire led them to play a critical role in creating ASEAN. A main reason was that the Malaysians often regarded Indonesians as "elder brothers," which caused Jakarta sometimes to take Kuala Lumpur for granted and in turn prompted Malaysian leaders to find some way to put their own stamp on ASEAN's foreign policy. Thus, in 1971, even before Mahathir came to power, Malaysia made its "ZOPFAN" proposal—a rather naive call for Southeast Asia to be recognized as a "zone of peace, freedom, and neutrality." Other than that initiative, Malaysia generally maintained a low posture.[21]

All that changed when Mahathir came to office. Trained as a physician—though that was not his preference—he had already become a prominent and often disturbing factor in Malaysian affairs.[22] Much of the reason was his long-banned book, *The Malay Dilemma.* Dr. Mahathir says its goal was to help the Malay population lift itself, but in the context of Malaysia's always precarious ethnic tensions (there were violent anti-Chinese riots in 1969), the book's sharp criticism of the economically powerful Chinese was indeed inflammatory. Unlike Indonesia, where the Chinese are a small minority of perhaps 4 million, Malaysia has a Chinese population totaling almost 35 percent of the country's 18 million people.

Dr. Mahathir's dislikes do not stop only with the Chinese. He has become extremely critical of what he calls "the West," but in fact he almost always means the United States. In 1991, in a fiery speech at the United Nations, he took the United States to task for seeking to impose its "human rights" views on others, and for attempting, in the wake of Moscow's decline, to impose a U.S.-run "new world order." He also included among his targets Israel and the "Zionists," though neither is directly involved with Malaysia or Malaysians. So extreme are his views that when he learned that the visiting New York Philharmonic would play a work written by a long-dead nineteenth-century Swiss composer who had also been Jewish, Malaysia insisted that the piece be removed from the program.[23] The Indian-born conductor of the orchestra refused, and Thailand's music-lovers quickly arranged a Bangkok concert instead! Dr. Mahathir would deny it, but, as in the case of Malaysia's Chinese, his deep animosities are so often ethnically based that it is difficult not to conclude they are essentially racist.

Whether or not Mahathir's attitudes toward the Chinese are literally racist, they have had an important effect on Malaysia's foreign policy. He has worked for very close relations with Japan and cited that nation as the best model for Malaysian development—although just next door, in Singapore, is an economic model at least as impressive. The two countries were joined briefly in the 1960s, and since then Singapore has made truly remarkable economic strides. Its status as a small city-state partly explains that progress, but its per capita income is nevertheless second in Asia only to Japan's. Many of its accomplishments and methods could be used as models from which Malaysia might learn—all the more so because it is so close—but not by Dr. Mahathir. He insists that Malaysia must instead "look East," to Japan, and once again it is difficult to avoid the conclusion the reason is Singapore's ethnicity: It is 75 percent Chinese.

Dr. Mahathir has told interviewers that his associations with Japan go back to his childhood in the 1930s, when his hometown had a Japanese-owned portrait studio and toy shop. Whatever the origins, his affinity for Japan has led him to be very supportive of an enlarged and special role for Japan in today's Asia. He continues to call for an East Asia Economic Group (EAEG) that would include Japan but not the United States, and the result has been a confrontation with Washington. The latter strongly supports a much wider organization, APEC—the Asia Pacific Economic Cooperation group. It was established in 1989 and includes *all* the Asia Pacific economies: the United States, Australia, New Zealand, and Canada, as well as ASEAN, Japan, China, Taiwan, South Korea, and Hong Kong. As the only regional effort with such wide membership, APEC has impressive promise.

This issue has great potential to be divisive in post–Cold War Asia. Some in Japan, already cool to the United States, are calling for a "return to Asia," and Malaysia's EAEG idea—which may in fact have originated in Tokyo—strongly parallels that notion. It has already disturbed U.S.–Malaysian relations and caused difficulty for official Tokyo as well: Japan hardly wants to face a "choice" between East Asia and the United States. Indonesia's skillful foreign minister, Ali Alatas, understands this problem and has used his influence in ASEAN to tone down the EAEG idea. It is now referred to as a "caucus" rather than a "group," but the issue will continue to trouble U.S.–Asian relations. One reason is that Dr. Mahathir can cite Washington's interest in a North American trade bloc as reason for Asia to establish its own—without the United States.

The Malaysian proposal reflects other irritants that Dr. Mahathir often directs especially at the United States. An example is his campaign against "environmental extremists": he calls them oblivious to the needs of developing nations. Thus at the 1992 Rio summit on the global environment, Malaysia charged the United States with seeking to impose its environmental views unilaterally on the rest of the world. (Ironically, the main Rio criticism of the United States was that it gave insufficient support to environmental causes.) Likewise, Mahathir has argued that the United States's stress on human rights in foreign policy shows it is oblivious to the "special" conditions of developing nations, particularly in Asia. On this he may gain support: Few governments anywhere share this concern over human rights, and Asia's often authoritarian regimes strongly resist what they see as interference in their internal affairs.

In sum, Malaysian foreign policy since Mahathir has become something of a loose cannon, reflecting little professionalism but much anti-U.S. tendentiousness.[24] When the USSR was still prominent, Malaysia was increasingly sympathetic to its presence in the Pacific region. Malaysia argued that Asia's needs would not be well served if only the United States was strong in the area, and its military became newly receptive to the USSR as a supplier of aircraft and other equipment. That interest has not ended with Moscow's decline: In 1992 Kuala Lumpur announced that although U.S.-built aircraft are far more advanced, Malaysia would nevertheless purchase cheaper MIG–29s from Moscow. Other, more petty anti-U.S. manifestations include a studied inability by Malaysia's military leaders to find time to meet with the visiting commander of U.S. forces in the Pacific. Such steps must reflect a deep leadership resentment and ignorance of everything American; especially odd since Malaysia long had good relations with the United States and now sells it $6 billion annually—only slightly less than to Japan.[25]

■ THE PHILIPPINES AND SINGAPORE: FOREIGN POLICY POLAR OPPOSITES

If Malaysian diplomacy appears increasingly amateurish and in its economic relations with the United States even self-defeating, the archetypical example of the species is the Philippines. In contrast to the foreign policy professionals in Bangkok, who worry so much about national security that they sometimes respond to every change in the wind, Manila has had no foreign policy design or leadership at all. The reason is easy to understand. With the U.S. Navy and Air Force in the Philippines and Filipinos' emotional connection with the United States, which predates even the World War II comradeship of Bataan and Corregidor, no Filipino has ever had to worry for a moment about foreign threats to national security.

In that respect the Philippines is diametrically opposite from Singapore, which never takes national security for granted. When it established its armed forces and looked for training and advice from another small state whose big neighbors might like it to disappear, Singapore turned to Israel. Similarly, when Manila set out to underline *its* independence—by insisting that the United States take away its military bases—it was Singapore that told the United States its Navy and Air Force could use bases in Singapore instead.[26]

A main explanation for Manila's behavior is a sense that, like Malaysia, its independence is less genuine because it was handed over. There was an armed Filipino struggle for independence from Spain at the end of the nineteenth century, but the Spanish-American War, and Dewey's defeat of the Spanish fleet at Manila Bay, ended it. Filipinos had seen the United States as liberator; instead the liberator "took" the Philippines and, with much brutality and great loss of Filipino lives, snuffed out the independence movement. Then, for forty years until Japan's invasion brought it to an end—and despite the United States's many misgivings about the morality of its own colonialism—the United States imposed on the Philippines its language, its culture, and its strategic and economic interests.

The result was a growing Philippine nationalism that was resentful of, and at the same time exploitative of the United States. Almost from the start of the postwar era, its focus was the presence on Philippine territory of that nation's largest naval station—at Subic Bay—as well as its expansive holdings at Clark Air Force Base. These and other installations, including one devoted to live-fire bombing exercises, ensured that the "bases issue" became both a cause around which to build much antiestablishment sentiment and the dominant subject of Philippine foreign policy thinking. True, Manila joined SEATO in 1954, and even before that it signed a Mutual Defense Treaty with the United States. But for most Filipino writers, educators, and intellectuals, such steps were more proof the United States controlled their politics and chose their presidents—and in the early postwar years there was evidence to support that argument.

Ferdinand Marcos, who became president in 1966, was clever enough to turn this perception to his own advantage. The United States had long given the Philippines much foreign aid and implicitly recognized the bases as part of the justification, but Marcos insisted on the payment of "rent"— and at that point the U.S.–Philippine alliance changed. No longer could it be said the relationship was one of "mutual" security: Instead it had now become essentially commercial. With that step the bases issue took on new form: Filipinos could now argue, with more justification than ever, that the bases served mainly U.S. interests, and therefore the main question for the Philippines was whether the price was right.

At the same time, Filipinos basked in the guarantee against foreign threat provided not only by the bases but also by their SEATO membership and the U.S. security treaty. Not surprisingly, foreign policy became the least important of all government concerns, and also not surprisingly, it became increasingly irrelevant and irresponsible. Few Filipino professionals were attracted to foreign service. Ambassadorships became even more blatantly political appointments than in the United States, and little serious intellectual or academic thought was given to issues of international or Asian politics. Beyond rhetorical comment about "rejoining

Asia" and exhortations regarding the value of greater "regional cooperation," there was no Philippine foreign policy.

It was largely in that shallow spirit that Manila became a founder of
ASA in 1961 and ASEAN in 1967. The result was that the Philippines' leaders were rarely taken seriously by their regional partners, and for good reason—what passed for a Philippine foreign policy "debate" was usually little
more than a question of who had spoken most flamboyantly against the
bases. Consequently, when Marcos finally was deposed and Mrs. Corazon
Aquino became president in the People Power Revolution, which included
the most emotional of the antibase forces, the ending of U.S. base rights became almost a foregone conclusion. At one point, as the two sides haggled
over how much the United States would pay to stay in the Philippines, Mrs.
Aquino refused even to see the visiting U.S. secretary of defense. Then nature intervened in the form of a 1991 volcanic eruption that destroyed much
of the immediate usefulness of Clark Air Force Base and also affected Subic
Bay Naval Station. With that event, which occurred simultaneously with the
collapse of the Soviet Union, the monetary value of the bases also collapsed,
and the United States announced that yes, it would leave.

Today the Philippines has accomplished its most earnest and long-
sought foreign policy goal: The United States has closed the bases. Sadly,
just before a presidential election in which she did not run, President
Aquino made frantic last-minute efforts to turn the issue around. But they
were marked by the same ineptitude that characterized not only her administration but Philippine foreign policy generally and came to nothing.
Ironically, the new president, to whom she gratefully turned over power—
Gen. Fidel Ramos—does have reason to understand national security issues. A graduate of West Point, he had never been among those demanding the departure of the United States and had long directed the battle
against guerrillas who call themselves "communist." But as he came to office in 1992, General Ramos faced a profoundly changed foreign policy
environment, lacking not only the money and security the bases had provided but also much of a foreign policy tradition on which to call.

Tiny Singapore—largely because it is tiny—is not so unprepared. It
has set out to make itself a remarkably prosperous homeland for its own
small population and something of major value to its neighbors. It has become a financial, commercial, and supply center for the region, as well as
an intellectual base—especially with regard to international security issues.
Much of this success reflects the impressive energies and intellect of Lee
Kwan Yew, Singapore's dominant and recently retired prime minister. His
domestic accomplishments were formidable, but foreign policy issues—
shaped by *realpolitik*—were never far from his mind. His approach to U.S.
efforts in the Vietnam War perfectly reflected his broader understanding of
international politics. Lee strongly supported the U.S. war effort because he

understood it represented a commitment of U.S. credibility. But he also recognized it had been an error to invest there in the first place. As he once put it, "Now that you have gotten on the tram, you must stay on until the last stop."

Before and since his retirement, Lee's voice has been the clearest and most consistent in Asia calling for a continued U.S. security presence. When the USSR was a factor in the region, Lee understood it was up to no good and drew constant attention to Moscow's troubling presence at Cam Ranh Bay. Even so, as a commercial enterprise, Soviet ships—no doubt heavily fitted out with electronic gear—were allowed at Singapore's repair facilities. As the defense minister once put it to me, "we let them dock here, but not too close to American ships."

The same realistic pragmatism has applied to Lee's—and Singapore's—approach to Japan. Whereas others continue to rail emotionally and without conviction at the unlikely prospect of a revival of Japanese militarism, Singapore has taken a different tack. Lee and others have stressed that Japan's Asian presence is a fact of life and that Japan and everyone else should treat that reality with maturity. Thus, to the Japanese he has consistently stressed the need to make a public, clear, and official apology for their World War II actions. Only in that way, he has said repeatedly, can the issue be put behind them "once and for all," and only on that basis can others in the region begin to treat Japan with a greater degree of trust than now.

But the core element in Singapore's approach—which in many ways encapsulates most of Asia's serious thinking about the post–Cold War era—pertains to the United States. Singapore recognizes, as U.S. leaders regularly insist, that the United States' most important political and security relationship is with Japan. That is a main reason Lee has so often urged the Japanese to close the book on World War II: He understands the resentment U.S. citizens still feel about Pearl Harbor, and he recognizes as well that it lies at the heart of much of their trade-related anger with Japan. It is for that reason that Singapore's leaders increasingly stress that if the U.S.–Japan connection stays close, there is little for Southeast Asians to worry about in the era after the Cold War. But if that relationship should sour, and if—as must then be expected—Japan were to rearm because it no longer felt safe under the U.S. security umbrella, all manner of tragedy would come to the Pacific.[27]

The end of the Cold War, in other words, has not lifted a security threat, in Southeast Asian thinking. As in other regions, it has only brought to new light much older strands of national interest. The question for Southeast Asians, as this chapter has aimed to show, is whether their widely different foreign policy traditions and levels of skill will enable them to handle that new challenge coherently and with sophistication.

Like the challenge they faced in the Cold War era, the new challenge has an economic as well as a politicosecurity dimension. In the Cold War era, the main economic challenge was to find the right path toward *internal* improvement. That has largely been accomplished: There is widespread agreement that export-led development, market forces, and intensive involvement with the global economy are most likely to achieve material well-being for their peoples. Each state has now embarked on that path; even Vietnam, as it seeks to emulate the progress its ASEAN neighbors have made, now searches for private foreign investment.

The new, post–Cold War economic challenge is more *external* in its focus. Here the question is bound up with the roles of Japan and the United States, the economic giants of the world and the region. The latter, with its massive, open market, has been the key to the region's success in achieving export-led development; the export accomplishments of Malaysia, Thailand, and Singapore are the clearest evidence of that U.S. role. But now, many in Southeast Asia fear that as the United States concludes its North American Free Trade Agreement accord with Mexico and Canada (and talks of building other free trade areas in the Western Hemisphere), it appears to be moving away from Southeast Asia just as the other giant, Japan, is moving in again. How to relate to these two giants—whether and how to keep the United States involved or whether, as Malaysia proposes, to cast their lot with Japan —represents the greatest economic challenge to Southeast Asians in the new era.

Of course, that issue involves political and security questions as well, and it is in this respect that the politicosecurity dimension today is so much more complicated than in the Cold War years. Then the main threat was communism, both internal and externally supported. That issue at least had a coherence rooted in Marxism-Leninism. Now that threat—as well as the certainty of a reassuring U.S. presence to counter it—is largely gone, but the security threats are not. The most troubling comes from China: Its unyielding stance toward the Spratly Islands and Vietnam reflects that great-power arrogance that all Southeast Asians have experienced and most fear. Indeed, China today evokes memories of earlier times, when it expected deference from the small nations on its southern rim. But to build security against Beijing means to depend on others, and in an era when there is no longer a USSR, that means, once again, Japan and the United States. Would Southeast Asians therefore welcome, even promote, Japan's rearmament? Does it mean to encourage the return of U.S. bases, and if so, when? Does it mean those in the region should embark on large and very extensive armaments programs, which will take the money so much needed for their people? As the king said in *Anna*, "It is a puzzlement!"

■ NOTES

1. In 1965–1966, Indonesia brutally suppressed and outlawed its domestic Communists, broke relations with China, and sharply cooled its ties with the USSR. For the origins of ASEAN and its predecessor groups, known as ASA and "Maphilindo," see Bernard K. Gordon, *The Dimensions of Conflict in Southeast Asia* (Prentice-Hall, 1966).

2. One of the most persistent and misleading myths of the Vietnam War era is that Cambodia had been peaceful and immune from the war until the U.S. extended the fighting there. The U.S. did bomb areas of eastern Cambodia adjacent to Vietnam and in 1970 briefly launched what President Nixon called an "incursion" into those areas. The reason in both cases was hopefully to interfere with Vietnam's flagrant violation of Cambodia's neutrality and use of its territory to supply and move Vietnamese troops from the north into South Vietnam. Hanoi began this practice in the mid-1960s at the latest, and it was the Cambodian leader at the time (Prince Sihanouk) who regularly asked publicly that the Vietnamese stop. He visited Moscow in 1970 to ask that the Soviets press Vietnam on the issue, and was literally on his way to China for the same purpose, when he was overthrown in a *coup* arranged by officers who were disgusted both by internal corruption, and by his inability to prevent Vietnamese use of Cambodian territory.

3. A discussion of the foreign policy environment surrounding the establishment of ASEAN is in Bernard K. Gordon, *Toward Disengagement in Asia: A Strategy for American Foreign Policy* (Prentice-Hall, 1969).

4. Average per capita GDP figures are useful to *compare* one nation with another, and they also can show change over time in a particular nation, but they should be used with caution. A per capita GDP figure does not necessarily mean that the "average" person in each country earns that amount, because income distribution is uneven in all countries and especially in developing nations. In this paragraph, ASEAN data is from *ASEAN-Japan Statistical Pocketbook 1991,* ASEAN Center, Tokyo, and Japan data from *U.S. and Japan in Figures,* Japan External Trade Organization (JETRO), 1991.

5. The term "Khmer Rouge" means merely "Red (i.e., Communist) Cambodians." It was coined by Prince Sihanouk, the first leader of independent Cambodia, as early as the late 1950s, and by the early 1960s he was using it in everyday speech. Sihanouk's aim was to criticize those native Cambodians (Khmer) who, with Vietnam's support, were opposing him and who he believed—correctly—sought his overthrow. In fact, almost all the Cambodian communists were linked to the Vietnamese, and many had been trained there. Some were more politically aligned than others with Hanoi. The more radical, especially those who had not been trained in Vietnam, were—like most Khmer—bitterly anti-Vietnamese. All were communists and therefore by definition "Khmer Rouge." The world knows the term "Khmer Rouge" as a synonym for the butchers who murdered hundreds of thousands, perhaps a million, of their own people while they ruled Cambodia from 1975–1978. The massacres were aimed to "cleanse" the nation of anyone who might have beliefs or connections less radical than the leadership's. Thus anyone who spoke French was a target, on the presumption such a person carried foreign ideas. Those who wore glasses were also suspect and often murdered on the assumption they could read foreign materials.

6. This point is also made by Michael Leifer: "The ostensible purpose of establishing ASEAN was to promote economic, social, and cultural cooperation but regional security was the prime preoccupation of its founders" (*ASEAN and the*

Security of South-East Asia, Routledge, London and New York, 1989, p. 1). I should note, however, that in the 1990s, Thailand has also taken the lead in promoting an ASEAN "free trade area." If successful, it will represent the first meaningful effort in ASEAN economic cooperation.

7. Leifer, *ibid.,* p. 97.

8. A good discussion of Thai policy is in Khatharya Um, "Thailand and the Dynamics of Economic and Security Complex in Mainland Southeast Asia," *Contemporary Southeast Asia,* December 1991, pp. 245–270.

9. It should be said that these actions came from a Thai government sometimes regarded by Thais as too "left-leaning" at the time and ousted in a *coup* not long afterward.

10. The settlement is threatened because the Khmer Rouge—though no longer in power—remains an armed force with continuing and even growing political support. Much of its endurance stems from its capacity for terror, backed by large *caches* of Chinese weapons. Every Cambodian knows the Khmer Rouge was responsible for mass murders from 1976–1978, but it is also known for its strong stand against Vietnam: Cambodia's most hated and feared historical enemy. If the Khmer Rouge comes to power again, that will be the main reason.

11. Details of the Thai military's business activities were reported in *The Economist* of July 11, 1992, and *The Financial Times* of July 14, 1992. Ironically, the 1990 *coup* that brought the civilian coalition initially to power was itself the work of generals parading as reformers. They charged that other officers had carried corruption to unbearable limits, but a cynic might say they merely had concluded it was *their* time to share in the spoils. As one general put it in a remark about the wife of another, "she has become a walking jewelry box."

12. Among other problems, few of Thailand's soldiers know how to do anything other than make money. On the very few occasions when the Thai military has been in or close to combat—as in the Vietnam War—it did not distinguish itself as a fighting force.

13. Indonesia's population is overwhelmingly Muslim, but so-called Islamic fundamentalism—though it has attempted a political role—has not been successful. The army in particular puts it down, and the composition of the army's leadership itself reflects Indonesia's commitment to religious tolerance. Stemming from their early training at Dutch-established schools, many senior officers are Catholic, and a number are Lutheran Protestant.

14. The Soviets were associated with Indonesia's navy and to some extent its air force, whereas the U.S. wisely chose to build its links with the much larger and more important army of Indonesia.

15. Indonesia's official view is that the PKI—with strong and secret support from China (but not the USSR)—attempted to destroy the army leadership and take power. Some U.S. and other Western analysts dispute this and argue that the army itself provoked the coup in order to destroy the Communists. I consider that view not persuasive, not least because several of the army's top leaders were killed on the night of the coup, and only a very close call allowed General Suharto, today and since then Indonesia's president, to escape.

16. Leo Suryadinata, "Indonesia-Vietnam Relations Under Soeharto," in *Contemporary Southeast Asia,* March 1991, pp. 331–346. This is one of the very few discussions of the Jakarta-Hanoi connection, and as Suryadinata points out, it has been more often Indonesia than Vietnam that has stressed the commonality in their backgrounds. A good illustration came in 1990, when President Suharto visited Hanoi. A leading Indonesian newspaper remarked that the two nations' common struggle against colonialists was the reason Jakarta had never broken relations with Hanoi.

17. Suryadinata, *ibid.*, p. 338, makes the point that the Indonesian military was particularly sympathetic to Hanoi's Indochina aspirations, partly because it saw in that effort a parallel with Indonesia's own needs to assure continued control over East Timor.

18. Quoted by Suryadinata, *ibid.* p. 338.

19. I discussed those attitudes in "Asian Angst: The U.S. in Asian Eyes," *Foreign Policy,* Summer 1982.

20. The history is discussed in Richard Stubbs, "Malaysian Defence Policy: Strategy versus Structure," *Contemporary Southeast Asia,* June 1991, pp. 44–56.

21. Some of the origins of ZOPFAN are explained in Mutiah Alagappa, "Regional Arrangements and International Security in Southeast Asia: Going/Beyond ZOPFAN," *Contemporary Southeast Asia* (Singapore), March 1991, pp. 269–305. He explains there that the concept was entirely born of Malaysia's "own circumstances and concerns," that it was met with a cool response from Indonesia and came as a "bombshell" with no warning to the other ASEAN foreign ministers.

22. He has said he wanted a political career from the outset, but the only available scholarship for a poor young man was in medicine, so he took that.

23. On another occasion he created a major furor when the nonpolitical president of Israel, who had been on an Asian visit that also included the Philippines, paid a similar visit to Singapore. Dr. Mahathir's government called that a direct affront, and made it clear Kuala Lumpur would not tolerate a repetition of the "offense" by its smaller neighbor.

24. Stubbs (*ibid.,* p. 51) notes that in Malaysia, "security decisionmaking can be 'highly political and irrational. . . . the voices at security meetings . . . may not be savvy about security and defence matters,'" quoting Noraini Haji Abdullah, "Leadership in Malaysia: Security Perceptions and Policies," in M. Ayoob and Chai-anan Samudavanija, *Leadership Perceptions and National Security* (Singapore: Institute of Southeast Asian Studies, 1989, p. 149).

25. On the same day as his vitriolic UN attack on the United States in 1991, Prime Minister Mahathir went across town in New York and appealed for more U.S. investment in his country. No doubt U.S. investors make their decisions principally on economic grounds, but it is difficult to believe their advisors are totally unconcerned with a Malaysian leadership that regards the United States and its values as the principal problem in today's world.

26. By mid-1992, after the transfer of the U.S. Seventh Fleet Logistic Command from the Philippines to Singapore, shipyards there were already doing a thriving business repairing naval vessels previously attended to at Subic (*Japan Times,* August 9, 1992).

27. One of many of Lee's comments on this point is reported in Chin Kin Wah, "Changing Global Trends and Their Effects on the Asia-Pacific," in *Contemporary Southeast Asia,* June 1991, p. 7.

■ 8

U.S. Power and Policy: Choices in the Pacific Region

Steve Chan

Concerns with change versus continuity have always occupied a central place in the research agenda of international relations analysts. Events such as the rise of Japan as a global economic power, the reunification of Germany, and the merger of the European Community after 1992 tend to abet speculations about a possible basic transformation of the international system and about the policy implications of such a transformation for the United States. These speculations have dwelled considerably on the extent, causes, and consequences of a decline in U.S. power in the world political economy. In this chapter I address one particularly popular formulation on this subject. It examines the analytic foundation and policy implications of the hegemonic stability theory, with particular reference to the Asia Pacific region. In this examination, several competing theories on international political economy will be introduced to offer contrasting perspectives.

■ WINDS OF CHANGE

It is somewhat ironic that the popularity of the hegemonic stability theory has coincided with the onset of East-West détente, the disintegration of communist regimes in Eastern Europe, and the reorientation of the socialist systems toward market economics. Thus, while the United States' chief ideological rivals seek international accommodation from a position much weakened by their severe domestic political and economic problems, concerns about the United States' power and policy have mounted concomitantly. Curiously, these concerns about the United States's world position have not abated substantially as a result of Washington's recent leading role in organizing the United Nations efforts to force Saddam Hussein out of Kuwait.

In the Pacific region, perceptions of a declining United States have undoubtedly been motivated to a large extent by the emergence of Japan as a formidable economic and technological contender. Following Japan's example, the other Asian NICs—such as South Korea, Taiwan, Singapore, and China—have established a strong commercial edge that has brought about substantial deficits for the United States in its bilateral trade with these countries. As the Asians increasingly dominate the U.S. market in a variety of product lines from textiles to electronics to automobiles, U.S. analysts begin to realize that their comparative advantage has shifted to the export of agricultural products (e.g., wheat, beef, oranges, wine, tobacco, lumber). Thus, there is a sense that the international division of labor is undergoing rapid and perhaps fundamental changes; the U.S. seems to be losing its manufacturing and technological competitiveness, whereas the Asian "trading nations" (Rosecrance 1986) continue to reach for higher stages in the international product cycle.

Surely, the "lessons of Vietnam" also weighed heavily on a sense of a U.S. decline. The general military retrenchment from Asia initiated under the Nixon doctrine and the shattered domestic consensus on foreign policy (Holsti and Rosenau 1984) have contributed to a more pluralistic and decentralized vision of international relations, where military force becomes a less prominent and acceptable tool of statecraft and where transnational politics among nongovernmental groups play a more important role (Keohane and Nye 1977). Understandably, in the context of the Pacific region, this vision is buttressed by several concomitant processes. The trends toward increasing interpenetration of product markets, crisscrossing investment patterns, monetary linkages, and technology transfers enhance the development of transnational networks of economic and cultural interactions and interests. At the same time, the processes of political and economic liberalization in some authoritarian regimes on the western Pacific Rim (e.g., South Korea, Taiwan, Thailand and, indeed, China) enable the formation of domestic interest groups that have a vested stake in deepening "complex interdependence." Finally, the onset of détente has diminished the premium placed on U.S. military protection by its Asian allies, whereas the revival of nationalism in countries such as South Korea, the Philippines, and Japan (e.g., Morita and Ishihara 1990) has obviously made subservience to Washington's hegemony less politically acceptable.

■ HEGEMONIC STABILITY

Charles Kindleberger (1973) is usually credited as the major advocate of the hegemonic stability theory. In his study of the causes of the Great

Depression, the absence of an international leader was given the most importance. During the interwar years, Great Britain was no longer able and the United States not yet willing to assume this leadership role. No other government had the wherewithal *and* the foresight to step forward to stabilize the international monetary order, serve as a lender of last resort, or open its domestic market to counteract sagging economic demand abroad. Instead, each country practiced a policy of "beggar thy neighbor," whereby their actions precipitated competitive currency devaluation and protectionist recrimination. Their myopic policies, according to Kindleberger, increased the severity and prolonged the duration of the Great Depression.

Underlying this view of international political economy is the theory of public goods. International peace, stability, and order are seen as public goods. All countries can consume these desiderata simultaneously without diminishing each other's enjoyment. Moreover, once these public goods are provided to any one party, it will be exceedingly difficult and perhaps even impossible to withhold them from others. This latter feature of public goods creates the temptation to free ride, thus accounting for the tendency of alliance leaders to bear a heavier burden for collective defense than their smaller counterparts (Olson and Zeckhauser 1966).

The key point about the hegemonic stability theory is that there must be a hegemon—a single dominant power—to ensure international stability. Only a hegemon can establish the international rules that facilitate orderly exchanges among nations, and punish transgressors with predictable penalties. Only a hegemon has the incentive to provide this public good, as it has the greatest stake in perpetuating the existing international system that gives it the dominant status. And, by definition, only the hegemon has sufficient resources to sustain and enforce an international regime.

The hegemonic stability theory therefore argues that the eras of Pax Britannica and Pax United Americana were characterized generally by peace and prosperity. For example, the institutions of the General Agreement on Tariffs and Trade (GATT) and the Bretton Woods monetary accord, both organized and sustained under U.S. auspices, provided the essential foundation for the remarkable global economic expansion subsequent to World War II. However, the demise of these institutions presages a possible return to the mercantilist practices of the 1920s and 1930s. According to this scenario, the socioeconomic dislocations stemming from the Great Depression contributed to the rise of protectionism, nationalism, militarism, and fascism.

Whereas Kindleberger's (1973) analysis focuses on global economics, other scholars have suggested that a preponderance of power enjoyed by one country helps to maintain international peace. The most well-known formulation is by Organski and Kugler (1980), who argue that wars are least likely to happen when the international distribution of power is lopsidedly in favor of a predominant country. Whether in the form of the

Roman legion or the British navy, a superpower can ensure order and stability. Conversely, armed conflicts among the great powers are most likely
to take place when an established leading nation is overtaken by a late-
comer, such as when Germany became more powerful than Great Britain
at the beginning of this century. Popularly known as the power transition
theory of war, this formulation explains armed conflicts as rear-end colli-
sions—when a hegemon's power declines and a challenger catches up.

Paradoxically, a hegemon's policies tend in the long run to bring
about its own decline (Kindleberger 1981; Krasner 1976; Stein 1984). The
free rides enjoyed by the hegemon's junior partners enable the latter to
catch up, at the same time sapping the hegemon's ability and incentive to
continue the provision of public goods. According to the theory's proponents, the very success of the hegemon's policies in fostering a stable and
open international political economy encourages the expansion of trade,
investment, and technology transfer to the relative advantage of the fol-
lower nations and thus eventually contributes to the hegemon's relative decline. Finally, to the extent that the hegemon's elites hold on to outdated
beliefs and practices—such as the gold standard and a conception of national security based on territorial control and military outreach (e.g.,
Blank 1978; Rosecrance 1986)—this decline is further accelerated. Typically, a heavy defense burden, unrestrained public and private consumption, and underinvestment in production combine to erode the hegemon's
leadership position (Calleo 1982; Kennedy 1987), thus helping to bring
about a power transition in the international system and the discord and
instability that accompany this transition.

■ LOST HEGEMONY OR
PERSISTENT DOMINANCE?

Much has been written about the decline of U.S. power and the challenge of Japan. Books such as *Japan as Number One* (Vogel 1979), *America Versus Japan* (McCraw 1986), *The Eastasia Edge* (Hofheinz and
Calder 1982), and *Trading Places: How We Allowed Japan to Take
the Lead* (Prestowitz 1988) forecast or warn against an ongoing or im-
pending power transition in the Asia Pacific region and perhaps even globally. This message of systemic transformation has been reinforced by
statements from Japanese officials and businessmen, with *The Japan that
Can Say No* (Morita and Ishihara 1990) offering perhaps the most well-
known example.

The leadership position of the United States in international economics and politics has clearly slipped since the days of Washington's
overwhelming superiority immediately following the end of World War II.
But has this slippage been so drastic as to signal a power transition? Does

this relative decline mean that the United States has lost its global dominance or hegemony?

Keohane (1984, p. 33–34) suggests that "to be considered hegemonic in the world political economy . . . a country must have access to crucial raw materials, control major sources of capital, maintain a large market for imports, and hold comparative advantages in goods with high value added, yielding relatively high wages and profits. It must be stronger, on these dimensions taken as a whole, than any other country." These criteria suggest that the United States is still the only credible claimant to the title of hegemon. Its resource base and domestic market far exceed those of Japan and Germany, both of which are highly dependent on foreign raw materials as well as overseas markets. Although the dollar has suffered recurrent setbacks, it still remains the preferred currency for international exchange and finance, thus giving Washington a major advantage in the control of international capital. Finally, although Japan and Germany have closed the wage and technology gaps separating themselves from the United States (and in some cases have even moved ahead), the latter still enjoys an overall edge in these dimensions. Thus, the U.S. position with respect to natural resources, economic size, financial leverage, and technological assets gives it a *combined* advantage over Japan and Germany, which are not able to challenge this U.S. superiority across the board.

Parallel to Keohane's formulation, Strange (1987, p. 565) suggests four elements of *structural power* that buttress and sustain a hegemon's global position: (1) the ability to threaten or protect other countries' physical security by resort to arms; (2) the ability to control the global system of production of goods and services; (3) the ability to shape the international capital market of finance and credit; and (4) the ability to direct the development, accumulation, and transfer of knowledge—defined broadly to include technology as well as ideology (e.g., intellectual fads and fashions).

Neither Japan nor Germany currently possesses the sort of military capabilities required to affect other countries' security. Although both have had significant successes in their overseas commerce, as shown by the rapid rate of their export expansion, U.S. companies still dominate in the international production of goods and services. Whereas the *location* of this production has increasingly moved outside the United States (as shown by the widespread tendency to engage in offshore manufacturing), the ownership and managerial control of these activities have remained in U.S. hands. Moreover, although the United States has experienced significant deficits in its trade balance and although its influence in international monetary and financial matters has clearly slipped a great deal, the dollar remains the dominant currency, and U.S. companies still play a leading role in international syndications for investment and loans. Finally, as attested by the frequency of Nobel Prize awards, U.S. researchers and research centers are still at the forefront in extending the frontiers of basic science.

In light of the above considerations, it is not surprising that on closer inspection, several authors have found the claim of lost U.S. hegemony to be premature and mythical (Nau 1990; Russett 1985; Strange 1987). Even though the *relative* international position of the United States has deteriorated, Washington remains the *prima inter pares* in international relations. A weakening of the United States' *bargaining power* on particular issues or occasions should not be confused with its still considerable *structural power* to influence the rules of international regimes. According to Caporaso (1978, p. 4), "bargaining power is power to control the outcomes of specific events . . . [whereas structural power] is a higher order power because it involves the ability to manipulate the choices, capabilities, alliance opportunities, and payoffs that actors may utilize."

■ PUBLIC GOODS OR PRIVATE GAINS?

As indicated earlier, hegemonic stability theory claims that there must be one dominant power to assure the provision of public goods such as international peace, monetary order, and free trade to the global community. Conversely, the theory contends, the disappearance of a hegemon and the concomitant shortfall in the provision of public goods tend to produce economic nationalism and military strife. However, one may legitimately question the extent to which a hegemon's policies produce public goods as opposed to private gains.

During the days of its domination, Great Britain did not always seek open trade. It was often unwilling to make tariff concessions to its trading partners in order to reduce protectionist barriers and to facilitate the free flow of merchandise (Stein 1984). Similar objections could be raised with respect to the institutional arrangements—such as NATO, GATT, the Bretton Woods monetary accord, and the annual G7 summit meetings—developed under U.S. hegemony. These "regimes" tend to be exclusive clubs of the advanced industrial and especially the North Atlantic countries. Certainly, the socialist countries were excluded from their membership—indeed, the very purpose of some such regimes was to impose a *cordon sanitaire* to contain communism. To a large extent, the less developed countries of Asia, Africa, and Latin America were also outsiders to these institutions. Therefore, the public goods supposedly supplied by the hegemon appear rather exclusionary upon closer examination.

It also appears that although the United States is attracted to the thesis of free-riding allies, the tendency toward an inequitable allocation of alliance burdens, initially observed by Olson and Zeckhauser (1966), has gradually diminished over more recent years. It may be politically expedient to criticize the United States' allies—especially Japan—for not contributing enough to collective welfare. This criticism, however, may often be empirically inaccurate. Thus, for example, if a country's contribution to collective welfare (e.g., global peace, international development, Third World stability, friendliness to the West) is measured by the relative size of its foreign aid program, the United States has consistently ranked close to the bottom among its peers in the Organization of Economic Cooperation and Development (OECD). Conversely, by allocating a higher share of their GNP to foreign aid, most U.S. allies, it may be argued, have assumed a heavier burden in the provision of this public good. Tokyo's expanding foreign aid program, its monetary interventions to provide capital liquidity and currency stability, and its fiscal stimulations to encourage greater domestic consumption belie the image of a myopic trading nation in pursuit of short-term gains (Boyer 1989; Rosecrance and Taw 1990). Thus, the U.S. tendency to focus on military spending as an indicator of collective burden sharing will only produce an outdated as well as partial picture. Moreover, even though the United States paid more dollars than its allies in military deterrence against communism, its allies paid more in territory and lives (Russett 1985).

The typical U.S. self-image also tends to be quite self-serving. It is rather more gratifying to see oneself as a generous provider of public goods than as a myopic egoist in pursuit of private gains. As mentioned earlier, a stable and orderly international monetary regime is considered a public good. To what extent have U.S. policies enabled this public good and to what extent have they exploited it? Beset by chronic budgetary and trade deficits, Washington has taken advantage of the dollar's premier position by exporting its domestic inflation and thus, in effect, forcing its trading partners to pay for its own fiscal extravagances. Without any international consultation, it suddenly and unilaterally announced in 1971 the cancellation of its longstanding commitment to convert dollars to gold (consequently bringing about an immediate and sharp devaluation of the dollar holdings of its trading partners). Strange's (1987, p. 568–569) commentary on this incident is especially instructive:

> In most countries, whether the balance-of-payments is in surplus or deficit indicates the strength or weakness of its financial position. With the United States, the exact converse can be true. Indeed, to run a persistent deficit for a quarter of a century with impunity indicates not American weakness, but rather American power in the system. To decide one August [1971] morning that dollars can no longer be converted into gold was a progression from exorbitant privilege to super-exorbitant privilege; the U.S. government was exercising the unconstrained right to print money that others could not (save at unacceptable cost) refuse to accept in payment.

The United States not only is the world's banker and treasurer, it also has had almost exclusive access to the printing press to issue new money. It is almost as if someone who cannot balance his expenditures with his income is able to keep putting off the necessary payments by giving himself ever larger lines of credit.

If hegemons indeed provide public goods such as peace and stability, they also tend to benefit most from the resulting international order. The regimes established by the hegemons, in other words, tend to promote rather than diminish their continued dominance. Thus, Russett (1985, p. 218) remarked, "[i]f one looks not at narrow issue-area regimes but at broad aspects of the international environment after World War II, one has to be impressed by the degree to which perceived U.S. interests, not just the interests of all states, were served."

Without much exaggeration, one can argue that the United States has won the Cold War. With few exceptions, such as Vietnam and Cuba, the containment policy worked. And, beyond the wildest expectations and fondest dreams of the advocates of this policy, communism was in a sense "rolled back" (though as a result less of foreign pressure than of domestic dynamics). The Soviet Union has been forced to quite literally relinquish its empire in Eastern Europe and has, along with its erstwhile Warsaw Pact allies and China, turned toward market economics and a reintegration into the capitalist world system. As the world's largest economy, biggest foreign investor, and leading technological power, the United States has the most to gain from this "opening" of the socialist economies. Just as the previous decolonization of European and Japanese possessions after World War II offered it access to various Third World markets and sources of raw materials, the United States is likely to benefit more than the Europeans and Japanese in the new commercial opportunities created by East-West détente.

In addition to military capability and industrial competitiveness, a country's ideological influence in the world is a key element of its power base. Under Pax Americana, the United States was able to promote its cultural dominance through the spread of the English language, the U.S. style of education, and the "American way of life." Sometimes called "coca-colonization," this less tangible but nevertheless basic component of U.S. power could not be matched by either Japan or Germany. In the words of a former official in the Reagan administration (Nau 1990, p. 11),

> Studies that focus primarily on power and politics exaggerate the costs of continuing American leadership in the world economy. They overlook the more homogenous political world in which America seeks to exert its power today, and they pay too little attention to the content of American economic policies that can enhance American power and to the market mechanisms by which America can less visibly and less expensively assert its power.

It does seem that in many respects a hegemon's policies produce private goods for itself. As remarked by Russett (1985, p. 231), "the characterization of hegemonic United States as predominantly supplying itself and others with collective goods is inaccurate. Even for those goods which can correctly be called collective the United States has not paid at all disproportionate costs." Moreover, these costs have been well worthwhile because they have been "recouped many times over" by offsetting gains.

■ CONFOUNDING CAUSE AND EFFECT?

The hegemonic stability theory argues that a hegemon's policies help bring about peace and order, which in turn foster global prosperity and the formation of security community. Thus, for example, its advocates claim that British and U.S. leadership in trade liberalization were responsible for the impressive global economic expansion in the late nineteenth century and mid-twentieth century, respectively. Concomitantly, the absence of a hegemon is alleged to have caused the economic contraction and trade discord during the late 1920s and early 1930s.

It is, however, possible to reverse the chain of cause and effect as presented by the hegemonic stability theory. One can plausibly argue that an expanding global economy, not British or U.S. hegemony, produces a more liberal trading regime. As countries experience domestic prosperity, they feel less need or pressure to engage in protectionism. Conversely, a declining global economy—such as the one during the Great Depression, characterized by banking panic, falling stock prices, weakening domestic demand, and severe deflationary pressure—inclines each country to adopt mercantilist policies of "beggar thy neighbor." According to this reasoning, macroeconomic conditions, not hegemonic power, tend to influence national policies. With respect to the recent rise in global protectionism, this argument suggests that the cause lies more with a weakening international economy than with a declining United States—even though the economic health of the latter, being the dominant power, also obviously affects the international economy.

But what causes a hegemon's power to decline? Proponents of the hegemonic stability theory point to the free-riding behavior of the secondary powers as a main reason. The latter countries supposedly exploit the generosity of the hegemon and benefit from the asymmetric exchanges that eventually sap the hegemon's willingness and capability to provide public goods. Here again, however, one could argue that the causes of hegemonic decline lie more with internal policies than external conditions.

As shown most dramatically in Lyndon Johnson's decision to pursue both the Vietnam War and the Great Society programs without raising taxes, successive U.S. administrations—with only partial exception of Ronald Reagan's (Russett 1982)—have persistently chosen to have both "guns" and "butter." In Calleo's (1982) words, these policies are tantamount to attempting to "get a quart out of a pint pot"—at the cost of abetting inflationary pressure, currency speculation, and ever increasing budgetary deficits. In 1991 these deficits are projected to rise to about $280 billion, and interest payments on national debt (about $216 billion) would represent the third-biggest spending item for the U.S. government, after social security and defense. These fiscal allocations give current consumption by both the public and private sectors precedence over future productivity. Capital investment and civilian exports suffer accordingly, because physical and human resources are diverted from long-range research and development to support immediate expenditures on defense and welfare.

Thus, the rise and fall of great powers seem from this perspective to be not so much products of some inexorable processes of uneven growth or differential technological change. These processes need themselves to be explained in terms of group dynamics, national purpose, and policy choices (e.g., Nau 1990; Olson 1982). Institutional sclerosis, distributional politics, and electoral cycling offer a more persuasive explanation of the poor policy performance by some political economies, hegemonic or otherwise. However, effort mobilization, institutional continuity, and policy adaptation must surely be a part of any explanation to account for the upward status mobility of other countries in the international system (Bobrow and Chan 1986). In other words, the environmental structure is a relevant but secondary variable in explaining cycles of leadership change (Modelski 1987); the primary influence has ultimately to be sought in the actor's purpose and choices.

■ PARTISAN MUTUAL ADJUSTMENT

Do chaos and discord necessarily have to follow in the wake of hegemonic decline? There is, of course, a large literature that associates international peace and stability with a diffused distribution of capabilities among the major national contestants and correlates international war and turmoil with a concentration of power in the possession of one country. The basic premise of the balance of power school (e.g., Morgenthau 1978) is that no country can be trusted with too much power and that the best antidote to any country's drive to increase its power is counterpower by other countries. According to this theory, war is prevented when there tends to be rough parity in the capabilities of the major countries. No one country has sufficient power to overwhelm its opponents, and every country is accordingly deterred from aggression because of the uncertainty of victory and the fear of defeat. Conversely, war is most likely to break out when government officials perceive that their country has a substantial capability edge over its rivals and thus feel that their aggression against others will be rewarded.

The empirical evidence is rather mixed with regard to the arguments of the balance of power theory and its rival, the power transition theory. In a particularly well-known analysis, Singer et al. (1972) hypothesized that if the balance of power theory is valid, fewer wars should be found during historical periods when the international system was characterized by a rough equivalence in the capabilities of countries, when capability changes were in the direction of greater parity, and when the international power hierarchy was relatively fluid. If instead the power transition theory is valid, they reasoned, they should find *more* wars during these periods. These authors discovered sharply divergent data patterns for the nineteenth and the twentieth centuries. Although the balance of power theory is better able to account for the occurrence of war during the nineteenth century, the power transition theory is more valid for the twentieth century. In the current century, therefore, when a leading country enjoys a preponderance of power, peace is more likely to prevail—as the hegemonic stability theory would predict. However, this theory's expectations are not supported by the patterns of war occurrence during the past century, when such preponderance actually led to more, not less, armed conflict.

Thus, it seems that hegemonic rule has not historically been a necessary condition for international order and stability. In fact, there is substantial theoretical and experimental evidence to suggest that self-interested actors can readily coordinate their policies for greater mutual gain. This collaboration can take place even in the absence of central guidance.

"Partisan mutual adjustment" describes political processes in a decentralized system where egoists compete for resources and where each egoist has the ability to help as well as hinder the others' goal achievement (Lindblom 1965). In this system, neither common purpose nor central authority offers guidance for allocating resources among the parties. The hallmarks of this system are instead partisanship, interdependence, and coordination. A partisan is someone who has an independent agenda and a private set of policy standards and assumes that others have theirs. Partisan actors believe that there are genuine disagreements about ends and means and that these disagreements cannot be resolved by appeals to known standards or universally accepted criteria. Interdependence means that given a set of actors, each one's pursuit of its interests impinges, whether out of necessity or inadvertence, on others' pursuit of their interests. Coordination refers to a set of interdependent decisions in which "each decision is adapted to the others in such a way that for each adjusted decision, the adjustment is thought to be better than no adjustment in the eyes of at least one decision maker" (Lindblom, 1965, p. 24). This coordination takes place without a centralized plan but emerges naturally out of experience, learning, and anticipation among the actors as a result of their frequent interaction.

The perspective of partisan mutual adjustment is obviously more suitable for a world of complex interdependence (Keohane and Nye 1977) than a world of hegemonic dominance. It addresses a world in which military power recedes from the center stage of international relations, where transnational linkages and nontraditional issues proliferate, where multiple policy agendas and crosscutting cleavages fragment familiar coalitions, and where the status rankings of countries become more fluid and less consistent across various capability dimensions. Competing interests, shifting alliances, reciprocal (even though often asymmetrical) sensitivities and vulnerabilities, weak and leaky regimes, and the necessity of mutual adaptation are the prevalent conditions of complex interdependence.

Such conditions do not necessarily mean chaos and disorder in international relations. In fact, even egoists have a collective interest in institutionalizing the rules governing their interactions and in eschewing defection in order take advantage of longer-term gains. These considerations led Keohane (1984, p. 221) to conclude that "[c]ooperation among independent governments in the absence of hegemony, to achieve joint gains, is possible, and . . . regimes can facilitate such cooperation by reducing transaction costs, providing information, and constructing rules of thumb to guide bureaucracies in making routine decisions." Lindblom (1965) went even further by arguing that, far from bringing upon themselves a Hobbesian world, actors tend in fact to be more strongly motivated to seek agreement, to search for coalition partners, and to move toward conditions of Pareto optimality in a situation of partisan mutual adjustment than in a situation of centralized coordination or hegemonic domination. By treating collective decisionmaking as a fragmented remedial process and by allowing multiple actors to become watchdogs for different particularistic interests, partisan mutual adjustment lowers the probability of political impasse and inefficient resource allocation.

Indeed, it would appear that the policy relevance of partisan mutual adjustment rises as a function of the complexity of issues, the variety of interests, and the multiplicity of actors at hand. The resulting system of decentralized interaction does not ban competition or rivalry among the participants, nor does it assure an equitable distribution of payoff among them. However, it is less likely in this system for the adverse consequences of any decision to go unnoticed or for the particularistic interests of any major actor to be unprotected. Indeed, Axelrod's (1984) well-known game theoretic evidence from experimentation with prisoners' dilemma suggests that the "shadow of the future" inclines egoists to eschew defection and to initiate cooperation, lest their myopic actions set off an "echo chamber" of mutual recrimination and collective disaster.

In short, hegemonic decline does not necessarily have to be followed by international anarchy. Historical as well as experimental data suggest that under certain conditions, cooperation can occur and indeed flourish in a decentralized and pluralistic system. Collaboration among egoists is possible and even likely in a situation of complex interdependence, whereby compromises and side payments are facilitated to the extent that there exists a dense network of interlocking ties, crosscutting (as opposed to overlapping) cleavages among the actors, and a large issue set that lends itself to policy linkages (Tollison and Willett 1979).

■ CONCLUSION

This essay has examined the theory of hegemonic stability as it applies to the U.S. position in the world system in general and in the Asia Pacific region in particular. Although acknowledging a relative decline in U.S. power, it has questioned the extent to which this relative decline has produced or is likely to produce in the near future a power transition between the United States and Japan. Moreover, it challenges this theory's premise that a hegemon's policies necessarily produce public goods and that its decline tends to be accompanied by international strife and discord. Finally, it suggests that adjustments in international power rankings are ultimately the product of human action and political choice, not the result of some impersonal processes.

It is plausible that a more equal distribution of capabilities among the major countries can incline the secondary powers to assume a greater role in contributing to collective welfare (Snidal 1985). Thus, to the extent that a relative decline in U.S. power has been offset by a concomitant status rise on the part of Japan and Germany, the latter two countries should now have more stake in and thus greater incentives to buttress the current international order. They will accordingly increase their relative contribution to the provision of international peace, monetary stability, financial liquidity, and free trade. This new and enhanced Japanese and German role is already quite noticeable in the G7's collective management of the Third World's debt crises during the 1980s and the Iraq-Kuwait conflict during 1990–1991.

In the Asia Pacific region, one may more appropriately speak of an emergent *bigemony* (i.e., shared hegemony) between the United States and Japan. Whereas the former continues to be the principal military power, the latter has increasingly become a primary source of technology and capital for its neighbors. Japan also absorbs the bulk of its neighbors' exports of foodstuffs and raw materials, such as petroleum from Indonesia, iron ore from Australia, and wheat and soybeans from the United States. In return, it is the chief supplier of manufactured goods for these neighbors. On the other hand, the United States still has a stronger cultural and ideological influence than Japan, even in former Japanese colonies such as South Korea and Taiwan.

More generally, however, international relations in the Asia Pacific region as well as in the world as a whole have increasingly taken on the features of complex interdependence. The trends point to a further global-ization or regionalization of production processes, a rising tendency to-ward interpenetration of national product markets, increasing patterns of cross-investment among the more advanced economies, and an accelera-tion of technology transfer and cultural diffusion. These trends promote the development and proliferation of dense transnational networks of interests. At the same time, they underscore the more acute mutual vul-nerabilities faced by the actors engulfed by these networks. The resulting interlocking ties encourage mutual partisan adjustment, as disruptive be-havior can cause severe and wide ripple effects. Thus, in contrast to the external coercion provided by a hegemonic enforcer, the actors are likely to be self-deterred from undertaking defection and aggression because of the prospect of such damaging reverberations.

Of course, complex interdependence does not deny differences in rela-tive national power. Nor does mutual partisan adjustment eliminate the need for effective statecraft. On the contrary, national purpose and policy capacity are crucial for upward status mobility in an international system characterized by these attributes. Comparative advantage goes to those ac-tors who have the requisite skills, personnel, and institutional wherewithal to collect timely information, to engage in effective communication, and to undertake anticipatory planning and coalition formation. Similarly, those who possess a steady and clear purpose, make realistic ends-means adjust-ments, and adapt quickly to changing conditions should do better in a world of complex interdependence than those without these characteristics.

Significantly, the qualities just mentioned refer less to a country's in-herited structural position in the world than to its policy capacity to man-age ongoing processes. Surely not all hegemons were favored with large size or abundant natural resources—the precedents of Portugal, Holland, and England come readily to mind. Moreover, some hegemonic contenders possessing greater size and more natural resources (e.g., Spain, France, and, most recently, the USSR) failed to achieve a leadership position. Therefore, structural position and the raw ingredients of national power (e.g., territorial and population size, mineral wealth) are not sufficient con-ditions for international preeminence. Analogously, one's seating position and the objective strength of one's hand are not enough to predict victory at the poker table. How skillfully one plays the cards is a more important consideration. By the same token, national purpose and policy capacity— that is, the skill with which an actor operationalizes the assets dealt to it by nature or history—matters more than the assets themselves in accounting for international ascendance and decline. And, unlike assets, national pur-pose and policy capacity should in principle be equally available to all.

Therefore, relative differences in national performance can be traced more to discrepancies in policy capacity than in objective assets. Holland and England overcame their comparatively meager tangible resources to claim dominance in international relations. On the other hand, Spain, Austria-Hungary, and Russia were unable to establish hegemony despite their much larger resource bases. It would therefore seem that the rise or decline of U.S. power in the Asia Pacific region as well as globally depends more on internal policy processes than on external structural conditions. A country's international position is a function rather than a determinant of its power, which is in turn shaped by national purpose and policy choice, among other things.

■ REFERENCES

Axelrod, R. 1984. *The Evolution of Cooperation.* New York: Basic Books.

Blank, S. 1978. "Great Britain: The Politics of Foreign Economic Policy, the Domestic Economy, and the Problem of Pluralistic Stagnation." In P. J. Katzenstein (ed.), *Between Power and Plenty: Foreign Economic Policies of Advanced Industrial States.* Madison: University of Wisconsin Press.

Bobrow, D. B. and S. Chan. 1986. "Assets, Liabilities, and Strategic Conduct: Status Management by Japan, Taiwan, and South Korea," *Pacific Focus* 1:23–56.

Boyer, M. A. 1989. "Trading Public Goods in the Western Alliance System," *Journal of Conflict Resolution* 33:700–727.

Calleo, D. 1982. *The Imperious Economy.* Cambridge, MA: Harvard University Press.

Caporaso, J. A. 1978. "Introduction to the Special Issue of International Organization on Dependence and Dependency in the Global System," *International Organization* 32:1–12.

Hofheinz, R. Jr. and K. E. Calder. 1982. *The Eastasia Edge.* New York: Basic Books.

Holsti, O. R. and J. N. Rosenau. 1984. *American Leadership in World Affairs: Vietnam and the Breakdown of Consensus.* Boston: Allen & Unwin.

Kennedy, P. 1987. *The Rise and Fall of Great Powers.* New York: Random House.

Keohane, R. O. 1984. *After Hegemony: Cooperation and Discord in the World Political Economy.* Princeton, NJ: Princeton University Press.

Keohane, R. O. and J. S. Nye. 1977. *Power and Interdependence: World Politics in Transition.* Boston: Little, Brown.

Kindleberger, C. P. 1981. "Dominance and Leadership in the International Economy," *International Studies Quarterly* 25:242–254.

Kindleberger, C. P. 1973. *The World in Depression, 1929–1939.* Berkeley: University of California Press.

Krasner, S. D. 1976. "State Power and the Structure of International Trade," *World Politics* 28:317–347.

Lindblom, C. E. 1965. *The Intelligence of Democracy: Decision Making Through Mutual Adjustment.* New York: Free Press.

McCraw, T. K. (ed.). 1986. *America Versus Japan.* Boston: Harvard Business School.

Modelski, G. 1987. *Long Cycles in World Politics.* Seattle: University of Washington Press.

Morgenthau, H. J. 1978. *Politics Among Nations* (5th ed.). New York: Knopf.

Morita, A. and S. Ishihara. 1990. *The Japan That Can Say No.* Tokyo: Kobunsha.

Nau, H. R. 1990. *The Myth of America's Decline: Leading the World Economy into the 1990s.* New York: Oxford University Press.

Olson, M. Jr. 1982. *The Rise and Decline of Nations.* New Haven, CT: Yale University Press.

Olson, M. Jr. and R. Zeckhauser. 1966. "An Economic Theory of Alliances," *Review of Economics and Statistics* 48:266–279.

Organski, A. F. K. and J. Kugler. 1980. *The War Ledger.* Chicago: University of Chicago Press.

Prestowitz, C. Jr. 1988. *Trading Places: How We Allowed Japan to Take the Lead.* New York: Basic Books.

Rosecrance, R. 1986. *The Rise of the Trading State: Commerce and Conquest in the Modern World.* New York: Basic Books.

Rosecrance, R. and J. Taw. 1990. "Japan and the Theory of International Leadership," *World Politics* 42:184–209.

Russett, B. M. 1982. "Defense Expenditures and National Well-Being," *American Political Science Review* 76:767–777.

Russett, B. M. 1985. "The Mysterious Case of Vanishing Hegemony; Or, Is Mark Twain Really Dead?" *International Organization* 39:207–232.

Singer, J. D., S. Bremer, and J. Stuckey. 1972. "Capability Distribution, Uncertainty, and Major Power War, 1820–1965." In B. M. Russett (ed.), *Peace, War, and Numbers.* Beverly Hills, CA: Sage Books.

Snidal, D. 1985. "The Limits of Hegemonic Stability Theory," *International Organization* 37:579–614.

Stein, A. A. 1984. "The Hegemon's Dilemma: Great Britain, the United States, and the International Economic Order," *International Organization* 38:355–386.

Strange, S. 1987. "The Persistent Myth of Lost Hegemony." *International Organization* 41:551–574.

Tollison, R. D. and T. D. Willett. 1979. "An Economic Theory of Mutually Advantageous Issue Linkages in International Negotiations." *International Organization* 33:425–449.

Vogel, E. F. 1979. *Japan As Number 1: Lessons for America.* Cambridge, MA: Harvard University Press.

■ 9

Alternative Directions for U.S. Strategy in the Changing Pacific Basin

David B. H. Denoon

Three broad issues may affect long-term development patterns in the Pacific Basin.[1] *Ethnic and religious friction,* particularly in Southeast Asia, have been submerged partly by skillful authoritarian governments and partly because economic improvements have been so dramatic. Yet these tensions are age-old and could reemerge as education levels rise and as more open political systems spread. It has been disappointing to see how religious and ethnic resentment has persisted in Yugoslavia, Belgium, Ireland, and Canada despite rising incomes. Given the elaborate mosaic in Southeast Asia, these tensions require adept responses and could derail various efforts at economic integration if they were crudely handled.

A second issue, one that is harder to evaluate, concerns the environment for and *manner of conducting business* in Southeast Asia. Put in their most favorable light, common business practices might be termed "highly personal" and "family-oriented." To many outside observers, however, there is deep suspicion about the extensive corruption and side payments that are frequently necessary to do business in the ASEAN (Association of Southeast Asian Nations) countries. Singapore is the striking exception to this rule. In fact, one reason that foreign multinational firms cite for being based in Singapore is that they can operate there without making side payments. Also, since many of the local firms are relying on foreign capital and outside technology, there is some uncertainty about whether they are developing sufficient technical and managerial talent to be self-sustaining in the future.[2]

A third issue, which can only be answered with time, is whether the *scale and diversity* of the geographic and cultural differences in the Pacific

Basin will make an economic community simply unmanageable.³ If one looks at the pace and character of economic integration in Europe in the 1950s and 1960s versus what is happening today in the Pacific Basin, there are both positive and negative comparisons. Western Europe had a more homogeneous culture and a clear external military threat, both of which tended to encourage cooperation. Yet as the Single European Act and the Maastricht Treaty came closer to being implemented, the European public began to express more and more serious reservations about single-market integration.

In the Pacific, now that the Cold War is over, cooperation for security purposes is less likely to be a cement throughout the region, but the current level of trade and capital flows within the region has established a set of personal networks and a financial stake in making cooperation work successfully. In the discussion below, part of the intent will be to explore the circumstances that would either further or hinder Pacific-wide cooperation.

In the period from the end of the Vietnam War (1975) to the end of the Cold War, the broad outlines of U.S. strategy were clear: (1) to the extent possible, contain the expansion of Soviet influence through formal treaties or tacit means of support; (2) discourage China from exporting communism, and use Beijing's concerns regarding Soviet intentions as a means for linking China more with the West; (3) provide adequate nuclear and conventional forces so that U.S. allies and friends would feel secure; and (4) offer various inducements (economic and military aid, tariff preferences, and essentially open access to U.S. markets) as a way to encourage general cooperation with the West and the United States in particular.

These U.S. steps were remarkably successful at the strategic level. Although the Soviet Union did briefly expand its influence by establishing bases in Vietnam and financing Hanoi's control of Laos and Cambodia, these moves proved quite costly and did not lead to further expansion of influence anywhere else in East Asia. Moreover, by 1986, when General Secretary Gorbachev gave his speech at Vladivostok offering economic cooperation, it had become clear that the USSR was fading as a military power and had little to offer as an economic partner. A mere five years later, the Soviet Union had literally disintegrated as a country.

Today the United States faces much more basic choices because there is not one adversary that warrants paramount attention. In addition, because the present is a period of limited strategic rivalry, there is no obvious boundary between taking prudent steps to prepare for future challenges and taking actions that could be perceived as threatening others and thus stimulate hostile responses.

Each year the top policymakers in the U.S. Department of Defense prepare a classified document known as the "Defense Guidance." In a draft of the 1992 "Defense Guidance" that was leaked to the press, one view suggested that the United States should define its political and military mission in the post–Cold War era. This view urges the United States to try to ensure that no rival superpower emerges in Western Europe, Asia, or in Russia. The draft stated: "The U.S. must sufficiently account for the interests of the advanced industrial nations to discourage them from challenging our leadership or seeking to overturn the established political and economic order."[4]

Then–Secretary of Defense Richard Cheney subsequently disavowed this draft and produced an alternative version that stressed cooperation rather than U.S. dominance. Nevertheless, if the Department of Defense (DOD) version of U.S. strategy were to be implemented, it would entail both an interventionist foreign policy throughout the globe and the acceptance by other nations that the United States was operating in their interests. Clearly, it would also be an implicit downgrading of the collaborative approach the United States has taken since 1949 with NATO and the bilateral security treaties with Japan and South Korea.

Current Secretary of Defense Les Aspin, then chairman of the House Armed Services Committee, released a series of studies during 1991 and 1992 in which he defined a very different vision of U.S. security commitments.[5] Aspin's prescription for U.S. forces called for a major reduction in overseas deployments and sizable cuts in both general purpose and nuclear forces but proposed an increase in air and sea capability to enable rapid intervention in distant conflicts.

Both the original DOD and the Aspin proposals focus on U.S. initiatives and assume a world in which there will be little direct resistance to U.S. action (as long as the United States takes the interests of the other major powers into account). There appear to be at least two fundamental flaws in these proposals: (1) both assume that the United States will have sufficient resources and public support to carry out major foreign interventions, and (2) they assume that the other principal powers will see U.S. actions as benevolent.

Both these proposals seem to be overgeneralizing from the very atypical circumstances of the 1989–1992 period. If all future challenges to the international order were similar to Saddam Hussein's invasion of Kuwait, then these assumptions might be valid. Yet the Iraqi conquest of Kuwait threatened oil supplies for both the European Community and Japan and was such blatant aggression that the Soviet Union, India, and China could find little justification for supporting it. Most future crises are unlikely to be so clear-cut and present such a nice complementarity between moral and national interest considerations.

Moreover, both the Soviet Union and China were preoccupied with internal problems, and Iran was devastated from its long prior war with Iraq. Hence, the ease with which the United States put together the anti-Iraq coalition is not representative of how the world's principal military actors will view crises in the future.

In addition, though the Aspin prescription is less expensive than the original DOD one, both assumed that the United States will maintain the ability to be the globe's preeminent power for the forseeable future. Doing so would require either: (1) other countries contributing to the costs of U.S. forces (as they did for the Gulf War coalition) *or* (2) a resurgence of the U.S. economy to facilitate the maintenance of high levels of defense expenditure.

In addressing the strategic choices for the United States in the Pacific Basin, the need for U.S. military intervention appears remote, and economic dilemmas are most salient. The trade imbalances (all favoring the East Asian countries) cannot continue indefinitely, and the burden-sharing arrangements for air and naval protection will need to be rethought.

Also, the current debates about what type of legal framework to have for economic cooperation in the Pacific are potentially divisive. The original Australian initiative to create the Pacific Economic Cooperation Conference (PECC) has been superseded by a second: the Asia Pacific Economic Cooperation (APEC). At the APEC meeting in Seoul in November 1991, there was agreement to establish a secretariat and a budget, but basic goals for APEC have not been delineated.

As long as APEC includes North America and is designed to be "pan-Pacific," it could be a useful forum for resolving economic differences. However, the recent Malaysian push to establish an East Asian Economic Group could lead to a grouping where the Japanese completely dominated and the United States was excluded. The other members of ASEAN thus got Malaysia to change the name to East Asian Economic Caucus (EAEC) and to keep it as a subgroup within APEC. Nevertheless, the potential for a split "down the middle of the Pacific"—i.e., between North America and Asia—still exists.

Here, it should be noted that during 1992 there was substantial personal friction between President Suharto of Indonesia and Prime Minister Mahathir of Malaysia. To date, this tension has been kept to tolerable levels by the desire of both leaders to appear reasonable.[6] Yet with President Suharto now chairing the nonaligned movement and Prime Minister Mahathir clearly trying to play a larger role in East Asia, there could be continuing distance between these key Muslim leaders.

The remaining discussion in this chapter will concentrate on three questions:

1. What are the major current problems facing the United States in the Pacific Basin?
2. What future problems warrant attention now from U.S. policymakers? and
3. What alternatives does the United States have for optimizing in dealing with this mix of current and future problems?

Obviously, in a single chapter these issues cannot be resolved in great detail, but the attempt will be made to provide enough discussion so the linkages between the issues are clear.

■ THEORETICAL CONTEXT AND SPECIFIC CASES

To be explicit on how these various issues fit together, it is worth noting that U.S. concerns with the Pacific Basin exist at *three* levels of intervention: global, regional, and direct bilateral.

The *global* concerns come from the geopolitical significance of the region. In a bipolar world,[7] the U.S. alliances and understandings with Pacific Rim nations created both a military and an economic dilemma for the USSR. Although the Soviet Union could project power through naval aviation based at Vladivostok and Petropavlosk and potentially be disruptive with its extensive submarine fleet, it never achieved the ability to sail and protect a "blue water navy" in the Pacific. Similarly, as the Soviet Union fell further and further behind the West in terms of economic performance, there was little incentive for the East Asian countries to seek close economic ties with the USSR.

In today's strategic environment, the United States is the only clear superpower, but there are a host of middle powers (Japan, Russia, the United Kingdom, France, India, and China).[8] Hence, the countries in the Pacific Basin have a broader range of potential alliance options. Moreover, the United States has less need than the middle powers for tight, binding alliances as long as no single middle power is organizing against its interests. Thus, at least in the near term, it appears that U.S. strategic dominance will not constrain flexibility for many countries in the Pacific Basin. Also, though the world may be "unipolar" in a military sense, for most political, diplomatic, and economic negotiations it seems more realistic to describe it as "multipolar."

If the global political scene will provide greater maneuverability for Pacific Basin countries, what are the alternatives at the *regional* level? Here the cultural and language diversity are almost certain to prevent the type of political union envisaged by the European Community. There will thus be two major regional concerns: (1) preventing local conflicts or tension from spreading to other parts of the region, and (2) deciding how to handle the growing economic integration within the region.

The two military issues that might become regionwide concerns are North Korea's obvious efforts at developing nuclear weapons and the simmering Cambodia conflict. To date, both issues are being handled at the global level because there are no specific regional institutions capable of dealing with them.

North Korea has come under considerable pressure from the International Atomic Energy Agency (IAEA) and bilateral pressure from neighboring countries to allow inspection of all its nuclear facilities. The North Koreans had briefly agreed to accept IAEA inspections, but in March 1993 backed out of the commitment. Yet the progress in its negotiations with South Korea on reunification of the peninsula and reciprocal inspection of nuclear facilities has at least temporarily allayed worries that the ever-volatile inner-Korean border will become a flashpoint for an actual military conflict. Nevertheless, the South Korean government has been sufficiently disappointed in the North Korean lack of candor about nuclear inspections that it has held up on various forms of trade and investment liberalization. In Seoul, there has also been a noticeable dimming of enthusiasm for quick reunification with the North as the assorted costs of reunification in Germany become more evident.

The Cambodia conflict will be discussed in greater detail below, but the current presence (after elaborate multinational and major power negotiations) of a massive UN peacekeeping force, is an indication that no Asian regional entity alone was willing to or capable of establishing a cease-fire.

The principal regionwide discussions focus on economic integration, where the key debate is over whether to pursue (1) a truly multilateral solution stressing GATT-type tariff and nontariff barrier reductions, or (2) various forms of regional or subregional integration as a first step. These economic choices obviously are related to decisions on preferred political alignments.

Japan and the United States are so dominant in the economic picture for the rest of the Pacific Basin countries that the easiest route would be to work out specific arrangements with those two powers. It is worth noting that most East Asian countries get 40–55 percent of their imports from the United States and Japan (see Appendix II). At the political level, this could result in a type of U.S./Japan condominium, or bigemony,[9] and the economic analogue would be a common market for countries in the Pacific that agreed to certain rules of policy management.

Subregional groupings might be an interim step. The ASEAN countries have already agreed to form an Asian Free Trade Area (AFTA),[10] with tariffs to be cut over a fifteen-year period that began January 1, 1993. Although the tariff cuts planned in AFTA are gradual, it will form an economic zone of 310 million people with a GNP of over $300 billion. It is also possible that Japan or the United States would sign other free trade agreements on a bilateral basis.

Most market-oriented economists prefer trade agreements that are multilateral,[11] and if the current GATT negotiations succeed there may be less incentive for forming subregional or bilateral arrangements. Nevertheless, the Asian countries are worried that the United States has moved so rapidly on the North American Free Trade Agreement (NAFTA). Also, if the United States were to turn in a clearly more protectionist direction, then the Asian countries in the Pacific Basin would almost certainly form their own protective cordon.

Another development that warrants attention is the growth of informal trading areas where business ties are close. Examples are Hong Kong's links with Guangdong province, Taiwan's links with Fujian province, and the growing prospect of Korean ties in northern China. Although these do not constitute formal free trade areas, as the trade and investment expands and people travel back and forth more frequently, the interchange could create a set of mutual expectations that are similar to those that have built up in Western Europe.

The *bilateral* issues for the United States in the Pacific Basin come from special historical links that have created either particularly close bonds or particular animosities.[12] The two countries that have close bonds but where there is now tension are the Philippines and Thailand, and the country where mutual bitterness remains is Vietnam.

Curiously, the Philippine elite seems to have been surprised with the speed of the U.S. withdrawal from Subic Bay once the Philippine Senate rejected the terms negotiated for the extension of the U.S. presence. U.S. bilateral economic and military assistance is likely to drop sharply. Moreover, there is broad disappointment among most of the aid donors with the slow progress the Aquino government made in carrying out economic reforms, and this may affect support through the Multilateral Aid Initiative. Philippine–U.S. relations could thus be moving into a period of increased distance. The election of Gen. Fidel Ramos as president of the Philippines and his subsequent appointment of pragmatic cabinet secretaries may make the mechanics of U.S.–Philippine relations work more easily than during the Aquino administration. Nonetheless, the quick reduction in aid and U.S. formal support will require both a psychological adjustment and a set of major economic changes inside the Philippines.

The problems in U.S.–Thai relations are much more limited in scope, and they stem from Bangkok's resentment that the United States is pressing hard for reciprocity and access to Thai markets.[13] The long history of a close working relationship between the United States and Thailand bodes well for resolution of the current specific irritants, but the generic problems that the United States faces with trade deficits in the Pacific Basin may mean that many small to moderate-sized countries will be pressured by the United States to open their markets. Although the rioting in Bangkok in May 1992 against an unelected prime minister (General Suchinda) created a temporary climate of instability, the king's intervention to restore calm and pave the way for a compromise led to a new election and an apparent return to stability in Thailand.

U.S. tensions with Vietnam are, obviously, deep-seated and not likely to fade until there is a generational change of leadership in both countries. Although the U.S. government has been pleased with the withdrawal of most Vietnamese troops from Cambodia, the POW/MIA issue is such an emotional one on Capitol Hill that achieving full diplomatic recognition will doubtless be a drawn-out process. The United States has agreed to supply some humanitarian assistance to Hanoi, but the Vietnamese are still unrealistic in their hopes for major U.S. bilateral aid.

The Cambodian conflict involves each of the three tiers of interaction identified above: global, regional, and bilateral. The present interim resolution of the conflict came about because the USSR was fading as a major power and was no longer willing to finance the Vietnamese occupation of Cambodia. Once the Vietnamese and the Soviets became more tractable, the Chinese then were willing to put pressure on their clients, the Khmer Rouge. At the regional level, it was also becoming clear that ASEAN cohesion was split when the Thai prime minister, Chatchai, broke from the previous ASEAN position and favored recognition of the Vietnamese-dominated Hun Sen regime.

Therefore, with many of the players willing to switch or modify positions that had been held throughout the 1980s, it became possible for the United States and France to play key roles in arranging the cease-fire under UN auspices. However, because the Khmer Rouge has a limited electoral constituency but a potent military capability, it is unclear if the UN peacekeeping force will be adequate to enforce the agreement.[14]

Thus, we have examples of issues in the Pacific Basin that are global in scope, some that are predominantly regional, some essentially bilateral, and others a blend of all three.

■ CURRENT REGIONWIDE PROBLEMS
FOR THE UNITED STATES

The United States must deal with three generic problems throughout the Pacific Basin: trade imbalances, differences in political culture, and arms control questions.

Trade imbalances are the most pressing and the most universal dilemma within the region. As Table 9.1 illustrates, the United States has a consistent trade deficit with all but three countries in the region (Australia, Brunei, and Papua New Guinea); even in those countries where it had a surplus in 1991, it only totaled $4.6 billion.

This imbalance poses a true conundrum for the United States, because since 1945 Washington has taken the lead in favoring open trading systems and has been particularly forthcoming with aid and tariff preferences for countries in the Pacific Basin. Yet, as the bottom line of Table 9.1 illustrates, the United States is now in rough trade equilibrium with all other parts of the world except Asia. In fact, the United States is in a *net surplus* of about $6.6 billion with all other parts of the world but in a *net*

Table 9.1   U.S. Trade Balance, 1989–1991
(in millions of dollars)

Country	1989	1990	1991
Brunei	(11.6)	47.1	135.8
Indonesia	(2,282.0)	(1,444.0)	(1,346.6)
Malaysia	(1,873.7)	(1,846.8)	(2,200.6)
Philippines	(866.1)	(913.4)	(1,202.8)
Singapore	(1,658.4)	(1,777.8)	(1,168.5)
Thailand	(2,091.4)	(2,293.3)	(2,367.8)
ASEAN	(8,783.2)	(8,228.2)	(8,150.5)
Australia	4,458.1	4,091.1	4,405.9
Burma	(12.4)	(2.6)	(2.9)
China	(6,234.5)	(10,430.9)	(12,689.0)
Fiji	6.1	(9.2)	(20.4)
Hong Kong	(3,430.9)	(2,804.9)	(1,146.1)
Japan	(49,058.7)	(41,104.5)	(43,436.2)
South Korea	(6,277.9)	(4,081.2)	(1,506.3)
Laos	(0.5)	0.4	(1.1)
Macao	(643.0)	(728.2)	(573.0)
New Zealand	(91.3)	(62.2)	(202.4)
Papua New Guinea	92.3	32.2	61.4
Taiwan	(12,978.1)	(11,175.1)	(9,844.9)
Other Asia Pacific	126.1	146.1	224.9
East Asia Pacific Total	(82,827.9)	(74,357.2)	(72,880.6)
World Total	(109,399.3)	(101,718.2)	(66,204.7)

Figures in parentheses are deficits.

deficit with Asia of $72.9 billion. In other words, even with all the oil the United States imports from Venezuela, Nigeria, and the Persian Gulf region, the country still exports more to Latin America, Africa, Europe, and the Middle East than it imports. Thus, U.S. trade problems are essentially Asian problems. Once the U.S. public fully understands this fact, there will be an extremely strong reaction.

Hence, it appears prudent for the United States and its Asian trading partners to work out means to reduce these deficits and their impact on U.S. employment. Unfortunately, the progress in changing U.S. macro-economic policy to encourage savings and increase productivity has been infinitesimal, if it has taken place at all. Moreover, there is now growing evidence that other countries in Asia are attempting to follow the Japanese pattern of industrial policy and export sector targeting as a means for garnering permanent niches in the U.S. market.[15] Also, progress at getting Japan to open its markets through efforts such as the Structural Impediments Initiative has been so slow[16] that there is reason to worry about comparable negotiations with other Asian countries in the future.

Clearly, there is no single answer to these trade problems, but if they are not resolved, the character of all U.S. relations in the Pacific Basin (political, military, and economic) will certainly be affected.

Differences in political culture also have the potential for creating major friction between the United States and countries in the Pacific Basin. Although most U.S. citizens are justly proud of their democratic system and its strong protection of individual rights, none of the principal cultures in Asia values open expression and individual freedom to the same extent.

In the early part of this century, when U.S. values were being presented as part of "Wilsonian internationalism,"[17] they appeared to be a benign mix of Western science, democratic government, and open trade that had considerable appeal to the intellectual elites in Asia. Some have argued that Western values and culture create a form of "soft power" that persuades and induces others to follow in creating a liberal international environment.[18] This argument might be true in the long run, but there are likely to be growing clashes between congressional assertiveness in this area and the conduct of routine relations with China, Singapore, Indonesia, Malaysia, Vietnam, and even Thailand. If trade relations are also a source of friction, then it is unlikely that these governments will be as responsive as they have been to pressure on both economic and human rights issues.

Arms sales and the proliferation of sophisticated weapons are also proving to be increasingly contentious issues in the Pacific Basin. Although Japan has a virtual ban on arms exports, the shipment of submarine tooling equipment in 1987 by the Toshiba Machine Co. was a major irritant with the United States, and the Japan Aviation Electronics Industry Co. was fined $10 million in 1992 for selling U.S. technology in fighter navigation equipment to Iran.[19]

Nevertheless, these complaints about Japan pale in comparison with the coming imbroglios over Chinese and North Korean arms sales. There are reports that China is assisting Syria in the production of surface-to-surface missiles and in improving the accuracy of Scud-C missiles.[20] There are also reports that Israel has transferred Patriot anti-ballistic missile technology to China.[21] Although the U.S. government could not confirm the transfer of Patriot technology, there is clear evidence of air-to-air missile technology being shared between Tel Aviv and Beijing. Additionally, the extent of Chinese participation in the international arms market is now well documented.[22]

The growing visibility of these arms transfers is reflected in the debate over whether the United States should have boarded North Korean vessels carrying Scud-C missiles to Iran[23] and what the Ukrainian motivations were in bargaining to hold onto their nuclear weapons.[24] Because Russia and the United States are still the world's two leading exporters of arms, it is unlikely that others will see Washington as having any particularly strong moral position on this matter.

Additionally, if Japan were to change policy and get legally into the arms sales business, then there would be not only an alternative supplier of sophisticated weaponry but also geopolitical significance to the move. Hence, if the United States is to make any inroads at limiting arms sales to volatile areas, Washington may need to exercise more control over its own arms purchasers, limit its own sales, and possibly approach the overall issue in a multilateral context.

■ FUTURE SCENARIOS

There is obviously no quantitative methodology that can allow us to predict precisely what long-term future economic and political trends will be for a region as complex as the Pacific Basin. Therefore, it would be misleading to try to make a single forecast. However, it is useful to try to identify what clusters of issues are likely to develop and how present choices for the United States might affect future alternatives.

Thus, for purposes of discussion, three broad scenarios are proposed and potential developments within three different subregions of the Pacific Basin are suggested. As outlined in Table 9.2 the scenarios are labeled: (1) "The Present as Prologue," (2) "Economics Reigns," and (3) "Regional Power Rivalry."[25] These scenarios are not meant to be rigidly mutually exclusive or to imply that other developments are implausible. Each of them appears possible, however, and each would call for a different U.S. response should it occur. I will not review each entry in Table 9.2, but instead will sketch out the basic differences between the scenarios.

The Present As Prologue is meant to project roughly the current strategic and economic situation into the future. Under these conditions, Japan, South Korea, and Taiwan lead economically in Northeast Asia, and China benefits from its ties with each of these fast-growing neighbors. Similar patterns hold true in ASEAN, and the entire Pacific Basin is politically stable, but there are growing tensions between the United States and its Asian trading partners. When there is policy gridlock in the United States (such as arising from difficulties between the executive branch and Congress), there could be stalemate on foreign policy as well. This outcome might prevent the ratification of NAFTA (which would please many in Asia), but it would also probably preclude any bold initiatives in the Pacific Basin.

If the present is a reasonable prologue for the future, we can also assume that both China and North Korea will retain their Communist

Table 9.2   Future Scenarios of U.S. Strategy in the Pacific Basin

Impact	I: The Present As Prologue	II: Economics Reigns	III: Regional Power Rivalry
Northeast Asia			
Economic	• Japan, South Korea, Taiwan lead; PRC gets technical and aid	• Tensions between southern, northern PRC; Russia, North Korea fall behind	• Mercantilism *redux*
Domestic Political	• Subregion stable	• Income splits grow	• External threats grow
National Security	• Negotiations between South and North Korea; no wars	• Military demobilization difficult in Russia, North Korea	• PRC/South Korea vs. Japan India vs. PRC ASEAN split
Southeast Asia and the Pacific Islands			
Economic	• ASEAN high growth (except Philippines)	• ASEAN enjoys high growth, Pacific Islands lose aid	• Intraregional trade slows
Domestic Political	• Political stability	• Heightened tension across income groups	• Nationalism increases
National Security	• Military quiet	• Military legitimacy declines	• Indonesia, Vietnam increase dominance
The United States			
Economic	• Slow growth	• Serious revitalization	• Trade barriers: 1930s?
Domestic Political	• Political gridlock	• Ethnic politics decline	• Asian minorities active
National Security	• Gradual downsizing: 30 percent	• Major military cuts: 50+ percent	• Rebuild conventional forces

governments and seek considerable autonomy in their foreign policy. This scenario would probably mean China continues to seek major power status and the submerged rivalry between China and Japan persists.

Economics Reigns would be a world of substantially reduced military tension and expenditures but enhanced economic competition. Although the Pacific Basin would presumably do well vis-à-vis-the rest of the globe, there would probably be resentment within East Asia over the differences in living standards and economic influence. Russia, North Korea, Indochina, and the Philippines would presumably fall further behind their neighbors. There might even be greater tension within countries if the differentials in income and growth between regions that are now evident, as between southern and northern China, continue in the future. The role of the military would decline, as would aid and diplomatic support that was previously provided for strategic reasons.

If economic competition becomes the centerpiece of Pacific Basin interaction, the informal trading areas discussed above (Hong Kong/Guangdong, Taiwan/Fujian, and Korea/northern China) could become more important in explaining regional relations. The respective business communities will be less concerned with sovereignty and more focused on freedom for capital and trade movements. If Vietnam continues in a pragmatic direction, it, too, will find growing commercial interaction, especially with Thailand but also with the rest of the ASEAN countries. These external linkages will eventually undermine the control the governments in Beijing and Hanoi have over their citizens.

Regional Power Rivalry now appears as only a distant possibility, but it should not be excluded because its implications are so significantly different from the other two scenarios. At present, both the Indians and Chinese are courting each other, but many factors could recreate the animosities that led to war in 1962. Similarly, China is now anxious for Tokyo's capital and technology and access to the Japanese market, but there could easily be circumstances (such as Japan's seeking broader preeminence in the region) that leads to Chinese resistance. Likewise, within ASEAN there are a host of potential splits.

If these sources of classic strategic rivalry dominate, it would also affect the character of economic relations, probably driving the region in a more mercantilist direction. The character and extent of the United States involvement in this rivalry would then depend upon how economic relations had developed and to what extent the United States felt threatened by the trends.

■ U.S. OPTIONS

There appear to be at least three main options the United States could take in attempting to deal with future developments in the Pacific Basin.[26]

For purposes of discussion, they have been labeled: (1) "Interlocutor," (2) "Active Balancer," and (3) "Strategic Withdrawal."

The United States is currently in the curious position of being the paramount military power but absorbing trade deficits with virtually every country in the region and losing key industries to Asian producers. This is not a sustainable stance. So, even though it would probably be most accurate to describe the current U.S. role as "Dominant Arbiter," it seems unrealistic to assume continued U.S. dominance unless there is a dramatic turnabout in the U.S. economic position.

Interlocutor would be the easiest role for the United States to perform. Washington is on good terms with all countries in the region except North Korea and Vietnam and was notably successful in brokering the recent Cambodia settlement. Now that the incubus of U.S. facilities in the Philippines has been resolved and U.S. naval forces will rotate their visits among several friendly countries (with certain home-porting advantages in Singapore), the United States can be less engaged than before yet still present. The interlocutor could thus be the supportive but nonthreatening stabilizer when needed.

An *Active Balancer* role would entail more than that of interlocutor, requiring shifting alliances or understandings as the circumstances warranted. This type of nineteenth-century balancing strategy does not appear necessary now. Yet it may become essential if the world moves in a more mercantilist direction and intense strategic rivalry develops in East Asia. As long as the U.S.–Japan relationship is solid, there would be little appeal in challenging that entente; however, if relations between Washington and Tokyo sour to the point of a split, then this approach may be viewed as necessary. Similarly, a modernized and more nationalistic China allied with Korea or even India might also warrant balancing. This is clearly not a role the United States would relish, as it would require frequent diplomatic subtlety and a continued engagement of major forward deployed forces in the region.

A *Strategic Withdrawal by the United States* from the Pacific Basin seems unlikely now, but there are elements of both the Republican and Democratic parties that would support it. Under present circumstances, this move would doubtless cede military dominance to Japan and thus create a strong counterresponse from China, Korea, and the ASEAN countries. However, if it were phased in over a period of several decades and a new set of military balances or security arrangements were established, the impact could be less destabilizing. Again, it should be noted that unless the United States reverses its economic imbalances in the region, there are likely to be a growing number of advocates for strategic withdrawal.

I cannot predict precisely what will happen, but it would be naive to assume that the current economic and strategic relationships the United States is maintaining in the Pacific Basin are a realistic blueprint for the future.

■ NOTES

1. For two different historical treatments of these frictions, see B. Gordon, *The Dimensions of Conflict in Southeast Asia*, (Englewood Cliffs, NJ: Prentice Hall, 1966) and D. G. E. Hall, *A History of Southeast Asia* (London: Macmillan, 1968).

2. For two skeptical views on this issue, see K. Yoshihara, *The Rise of Ersatz Capitalism in Southeast Asia* (London and New York: Oxford University Press, 1988) and J. Cladd, *Behind the Myth: Business, Money and Power in Southeast Asia* (London: Unwin Hyman, 1989).

3. For a balanced assessment of these issues, see G. Segal, *Rethinking the Pacific* (London and New York: Oxford University Press, 1990).

4. Tyler, P. 1992. "U.S. Strategy Plan Calls for Insuring No Rivals Develop," *New York Times* March 8, p. A–1.

5. See, for example, L. Aspin, "Four Options for a Defense That Works," *mimeo.* (Washington, D.C.: House Armed Services Committee, February 27, 1992).

6. Vatkiotis, M. 1992. "The Mahathir Paradox," *Far Eastern Economic Review*, August 20, pp. 16–18.

7. See S. Bialer and M. Mandelbaum, *The Global Rivals—The 40 Year Contest for Supremacy* (New York: Knopf, 1988) for a discussion of the implications of bipolarity.

8. For a discussion of potential directions for the global political system, see R. Jervis, "The Future of World Politics: Will It Resemble the Past?" *International Security*, Vol. 16, No. 3, Winter 1991–1992, pp. 39–73.

9. See S. Chan, "Power and Policy: America's Choices in a Changing Pacific Region," Chapter 8 of this volume, for a discussion of bigemony and its implications.

10. In the ASEAN free trade area, it was agreed that all tariffs must be down to 5 percent by the year 2008. See P. Shenon, "Southeast Asian Nations Sign Free Trade Accord," *New York Times,* January 29, 1992, p. D–5.

11. For a detailed analysis of Pacific Basin trade and estimates of future developments from a multilateral perspective, see M. Noland, *Pacific Basin Developing Countries—Prospects for the Future* (Washington, D.C.: Institute for International Economics, 1990).

12. For an overview of U.S. bilateral relations with East Asia, see S. Bosworth, "The United States and Asia," in *American and The World 1991/92, Foreign Affairs,* Vol. 71, No. 1, pp. 113–129.

13. Bresnan, J. 1992. "Economic Development in Southeast Asia and the Implications for U.S. Policy," *mimeo* (New York: Council on Foreign Relations, February), pp. 39–42.

14. Shenon, P. 1992. "Cambodia Pact Founders on Attacks and Distrust," *New York Times,* August 18, p. A–1.

15. Office of Technology Assessment, *Competing Economies—America, Europe, and the Pacific Rim* (Washington, D.C.: O.T.A., October 1991).

16. U.S.–Japan Working Group, *First Annual Report on the Structural Impediments Initiative* (Tokyo: 1991).

17. Iriye, A. 1991. "The American Experience in East Asia," in M. Bullock and R. Litwak, eds., *The U.S. and the Pacific Basin: Changing Economic and Security Relationships* (Washington, DC: Woodrow Wilson Center Press), pp. 13–32.

18. Nye, J. 1990. "Soft Power," *Foreign Policy,* No. 80, pp. 153–171.

19. Sanger, D. 1992. "Japanese Plead Guilty in Iran Arms Sales," *New York Times,* March 12, p. D–1.

20. Safire, W. 1992. "China's 'Hama Rules,'" *New York Times,* March 5, p. A–27.

21. Sciolino, E. 1992. "U.S. Said to Suspect Israelis Gave China American Arms," *New York Times,* March 13, p. A–12.

22. Bitzinger, R. 1990. "Arms to Go: Chinese Arms Sales to the Third World," *International Security,* Vol. 17, No. 2, pp. 84–111.

23. Tyler, P. 1992. "U.S. Weighs Boarding Korea Arms Ships," *New York Times,* March 6, p. A–9.

24. Randolph, E. 1992. "Kiev Halts A-Weapons Transfers," *Washington Post,* March 13, p. A–1.

25. These three scenarios and related arguments are presented in D. Denoon, *Real Reciprocity: Balancing U.S. Economic and Security Policies in the Pacific Basin* (New York: Council on Foreign Relations, 1993).

26. There is a fourth plausible option: some type of U.S.–Japan bigemony. Yet there is currently sufficient resentment of Japan in many parts of Asia to make this unattractive for the United States—as long as it can deal effectively on a direct basis with most countries in the region.

Appendix 9.1 1991–1992 Forecast of Real Economic Growth and Increase of Consumer Prices of Fifteen Economies (percent)

	Real GDP/GNP			CPI		
	1990	1991	1992	1990	1991	1992
Australia	1.4	2.2	2.7	7.3	5.6	6.3
Brunei Darussalam	2.9	3.2	3.3	2.1	4.3	2.0
Canada	0.9	-1.1	3.6	4.8	5.2	3.0
China	5.0	5.7	6.8	2.4	7.8	7.5
Hong Kong	2.4	2.8	5.5	10.0	9.6	8.0
Indonesia	7.1	5.5	6.6	9.4	6.7	6.5
Japan	5.8	3.0	4.3	3.0	2.5	2.9
Korea	9.0	8.5	8.0	8.6	10.0	8.0
Malaysia	10.0	8.3	8.0	3.1	3.7	4.2
New Zealand	0.4	1.5	1.3	4.3	2.9	2.8
Philippines	3.1	1.9	4.0	12.7	14.3	8.3
Singapore	8.3	7.0	7.5	3.4	4.1	4.0
Chinese Taipei	5.3	6.2	7.2	4.1	4.5	3.8
Thailand	10.0	9.0	6.8	6.0	6.0	5.9
United States	0.9	0.4	3.0	5.4	4.7	4.4
Weighted Average	3.2	2.3	4.3	5.2	5.2	4.6
Average excluding U.S. and Japan	4.5	4.0	5.7	6.0	6.7	5.5
Simple Average	4.8	4.3	5.2	5.8	6.1	5.2
Average excluding U.S. and Japan	5.1	4.7	5.5	6.0	6.5	5.4

The weighted average is based on the respective countries' exports from 1987 to 1989.
Source: Pacific Economic Outlook 1991–1992, U.S. National Committee for Pacific Economic Cooperation, (San Francisco, CA: PECC, May 1991). Reprinted with permission.

Appendix 9.2 Percentage of Total Imports from Japan and the United States, 1990

South Korea:	
Japanese source	29.0
U.S. source	25.0
Taiwan:	
Japanese	29.2
U.S.	23.1
Singapore:	
Japanese	20.2
U.S.	16.0
Philippines:	
Japanese	23.0[1]
U.S.	20.4
Malaysia:	
Japanese	24.1
U.S.	16.9
Indonesia:	
Japanese	24.0[2]
U.S.	16.9[2]
Thailand:	
Japanese	30.0
U.S.	11.0

1. Estimated from prior year growth rates.
2. These figures are 1991 estimates, not for 1990.
Data Source: U.S. Department of Commerce, "Fact Sheets," Office of the Pacific Basin, March 1992.

■ 10

Asia Pacific Economic Integration in Global Perspective
Peter C. Y. Chow

The development of regional trading blocs in the world economy gained momentum in the early 1990s. This trend was in fact heralded by a number of phenomenal turns of events in the second half of the previous decade. On the global horizon, the 1980s saw the deadlock of the Uruguay Round of trade negotiations, the decision of the European Community (EC) on the single-market initiative, and the hatching of the North American Free Trade Agreement (NAFTA). Within the Asia Pacific region, the East Asian NIEs and some ASEAN nations were buoyed by an economic dynamism that registered consistently faster growth rates in GNP and in exports than the rest of the world. What is more, intraregional trade and investment flows, among other things, contributed to a sense of community ripe for the advance toward regional integration.

Despite political constraints and unsettled debates on the formation of an Asia Pacific economic bloc, the undercurrents for a forum for regional coordination in economic cooperation were running perceptibly (Frankel 1992). There are several scenarios for economic integration in the region, each with somewhat different groupings. At least five or six groups of countries accounting for the bulk of the trade and investment flows in the region must be included as the key participants. In the first tier, there are two groups: (1) Japan, and (2) the East Asian NIEs (to wit: South Korea, Taiwan, Hong Kong, and Singapore). In the second tier is a third group: ASEAN-4, the four largest members of the Association of Southeast Asian Nations (namely, Indonesia, Malaysia, Thailand, and the Philippines). To these are to be added another tier, which consists of two additional groups:

China, and the two Oceanic countries of Australia and New Zealand. A broader definition of Asia Pacific also includes the United States, Canada, and Latin American countries with littorals on the Pacific. The first five groups, comprising twelve countries, are the most common components in the various scenarios for Asia Pacific integration (Kim 1992).

In 1989 the combined GNP of the first five groups of nations (i.e., excluding the United States and Canada) stood at a hefty $4,245.6 billion, or 21.3 percent of total world GNP. Total exports from these five groups were $646.8 billion, or 22.3 percent of total world trade. Despite the region's lopsided trade flows to the U.S. market in the last decade, intraregional trade among these twelve countries has increased much faster than the overall export growth since the mid-1980s. Moreover, Japan and the NIEs, particularly Taiwan and South Korea, have substantially increased their direct foreign investments in neighboring, less developed areas such as ASEAN–4 and China. Taiwan became the largest foreign investor in Indonesia and Malaysia, as well as one of the top investors in other ASEAN countries in 1991. The phenomenal growths in intraregional trade and investment flows, since the late 1980s, have made these Asia Pacific economies much more interdependent than ever before.

These developments are abetted by the currency realignment after the Plaza Accords of 1985 and the internal as well as external environments in the NIEs. The increases in labor costs in Taiwan and South Korea, as their economies moved a few notches up the high tech ladder, created opportunities for the less developed ASEAN countries and China to enter the world market with their traditional labor-intensive products. The change both facilitated their structural transformation and further enhanced the division of labor among nations in the region.

However, economic integration is partially motivated by noneconomic factors. The experience of the EC has demonstrated that noneconomic considerations have a dominant influence on further integration in Europe. Hence, despite favorable economic conditions, there is still a long way ahead before institutionalized economic integration of any type can take shape in the Asia Pacific region.

In order to describe the various scenarios of regional economic blocs, it is necessary to briefly review the formats or stages of economic integration. The lowest level of integration is a preferential trading arrangement, under which member countries *reduce* their trade barriers for one another yet determine their own separate trade policies toward nonmember countries. The next level is a free trade area (FTA), under which participating countries *eliminate* trade barriers within the area but maintain their own trade policies toward nonmember countries. A more cohesive trading group is a customs union, which, in addition to the functions of FTA, also decides a common commercial policy toward nonmembers. A common market further integrates the economies among member states by extending the dimension of free trade policy to factor markets, allowing, for example, free capital and labor flows across national boundaries. The most comprehensive integration is an economic union, which maintains common economic policies as well as a common currency for all members.

A few questions about the prospects of Asia Pacific integration may be asked. Will the internal and external forces of economic integration become so compelling that the various groups of countries mentioned above will be pushed toward a regional economic bloc? What are the alternative scenarios of economic integration in the region? These and other questions are interesting not only to economists but also to those concerned with Asia Pacific regional development.

The purpose of this chapter is to examine the problems and prospects of economic integration in Asia Pacific and to critically assess various alternative scenarios with different country groupings in global perspective. It starts with a discussion of economic interdependence in the region, such as can be ascertained by analyzing the increased intraregional trade and investment flows. However, it argues that because of political constraints, a formal regional economic bloc is still in the process of evolving. Thus far, the annual ministerial meeting of the Asia Pacific Economic Cooperation forum (APEC) is the highest intergovernmental hierarchy for promoting trade and economic cooperation in the region. The chapter concludes that a discriminatory trading bloc is detrimental to the multilateral trading system and that a loose, open confederation with gradual integration based on increasing economic linkages is the best approach toward regional harmony and development.

The chapter is organized as follows: After the introductory remarks in the first section, the second section will discuss the question of increased interdependence and the driving forces of economic integration within the Asia Pacific region. The third section will address the evolving process of formulating an institutional framework for economic cooperation in the region. The fourth section will analyze the open regionalism of the APEC and subregional economic blocs. The final section will conclude by placing the Asia Pacific regional economic integration in the global perspective.

■ INTERDEPENDENCE WITHIN ASIA PACIFIC

The Asia Pacific countries are at different stages of economic development and have diverse sociopolitical structures domestically. Japan, the indisputable leader in industrialization, has already reached a point where it can easily compete with other OECD countries such as the United States and EC members. Japan is also the major supplier of advanced technology and capital in the region through its direct foreign investment in East and Southeast Asia.

The four resource-poor NIEs are in a stage of transformation from an economy of predominantly labor-intensive, light manufactures to one with relatively more technology-intensive and human-capital-intensive industries (Chow and Kellman 1992). After the mid-1980s, the NIEs, notably Hong Kong, South Korea, and Taiwan, shifted their status from capital-recipient countries to major foreign investors in the region, especially in the neighboring ASEAN–4 and Pacific coastal provinces in China. The interrelationship between the NIEs and ASEAN–4 in the 1990s was similar to that between Japan and the NIEs in the 1960s through 1970s. By gradually shifting their comparative advantage in standardized, labor-intensive production technologies to the lesser developed countries through foreign direct investment, the NIEs are gradually upgrading their industrial structures and commodity composition of exports to more technology-intensive and human-capital-intensive products.

The ASEAN–4 are generally considered the next tier of NIEs (Bradford, 1987). Whereas China used to be regarded as a "sleeping tiger" that just yawned to wake up about ten years ago, when it initiated its economic reform and "open door policy,"[1] assessments of its potential as the next NIE have changed (see Chapter 12). Generally speaking, the ASEAN–4 and China are relatively abundant in natural resources and low-cost labor supply and are at a less developed stage than the four existing NIEs. Australia and New Zealand are usually classified as industrialized countries with rich endowments of natural resources. The two Oceania countries and some of the ASEAN countries are among the few exceptions that have ever run trade surpluses with Japan, which they did by exporting some raw materials and resources-based intermediate products to Japan.

In the past decade, Pacific dynamism was largely marked by the rapid growth of exports from the Pacific Basin countries to the industrial markets. As a result, the "center of gravity" of the world economy is said to have shifted toward the Pacific Basin. As noted by Chow (1989), the trade flows of these countries were lopsided and leaned heavily to the United States as the major market. Japan and the Asian NIEs were responsible for more than 60 percent of the cumulative U.S. trade deficits of the 1980s. Recently, China has become another country that runs a trade surplus against the United States. The latter's persistent trade deficits and the resultant protectionism mandated that trade-surplus countries in Asia diversify their trade. The currency revaluations, following the Plaza Accords of 1985, substantially enhanced the intraregional trade within the Asia Pacific region after the mid-1980s.

Moreover, the structural transformation in the NIEs also contributed toward integration in Asia Pacific through increased intraregional trade and investment flows. In addition to facing rising labor costs and environmentalist sentiments at home and resurgent protectionism in the industrialized countries, the NIEs are confronted with new challenges from less developed members in the region, who are now strong competitors on the traditional labor-intensive product lines in the industrial markets. Hence, many business firms in the NIEs—particularly Hong Kong, South Korea, and Taiwan—have instead exported various kinds of domestically produced industrial components to be processed at offshore assembly lines in the neighboring ASEAN–4 or coastal provinces in China for reexport to the world market. The resultant foreign direct investments (FDI) from the NIEs have generated another favorable momentum toward regional economic integration.

By the end of 1991, business firms from Hong Kong had employed more than three million workers in adjacent Guangdong province, whereas more than 3,000 Taiwanese firms invested in China with a total investment of more than $3 billion. South Korea started its direct investment in China later than the other NIEs; yet by the end of 1991, there were 141 Korean firms pledged to a total of $1.4 billion.[2] Following its diplomatic recognition of China in August 1992, South Korea signed a number of trade and investment agreements with Beijing, and became China's newest close trade partner. It seems that the resource-poor NIEs have their eyes on China as their hinterlands to make up for their own poor natural resource endowments.

Taiwan's direct foreign investments in ASEAN–4 also went up substantially after Taipei liberalized foreign exchange control in 1987. In the last six years, Taiwan invested more than $12 billion in Southeast Asia. By the end of 1991 it ranked as the largest foreign investor in Indonesia and Malaysia and one of the top investors in Thailand and the Philippines. In short, in the second half of the 1980s the region seemed to move closer and closer toward economic integration in spite of political constraints.

China's outward-looking development strategy also seemed to further integrate its socialist economy into the region (Wong 1988). China is in need of capital and advanced technology to speed up its "four modernizations" drive, which, it is proclaimed, will quadruple the nation's per capita income by the year 2000. This modernization drive and the open door policy have substantially increased China's involvements with other Asia Pacific economies and greatly contributed to the growing integration in the region.

The sustained growth of China's economy has substantially enhanced political stability in the neighboring countries. Except for some uncertainties in Beijing's policy toward the future of Hong Kong after 1997 and the chronical debates on the overlapping sovereignty claims with Taipei, which challenged Taiwan's international status, China's open door policy presents little threat to Japan or the NIEs, at least in the short run. Reiterated statements upholding this policy during Deng Xiaoping's "southern visit" to the Special Economic Zones in early 1992 seemed to illustrate that China's pragmatism would definitively shut off, if not totally terminate, the ideological disputes constraining China's economic reforms and foreign economic relations after Tiananmen. The massive capital flows and the ever-expanding two-way indirect trade across the Taiwan Strait, totaling $5.6 billion in 1991, seems to work smoothly with little or no direct official contact.[3]

To some extent, China's open door policy probably will challenge the ASEAN–4 more than it does any of the NIEs. Being latecomers to industrialization, China and ASEAN have been enjoying a comparative advantage in similar product lines in their major exports. China's exports have predominantly been concentrated in labor-intensive light manufactures, as well as some resource-based products such as crude oil and other raw materials upon which the ASEAN–4's exports rely. In an earlier study, Chow (1992) applied the "export similarity index" (Finger and Kreinin 1979) in an evaluation of the overlapping of exports between China and ASEAN–4 in OECD markets. Other things being equal, the higher the export similarity index, the higher the overlapping of exports between a pair of countries in a third market; hence, the higher the export similarity index, the greater the potential competition between two countries. Table 10.1, replicated from Chow (1992), illustrates the similarity index between China and ASEAN–4.

One can find from Table 10.1 that the degree of export overlap between China and ASEAN–4 has substantially increased after China adopted the open door policy in 1979. By 1990 more than 50 percent of China's exports overlapped with those from the Philippines and Thailand in the U.S. and EC markets, and greater than 40 percent with those from Indonesia in the same markets. Among the ASEAN–4, Malaysia seems to have the least degree of export similarity with China. Relatively speaking, China's challenge to ASEAN–4 in export similarity is more serious in the U.S. and EC markets than in the Japanese market. As noted, the above figures only include exports of manufactures (three-digit SITC 5 through 8, except for SITC 688). If one includes agricultural commodities and mineral products (SITC 0 to 4), the index would be much higher. Therefore, potential clash between China and ASEAN countries because of competition on similar product lines in the same markets could be a detriment to regional economic bloc cohesion.

However, in a dynamic sense, the export-overlap factor alone should not be an obstacle to further economic integration in the region, because growing economies in export markets would absorb more imports from the ASEAN–4 and China as well. Also, alternative markets can redirect the current trade flows for these nations so as to reduce their severe competition in the same market. Moreover, there are indications that China will gradually open its own domestic market to foreign investors. Therefore, to evaluate the net impact of economic integration within developing countries, one has to consider the dynamic aspect of economic growth

Table 10.1   China's Export Similarity Index with ASEAN–4 (in percent)

	EC	Japan	United States
Indonesia			
1979	24.3	18.2	13.9
1985	32.0	14.2	47.2
1986	31.4	13.8	48.6
1987	39.8	13.9	47.0
1988	42.9	20.4	40.3
1989	42.2	18.0	44.9
1990	45.7	22.8	49.0
Philippines			
1979	30.6	34.5	44.1
1985	43.1	23.0	46.2
1986	44.1	27.5	50.6
1987	44.3	31.0	54.3
1988	42.4	34.4	49.6
1989	45.4	33.6	51.6
1990	52.6	38.6	50.3
Malaysia			
1979	14.5	11.0	6.0
1985	12.9	16.3	20.9
1986	16.3	15.7	24.5
1987	17.4	18.4	29.5
1988	23.7	20.4	35.4
1989	28.7	23.9	37.1
1990	33.2	28.6	36.5
Thailand			
1979	36.8	32.6	29.5
1985	53.7	28.7	50.1
1986	52.8	25.2	40.0
1987	55.8	28.6	44.2
1988	54.3	33.4	42.7
1989	56.9	36.0	52.1
1990	62.8	36.0	56.2

Coverage of export commodities: 3-digit Standard International Trade Classification (SITC) commodities from SITC 5 through 8, excluding SITC 688.
Source: Reprinted with permission from Peter C. Y. Chow, and M. Kellman, *Trade— The Engine of Growth in East Asia* (New York: Oxford University Press, 1992).

rather than the static cost-benefit basis of trade creation and trade diversion (Lipsey 1988). In other words, an integrated regional economic bloc is not necessarily a "zero-sum" game for participating countries.

Hence, China's open door policy should be welcomed by all Asia Pacific countries for its conducive effects on political stability in the region. Further integration of China's economy may generate even greater pressure within China for upholding the momentum of the reform toward a market economy, which will be in the region's interests.

The patterns of foreign investment from the NIEs have also spawned further linkages with ASEAN–4 and China. Just as Japan shifted its labor-intensive production technologies to the NIEs through foreign direct investment during the 1960s and 1970s, the NIEs today are replicating a similar technology transfer to the lesser developed ASEAN–4 and China. In this regard, Lee (1990) tried to make an analogy between Akamatsu's (1961) "flying geese" pattern of trade and industrial development and the patterns of foreign direct investment. The NIEs, particularly South Korea and Taiwan, are now in the intermediate position of catching up to the advanced industrial leader, Japan, whereas the ASEAN–4 and China are moving into the tier of the NIEs. Taiwanese and South Korean FDI in ASEAN–4 and China is heavily concentrated in resource-based industries and labor-intensive manufactures. But Taiwanese and South Korean FDI in the United States and EC are motivated by the "defensive" desire to protect their export-market shares of technology-intensive and skill-intensive products in the industrialized countries. The divergent directions in FDI of the NIEs is a new phenomenon that illustrates their ambitious drive in speeding up their respective structural transformations, which will leave more room in the world market for the lesser developed ASEAN–4 and China to expand their traditional, labor-intensive exports.

The unique pattern of mutual interdependence among these countries is summarized in Figure 10.1.

■ EVOLUTION OF REGIONAL ECONOMIC INTEGRATION IN ASIA PACIFIC COUNTRIES

Figure 10.1 suggests that there exist some real complementarities among these countries. The potentials for them to integrate into a regional economic bloc are inherently strong. However, mutual economic interdependence alone does not automatically lead to a regional economic bloc; noneconomic factors usually override economic ones. As Wallace (1981, p. 221) pointed out a long time ago, "a political commitment to override immediate economic concerns was the necessary condition for the transformation of European cooperation into [economic] union." Hence, the lesson from the successful experience of the EC indicates that the first and most important condition for any economic integration is the minimum political commitment of mutual recognition of the political entities of all participants.

Figure 10.1   Japan, China, ASEAN, and the NIEs

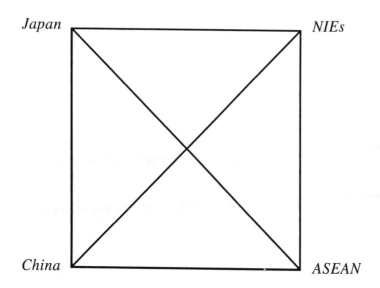

Notes:
Japan
i)   net exporter of technology and capital
ii) trade surplus against the NIEs, but trade deficit with Oceania states and ASEAN–4
iii) relies on external market to maintain its industrial capacities and scale economies
     production

China
i)   vast natural resource endowments and huge domestic market
ii) in need of capital and technology for further modernization
iii) regional center of geopolitics

the NIEs
i)   semi-industrialized states in transitional stage to technology advancement
ii) lack of natural resources and limited size of domestic market
iii) exporter of capital and labor-intensive production technology for ASEAN–4
     and China

ASEAN–4
i)   net exporter of raw materials and natural resource–based products
ii) capital recipient countries with low-cost labor supplies
iii) dependent on exports of primary commodities and light manufactures

Historically, few countries would be willing to voluntarily trade off
political sovereignty for economic interests. With the end of Cold War in
the 1990s, ideological obstacles to further economic cooperation among
nations have substantially diminished. But even under such a favorable

international environment, one has reason to expect that the creation of a regional economic bloc will be completed through the gradual, evolutionary formation of linkages among nations. As the evolutionary developments in the 1990s become more favorable, the economic and political boundaries will eventually become blurred, and the political constraints to regional economic integration will be minimized. But in the current international environment, one can only guess whether the Asia Pacific countries will gradually depoliticize when they handle their foreign economic relations.

However, despite political constraints that prevent the institutionalization of any formal organization for economic integration in the region, there are several informal groups dedicated toward this purpose. Each of these informal groups is very conducive to the process of developing a formal institutional framework for regional economic cooperation. The Pacific Basin Economic Council (PBEC), established in 1967, is a private organization that includes businessmen from all Asia Pacific nations except North Korea and Cambodia. Its main purpose is to provide a forum for active exchange of views among private businessmen so as to provide advice to their respective governments and international agencies on a whole spectrum of economic affairs affecting the region's economic development.

The Pacific Economic Cooperation Conference (PECC), founded in 1980, is an informal group consisting of representatives of government, business, and academia from fourteen Asia Pacific countries, including Brunei, Canada, the United States, and eleven of the twelve countries from the first five groups mentioned at the beginning of the chapter (the sole exception being Hong Kong). The PECC provides dialogues for different participants from the Asia Pacific region. In 1986 a significant consensus among participants in the PECC created a historic communiqué calling for economic cooperation in the Pacific. As a result, APEC was formed in 1989, encompassing all of the PECC countries except China and Taiwan. The latter two, along with Hong Kong, were admitted to APEC during the 1991 annual ministerial meetings in Seoul, bringing that organization's membership to a total of fifteen.

APEC is a significant step toward coordination of trade and economic policies within the Asia Pacific region on an intergovernmental basis. Its creation provides a forum for regular meetings of government officials, at the ministerial level, from all members in the interest of fostering cooperation on broad economic issues. There are some discussions that parliamentarians from APEC members will also hold meetings in the future. Moreover, APEC has decided to set up a permanent secretariat office in Singapore to operate the routine functions of coordinating economic and commercial policies among member countries. One can conclude that, although conceptually it is long overdue for Asia Pacific countries to work closely on economic cooperation, there are divergent views on the nature, structure, membership, and functions of the institutional framework of economic cooperation in this region.

■ ALTERNATIVE SCENARIOS OF REGIONAL ECONOMIC BLOCS

From the above discussion, it seems that the creation of APEC is the most promising development so far for the emergence of a formal inter-governmental organization for regional economic cooperation. The APEC countries account for 38.2 percent of world trade and nearly one-half of total world output. More than 65 percent of their exports are intrabloc trade. Hence, APEC, which includes the United States and Japan, outpaces the integrated EC in terms of the volume of trade and total output. However, if APEC becomes a "closed" regional economic bloc and adopts discriminatory trade policies toward nonmember countries, the frictions and confrontations with the integrated EC and/or North American countries would intensify.

One might ask: What if a preferential trading arrangement should be created within East and Southeast Asia? My answer is that, by excluding the North American countries from the region, such an arrangement would result in three defensive trading blocs in the world economy. As noted before, the United States has been and still is the largest export market for most East and Southeast Asian countries. Any regional trading alliance that discriminates against the U.S. market and undermines the multilateral trading system would not be advantageous to them. The possible gains from *intra*regional trade would be offset by the loss of *inter*regional trade caused by exclusion of the United States from the region as an "outsider." Moreover, Krugman (1992, p. 18), who presented a simulation model of three trading blocs with various elasticity of substitution between products of any two, concluded that "world welfare is minimized for a world of three [exclusivist] trading blocs."

Therefore, to sustain the multilateral trading system under the guiding principles of the General Agreement on Tariffs and Trade, the APEC should adopt neither the EC nor the NAFTA formula. Although there is a strong potential for the Asia Pacific countries to organize a regional economic bloc, it is not in their best interest to undermine the multilateral trading system upon which the region's growth and prosperity relies.

Given this institutional constraint, APEC can only be expected to be a loose, open intergovernmental organization of economic cooperation with limited objectives regarding regional development (Elek 1992; Kim 1992). APEC is not and cannot be discriminatory against others. Participating countries must be open-minded, and membership has to be based on economic linkages with other member countries. The nonexclusion principle warrants that trade liberalization should not come at the expense of non-APEC members so as to be consistent with the fundamental nondiscrimination principle of the GATT.

Within APEC, however, there are several subregional trading blocs that have closer economic relationships and even have more formal institutional frameworks than APEC itself. They are:

1. The U.S.–Canada partnership under NAFTA, which will also include Mexico soon;
2. The Australia–New Zealand group;
3. The preferential trading area within ASEAN and its development of prospective free trade when ASEAN phases out internal tariffs and nontariff trade barriers in the next fifteen years or sooner; and
4. The widely speculated Greater China Economic Community among Chinese economies (still in the making).

The first one is a mixed blessing for other Asia Pacific countries, in that the potential trade creation effect may be concentrated in North America, leaving the burden of the trade diversion effect to be borne solely by other Asian countries. Despite repeated assurances from Washington and Ottawa that NAFTA will not divert the major trade flows from East and Southeast Asian countries, few are convinced that the current trade flows will not be distorted.

The Australia–New Zealand group presents a typical model of harmonization between countries by agreeing that "antidumping actions will no longer be taken between them" (Elek 1992, p. 75). If the format of closer economic relations between Australia and New Zealand can be broadly expanded to other countries, market accessibility among Asia Pacific nations will be greatly enhanced.

The ASEAN is by far the most politicized intergovernmental organization. Yet its primary function, in effect, has been to deal with security concerns rather than economic interests. But as the momentum of regional economic cooperation prevails, the ASEAN will gradually reduce its trade barriers and possibly become a free trade area within the next ten to fifteen years. Nevertheless, the combined GNP of ASEAN–4 in 1989 was only 55 percent of that of the NIEs, and its total exports were only 36.8 percent of the latter. It would be hard for ASEAN–4 to maintain a separate trading bloc identity in direct confrontation with the NIEs, given the former's insignificant economic weight and dependency on foreign capital from the NIEs. For their own good, ASEAN countries should extend trade liberalization policies to some of the NIEs that have invested heavily in their countries. Integrating ASEAN with the NIEs will have a less polarizing effect than integrating it with industrialized Japan (a strong factor of apprehension has long existed in the ASEAN countries).

There are several scenarios of the Greater China Economic Community, each with different economic and political contents. Among them, the South China Economic Zone is the one most commonly referred to. The underlying rationale is to integrate Hong Kong with Guangdong province and Taiwan with the neighboring province of Fujian and/or other Pacific coastal provinces of China. Thus, China's abundant natural resources will be integrated with the capital and the technological and managerial know-how of Taiwan and Hong Kong. The resultant conglomeration will further prod the development of the three Chinese economies. However, if the basis of grouping is purely based on Chinese ethnicity, it will inherently create strong apprehensions in Southeast Asian nations.[4] If the Greater China Economic Community is formed by the establishment of an FTA or even a preferential trading area among the three Chinese economies only, then Singapore, which would not be willing to be identified as the "Third China," would be in a very awkward position, facing the dilemma of "Hobson's choice." Moreover, the numerous native businesspeople with an ethnic Chinese background, who have long been said to dominate the local economies in ASEAN countries, might be in for hostile treatment from the respective ASEAN governments.

What if the third (ASEAN) and fourth (mainland China, Taiwan, and Hong Kong) groups of countries should merge? Historically, assimilation by ethnic Chinese in the ASEAN countries has been difficult. Nationalism within ASEAN has generated such movements as the "Filipino First policy," Malaysianization, and Indianization in the respective countries (Herschede 1991). Although the ASEAN, as a whole, welcomed the open door policy adopted by Beijing, many ASEAN governments, especially Malaysia, are concerned that their ethnic Chinese residents might give first priority to participating in the "four modernizations" in their motherland at the expense of investing in the local economies in ASEAN (Herschede 1991).

A frequently mentioned scenario is a "yen bloc." What are its prospects? What would it entail? Jeffery Frankel (1992, p. 28) presented eight major findings and concluded that, though there is a growing role of the yen at the expense of the dollar in the Asia Pacific region, "it is difficult to see signs of deliberate policy actions taken by the Japanese government to increase its financial and monetary influence in Asia." So far, Japan has not been able to, and probably will not, provide a strong domestic market to absorb the exports from the region's members. Moreover, many of the East and Southeast Asian nations are still antagonistic to the Japanese design of a Greater East Asia Co-Prosperity Sphere before and during World War II. Hence, it is one thing to acknowledge Japan's critical role in the region. It is entirely another to assume that Japan's leadership will create a regional economic bloc. After surveying the developments in this region since the mid-1980s, it seems fair to conclude that open regionalism with subregional trading blocs is the most concrete evidence of what is at best an embryo of regional economic integration in Asia Pacific.

■ CONCLUSION

It is much more difficult to assess the outlook of regional economic integration than it is to appraise the actual trade and investment flows in the region. Common economic interests among nations can reduce political constraints that block the way of economic cooperation among nations, but it cannot totally overcome institutional constraints. From the above discussion, it seems that APEC's open regionalism with gradual integration through trade and investment flows is the most feasible approach toward economic integration in the Asia Pacific region.

Any scheme of economic integration in Asia Pacific that visualizes it as the third defensive trading bloc, side by side with NAFTA and EC, is premature in the current international environment. Besides, in view of the divergent sociopolitical characteristics and uneven levels of economic development in Asia Pacific thus far, any such move toward regional integration here would only intensify the fissures between Asia and the United States (Europe as well). Premature integration would transform the APEC group from its current structure into a formalized trading bloc.

What, then, is the possible role for Asia Pacific countries in the world economy? The following assessments are only tentative, pending further development:

1. The United States and Japan will probably have to share the leadership in pushing for a more open and liberal trading system. Bilateral trade negotiations and sectoral liberalization will continue to operate as usual, and an evolutionary process of more comprehensive economic cooperation in the entire region will gradually be heightened because of increased intraregional trade and investment flows.

2. Open regionalism under the framework of APEC will continue, and consensus for economic cooperation among nations will spur APEC to become a more formal organization for regional development.

3. Subregional trading blocs, such as a free trade area within ASEAN, and closer economic relations in the Oceania states will continue. There is a high possibility that a preferential arrangement on trade and investment between China and Taiwan will materialize to protect the status of Taiwan's investors in China, even without mutual recognition between the two as coequal "political entities."

4. China's open door policy will pretty much continue regardless of power shifts in Beijing's leadership. Further integration of China's economy with the NIEs and other countries will make it difficult for Beijing to turn back to its socialist path of development. This state of affairs is conducive to political stability and economic prosperity in the region.

5. Access to the domestic markets of Japan and China will be crucial for further integration in East Asia. Beset by its swelling twin deficits, the

United States will be unable to continue as the major export market for East and Southeast Asia. The lopsided trade flows from Asia Pacific countries to the U.S. market will become unsustainable. China's domestic market has been and still is an irresistible attraction for all foreign investors. Access to the Chinese market by external investors is a prerequisite for further integration in the region. Moreover, further opening of Japan's market to the NIEs and ASEAN–4 alike will greatly enhance economic integration in the region.

6. Membership of any formal organization of economic cooperation will still be dominated by noneconomic factors such as mutual recognition as international entities among all participants, especially between Beijing and Taipei. But political and economic boundaries will become even more blurred as economic linkages between nations strengthen through trade and investment flows.

Therefore, in the foreseeable future, Asia Pacific countries will still be flirting with a loose, nonexclusive, noncollusive, and open regionalism, gradually moving toward greater economic cooperation and mutual development. It will emulate neither the EC model nor the NAFTA formula. But the momentum of intraregional trade and investment flows will generate a strong feeling of belonging, a sense of "economic symbiosis" or "economic condominium" in the region.

■ NOTES

1. After Deng Xiaoping, the elder Chinese leader, reiterated the pursuit of "open-door" policy in his southbound visitations of coastal areas in spring 1992, there were some aspirations within Chinese leadership to build Guangdong province to become the fifth Little Dragon in the coming decade.

2. Statistical Book of Overseas Investment 1991, Foreign Exchange Department, Bank of Korea.

3. Despite the official stand of "three Nos" in Taipei—no Contact, no Compromise, no Negotiation—Taipei has set up a semiofficial Association for Relations Across the Taiwan Straits to deal with the routine business of civic affairs with its counterpart in Beijing, the Straits Coordination Society.

4. For the problems and prospects of various scenarios of grand China economic zone, see Peter C. Y. Chow (1992).

■ REFERENCES

Akamatsu, K. 1962. "A Historical Pattern of Economic Growth in Developing Countries," *The Developing Economies,* No. 1 (March–April), pp. 3–25.
Bradford, Collin, Jr. 1987. "Trade and Structural Change: NICs and Next Tier of NICs as Transitional Economies," *World Development,* Vol. 15, No. 3, pp. 299–316.

Chow, Peter C. Y. 1989. "Economic Integration in the Pacific Basin Countries." In Bernard T. K. Joei (ed.), *From Pacific Region Toward Pacific Community.* Taipei: Center of Area Studies, Tamkang University, pp. 331–348.

———. 1992. "Coordination of Chinese Economic Systems," *Issues and Studies* (Taipei), Vol. 29. No. 1 (Jan. 1993), 99–118.

Chow Peter C. Y. and M. Kellman. 1992. *Trade—The Engine of Growth in East Asia.* New York: Oxford University Press.

Elek, Andrew. 1992. "Trade Policy Options for the Asia-Pacific Region in the 1990s: The Potential of Open Regionalism." *Americana Economic Review,* Vol. 82, No. 2, pp. 74–78.

Finger, J. M. and M. Kreinin. 1979. "A Measure of Export Similarity and Its Possible Use," *Economic Journal,* Vol. 89, pp. 905–912.

Frankel, Jeffrey. 1992. "Is Japan Creating a Yen Bloc in East Asia and Pacific?" National Bureau of Economic Research Working Paper No. 4050.

Herschede, Fred. 1991. "Trade Between China and ASEAN: The Impact of the Pacific Rim Era," *Pacific Affairs,* Vol. 64, No. 2, pp. 179–193.

Kim, Duk-Choong. 1992. "Open Regionalism in the Pacific: A World of Trading Blocs?" *United States Economic Review,* Vol. 82, No. 2, pp. 79–83.

Krugman, Paul. 1992. "The Move Toward Free Trade Zones," *Policy Implications of Trade and Currency Zones: Policy Implications of Trade and Currency Zones.* Federal Reserve Bank of Kansas City, pp. 7–41.

Lee, Chung H. 1990. "Direct Foreign Investment, Structural Adjustment, and International Division of Labor: A Dynamic Macroeconomic Theory of Direct Foreign Investment," *Hirtotsubashi Journal of Economics,* 31:61–72.

Lipsey, Richard G. 1988. "Global Imbalance and United States Trade Policy," *Atlantic Economic Journal,* Vol. XVI, No. 2, pp. 1–11.

Wallace, W. 1981. "Economic Divergence in the European Community." In M. Hodge and W. Wallace, eds. London: George Allen & Unwin. Reprinted in John M. Letiche, ed., *International Economic Policies and Their Theoretical Foundations.* New York: Academic Press, 1982, pp. 183–223.

Wong, John. 1988. "Integration of China into the Asia Pacific Region," *The World Economy,* 11:327–354.

Appendix 10.1 Major Economic Indicators of Asia Pacific Countries

	GDP (billions of dollars)	1989 Population (in millions)	1989 Exports (billions of dollars)	1989 Imports (billions of dollars)
China	417.8	1,113.9	52.5	59.1
Japan	2,818.5	123.1	275.0	207.4
NICs				
Korea	211.9	42.4	62.3	61.3
Hong Kong	52.5	5.7	28.7	72.2
Singapore	28.4	2.7	44.6	49.6
Taiwan	147.6	20.1	66.5	50.5
Total NICs	440.4	70.9	202.9	233.6
Indonesia	94.0	178.2	21.7	16.4
Malaysia	37.5	17.4	25.1	22.5
Philippines	44.4	60	7.7	10.7
Thailand	69.7	55.4	20.1	25.8
Total ASEAN–4	245.6	311	74.6	75.4
Oceania				
Australia	281.9	16.8	33.2	39.9
New Zealand	41.4	3.3	8.6	8.8
Asia Pacific Total	4,245.6	1,639	646.8	623.9
Percent of World Total	21.25	31.48	22.28	20.48
United States	$5,156.4	248.8	$347.0	491.5
Canada	$ 488.6	26.2	$114.1	113.2
Pacific Rim Grand Total	$9,890.6	1,914	1,107.9	1,228.6
Percent of World Total	49.50	36.77	38.17	40.33

Sources: The World Development Report 1991. © The International Bank for Reconstruction and Development/The World Bank. Reprinted by permission of Oxford University Press, Inc. *Taiwan Statistical Data Book 1990.* CEPD, Executive Yuan, Taipei.

■ 11

Asia Pacific in Perspective: The Impact of the End of the Cold War

James C. Hsiung

In this chapter, our task is to step back to take another look at the Asia Pacific landscape and visualize how it is going to blend into the panorama of twenty-first century world politics. The best way to do so is to cast a long glance at history and very briefly trace, first, the identity of Asia Pacific and, second, the rise of the region as a center for world attention. Only then shall we be able to dwell adequately on the ultimate question of what lies ahead for Asia Pacific beyond the dawn of the next century, which is only a short seven years away. As its title suggests, this chapter will try to put Asia Pacific in perspective, reassessing the evolution of the region and the impact of the end of the Cold War from hindsight. In the next (and final) chapter, I shall indulge in some horizon-gazing prognostications about the future.

■ IDENTITY OF THE REGION

The emergence of an Asia Pacific regional identity is a mid-twentieth-century affair. When Europeans (Portuguese) first came to East Asia in the fifteenth century, the area was only a geographical name; its components were as disparate as they were unrelated. In the nineteenth century, when commercial capitalism was first brought by the British and other Europeans to China, India, and other parts of Southeast Asia (Borthwick 1992, p. 77–118), there was no sense of Asia Pacific as a distinct region. The reason was simple: There was no regional community to speak of, if community presupposes a certain extent of regular contacts—trade, diplomatic, or

otherwise—and a set of institutions sustaining these contacts. The area became known loosely either as the Orient or the Far East. (The latter
nomenclature reflected the British perspective, looking east from London,
the world's capital at the time.) Despite the legendary 1853 "opening" of
Japan by Commodore Matthew Perry, the United States came to the region
only after 1898, when the Philippines were ceded to it after the Spanish-
American War.

The Pacific came to journalistic prominence only after Pearl Harbor in
1941. The Pacific War, which started almost as an adjunct to the European
phase of World War II, made the Pacific no longer a quaint reference as
before. It was, however, Japan's defeat that brought the United States to
the Pacific in force. The Japanese briefly occupied what had been European colonies, from Indochina to the Dutch East Indies to Malaya, dis-
placing their former European masters. Japan's defeat in the Pacific War
was followed by the independence of these colonies (Lach and Wehrle
1975, p. 1–9). The United States came to Asia Pacific not only as the pro-
consul in Japan (until 1952) but also as the big brother in the entire region,
replacing the Europeans. U.S. contacts expanded as U.S. security involvement spread and business in the region flourished. The wars in Korea and
Vietnam, moreover, brought thousands of U.S. citizens across the Pacific
Ocean to East Asia (Borthwick 1992, p. 212–240). (Germany's defeat in
World War II did not result in as heavy a U.S. turnout in Europe; the U.S.
military presence there is no comparison to its presence in Asia Pacific
([Muller and Schweigler 1992].)

The Cold War, which soon extended to the Asia Pacific region, took
the form of U.S.–Soviet rivalry across the board—in the Korean Peninsula,
in Indochina, over China, and, furthermore, over waters in the Pacific
stretching all the way to the Indian Ocean. That the Soviet Pacific Fleet
was the largest of the Soviet naval forces was perhaps a good indicator of
the intensity of the U.S.–Soviet conflict in the Pacific. Equally, the United
States' bilateral mutual security pacts with Japan, South Korea, the Republic of China (Taiwan), and the Philippines, along with ANZUS (the security pact encompassing Australia, the United States, and New Zealand)
and SEATO (Southeast Asia Treaty Organization)—all of these, although
a tribute to Secretary of State John Foster Dulles's "pactomania," were a
measure of the Cold War conflict. The identity of the Asia Pacific region
was thus abetted by its emergence as a security community (Lach and
Wehrle 1975). Increased trade and other contacts among its members,
which developed after the 1960s, further sharpened the region's identity.

■ RISE OF THE REGION

The ascent of Asia Pacific as a region deserving worldwide attention
probably came only after the 1960s, for a combination of reasons. First,

the fixation of the Vietnam War, beginning in 1965, increasingly riveted the world's attention on the region. By coincidence, this period saw a number of other important developments. For one, the market economies of the western Pacific Rim, with few exceptions, registered average growth rates of 6 percent or more. Those of China and some Southeast Asian nations were only slightly slower (Borthwick 1992, p. 274). By 1970 Japan, the premier economy of the region, accounted for 50 percent of the area's income and 9 percent of that of the world. As if by design, Taiwan, South Korea, Hong Kong, and Singapore—the so-called "four Little Dragons"—all embarked upon a similar structural transformation from import substitution economies into export-driven ones. Since the mid-1970s, the cutting edge of economic growth in the region has moved west and south, from the Little Dragons to resource-rich Southeast Asia (especially Malaysia, Thailand, and Indonesia) and eventually to the People's Republic of China (Borthwick 1992, p. 276ff).

Asia Pacific today is a region that embraces not only Japan and the Asian NIEs, but also the ASEAN nations and China, as well as the Pacific Coast of North America. This is the region that most observers agree will most probably continue to surpass other regions in economic growth. Asia Pacific's GDP will have risen from 15 percent to 20 percent of world GDP between 1980 and 2000. It will be 75 percent of the *combined* U.S. and European GDP—90 percent if the Chinese GDP is added to it (Linder 1986, p. 13–14). In a survey of eight Asian and Southeast Asian economies—including the four Little Dragons, ASEAN–3 (Thailand, Malaysia, and Indonesia), and China—the *Economist* (November 11, 1991) pronounced them as forging "the fastest industrial revolutions the world has ever seen. All eight have proved that they can sustain growth rates of over 7 percent a year," or two to three times faster than the older industrial countries. At that speed, an economy doubles in a decade. By 2050, the survey added, "there will be a shift in economic power away from Europe and North America to the western side of the Pacific Rim."

Mutual and synergistic growth in the region's economies naturally led to a growing self-awareness that both spawned and was abetted by an ever-rising expansion of intraregional trade. In 1987 Asia Pacific intraregional trade rose nearly 30 percent, to $189 billion. If the trend continues, as is expected, the value of intraregional trade will, by the mid-1990s, overtake the region's total trade with North America (Hsiung 1989, p. 44). The regional self-identity was given an institutional boost in the creation of the Asian Pacific Economic Cooperation (APEC) forum at the end of 1989 in Australia. By 1991, at APEC's third ministerial meeting in Seoul —when all the three Chinese economies (mainland, Taiwan, and Hong Kong) joined by prior agreement—nearly all economies of scale in the Pacific Basin had joined the forum.

As the focus of this volume is international, not domestic, politics, I have chosen not to get into the causes or noncauses for the region's economic developmental phenomenon. I only wish to make a few passing comments on the challenge posed by this "miraculous" experience to theory and by extension to other nations. Of the various theories of development (or modernization), two stand out, both in their own right and for the frequency with which they have been invoked in studies of development and underdevelopment in other regions. They are broadly identified here as *developmentalism* and *dependencia*. Below, I shall note why they cannot explain the East Asian model.

■ IRRELEVANCE OF DEVELOPMENTALISM

Although it has various forms, the developmentalist theory, to put it in the simplest terms, posits that a prior condition for economic development is political development, which translates as democratization (W. W. Rostow 1960; Seymour Martin Lipset 1963). The theory also shares much in common with the Weberian thesis that modernization, or industrialization, denotes the spread of capitalism, which in turn is based on an entrepreneurship as conceived in the Protestant ethic (Weber 1958). Although less well-known but nonetheless a part of the developmentalist genre, there is the customary notion that societal instability is expected as a consequence of inequitable distribution of the benefits from initial growth (Midlarsky 1988; Muller 1985). But in the actual developmental experience of East Asia, none of these facets of the theory is empirically borne out to any notable degree, if at all.

In the first place, the East Asian experience followed the opposite sequence from that which developmentalism prescribes: Economic success came before, not after, political reforms leading to democracy. Perhaps the sole exception is Japan, where the two processes seemed to coincide. In South Korea and Taiwan, where the economic miracle was achieved in the late 1960s, democratization began only in the late 1980s, after an interregnum of almost two decades. Hong Kong has flourished under colonial rule, which by definition is nondemocratic. Singapore is ruled *by* law but is yet a distance away from the rule *of* law, an ingredient indispensable to the Western definition of democracy.

Second, all the Asian Little Dragons, together with Japan, are distinguished by a shared cultural heritage—i.e., a Confucian tradition—adapted in various combinations with their respective native cultures. This fact defies the Weberian (1964) thesis that the Confucian ethical system is inimical to the development of capitalism (read: economic success). According to the Weberian thesis, the trouble with a Confucian system is that (1) it lacks the dynamic motivation essential for entrepreneurship, which is indispensable to capitalist development, and (2) it contains negative and conservative values incapable of developing a dynamic social orientation toward capitalism. However, it would be hard to dissociate the East Asian developmental experience from the cultural influence of Confucianism. If fact, the opposite case can be made—i.e., that the miraculous achievement is precisely consequential upon the commonality of a Confucian tradition—as Herman Kahn (1979) first argued. Following Kahn's lead ten years later, Hung-chao Tai (1989) and associates also labored to show more than a casual, coincidental link between East Asian development and Confucianism.

Third, the miraculous economic growth in East Asia did not similarly bring, in its wake, social instability and social unrest, as developmentalism forecasts. Whatever turmoil there was in Kwangju, Korea, and in Chungli and Kaohsiung, Taiwan, came as a prelude to the advance toward democratization following on the heels of economic success rather than as a consequence of economic development.

■ IRRELEVANCE OF DEPENDENCIA

The other theory often invoked in the literature on Third World underdevelopment, the theory of dependency (or dependencia), is at a loss to explain why economic development was possible in East Asia in the first place. Dependencia argues that to the "core" occupied by the industrial West (led by the United States), much of the rest of the world constitutes the "periphery." The core-periphery relationship is one of subordination, and it is maintained by the capitalist core through either direct political control (i.e., colonialism), the exercise of monopoly economic power (neocolonialism), or the formation of alliances with internal elites in the Third World who oppose change for fear of losing their vested interests (Frank 1969; Wallerstein 1980). These dependency structures, therefore, foredoom the nations in the nonindustrial periphery to underdevelopment.

Without question, the dependency of their export-oriented strategy qualifies the Asian NIEs as dependent economies on the Western capitalist core. If one applies the logic of dependencia, none of the Asian NIEs would be expected to develop for as long as the capitalist core exists. From the perspective of the core-periphery paradigm, there is no reason any of the Asian NIEs should have a better chance to develop than, say, Brazil (Evans 1979). Thus, the very incidence of East Asia's miraculous economic success poses a formidable challenge to the dependency theory (cf. Chan and Clark 1992). An even greater challenge to the theory is the spread of the East Asian experience to other neighbors similarly in the "periphery," such as Thailand and Malaysia, often cited as the next Little Dragons waiting in the wings.

Recently, questions were raised as to what will happen to dependencia or, more specifically, to the core-periphery relationship of nations, following the end of the bipolar world. Goldgeier and McFaul (1992) postulated a "tale of two worlds" thesis. In the core states, they maintain, the growth of shared norms concerning democracy and markets not only will make balance of power politics a thing of the past but also will make nuclear weapons less important for maintaining stability than they were during the Cold War. In the peripheral states, however, the absence of shared norms about democracy and markets, no less than the absence of absolute deterrents to war, will make old-style balance of power politics the norm, according to their thesis.

Because it is predicated on the same core-periphery assumptions inherent in dependencia, the Goldgeier and McFaul thesis is no more or no less valid than the theory itself. It is incumbent on us to assess the Goldgeier-McFaul thesis if we are to evaluate the future of dependencia in the post-bipolar world. As will become clear below, the sweep of the Goldgeier-McFaul thesis touches on much more than just the future of the dependencia theory. It bears on the very question of what the future holds for relations among nations as they sail into the next century.

■ IMAGERY OF THE "TWO WORLDS": IS BALANCE OF POWER DEAD?

Conventional wisdom has it that if the East-West divide of the world disappears, the remaining divide must be between the industrial northern and the underdeveloped southern nations. The Goldgeier-McFaul thesis lends sophisticated theoretical corroboration to this view. We will examine the two cardinal propositions in their thesis. The first is that, with respect to the core states, their shared norms concerning democracy and markets will make balance of power obsolete and reduce the value of nuclear weapons. I have already dwelt on the declining value of nuclear weapons (see Chapter 1), so I will skip this part in my commentary here. However, I find a number of problems with the notion about the alleged future obsolescence of major-state balance of power and the reasons given for it.

First, empirically, democracies are found not to war with other democracies but to prevail in wars with autocratic states (Small and Singer 1976; Maoz and Abdolali 1989). Although there is agreement on these findings, the reasons for the phenomena are not clear. Few attempts, it seems, have been made to explain the regularity with which these two findings recur in history. David Lake (1992) offered an insightful explanation drawn from a microeconomic theory of state. State "rent-seeking," according to Lake, creates an imperialist bias (i.e., the propensity to exact rents from other states) in a country's foreign policy. This bias is the smallest in democracies, where the costs to society of controlling the state are relatively low. Hence, democracies are less war prone, especially in their relations with each other. Besides, because they are constrained by their societies from earning rents (Lake, p. 26f), democracies will devote greater absolute resources to security, enjoy greater support for their polcies, and will be more likely to win wars fought against autocracies (Lake, pp. 30–31).

There is no empirical evidence, though, that democracies do not form coalitions and countercoalitions (balance of power). Empirically, democracies are found disposed to ally with other democracies (Siverson and Emmons 1991). Goldgeier and McFaul call this "bandwagoning," but I disagree. Balance of power, in fact, is an art perfected in the nineteenth century by Great Britain, which as the existing hegemon played the world's ultimate balancer. Against this evidence, it is impossible to conceive, with Goldgeier and McFaul, that the growth of shared norms concerning democracy (and markets) will ever render balance of power obsolete in the foreign relations of the core states beyond the end of the Cold War. For obvious reasons, I shall not go into the question whether balance of power is coterminous with military alliance making and military operations alone. (Increasingly, it is not.) Suffice it to say that balance of power may take alternative forms, including that of macromanagement of free trade vs. state sovereignty.

The second proposition in the Goldgeier-McFaul thesis about future core-periphery relationships is that balance of power will survive the end of the Cold War *only* in the peripheral states. The reason given is that the world system's periphery suffers from an absence of deterrents to war as well as an absence of shared norms about democracy and markets. Likewise, I have difficulty with this proposition because of its two implicit assumptions: (1) an alleged perpetual polarization between the market and nonmarket economies; and (2) an alleged lack of absolute deterrents to war by the periphery states.

Since the late 1980s, even before the collapse of communism in Eastern Europe, a number of countries saddled with a Stalinist type of planned economy were already groping for a rendezvous with the market. Poland was the first in East Europe. In Asia Pacific, China's search for marketization commenced even earlier, as far back as 1978. By 1992 there were so many new converts to marketization that one could scarcely find a centrally planned economy that was inimical to the market. As the post–Cold War era wears on, the rigid dividing line between the market and nonmarket economies will be increasingly harder to maintain. The line is fast blurring. In the euphoria generated by the retreat of communism, chances are that the message of democracy will spread and become a "shared norm" among an increasing number of states that occupy places the dependencia theorists call the periphery. If this extension of the shared norms of democracy and market comes true, what appears to be the rigid divide between the core and the periphery states will likely diminish. It will be hard, under the circumstances, for the "tale of two worlds" thesis to be supported by the hard facts of an ever-evolving reality in the new age.

On the Goldgeier-McFaul allegation that states in the periphery are totally without absolute deterrents to war after the withdrawal of Soviet power, I am troubled by its two inherent major premises: (1) a blanket notion that the states in the periphery lost a patron with the dissolution of the Soviet Union and, hence, the nuclear umbrella that the latter used to provide; and (2) a notion that these peripheral states are now left without adequate means of self-defense and therefore remain totally at the mercy of the industrial core. I shall comment on these two assumptions separately.

First, if the nuclear umbrella was necessary before, it was only because the world was caught in a nuclear bipolar confrontation, which applied to the followers on both sides. The end of the Cold War, it follows, removed the Democles' sword from over the heads of all nations, including those in the periphery. The upshot is that national means of defense will replace the nuclear umbrella that each superpower was able to provide to its client states: Now that the nuclear bipolar confrontation is gone, so goes the need for the nuclear umbrella. The question of whether the Third World states will be able to deter wars on their own, in the absence of their Soviet patron, hinges on whether they can afford to maintain adequate national means of defense. The answer is: Not all Third World states are equally vulnerable. One measure of these states' ability to take care of their own defenses is their military expenditures (i.e., the costs paid in weapons acquisition in the name of national defense).

Some of the small states have been big spenders. Between 1981 and 1988, the years immediately before the end of the Cold War, Third World states spent an aggregate of $341 billion on imported arms, according to a Congressional Research Service report. Some of these included tanks, self-propelled cannon, artillery pieces, combat aircraft, warships, and even air-to-air missiles (Grimmet 1988). Twelve Third World countries can produce combat aircraft, eleven produce armored vehicles, twelve produce major fighting ships, and about forty produce small arms and ammunitions (SIPRI 1985).

Michael Klare (1991, p. 172) notes three converging trends that started in the last decade and are likely to become significantly more pronounced in the 1990s: (1) the steady accumulation of large stockpiles of sophisticated arms by highly militarized states in Third World areas of potential conflict (e.g., Middle East and South Asia); (2) the continuing proliferation of nuclear and chemical weapons technology to emerging Third World powers (including Brazil, Iraq, Israel, Libya, the two Koreas, and Taiwan); and (3) the acquisition by Third World nations with nuclear and/or chemical weapons of sophisticated aircraft and missiles capable of delivering such ammunitions over considerable distances. Many of the states named above also acquired ballistic missiles with the ability to deliver nuclear or chemical weapons over ranges of several hundreds or even thousands of miles (Klare 1991, p. 173)

The Iraqi invasion of Kuwait in 1990 showed, among other things, the extent to which unscrupulous Third World states such as Iraq can be so heavily armed as to be able easily to prey on a weaker target like Kuwait. In this connection, an inherent lesson taught by the ensuing Gulf War was that the interests of the core and those of a peripheral state such as Kuwait were in no way "decoupled," as Goldgeier and McFaul (1992, p. 487) asserted they would be. The coauthors argued that the region's oil was a decisive factor in the core's rapid and resolute response to Iraq (*ibid.*). If indeed it was, it simply shows that the lopsided sort of dependent relationship between core and periphery, alleged by dependencia as always in the core's favor, has another side to it: The core is dependent on the periphery as well. In a world in which interests of economic security will gain increasing importance because of the dictate of geoeconomics (see Chapter 1), this reverse dependency (i.e., by the core on the periphery) will accelerate, if only because the periphery has the vital resources essential for the core's economic security interests.

The Iraqi episode also demonstrated that balance of power has not ceased for the core states, contrary to the prognostication by Goldgeier and McFaul. What has changed is the reason for which balance of power is played out. Before, in the bipolar world, the motivation would be to counteract the expansionism of the other superpower or to forestall the likelihood that the latter would fill a power vacuum if no appropriate countervailing action were taken in time. In the post–Cold War world, on the other hand, the likely reason for balance of power is to check a local bully's expansionism, as in the Iraqi case. As such, it is typical of the central question asked in balance of power: Who in our midst is too strong (Claude 1962)? The oil concern was an additional desideratum for the core's speedy action in Operation Desert Storm, but it was not the decisive one. The oil factor may confirm the onset of the geoeconomic age, but in no way does it refute the survival of balance of power in the core's relations with the periphery in the post–Cold War era. If oil were the only concern for Desert Storm, then why would the war be so prematurely ended before Saddam Hussein was evicted from power? Without his eviction, Saddam remained a threat to the core's access to Persian Gulf oil. The decisive consideration that accounted for the premature end of the campaign was that a premature political demise of Saddam Hussein might lead to the rise to dominance in the Middle East of another tyrant who might be even more menacing to regional peace and stability. That consideration, too, was typical of balance of power calculations.

Goldgeier and McFaul used the lack of an oil desideratum as the reason for the core's failure to act, or engage in balance of power, in the cases of Liberia, Sudan, and Ethiopia. In these cases, I submit, the core did not act precisely because they involved civil conflicts, fought properly within national boundaries and without visible foreign intervention. In bona fide civil war situations such as these, there is very little the core can do to help.

It would be hard to place Yugoslavia on the core-periphery map of the dependency theorists. But, as one of the founding trio (the other two are India and Egypt) of the nonaligned movement, Yugoslavia should, I surmise, be part of the "periphery" in the world system of dependencia. The fact is that the European Community and the UN Security Council (the United States included) were the force behind the cease-fire plans and peacekeeping operations. If the implicit concern of the West was to forestall or minimize the destabilizing fallouts on Central European regional politics from the breakup of Yugoslavia, then this would be a bona fide case of balance of power at the initiative of the core states. Significantly, it came after the end of the Cold War, thus refuting the Goldgeier-McFaul claim about the demise of major-state balance of power.

In the Iraqi case, when the Western states acted in unison on the U.S. side, Goldgeier and McFaul (1992, p. 480) saw them as "bandwagoning" rather than balancing. If the same logic is applied, they would consider the concerted Western intercession against Serbia in behalf of Bosnia during the height of the Yugoslav civil war as "bandwagoning." But the very nature of the two cases, which left the intervening core states no choice, has to be considered. The Iraqi case involved an outright act of aggression, in that one state (Iraq) invaded and annexed another sovereign state (Kuwait) by force. More than that, if left unchecked, the Iraqi act would have been the first successful assault on the sanctity of postcolonial boundaries, something few, if any, members of the world community (particularly the West) could stomach. Again, in the Yugoslav case, the severity of the onslaught on Bosnian civilian lives by Serbian nationalists, mobilizing one of Europe's powerful military forces in the name of "ethnic cleansing," was such that it amounted to another holocaust. To say that the Western powers were "bandwagoning" instead of splitting on opposing sides would be like saying that balance of power is senselessly mechanical (balancing for balancing's sake) and should put a blind eye to acts of blatant aggression or near-genocide. This position would both be morally indefensible and misrepresenting what balance of power really is as a diplomatic institution.

The above critique on the "two worlds" thesis advanced by Goldgeier and McFaul is motivated more by our interest in probing what is the likely shape of future world politics than in passing judgment on the thesis per se or on the assumptions it shares with dependencia. Nonetheless, in the course of our commentary, we have done more than question the validity of the dependencia theory. We have also touched upon three important aspects of future international relations. First, we have discussed the continuing role of balance of power for the core states: It has survived the onset of the post–Cold War era, contrary to allegations by Goldgeier and

McFaul. Second, we have suggested that the lines of division between democracies and autocracies and between the market and nonmarket economies are blurring or wearing thin. In this connection, we have also questioned whether some of the peripheral states are really as defenseless, after the Soviet retreat, as they are sometimes portrayed to be. Third, we have argued that the security interests (albeit redefined to accommodate economic security) of the core and the periphery are in no way decoupled, as alleged. Here, too, we have further argued that while the balance of power concerns of the core states will continue as before, the motivation for them may vary as geoeconomics rivals with geopolitics.

■ EFFECTS OF THE SOVIET RETREAT ON THE ASIA PACIFIC REGION

Paradoxically, the retreat of Soviet power will affect the balance of forces and stability in Asia Pacific relatively less acutely than in some of the other regions, such as Europe and the Middle East. A number of reasons underscore this conclusion.

First, unlike European nations, the Asia Pacific nations were not split into two opposing alliance systems. Among the noncommunist states of Asia Pacific, there was no multilateral institution building such as NATO, the EC, or the Helsinki process (all of which were premised on a Western solidarity against a colossal adversary such as the Soviet bloc once represented). Here the Soviet threat was felt only in spasmodic fashion—in the Sea of Japan, on the Korean Peninsula, along China's northern borders, in Indochina, and in relation to the Pacific waters. Its retreat, therefore, did not similarly lift the spectre of a continentwide war such as NATO had been prepared to fight for over four decades—that spectre had never been known to Asia Pacific. The Soviet bowing out removed the last barrier for Sino-Vietnamese normalization, and resulted in a decided pro-China tilt in Mongolia's and North Korea's foreign policy posture. It nevertheless did not produce anything as harrying as, say, the restructuring of Franco-German relations following German unification and the total collapse of the Eastern bloc. If the end of the Cold War tipped the scales toward nationalism in Europe, so much so that it might even tangle with the progress toward single-market integration, the fact is that nationalism was never held back in Asia Pacific during the Cold War to the same extent as it was in Europe. Thus, there is no similar upsurge of nationalism now that the external threat has receded.

Across the Atlantic, members of NATO now find themselves ambivalent about an organization whose raison d'être came into question with the disappearance of the Soviet threat. One indication of the quandary is that NATO proved unable to do anything in the midst of the messy Yugoslav civil strife. By contrast, the Asia Pacific nations have been spared any such problems.[1] Other than the relatively short-lived SEATO, there have been only bilateral security bonds in this region. Therefore, the Soviet retreat did not similarly affect the viability of existing multilateral security institutions, simply because there were none. The bottom line is that the dawn of the post–Cold War era required relatively fewer adjustments in the relations among members of the Asia Pacific region than among European nations.

Second, unlike Eastern Europe, Asia had few Soviet client states. After the falling out of Beijing and Moscow in the 1960s, only North Korea, Mongolia, and Vietnam qualified as Moscow's "satellites." Soviet relations were nowhere near as close with these client states as with the Warsaw Pact nations. Another difference is that in Eastern Europe the other communist regimes fell before the Soviet Union did. In East Asia, the fall of the Soviet regime was not preceded, nor accompanied, by the collapse of communism in all of its [former] satellites. Only Mongolia saw the bowing out of communist rule in favor of electoral politics (the former Communist Party still holds the absolute majority seats in parliament). In North Korea and in Vietnam, no less than in China, the communist regime survived the fate that befell communism in Eastern Europe and the Soviet Union.

Third, if measured by past arms imports from Moscow, the dependency of Asia Pacific states on the Soviet Union was low. Aggregate data on regional shares of world arms imports for 1985, before the decline of Cold War hostility, indicate that the Middle East led all other regions in dependence on external arms supplies. Its 35 percent share stood head and shoulders over Africa's 12.1 percent, East Asia's 11.5 percent, the 10.1 percent share for Southeast Asia and Oceania, and the 8 percent share for Latin America (Gallik 1987, p. 7). The Soviets were the number one supplier of arms imports to the Middle East, accounting for a third of the region's total imports for 1982 through 1986 (*ibid.*). By comparison, East Asia and South Asia were far less dependent on Soviet arms imports (ranked fourth and fifth, respectively), suggesting that neither region is as adversely affected as, say, the Middle East, by the disappearance of the Soviet Union from the scene.

■ ALLIES AND ADVERSARIES: THE BLURRING LINES

At the risk of being redundant, I reiterate that a consequence of the end of the Cold War is the decline of nations' concerns for military security in favor of economic security. Under the circumstances, former allies may turn out to be potential adversaries (such as in trade matters), and former neutrals may turn out to be real or potential allies. The lines between allies and adversaries are blurring. To fully develop this point, I will make pertinent comparisons of relations before and after the end of the Cold War.

☐ Asian Nations vis-à-vis the United States

Throughout the Cold War, successive U.S. presidents subordinated economic interests to perceived geopolitical requirements (Huntington 1988). As the price for the military and diplomatic cooperation of Japan and the other East Asian allies (South Korea and Taiwan), Washington pursued a policy that eventually helped boost their economic power at the expense of U.S. economic interests. The U.S. policy of accommodation to East Asia began in late 1948 and early 1949 with the Dodge Plan. It aimed at reviving Japanese industrial productivity and boosting the other East Asian economies in return for their military cooperation (McCormick, p. 89). At little or no charge, for example, critical U.S. technology and industrial know-how were transferred to these allies. Washington accepted a trade and investment relationship based on the understanding that the U.S. market would be relatively open even though those of its Asian partners could be much more restrictive (Harrison, Selig, and Prestowitz 1990). For evidence of the long-lasting U.S. willingness to put security ahead of economic interests, one need only cite Washington's decisions in 1990 to join in codevelopment and coproduction of the Japanese FSX and South Korean FA–18 fighter aircraft. Washington decided on the moves against strong domestic criticisms that the deals, involving sensitive high tech transfers, would accelerate the ability of East Asian firms to compete against their U.S. counterparts in avionics (Mancini 1989). These instances were but the latest of what was a "40–year behavior pattern in which the United States has sacrificed its economic interests for what it regarded as military imperatives" (Harrison, Selig, and Prestowitz 1990, p. 192).

But with the winding down of the Cold War, the priorities were reversed, and Washington reacted to the trade surpluses of its East Asian trading partners, principally Japan, South Korea, and Taiwan. These three together accounted for 62 percent of the United States' $109 billion trade deficit in 1989. In addition to the use of voluntary export restraint (VER)—on Japanese car imports, for example—Washington found another weapon with which to bring down the East Asian trade imbalances. Starting in 1989, the United States piously enforced the so-called "Super 301" under the 1988 Omnibus Trade and Competitiveness Act (modeled after Section 301 of the 1974 Trade Act). Under Super 301, the U.S. government has the right to retaliate against countries named by the United States trade representative (USTR) as engaging in unfair trade practices against the United States, unless such countries correct those practices within twelve to eighteen months, under agreement with the USTR. The United States alone defines what is "unfair trade" under the law.[2]

At the same time, the United States undertook a number of negotiations with Japan and other East Asian nations with the specific purpose of removing what were called "structural" barriers. Similar talks were going on for the protection of intellectual properties, such as copyright of computer softwares.

The important thing for our purpose here is that the end of the Cold War finally brought change to a legacy in U.S. policies toward East Asia: the doctrine of essential similarity. The doctrine held out a compatibility between Washington and its East Asian protégés in the principles and purposes of their economies. During the Cold War, as part of its grand strategy, Washington averted its eyes and clung to the doctrine of similarity (with which to rally public and congressional support), even if it meant losses to U.S. businesses in unfair competition with East Asian trading partners that constrained U.S. imports (Harrison, Selig, and Prestowitz, p. 192).

Another indication of the winding down of the Cold War was Washington's increasingly strident demands for greater defense "burden sharing" by Japan and other East Asian allies to offset U.S. trade imbalances. Although Washington argued that the East Asians should feel a debt to Uncle Sam for military and economic assistance, the argument did not play well in the dusk of the Cold War. Most South Koreans, for example, think of themselves as victims of a partition imposed by the superpowers. As the memory of the Korean War recedes to the background, South Korean gratitude for U.S. help also fades, and it yields to an increasing sense that the United States *owed* South Korea military protection and special economic treatment in return for the use of their territory for nuclear-equipped U.S. military bases (Harrison, Selig, and Prestowitz, p. 194).

Similarly, the United States may complain about the nonreciprocated "free rides" the Japanese have been getting in terms of free security benefits and preferential treatment in trade relations. But looking back to the Cold War days, the Japanese now flatly reject the idea of "debt." Many in Japan believe, as ever before, that the United States rebuilt Japan after V-J Day for its own strategic reasons as an industrial bulwark against the Soviet Union and Communist China (Harrison, Selig, and Prestowitz, p. 194).

Just to show how curtly Japan now can say "no" to America, a recent report by the powerful MITI (Ministry of International Trade and Industry) countered U.S. complaints about unfair Japanese trading practices by calling the United States itself an "unfair trader." The report chastised Washington for its trade policy, which, it says, is characterized by unilateral action inconsistent with international agreements, including the General Agreement on Tariffs and Trade. The report singles out Super 301 as circumventing GATT's trade-dispute settlement procedures.[3]

Taiwan is a slightly different case. From 1949 to 1965, the United States pumped massive aid to Taiwan and, as a result, got the island to the point where it could start on the road to economic takeoff. It became an economic heavyweight a few years later. By 1990, as a gauge of its economic prosperity, Taiwan had replaced Japan as the world's largest holder of foreign-exchange reserves, well over $67 billion (figure for 1992: $84.5 billion). Taiwan had likewise replaced Japan by 1991 as the largest buyer of U.S. Treasury bills, totaling over $10 billion per year.[4] Yet people on Taiwan may have similar reasons to not feel a debt to the United States, precisely because the latter had built up Taiwan as a counterweight against mainland China (Harrison and Prestowitz 1990, p. 193). When it suited the convenience of changing U.S. strategic needs (as in the 1970s), Washington never hesitated to flirt with Beijing. The derecognition of Taiwan in 1979 was the crowning event in Washington's playing of the "China card" in its intense feud with the Soviet Union. In the post–Cold War era, however, when the rationale for the China-card strategy is a thing of the past, Taiwan's relations with Washington have gotten better than at any point since 1979. Relative to other East Asian nations, Taiwan may be an "oddball," in that its people still concede a link between their success and U.S. help, past and present.

A caveat has to be entered here, though: Faced with the formidable mainland Chinese threat from across the strait, Taiwan is still dependent on the United States for its security, to a degree not seen elsewhere. It is a fact not changed by the end of the Cold War. For instance, President George Bush on July 19, 1992, approved the lease of three Knox-class antisubmarine frigates to Taiwan for five years.[5] Later, in the heat of the presidential campaign, President Bush approved the sale of 150 F–16 aircraft to Taiwan.

The Japanese and Korean ambivalence about the value of having a U.S. connection caught on in the Philippines. After a Senate vote rejected the August 1991 bases treaty, the Manila government gave Washington a year to leave its last Philippine military base, Subic Bay. The rejection adds to the testimonies to the demise of the East-West conflict in the Pacific.

However, as some of the former allies were falling out with the United States, two former Asian neutral nations in the East-West conflict came forward as candidates to replace the Philippines as potential U.S. allies for the future. Even before the final conclusion of the U.S. talks with the Philippines, Singapore in November 1990 gave Washington timely leverage by offering itself as an alternative base. The Singapore–U.S. Trade and Investment Framework Agreement was signed in October 1991. This move, which could lead to a bilateral free trade pact, came after Singapore had openly espoused having a place in Southeast Asia for U.S. trade. Singapore may have created a model for U.S. relations with other Southeast Asian nations in the post–Cold War era (Conboy 1992).

In the more relaxed post–Cold War atmosphere, in April 1992 Malaysia and the United States unveiled a heretofore secret agreement on bilateral training and educational cooperation signed in 1984. Officials in Kuala Lumpur and Washington announced that joint annual military exercises between the two countries had been going on since the early 1970s. The agreement formalized the informal military cooperation, but it had been kept secret until April 1992, because Malaysia has been a champion of nonalignment and strongly advocated the creation of ZOPFAN, a zone of peace, freedom, and neutrality in Southeast Asia.[6] These new developments indicated a commonly shared concern, at least in Singapore and Malaysia, about the power vacuum that is going to be created by the imminent pullout of the U.S. military presence from the Philippines. More important, they indicated that some former neutrals during the Cold War era had turned into new U.S. allies, in contrast with the changing mood in the opposite direction among former allies Japan, South Korea, and the Philippines. With these former allies, U.S. ties have tended to cool as the Cold War recedes into the background. Such is the paradox created by the vanishing of the Cold War.

□ *Asian Nations vis-à-vis One Another*

The end of the Cold War and the retreat of Soviet power will likely create expectations in Asia that before long Washington will be pressured by Congress for a phased withdrawal of U.S. forces from the region. The area states, in turn, will be poised to rely more heavily on their own resources for national defense. A competitive arms race, typical of what is known in international relations theory as the "security dilemma," will therefore set in.

Already, Indonesia, Malaysia, and Thailand, in competition with China, are expanding their naval forces (see Chapter 4). In a parallel bid to expand its influence in the Indian Ocean to counter China, the Indian navy plans to deploy three aircraft carrier battle groups by 2010 (Vlahos 1991, p. 125). Taiwan is also shopping for weapons, from the French Mirage 2000 attack aircraft to the U.S. F-16, in anticipation of the need for increased national defense capabilities. With a total population of 21 million, the island earmarked $10.3 billion (or 24.8 percent of its $42.8 billion government budget) for defense expenditures for 1993,[7] nearly 35 percent more than mainland China's defense budget of $7.5 billion (1991). Yet, Taiwan is 267 times smaller in territory and 56 times smaller in population than the Chinese mainland.

In Chapter 1, I noted that by 1990 Japan's defense spending was below only those of the United States and the Soviet Union. Now, with the demise of the latter superpower, Japan has moved up to the world's number two position on the scale of global defense expenditures. The grave implications of this change, it seems, were not lost on the Chinese, who in an unprecedented move in May 1991 made a package proposal on nuclear disarmament.[8] Space does not allow me to go into details, but I do wish to note that the full import of the latest Chinese proposal becomes clear only in view Beijing's long-standing position since its first successful atomic detonation in 1964. That position had always been that nuclear disarmament was a collusion between the two superpowers to perpetuate their nuclear monopoly by denying other states the right to develop their own nuclear weapons (Leng 1980). Given the increasing Chinese uneasiness over Japan's expanding military potential, it is likely that the latest reversal of their position was prompted by an urge to constrain Japan through arms control (cf. Harrison, Selig, and Prestowitz 1990, p. 198).

Within the region, one finds a coincidental improvement in the political and security picture as the Cold War phases out. There has been smooth transition to democracy in South Korea, Taiwan, and the Philippines from the late 1980s through the early 1990s. In addition, the Soviet retreat from Indochina was followed by a number of international breakthroughs: the Sino-Vietnamese normalization (November 1991), the Cambodia peace agreement (early 1992), North Korea's brief acceptance of International Atomic Energy Agency (IAEA) inspections of its nuclear plants, and the Chinese acceptance of nuclear nonproliferation.

Despite remaining problems (such as human rights, the 1991 coup in Thailand, and Indonesia's long personal rule under President Suharto), the Asia Pacific region looks remarkably stable in the initial period after the close of the Cold War, particularly if compared with South Asia, the Middle East, or southern Europe.

The region's impressive economic growth was apparently not affected by the changeover to the post–Cold War era. A potential problem, however, which may be exacerbated in the new era, is the persistence of trade imbalances within the region. South Korea, Taiwan, and the ASEAN–5 (minus Brunei) invariably draw 40 to 50 percent of their imports from Japan and the United States (Appendix 2, Chapter 9). Almost without exception, Japan's annual trade with countries in East and Southeast Asia has enjoyed a surplus in the last decade. The Japanese surplus grew about 33 percent in 1991, to $37.4 billion.[9] Following Vietnam's unification in 1975, the political elites in ASEAN have expressed fears that, rather than facing direct external threat, their countries are in danger of economic (and cultural) "aggressions" from abroad (Ball 1991, p. 201; Maynard 1978, pp. 148–50). The trade deficits with Japan incurred by these fellow Asian nations, if continued over prolonged periods of time, could lend new fillips to those fears (Sayigh 1990, p. 63). Already, Prime Minister Lee Kwan Yew was sounding the common, if alarmist, fear of "more conflicts and eventually a return of war to settle economic problems.[10]

■ BONUSES FOR THE UNITED STATES

The new era brought to the United States more concrete gains than just the general relaxation of atmosphere in Asia Pacific. It meant that Washington was freed from being a hostage to its security concerns, which had subsumed economic interests (as discussed above). It also gave Washington great leverage in its dealings with former allies and foes alike. For example, Washington can more than before pursue a trade policy toward Japan that is based on *reciprocity* and designed to assure the survival of strategic U.S. industries such as aerospace, electronics, semiconductors, supercomputers, electronics, and so on.

Similarly, freed from the anti-Soviet security baggage, Washington can now play an evenhanded game with both Japan and China in the United States–Japan–China triad. U.S. transfers of defense technology and weaponry to Beijing in the past, which were considered necessary to offset the Soviet threat, inadvertently created a Chinese threat to Taiwan and Japan. To compensate for that, Washington had to keep up its arms sales to Taiwan (to the tune of $800 million a year) against recurrent Chinese complaints and, worse still, to make trade concessions to Japan (Harrison, Selig, and Prestowitz 1990, p. 200f). Now, in the post–Cold War era, the United States has regained its prudent discretion in foreign and defense policy. For one thing, it can now start building a balanced and durable interdependence, emphasizing reciprocity and aimed at bringing down its annual trade deficits with Asian nations—$44 billion annually with Japan alone (1991). Under normal conditions, an even-keeled U.S. relationship with China will also help increase U.S. bargaining power vis-à-vis Japan, as Washington will not be so dependent on Japanese goodwill in the new strategic triad.

Freed from its erstwhile security baggage, Washington will also be better able to consider a more ideology-free policy toward Vietnam and North Korea. In view of the Singaporean and Malaysian shifts toward greater security linkages with the United States, U.S. prominence in the waters stretching from the southwestern Pacific to the Indian Ocean is assured, even after its departure from the Philippine bases. That, too, is a bonus.

In all, the new era has rendered obsolete the old patterns of international alignments in Asia Pacific. More important, it has called into question previous concepts of allies and adversaries, now that security has taken on more and more economic overtones. Allies and adversaries now are separated by a blurring line at best. In essence, the post–Cold War era is not a zero-sum game as before; in terms of strategic planning, it is a new ballgame for all countries. But, as we took pains to show, balance of power has not phased out among the core states, as alleged by some. And our educated guess is that, as long as we live in an "anarchic" international system (i.e., without a world government or overarching authority over and above sovereign states), balance of power will not vanish, even in core-periphery relations.

■ NOTES

1. My views on this point are opposite to those of John Ruggie, "Multilateralism: The Anatomy of an Institution," 46 *International Organization* 3 (Summer 1992), p. 563.

2. Cf. "Survey: World Trade," *The Economist*, September 22, 1990.

3. *Japan Times Weekly* (international ed.), June 22–28, 1992, p. 1.

4. *Asian Wall Street Journal Weekly*, July 20, 1992, p. 21.

5. *Free China Journal* (Taipei), July 24, 1992, p. 1.

6. "Nonaligned Nations Are Tied to U.S. Forces," *Asian Wall Street Journal Weekly* (April 6, 1992), p. 1.

7. *Free China Journal* (Taipei), June 2, 1992, p. 1. A publication of the Government Information Office.

8. "China Proposes Measures for Nuclear Disarmament," press release of the Chinese Mission to the United Nations, New York (May 1992). I am indebted for this information to Gen. Kuanyi Du, head of the Chinese military delegation to the Military Staff Committee, Security Council, United Nations.

9. "Japan's Trade Gap Is Growing Again," *New York Times*, July 4, 1992, pp. 1 and 33. A breakdown of Japan's trade surpluses worldwide, provided by the Bank of Japan, was reproduced on p. 33.

10. Michael Richardson. 1989. "A Warning From the Pacific," *International Herald Tribune*, January 10; quoted in Sayigh 1990.

■ REFERENCES

Ball, Nicole. 1991. "Militarized States in the Third World." In *World Security,* eds. Michale T. Klare and Daniel C. Thomas.

Blair, John. 1976. *The Control of Oil.* New York: W. W. Norton.

Borthwick, Mark. 1992. *The Pacific Century.* Boulder, CO: Westview Press.

Chan, Steve, and Cal Clark. 1992. *Between Scylla and Charybdis.* London: Rutledge.

Claude, Inis. 1962. *Power and International Relations.* New York: Random House.

Conboy, Kenneth. 1992. "The U.S.–Singapore Relationship: A Model for Southeast Asia," *Backgrounder* No. 120 (March 12, 1992). Washington, D.C.: Heritage Foundation.

Evans, P. B. 1979. *Dependent Development: The Alliance of Multilateral, State, and Local Capital in Brazil.* Princeton, NJ: Princeton University Press.

Feldstein, Martin. 1988. *The United States in the World Economy.* Chicago: University of Chicago Press.

Frank, A. G. 1969. *Capitalism and Underdevelopment in Latin America.* New York: Monthly Review Press.

Gallik, Daniel, ed. 1987. *World Military Expenditures and Arms Transfers: 1987.* Washington, D.C.: Arms Control and Disarmament Agency.

Glickman, Norman, and Douglas Woodward. 1989. *The New Competitors.* New York: Basic Books.

Goldgeier, James, and Michael McFaul. 1992. "'A Tale of Two Worlds': Core and Periphery in the Post–Cold War Era," 46 *International Organization* 2: 467–492 (Spring).

Grimmet, Richard F. 1988. *Trends in Conventional Arms Transfers to the Third World by Major Suppliers, 1981–1988.* Washington, D.C.: Congressional Research Service.

Harrison, Selig, and Clyde Prestowitz, Jr. 1990. "Pacific Agenda: Defense or Economics?" *Foreign Policy* 79 (Summer 1990); reproduced in *The Future of American Foreign Policy,* eds., Charles Kegley, Jr., and Eugene R. Wittkopf. (New York: St. Martin's Press, 1992).

Hsiung, James C., and Samuel S. Kim, eds. 1980. *China in the Global Community.* New York: Praeger.

Hsiung, James C. 1985. *Beyond China's Independent Foreeign Policy.* New York: Praeger.

Hsiung, James C. 1989. "Balance of Power in the Pacific Century." In *From Pacific Region Toward Pacific Community,* ed. Bernard Joei. Taipei: Tamkang University Press.

Huntington, Samuel. 1988. "Coping with the Lippmann Gap," 66 *Foreign Affairs* 3:474.

Jacobson, Harold, and Michel Oksenberg. 1990. *China's Participation in the IMF, the World Bank, and GATT.* Ann Arbor: The University of Michigan Press.

Kahn, Herman. 1979. *World Economic Development, 1979 and Beyond.* Boulder, CO: Westview Press.

Klare, Michael. 1991. "Dealy Convergence: The Arms Trade, Nuclear/Chemical/Missile Proliferation, and Regional Conflict in the 1990s." In *World Security: Trends and Challenges at Century's End,* eds. Michael T. Klare and Daniel C. Thomas. New York: St. Martin's.

Lach, Donald, and Edmund Wherle. 1975. *International Politics in East Asia Since World War II.* New York: Praeger.

Lake, David. 1992. "Powerful Participants: Democratic States and Wars," 86 *American Political Science Review* 1:24–37 (March).

Leng, Shao-chuan. 1980. "Arms Control and Disarmament in Chinese Global Policy." In *China in the Global Community,* eds. James C. Hsiung and Samuel S. Kim.

Linder, Staffan Burenstam. 1986. *The Pacific Century: Economic and Political Consequences of Asian-Pacific Dynamism.* Stanford, CA: Stanford University Press.

Lipset, Seymour Martin. 1963. *Political Man: The Social Bases of Politics.* Garden City, NY: Doubleday.

Macchiarola, Frank, and Robert Oxnam, eds. 1991. *The China Challenge: American Policies in East Asia.* New York: Academy of Political Science.

McCord, William. 1991. *The Dawn of the Pacific Century.* New Brunswick, NJ: Transaction Publishers.

Mancini, John. 1989. *Testimony Before U.S. Congress, House Committee on Science, Space, and Technology, FSX,* 101st Congress, 1st Session (April 6 and May 11, 1989), pp. 110–126. John Mancini testified as Vice-President, American Electronics Association.

Maoz, Seev, and Nasrin Abdolali. 1989. "Regime Types and International Conflict," *Journal of Conflict Resolution* 33:3–35.

Maynard, Harold. 1978. "The Views of the Indonesia and Philippine Military Elites." In *The Military and Security,* ed. Sheldon Simon.

Midlarsky. M. I. 1988. "Rulers and the Ruled: Patterned Inequality and the Onset of Mass Political Violence," *American Political Science Review* 82:491–509.

Muller, E. N. 1985. "Income Inequality, Regime Repressiveness, and Political Violence," *American Sociological Review* 51:47–61.

Muller, Steven, and Gebhard Schweigler, eds. 1992. *From Occupation to Cooperation*. New York: W. W. Norton.

Rostow, W. W. 1960. *The Stages of Economic Growth: A Noncommunist Manifesto*. Cambridge: Cambridge University Press.

Sayigh, Yezid. 1990. "Controlling the 1990s: Security in the Developing Countries," *Adelphi Papers* No. 251 (Summer 1990).

Simon, Denis. 1991. "China in the World Economic System." In *The China Challenge*, eds. Frank Macchiarola and Robert Oxnam.

Simon, Sheldon. ed. 1978. *The Military and Security in the Third World*. Boulder, CO: Westview Press.

Siverson, Rudolph M., and Juliann Emmons. 1991. "Birds of a Feather: Democratic Political Systems and Alliance Choices in the Twentieth Century," *Journal of Conflict Resolution* 35:285–306.

Small, Melvin, and David Singer. 1976. "The War-Proneness of Democratic Regimes, 1816–1965," *Jerusalem Journal of International Relations* I:57–69.

Stockholm International Peace Research Institute. 1985. *SIPRI Yearbook 1985: World Armaments and Disarmament*.

Tai, Hung-chao, ed. 1989. *Confucianism and Economic Development: An Oriental Alternative?* Washington, D.C.: Washington Institute for Values in Public Policy.

United Nations. 1990. *World Statistics in Brief*, 3rd ed. New York: United Nations.

Vlahos, Michael. 1991. "Middle East, North Africa, and South Asia," *U.S. Naval Institute Proceedings* (March 1991).

Wade, Robert. 1992. "East Asia's Economic Success: Conflicting Perspectives, Partial Insights, Shaky Evidence," 44 *World Politics* 2:270–320.

Wallerstein, I. 1980. *The Modern World System II: Mercantilism and the Consolidation of the European World Economy, 1600–1750*. New York: Academic Press.

Weber, Max. 1958. *The Protestant Ethic and the Spirit of Capitalism*. New York: Scribner's.

Weber, Max. 1964. *The Religion of China: Confucianism and Taoism*, with an introduction by C. K. Yang. New York: Macmillan.

■ 12

Gazing into the Twenty-First Century: A Pacific Era?
James C. Hsiung

■ OUR CENTURY'S BEQUESTS

In this concluding chapter, it is tempting to try to conjure a sensible prevision of what is likely to be the shape of Asia Pacific, in terms of both its intraregional relations and its place in the context of twenty-first century world politics. A logical starting point is to assess the most important legacy that our century bequeaths on the next. Strictly speaking, the full meaning of "legacy" in this sense could encompass things such as: (1) the systemic configuration of power, including distribution of wealth and capabilities, that will determine the hierarchy in the world system and will likely shape its alliance patterns; (2) the prevailing norms, including ideals and values, about how the international system and the domestic society ought to be ordered; and (3) the established modes and processes by which transactions are conducted among nations and/or other international entities (such as multinational corporations and the UN). Quincy Wright (1955) would probably subsume most of these headings under entities, processes, forces, and relations.

Because of the constraint of space, nevertheless, I shall merely note three genres of change that dramatize the legacy of our century and are likely to affect world politics of the next century. The first is the spread of wealth beyond the core to Asia Pacific. Second, the spread of democracy not just as an ideal but as a functioning political institution from Western Europe and North America to Asia Pacific is an unprecedented development in the history of the Westphalian system; it is a trend most likely to continue. Third, the fall of communism in Eastern Europe and in the Soviet Union, the very progenitor of Leninist Marxism, will give pause to many in the Third World to reflect on whether the West is justified in calling it proof of the "victory of capitalism."

These three sea changes may be interrelated, but they need not be. A Western ideologue may typically argue, for example, that democracy has brought wealth to the East Asian countries in a process that proves the victory of capitalism. But, as argued in the preceding chapter, the Asian NIEs achieved their phenomenal economic success nearly two decades before their trek to democracy. Only in Japan did the two paths converge, and then only because of U.S. tutelage. Whether the East Asain economic "miracle" is proof of the victory of capitalism depends largely on how much one attributes it to the region's Confucian cultural mix (or other causes).

Regardless of one's views on the relationship among the three elements, it is highly conceivable that, after the tumultuous end of communism in Eastern Europe, the torch of democracy and the nonsocialist path of economic development, as exemplified by the East Asian bellwethers, will likely pass on far and wide in the Third World, as never before. The next question is: Will the spread of wealth extend further beyond East Asia? The answer to this crucial question is important not just for development theory but also for a larger reason: In terms of the future shape of the international system, it makes a decisive difference how economic power is distributed across the system. This distribution will determine how nations line up along the remaining divide separating the rich and the poor, the developed and the underdeveloped. It will in turn determine how hierarchy will form in the structure of the larger system and how many centers of power there will be around which states will align.

■ CAN THE ASIAN EXPERIENCE BE DUPLICATED?

In order to ascertain whether it is possible for the spread of wealth to extend to other regions, we have to ask whether the Asian experience can be duplicated. For that purpose we have to identify which *part(s)* of the Asian experience can be duplicated. We must first identify which country cases are unique. Displaying a self-confidence not shown before, Japan began in 1992 to sell itself as a best model for ex-Soviet republics and other ex-communist countries in Eastern Europe struggling to find their place under the sun.[1] Despite Japan's transparent underlying motive of trying to sell its own economic influence, the fact is that the Japanese experience *is* unique in a number of ways. In addition to its quasi-religious work ethic (recalling the mystic Bushido), its peculiar group consciousness and social structure (which Nakane [1985] calls "vertical grouping"), and its unusually high level of education, Japan had two other important attributes in its favor: One, a successful capitalist system was already functioning before World War II (Takahashi 1969; Lockwood 1964): Two, after the U.S. occupation (1945–1952), Washington consciously helped Japan to become a model of prosperity in the Far East as a counter to the lure of socialism. For that reason, the United States tolerated for four decades Japan's restrictive, aggressive trade and investment policy, an issue that did not catch fire in Congress until after the mid-1980s.

One test of uniqueness is that the Japanese success route finds no duplication. The route of the Asian NIEs, conversely, has been taken at least four times (in the four cases of South Korea, Taiwan, Hong Kong, and Singapore). Hence, in our search for an answer to the question of whether wealth will spread further, we should look for clues from the Asian NIEs.

Granted, domestic attributes (such as political stability, educational overhead, capital formation, development strategy, etc.) are important. There is abundant literature on this topic (Belassa, Berger, Fei, Hofheinz, McCord, Rabushka, and Wei, to name just a few). Because this book is concerned with international relations, however, it is only appropriate that I focus on the international factors that may account for the rise of the Asian NIEs. The external contributing factors to development are a topic most often neglected in the existing literature.

The most pertinent discourse on this topic, to the best of my knowledge, is that of Robert Wade (1992). In addressing the external factors responsible for South Korea and Taiwan's rapid rise up the world wealth hierarchy in the early to mid-1960s, Wade (1992, p. 311) listed three factors: (1) transport costs and trade barriers in the core markets (North America and northwestern Europe) were tumbling down; (2) competition intensified in the United States, especially after the entry of Japanese manufactures; and (3) the accumulation of higher skills in the core's labor force made unskilled labor scarce and more expensive, which enhanced the comparative advantage of the lower-income countries with a less skilled labor force. All three combined to create an insatiable demand by U.S. buyers for imported goods made at low costs from faraway places. That demand in turn paved the way for South Korea's and Taiwan's export-oriented strategy to pay off.

The explanatory power of this point becomes clearer and more convincing when one tests the three factors against other cases, as Wade did with Latin America (*ibid.*). Thus, I will speculate on whether these international factors are reproduceable for other aspiring nations in the near future. First, after 1973, the oil majors lost control over the world's oil pricing to the Organization of Petroleum-Exporting Countries (OPEC), which drove up oil prices (Blair 1976) and made low transport costs a thing of the past. Moreover, after the 1980s, protectionist sentiments ran high in the core states. By 1986, 21 percent of all manufactured goods imported to the United States and Europe were restricted by quantitative barriers (UNCTAD 1987, Table IV.4). If the deadlock in the Uruguay Round is any indication, there is no sign of a tumbling down of trade barriers anywhere soon.

Second, competition in the United States has shown a different twist because foreign companies (Glickman and Woodward 1989) increasingly are buying their way into the United States through FDI (foreign direct investment). U.S. productivity has declined (Feldstein, p. 283); but demand has also dropped in basic industries, especially in steel after 1978 (Feldstein, p. 299). Although the implications from these different indicators are not absolutely clear, one thing is certain: Foreign-owned suppliers competing in the U.S. market provide a wider range of choices (sometimes at lower prices, as some product parts are imported from parent companies abroad). The Japanese, for example, often use their U.S.-based subsidiaries as conduits for importing product components from Japan. Though this approach helps bring down the trade imbalance on paper, it only substitutes one form of imports ("intracompany") for another (country to country) (Glickman and Woodward 1989, p. 152). Some of the Japanese direct investments in the United States were meant to circumvent U.S. import restrictions, enabling Japanese-owned factories to produce manufactures in the United States (Feldstein, p. 588). This maneuver has the effect of putting a lock on a part of the local market and increasing competition with indigenous U.S. industries from within. The cumulative effect of the prolonged, decades-long onslaught of less-expensive imports from East Asian competitors is that U.S. workers have become increasingly upset by the impact of cheap imports on the job market at home. The opposition by the AFL-CIO and other major unions (and thus Democrats in Congress closely affiliated with labor) to Chinese imports allegedly made by even-cheaper prison labor is a case in point. This condition does not seem hospitable for other Third World nations hoping to follow the route by which the Asian NIEs got where they did.

Third, in the core states there has been a shift in growth patterns from manufacturing to the service industry after 1979 (Thurow 1989). The job market has shifted accordingly, creating problems for workers trained in the traditional curriculums emphasizing engineering and manufacturing. In the meantime, wages have gone up considerably in the East Asian NIEs over previous levels, so much so that they now farm out work to places such as Malaysia and Thailand. Instead of selling goods made by cheap labor to the United States, many East Asians now invest in U.S. capital-intensive technologies (Thurow 1989, p. 14) .

This FDI development poses two separate problems. In the first place, for the United States, Asian investments in capital intensive technologies may result in displaced labor and hence unemployment (for example, the parking attendant may be replaced by a plastic card). Second, for lower-income Third World nations, this development adds one more challenge to their troubled bid to imitate and catch up with the Asian NIEs. They can no longer capitalize on cheap labor (as the Asian NIEs used to) trying to get into the core markets and find themselves in competition with the core states trying to attract FDIs from new capital-exporting countries such as Japan and the Asian NIEs.

The world economy of today is no longer in the same expansionary phase as it was in the 1960s, when South Taiwan, South Korea, and Japan made big inroads into Western markets. Growth in world output slowed from 4.1 percent in the 1970s to 2.6 percent in the 1980s, for example. Along with that came a dramatic fall in the demand for unskilled labor and raw materials per unit of industrial production (Wade 1990, p. 346). Besides, with the North American Free Trade Agreement taking shape, the U.S. and Canadian economies can draw on the low-cost Mexican labor. That is bad news for the other Third World countries who count on a comparative advantage in low-wage labor.

In sum, all the above changes will conspire to make emulation of the East Asian success a prohibitively robust task. Another hurdle for a late bloomer is that it will have to compete with all the East Asian Little Dragons, not to mention Japan, in an already saturated world market. With the Cold War over, the eagerness with which the United States used to assist first Japan and then the Asian NIEs (by subjecting its own economic interests to Cold War security considerations—see Chapter 11) is not to be seen again. Future imitators of the Asian NIEs—more specifically, of their import-substitution and export-oriented strategy—cannot count on the United States to open its markets or offer other "free rides" the way it did for the East Asians before. Besides, as the dawn of the new era coincides with the U.S. "hegemonic decline," there is a limit to what the United States can do to accommodate "foreign distress goods," to use Kingdleberger's (1986) term, even if Washington were willing to do so.

To make things comparable, let us assume for a moment that an aspiring Third World nation can achieve the necessary domestic attributes (including adoption of the export-oriented strategy). What we see is that the international environment of the 1990s and beyond is by no means hospitable to any nation trying to duplicate the East Asian path to riches, *even if* the necessary domestic conditions are present. Barring unforeseen circumstances, the most probable outcome is that the present Asian NIEs are unlikely to see a new generation of NIEs joining their ranks soon (McCord 1991, pp. 143–160). The only exceptions are probably some of the Southeast Asian countries such as Thailand, Malaysia, and Indonesia.[2] But these are potential NIEs on the ladder to succes, and hence not in the same class as any other Third World countries just beginning in their economic climb.

The relevance of this discussion will become more obvious as I get into my ultimate analysis of the global and regional balance of forces. While I am on the subject of the future distribution of economic power, this is a good place to digress into a brief discussion of China's economic potential.

□ *The Prospects of China as an Economic Power*

For two reasons, China's economic potentials must be addressed separately. First, it is a nuclear power and, because of its size, is considered one of the four major powers (along with Japan, the United States, and Russia) to be reckoned with in Asia Pacific regional politics. Exactly how prominent a role the PRC will play, however, will depend largely on what economic heights it is able to reach. Second, despite its obvious potential as a regional economic power, China has been dogged by a number of real or perceived problems. Not the least of these are: memories of the Tiananmen turmoil of 1989; its contentious human rights problems; the uncertainty surrounding its leadership transition; and above all its burdensome communist legacy. In my assessment of China's economic future, I will by necessity have to examine first whether there are offsetting factors in its favor. Then the indicators of its potential will gain a new meaning, and the forecasts by external authorities, including foreign academics and intelligence sources, will be seen in the proper light.

The PRC has a number of advantages (i.e., offsetting factors) over other communist or ex-communist regimes. Its economic reforms began not in the late 1980s but in 1978 (Byrd 1991). Because of this head start, Chinese marketization and privatization have taken deeper roots: By 1991 the private sector was able to claim 47.2 percent of the country's total industrial output.[3] The Chinese had opened up 167 cities to external investment, attracting an aggregate $102 billion in foreign capital by the end of 1991.[4]

A few indicators will suffice to show the viability and dynamism of the Chinese economic reforms: (1) Even in the midst of a world recession in the early 1990s, as a CIA report pointed out, Chinese industrial output increased by 14 percent and GNP by 7 percent, and exports rose 16 percent to $72 billion:[5] (2) After only a brief lull since Tiananmen, foreign investors were once again flocking back to China. In the first quarter of 1992 alone, foreign companies contracted to invest $6.5 billion in 3,837 enterprises—an average of 42 foreign financed ventures in China each day. Investors came from the United States (5 percent), Japan (6 percent), Taiwan (9 percent), Germany (12 percent), and Hong Kong and Macao (55 percent), as well as other sources (10 percent);[6] (3) Despite scary talks about 1997, about 36 percent of Hong Kong's industry has moved across the border to the Pearl River delta on the Chinese side, and;[7] (4) Taiwanese investors have also responded to what they perceive as strong signs of the mainland economy: Their average investment size has upped from the previous $1 million or less per project. There are now more solely owned (as opposed to joint) ventures. Investment locales have extended from the previous heavy concentrations along the southeast China coast to inland areas. All these demonstrate a greater confidence in the mainland on the part of Taiwanese investors.[8]

Foreign forecasts about China's economic future range from the grossly fantastic to the less fantastic. The eminent Swedish economist Staffan Linder (1986, p. 14) foresees China's GDP as able to "equal the GDP of the United States and Europe by the year 2000." Linder's forecast was based on two premises: that the post-1978 economic reforms would go on and that the growth rate would continue at 4 percent annually. Both seem to be more than borne out by post-Tiananmen events. After Deng Xiaoping's "southern tour" in the spring of 1992, a "Document Four" issued by the Central Committee formally reiterated the Party's determination to continue the economic reforms unswervingly. Even the godfather of conservatism, Chen Yun, came out explicitly in support of the reforms. Despite the original plan to keep the growth at 6 percent to avoid repeating the woes of the overheated economy of 1988–1989, Beijing by mid-1992 conceded that the economy would grow at least by 10 percent for the current year.[9]

Taiwan's official estimates of the mainland's economic potential also changed recently. After a visit to observe personally the reforms on the mainland, Chao Yao-tung, a presidential advisor and former minister of economic affairs in Taiwan, offered his seasoned conclusion that the economic reforms there "are not going to turn back." Besides the successful rural industrialization and the general improvement of living standards, an equally impressive asset on the mainland is the solid high tech base, which, he said, is second only to that of Japan.[10] Chao's glowing report anticipated two interesting revelations. One was the publication in Taipei of official statistics showing that mainland labor conditions were already superior to Taiwan's in terms of the quality of work and the wage/productivity ratio.[11] The other was the release of a report by the Chung-hua Economic Research Institute, a government think tank in Taipei, that the mainland's export growth rate for 1991 had outstripped that of Taiwan, 15.9 percent to 13.3 percent.[12]

An ambitious new goal announced by Beijing after Deng's southern tour was for the southern province of Guangdong to catch up with the four Asian NIEs in twenty years, becoming the fifth Dragon. Accordingly, officials in Guangdong laid out a two-stage plan. In the first stage, during the last decade of the twentieth century, Guangdong would strive to attain the 1990 level of economic achievement of Taiwan and South Korea. In the second stage, during the first decade of the twenty-first century, Guangdong's economy was to reach the level of Taiwan's and South Korea's economies of the same year. A number of major undertakings to be launched by Guangdong were also announced,[13] but they need not be examined here. What is interesting is that this bid for Guangdong to catch up with the existing four Dragons was well received by knowledgeable economists in Taiwan and the United States. In a paper delivered at an international conference in Taipei, for example, Professor Chu-yuan Cheng, a Chinese-American expert on China's economy and well known for his usual pessimistic views on it, came out on high notes for a change. After analyzing the economic growth and potential of mainland China, especially in the coastal areas, Cheng came to the conclusion that, if the current growth rates continue, it will not be far-fetched to expect Guangdong to catch up with the four Dragons in twenty years.[14]

It is necessary to reiterate, however, that the obstacles to the spread of wealth beyond East Asia are formidable, and some of the ASEAN countries, as well as China, may be the only exceptions to buck this gloomy trend. It bears noting, however, that the idea of a "right to development" has caught on in the developing lands. In an adverse international setting, the less developed world will demand that its "right to development" is a human right to be achieved by requiring the more fortunate—that is, the industrial states—to help out (cf. Resolutions 1988/26 and 1989/45, UN Commission on Human Rights). The idea of an obligation for the developed states to help others lies at the heart of the Third World's alternative vision of what a new world order ought to be (Chapter 4). Further, at the United Nations Conference on Development and the Environment in Rio de Janeiro in June 1992, there was a chorus among Third World countries on two points: (1) that the developed countries should invest in helping the developing countries fight environmental pollution, and (2) that industrial polluters must pay for cleaning up.[15] In the new century, the development-environment linkage will receive further fillips. So will the Third World's insistence that the core states have an obligation to help the periphery. More important, the concept of the core, in the new era, will most likely be extended to include all the economically successful nations in Asia Pacific (the NIEs as well as Japan).

Such is the first important bequest of our century on the twenty-first century. Two other bequests are also worthy of note: (1) a new form of complex interdependence, and (2) the rise of complex multilateralism. I shall discuss them separately.

☐ Complex Interdependence in New Form

The term "complex interdependence" in international relations was first introduced by Keohane and Nye (1977, p. 8) to denote "situations characterized by reciprocal effects among countries or among actors in different countries." The "effects" mentioned in this definition result from international transactions, or flows of capital, people, goods, and messages across international boundaries. With the extensive increases in these international transactions after World War II, interdependence became increasingly more complex, and the ultimate consequence was *mutual vulnerability* among nations (Keohane and Nye, p. 15).

These traits will continue in the new age, but complex interdependence will take on a new coloration. In the first place, the complexity will manifest itself in a new breed of mixed free-trade and security communities. With the Cold War over, there is no longer an East-West ideological divide. The earlier dominance of national security concerns to the exclusion (or at the expense) of economic interests will give way to the increased salience of a mixed economic-military approach. In other words, as economic security interests swell in importance, military security will integrate with, or even be dominated by them. How to enlarge and safeguard a country's interests in free trade, for instance, will be part of its national security strategy. In the post–Cold War era, there is a leveling effect on international relations between the militarily powerful and the militarily weak. This phenomenon in part recalls the long-standing relationship between the United States and Canada. The implausibility of force ever being used made the U.S.–Canadian relationship a product of pragmatic decisions on primarily utilitarian grounds; force became irrelevant. In the new era, the universal extension of similar nonmilitary relations will make future complex interdependence very different from that of the 1970s and 1980s. The other side of the coin, though, is that there is nothing to guarantee that acute commercial frictions—as distinct from military feuds—between economically powerful nations will not result in more serious conflicts involving the threat or use of force as a backup.

A second characteristic of the new type of complex interdependence is the mutual penetration of the economies of the core and the periphery as the lines separating them vanish. As more FDI ventures result in the introduction of foreign-owned companies into one another's territories, mutual penetration of economies will make it hard to maintain the distinction between the various sovereign jurisdictions and between native and foreign private sectors. This blurring will happen between the Asian and the North American members of the Pacific community, especially if the FDI trends keep up. To distinguish this new type of complex interdependence from the old, we may call it one of a "pure" genre—i.e., unadulterated by *a priori* military security considerations.

Third, this pure complex interdependence will become manifest in a symbiosis of intraregional and transregional strategic interactions. For instance, in a hypothetical scenario in which the Japanese economic threat should replace the erstwhile Soviet military threat, it would be an intraregional cause célèbre, in the sense that it is a problem within the Pacific community. But in response, the United States may go beyond aligning itself with the other Asia Pacific members and reach out to co-opted members of the European Community. If that happens, it would be an instance of an *intraregional* economic conflict giving rise to a *transregional* response: hence, a symbiosis of intra- and transregional strategic interactions.

In the original Keohane-Nye formulation, an ideal complex interdependence model would have three characteristics: (1) multiple channels of varying degrees of formalness connecting nations, societies, groups, and elites; (2) an agenda of multiple issues that do not fall into a hierarchy, so that "high politics" (involving military security) do not dominate "low politics" (social/economic issues); and (3) an avoidance of the use of military force toward other governments within the region (Keohane and Nye, p. 24f).

Paradoxically, the state of affairs described in (2) and (3) did not exactly exist, and could not have existed, before the Cold War phased out. In the new era, without overriding national security considerations as before, the world will not have to worry about high politics dominating low politics. Moreover, the use of military force will not be a best option, because with the increased mutual vulnerability in the new pure complex interdependence, the use of force to settle what essentially will be nonmilitary disputes may boomerang on the aggressor.

As such, this pure complex interdependence will challenge the foremost assumption in the Realist statecentric view of international relations—namely, that the states as coherent units are primary actors on the world scene. To begin with, states may no longer be coherent actors. Mutual penetration of economies may result in a splintering of vital public and private interests within individual nation-states, resulting in a strategic divergence on issues to an extent unknown before. At worst, it may create cross-national business alliances that have agendas of their own, transcending those of the sovereign states. In the Cold War era, the unifying force of conflicting domestic interests was the common fear of external military threats to one's national survival. The age of geoeconomics will find this potential unifying force gravely weakened. Moreover, contrary to the Realist assumption, states may no longer even be the primary actors on the world stage: The multinationals and certain international organizations may compete with nation-states for the spotlight of international relations. In short, the pure complex interdependence of the twenty-first century may indeed create what Rosenau (1989, p. 9) calls a "multicentric" world.

A concrete example of this new complex interdependence would be the so-called international "strategic alliances" formed between businesses of different countries. Some prototypes of these alliances have begun to appear between U.S. and Japanese firms that are in the same fields and can complement each other to mutual gain (Johnson 1992). These cross-national business alliances will help U.S. firms become more competitive and penetrate the Japanese market and vice versa. A few examples will suffice:

• An alliance between Japan's Canon Ltd. and IBM to jointly produce notebook computers, to be sold under IBM's brand name. Under the arrangement, announced in December 1991, Canon will produce the liquid crystal displays for the product, and IBM will make most of the other components. This partnership will allow IBM to produce state-of-the-art notebook computers, an area it would usually stay away from.

- Mitsubishi Electric of Japan and AT&T announced last October an alliance to manufacture new kinds of gallium arsenide computer chips that can be used in mobile and cordless telephones. If all goes well, the two companies working together will be able to produce the new chips more quickly than if each worked on its own.
- U.S.–Japanese steel alliances. These arrangements give U.S. firms access to superior Japanese production techniques. There are currently twelve major alliances between U.S. and Japanese steel companies. For example, Nippon Steel Corp. of Japan and Inland Steel Industries of Chicago have a fifty-fifty alliance called I/N Kote to produce galvanized coating line, a special steel tubing product.

Full flowering of these international business alliances beyond the prototype stage, however, will have to await the repeal or modification of U.S. antitrust laws. At the present stage, the U.S. companies that stand to gain in competitiveness through the strategic business alliances may see their interests in conflict with existing laws. If the administration follows these laws, however, it will diverge from the interests of the U.S. business community. This scenario would be a textbook example of how a state is no longer a "coherent actor," as the Realists assume it to be. Indeed, as mutual penetration of economies further expands, it is conceivable that the business "tail" will wag the government "dog." It is also conceivable that domestic businesses (in addition to the multinationals) locked into alliances with foreign firms will act on the world scene quite independently of their home government. In that circumstance, these firms, as well as the multilaterals will compete with the nation-states as the "primary" actors, depriving the latter of their heretofore sole right to claim to being such, as the Realists maintain.

☐ Multilateralism on the Rise

Before we discuss the rise of multilateralism in the new era, let us digress briefly on the question of whether international cooperation will be hampered by hegemonic decline (cf. Chapter 8). The final collapse of Soviet power happened to coincide with the gradual path of fading U.S. hegemony (Krickus 1987). This hapless coincidence creates a problem for theorists. According to the theory of hegemonic stability, the international order depends on the availability of a hegemon that by its size and high productivity is in a position to function as the banker of last resort and to open its market to the "distress goods" of other nations (Kindleberger 1986; Lake 1984). From this perspective, the function of the hegemon is essential for international cooperation. The problem posed by the hegemon's decline is in the form of a paradox: From the Realist perspective, the diffusion of power resulting from the loss of U.S. hegemony should have undermined the ability of anyone to create international order and cooperation. But Robert Keohane (1984, pp. 9, 215; Chapter 6) finds that, on the contrary, the decline in U.S. hegemony does not necessarily sound the death knell to international cooperation. According to Keohane, economic interdependence in the world has continued to grow, and the pace of U.S. involvement in the world economy even accelerated after 1970 (Keohane 1984, p. 7).

Keohane's argument, by coincidence or not, confirms the position of the Institutionalists. From the latter's perspective, the increasing need for coordination of policy created by interdependence should have led to more, not less, cooperation. Thus, from this perspective, a hegemon is not necessary for fostering international cooperation. If we assume for a moment that the role played by the Soviet Union within the former Communist camp approximated that of a hegemon of sorts, then the combination of the Soviet collapse and the U.S. hegemonic decline calls into question, for the Realists, the very prospect of international cooperation. It is not our intention to pass judgment on whether Keohane's data and analysis supports his conclusion, nor on the Realist-Institutionalist dispute. We do wish, however, to point out that, with a little imagination, the seeming paradox can be reconciled within the theory of hegemonic stability itself. In brief, the theory posits that where collective action is failing, hegemonic leadership plays a role equivalent to that of governmental coercion. It thus substitutes for collective action in the provision of "collective goods" such as order, peace, and so on.

But substitution works both ways: If cooperation can be brought about by collective action, then the decline (even removal) of hegemonic leadership need not depress cooperation. In reality, the falling importance of the United States in the global economy has been balanced by the rising importance of Japan and Germany. The three form a subset such as Olson's (1955) "privileged group." In a privileged group, some or all of the members have an incentive to see that the collective good is provided, even if they have to bear the full burden of providing it alone (Olson 1955, p. 50). The aggregate size of this subset (the top three economic powers) in the world has not changed appreciably.[16] Two implications ensue from this fact: (1) cooperation may be relatively more difficult within the subset with the erosion of the U.S. hegemonic power (hence, the U.S.–Japan trade problems assumed distorted proportions after 1985), and (2) when members within the subset are in full agreement, (e.g., over the flexible currency-exchange rates; and pledges to improve trade conditions, such as lifting domestic barriers), cooperation can be sustained. Once begun, cooperation may extend beyond the subset itself. In the G7 economic summitry, for instance, the subset has been extended to four other nations (Snidal 1985).

The moral is not that cooperation has increased with hegemonic decline, as Keohane believes, but that *despite* hegemonic decline, cooperation has been sustained by collective action involving the initiatives of a subset that includes the former hegemon. Therefore, the coincidence of Soviet collapse and the weakening of U.S. hegemony is no reason international cooperation should suffer—collective action can take over, substituting for hegemonic leadership.

Empirically, this point is borne out in what is happening in Asia Pacific in both the security and the economic areas. In the former area, multilateral approaches to security are slowly emerging, as in the Cambodian peace process or the semiofficial forum on the contested outlying islands of the South China Sea, hosted in the summer of 1992 by Indonesia and attended by all the parties with competing claims to the islands. Another area in which stability may increasingly be maintained in multilateral form is the Korean Peninsula (Baker 1991, p. 5).

In the economic domain, similarly decentralized approaches have led to the founding of APEC (Asian Pacific Economic Cooperation), a multilateral body for planning and coordinating national efforts across the Pacific region and meeting the challenges of "pure" complex interdependence.

At the regional level, the "pure" complex interdependence has spawned multilateral cooperative projects in what Robert Scalapino (1991, p. 21) calls "natural economic territories" (NETs), often cutting across political lines. Scalapino lists five such NETs: (1) China's Guangdong province, Hong Kong, and Taiwan; (2) China's Shandong province and South Korea; (3) the Sakhalin–Kuriles–north Japan NET; (4) the Siberian ports of Vladivostok and Nahodka linked up with regions such as Niigata in west Japan; and (5) Singapore, Malaysia, and Indonesia. To these is to be added a sixth NET, the Tumen project, involving the cooperation of China, Russia, North Korea, South Korea, Mongolia, and Japan in an area that intersects the boundaries of China, Russia, and North Korea (as discussed in Chapter 4).

The proliferation of the NETs is a testimony to the rise of both "pure" complex interdependence and the decentralized approach to international cooperation, as is made possible by the end of the Cold War and necessitated by declining hegemonic leadership. The NETs' spread is an indication that multilateralism will be the functional equivalent of such leadership in the provision of "collective goods" (which the hegemonic stability theory expects a functioning hegemon to provide). It does not, however, obviate the role of the United States as a participating partner. Only the past patron-client relationship between the United States and the other members in the region has changed. Besides, the competition between the United States and Japan in the subset defined above will tend to generate more, not less, multilateral cooperation. The reason is that the competition will translate into their competitive support for the other Pacific members on multilateral cooperative projects such as the NETs.

■ A PACIFIC ERA?

Many commentators have ventured the ticklish idea that the twenty-first century will be the Pacific Century or Pacific Era. Will it be? Before I come back to this question, let me raise another question: Why ask whether there is going to be a Pacific Era in the first place? Does it matter? I wish to note that it does matter for three reasons: (1) deciding whether there will be a Pacific Era requires designing a conscious set of criteria to be applied comparatively to the different regions; (2) doing the necessary crossregional comparisons makes one consider which region may offer a suitable developmental model for others to emulate; and (3) the answer to whether there is to be a Pacific Era holds the key to another crucial question, namely: What strategic planning should the United States undertake in preparation for the future?

I have already addressed the concerns in (2) above. The gist of my discussion was that the East Asian experience, more particularly its import-substitution and export-oriented strategy, by itself may offer a model for other developing countries to follow. But as I was quick to point out, the international environment is not as hospitable now as it was at the time (1960s) the present Asian NIEs were beginning their climb up the ladder of economic success. The discussions below, therefore, will focus on (1) and (3) only.

□ *Three Super Trading Blocs*

When the same criteria are applied across the board (e.g., share of world trade, GDP growth, etc.), it becomes apparent that there are three super trading blocs: (1) Europe, whose exports are 50.2 percent of the world's total; (2) Asia Pacific, 27.3 percent; and (3) North America, 20.1 percent.[17] Asia Pacific is the United States' largest trading partner; two-way trade is $300 billion (1989).[18] But Europe has the largest intraregional trade (75 percent of all trade is conducted within the region), reflecting its strength in terms of self-sufficiency and institutional cohesion (regional integration).

Because the chances of economic power extending to currently underdeveloped regions are not great, the present configuration of the three super trading blocs is not likely to change so precipitously as to thwart the logic of my reasoning here for the foreseeable future. Admittedly, the relative weights of the three trading blocs may change over time, requiring adjustments in U.S. strategic thinking on the shifting balance of power.

Those who believe in a Pacific Era invariably point to two sets of data. One is related to Asia Pacific's sustained high growth rates: 8.6 percent for the period 1965–1980 and 6.6 percent for 1980–1988, as against the United States' 2.7 percent and 3.0 percent; Canada's 5.0 percent and 3.5 percent; and Europe's 3.9 percent and 2.9 percent for the same periods, respectively (see Table 12.1). The other set of data documents Asia Pacific's trade with the United States. The combined trade of Japan and the Asian NIEs with the United States for 1980–1987 was $1,066 billion, nearly 20 percent more than the $909 billion EC–U.S. trade for the same period (see Table 12.2). However, the extreme edge of Europe is revealed only when one examines other important data:

1. Europe still is the world's largest trading bloc, accounting for 50.2 percent of the world's total exports. The combined GNP of Western and Eastern Europe is 36.1 percent of global GNP (Thurow 1992).
2. Europe is the most advanced in regional institution building. Regardless of the fate of the Maastricht Treaty, not even the most pessimistic analysts expect the EC's single-market integration to reverse itself. One sign of the region's self-confidence, as well as self-sufficiency, is its high proportion of intraregional trade.
3. The merger of the EC and EFTA (European Free Trade Association) to become the EEA (European Economic Area), which includes ex-Communist nations, has created the biggest trading area on earth.[19]

Other indicators of Europe's strength are that members of the Organization for Economic Cooperation and Development (OECD) account for 55.6 percent of the world's developmental aid; 47.3 percent of contributions to the United Nations; 70.5 percent of the troops committed to NATO; and 54.0 percent of the books published.[20] The EC's GDP, at 33.3 percent of world GDP, is larger than those of the United States (32 percent) and Japan (18.1 percent).

Table 12.1 Average Annual Growth Rates in GDP (in percent)

	1980–1988	1965–1980
China	11.4	6.4
Asia Pacific countries	6.6	8.6
Japan	4.1	6.3
Canada	3.5	5.0
United States	3.0	2.7
EC and EFTA	2.9	3.9

Source: The Economist Book of Vital World Statistics (London: The Economist Books, 1990) pp. 44–45.

Table 12.2   U.S. Merchandise Trade with Selected Countries and Areas, 1980–1987 ($ billions)[a]

	Canada[b]	Japan	East Asian NICs[c]	Western Hemisphere Developing Countries[d]	EC-12[e]
Exports					
1980	40.3	20.8	14.7	38.7	58.9
1981	44.6	21.8	15.1	42.1	57.0
1982	37.9	21.0	15.6	33.6	52.4
1983	43.3	21.9	16.9	25.7	48.4
1984	51.8	23.6	17.7	29.7	50.5
1985	53.3	22.6	16.9	31.0	49.0
1986	55.5	26.9	18.3	31.1	53.2
1987	59.8	28.2	23.5	35.0	60.6
Imports					
1980	42.0	33.0	18.8	38.7	39.9
1981	46.8	39.9	22.1	40.8	45.6
1982	46.8	39.9	23.8	39.6	46.4
1983	52.5	43.6	29.6	43.6	47.9
1984	66.9	60.4	39.1	50.1	63.4
1985	69.4	72.4	41.9	49.1	71.6
1986	68.7	85.5	41.1	44.1	79.5
1987	71.5	88.1	61.3	49.1	84.9

Notes:
a. Exports valued free alongsideship; imports valued cost, insurance, and freight.
b. Includes undocumented exports to Canada (about $6.4 billion in 1987).
c. East Asian newly industrialized countries: Hong Kong, Singapore, South Korea, and Taiwan.
d. Western Hemisphere Developing Countries: all countries of North and South America (including the Caribbean island nations) except for Canada, Cuba, and the United States.
e. European Community: Belgium, Denmark, Federal Republic of Germany, France, Greece, Ireland, Italy, Luxembourg, the Netherlands, Portugal, Spain, and the United Kingdom.
Source: United States Trade Representative, *United States Trade Performance in 1987,* 1987, Tables 20–23, 25, 26.

In each of the above categories, Asia Pacific does not come close to Europe. Besides, in comparison with Europe, the Asia Pacific region manifests far wider gaps in income distribution and lacks the unity and diplomatic influence of the EC (Borthwick 1992, p. 532).

There is another way of comparing Asia Pacific and Europe. In the first place, Europe's per capita income tripled in four decades, from $4,860 in 1950 to $20,880 in 1990 (Thurow 1992). But Asia Pacific's per capita income remained a dismal $340 (IBRD 1991, p. 182). Second, West Europeans' average life expectancy increased from sixty-seven to seventy-six years, and educational opportunities tripled in four decades. In contrast, average life expectancy in Asia ranged widely, from fifty-seven/fifty-seven (male/female) to sixty-eight/seventy-two (m/f) in 1987 (UN 1990, p. 96). Levels of education and modern public health conditions in Asia Pacific are not as evenly distributed as in Europe. One-third of the residents in Kuala Lumpur, Jakarta, and Manila still live in slums. By 2000, only 37 percent of the population in Indonesia is expected to become urbanized. Moreover, environmental degradation is serious throughout the Asia Pacific region (Borthwick 1992, pp. 536–538).

On the basis of these indicators, it is not surprising economists such as Lester Thurow came to the conclusion that the twenty-first century will be the European Century again. Given the comparative evidence, it would be hard not to agree with this prognostication. I only wish to enter one caveat—namely, that the European advantage will last probably only until 2010. After that, Asia Pacific will quickly catch up with Europe on all counts. For example, the total Asia Pacific GDP will reach the same level as that of the United States and Western Europe (OECD), approximately in the 32–34 percent range as a share of global GDP. This conclusion is reached by projecting from the present percentages, taking into account Asia Pacific's faster growth rates. This projection coincides with an OECD estimate that by 2010 Asia Pacific's GDP will be one-third of world GDP (or a quarter more than in 1990).[21] With the increases in total GDP, the other scores for Asia Pacific will in turn improve—e.g., its share of total world trade and developmental assistance. Regional institution building, which is the weakest in Asia Pacific today, will also advance. One sign in that direction already was the murmuring about the inauguration of an "Education Forum" following the Asian Pacific Educational Ministers Conference held in Washington in the summer of 1992.

If our projection as such makes any sense, then the so-called Pacific Era will come only after 2010. Two logical questions then follow: (1) Which country will be the regional leader in the Pacific Era? and (2) How should the United States respond accordingly? What should be its strategy?

☐ Alignments Within Asia Pacific

Without question, the area's four major powers will be the United States, Japan, China, and Russia. But by geography, culture, or commitment, neither Russia (assuming it is fully recovered from its post-Communist chaos) nor the United States is a fully Pacific nation. That leaves Japan and China as the two contenders for regional hegemony. By its existing economic strength alone, Japan will most likely be the region's hegemon during the first half of the new century. However, with its growth rate almost three times as fast as Japan's, 11.4 percent to 4.1 percent (1980–1988), China—barring unforeseen disasters—may well catch up with Japan by 2050 at the latest or by 2010 at the earliest. Thus, it is reasonable to assume that China will likely race forward to become the region's hegemon sometime by the second half of the century. That date may come sooner if, for example, Beijing's Greater China scheme works out and pays off. The scenario is premised upon the successful absorption of Hong Kong after its 1997 reversion and the mainland's deepening economic integration with Taiwan with or without reunification (Hsiung 1992).

☐ *U.S. Strategy for the Pacific Era*

With the end of the Cold War, U.S. strategic thinking is at a crossroads. U.S. global strategy, culminating in the containment of the Eurasian heartland power, was deprived of its raison d'étre by dint of the Soviet disintegration. Now the heartland is weak, and the periphery is strong. These changes will do violence to the "rimland strategy" à la Nicholas Spykman, which provided the geopolitical justification for the containment policy that was to last over four decades. The logic of the strategy was premised upon the threat to world security posed by the heartland. It prescribed that the Western European rim and the Asian rim (the Chinese subcontinent) must be defended at all costs (by the United States) to contain the heartland power in order to assure world peace and stability (Spykman 1942; Gray 1977). Although the adequacy of the rimland strategy after 1991 has come into question, the United States has yet to work out a new strategy for the changing times. The first hurdle for this task is the difficulty in targeting a new source of threat to replace the former Soviet Union.

My answer is that, in the geoeconomic age, one has to follow a different tack in one's thinking about who will be the gravest threat to U.S. security. First, the definition of security has shifted from military to economic interests. Second, the concept of "enemy" will have to be revamped, to allow the possibility of some country being both a [trading] partner and an adversary at the same time. Third, in the days of rival trading blocs, an adversary may very well be a group of nations such as the EC more than any one country such as Japan or Germany.

In this respect, I take exception to the view espoused by some that the future world order will be a state-centric tripolar system comprising the United States, Germany, and Japan. It is my argument that in the geoeconomic age, balance of power will no longer be drawn along state-centric lines but along lines delineating trading blocs. It is important to keep in mind the three super trading blocs outlined above. In thinking about future balance of power, it is instructive to keep in view the relative "sizes" of the trading blocs, as measured by their respective share of the world's total GDP and trade volume. Within each trading bloc, power configurations will determine how intrabloc alignments will be drawn.

Before going on, I will pause to make a comment on what the arrival of the three super trading blocs signifies for international relations (IR) theory. In the traditional geopolitic setting of world politics, nation-states experience what John Herz (1976, p. 72) called a recurrent "security dilemma." In the "anarchic" world they live in, states are "driven to acquire more and more power in order to escape the impact of the power of others." Yet this renders the others insecure and compels them to attempt the same power acquisition; hence the arms races. The resultant vicious cycle of security and power accumulation only reinforces the insecurity of nations and makes them at times feel even less secure, relative to each other, than before (Herz 1976, p. 73). There are two aspects to this dilemma. First, one nation's security entails the relative insecurity of others. Second, caught in the cycle of competitive power acquisition, a nation may end up feeling less secure than before. The phenomenon was not new when John Herz addressed it. His term "security dilemma" has since been quoted and requoted in the IR literature.

What we are witnessing now is a geoeconomic counterpart of the security dilemma. First came the European Community, which loomed ever larger on the international horizon. Its threat to other regions' economic security was concretized, for example, by New Zealand and Australia's loss of their traditional British market for agricultural exports when the United Kingdom joined the EC in 1973. In their bid to diversify their markets, the New Zealanders and Australians found common cause with members of the Asia Pacific region. Thus, to the EC's announced single-market initiative, APEC was the answer. I do not wish to repeat what has already been said about APEC, but it is important to note that (1) the APEC idea was given institutional form at the initiative of the Australians, under Prime Minister Bob Hawke, and (2) its inaugural session was held in November 1989, coinciding with the tumbling down of the Berlin Wall, an unmistakable sign of the end of the Cold War and (by extension) the dawn of the geoeconomic age. Then, too, in reaction came NAFTA, signed by the United States, Canada, and Mexico on August 13, 1992. A revealing element of NAFTA is its expressly stated goal to set up obstacles to prevent Asian and European companies from bypassing American tariffs by shipping goods through Mexico.[22]

One trading bloc thus gave the impetus to the making of a second and then a third trading bloc, in a process that reminds one of the "security dilemma" about which John Herz spoke. The origin of the insecurity and competition cycle is the same. The intention of maximizing one's own security to the exclusion of outsiders, or, to be more exact, non–bloc members (e.g., NAFTA's goal of thwarting Asian and European exports slipped through Mexico) is the same. The end result from this cycle of mutual power enhancement and competition will probably be that each bloc will end up feeling relatively less secure than before, although to what extent remains to be seen. One principal difference is that the nature of "security"

254   *James C. Hsiung*

has changed. Instead of (or in addition to?) arms races, we are going to see "trade wars" in furtherance of economic security interests. A competitive round of currency devaluations (to mitigate trade imbalances) or of protectionist measures within each bloc (to keep out unfair imports) are two possibilities that immediately come to mind. (A recent instance was the U.S. decision in November 1992 to impose a 200 percent tax on all white wines imported from Europe, a retaliation against the EC's farm subsidies). Another major difference between economic and military competition can be seen in the way this latest round of security buildup is taking shape. Instead of state-centric efforts, it involves a concerted reaction by the whole trading bloc. Assuming regional integration is different from the traditional coalition making, the difference in this sense is truly qualitative—one of sort, not just of degree.

It can appropriately be observed that the competitive formation of the super trading blocs is an updated version of the security dilemma in the geoeconomic age. Accordingly, the strategic response of the United States will follow a two-stage scenario. In the first stage, between now and circa 2010, its immediate concern is to determine which of the other two economic blocs constitutes a more formidable threat: Asia Pacific or Europe? As I have tried to show, of the three super trading blocs, Europe outweighs both East Asia and North America. Despite Asia Pacific's faster growth rates and its larger share of total U.S. foreign trade, Europe is by far the more virile as a competing economic bloc. The logic of balance of power, therefore, dictates that the United States align itself with Asia Pacific as the weaker of the two competing blocs to fend off the threat posed by the larger bloc. The logic for aligning with the weaker of the other two in a set of three is that, in our "anarchic" world (i.e., in the absence of a supranational authority), nations are after not absolute gains but relative gains in alliance making (Grieco 1990, pp. 40–49). As Kenneth Waltz (1979, p. 105) aptly puts it, the question states ask is not "Do we both gain?" but rather, "Who gains more?"

In my earlier study (Hsiung 1985, p. 110ff) of the U.S.–Soviet–Chinese triad, I drew upon tests made by social psychologists Edgar Vinacke and Abe Arkoff of a formulation by sociologist Theodore Caplow. These tests suggested that under certain conditions the formation of particular coalitions depends upon the initial distribution of power in the triad and may be predicted to some extent once the initial power distribution is known. Following this exercise, it was possible to show why the U.S.–PRC coalition against the Soviet Union could be predicted by the theory of triadic games. Similarly, using the same logic, one can almost predict why a North America–Asia Pacific alignment vis-à-vis Europe is in the offing. Without going into great detail, I will extrapolate from my 1985 study. Assuming the power ratio among the three super trading blocs to be 4:3:2:, there is a 67 percent chance that North America (with a weight of 3) and Asia Pacific (with a weight of 2) will align on the same side, against Europe's power weight of 4 (Vinacke and Arkoff showed that in 59 out 88 games, or 67 percent of the time, the subjects chose a "BC," or 3:2, alliance, as opposed to a 4:3 or a 4:2).

In the second stage of its strategic scenario for the future, the United States' concern will be with the power alignment within the Asia Pacific region itself. For by 2010, when Asia Pacific will have caught up with Europe, U.S. strategic concerns will be: (1) Should we continue the earlier BC (North America–Asia Pacific) bond against A (Europe)? and (2) if so, what about the power alignments within Asia Pacific?

To go back to the Caplow formulation, in a power ratio of 1:1:1 (that is, with the three trading blocs approaching an equilibrium), there is an equal chance of the AB, BC, or AC bonds being picked (Hsiung 1985, p. 110). That being the case, the outcome will depend on intervening variables that are not foreseen. Our attention therefore will turn to the power alignments within the Asia Pacific itself. This question will be with us, in fact, from the first stage (between now and 2010) on. Because the United States (through NAFTA) has to count on an alliance with Asia Pacific to cope with the European economic power, it is imperative that Washington be able to lead in Asia Pacific. Japan, which now stands head and shoulders over all other Asia Pacific members, is the only country with the economic clout to defy the U.S. leadership. The following projections by Linder (1986, p. 12) should help us visualize the distribution of economic power in the region by the year 2000:

Country	Share of World GDP
Japan	13.5 percent
Remainder of Asia Pacific (not including United States)	9.8 percent (13.1 percent if higher estimates for China used)
United States	27.6 percent
U.S. Pacific	4.19 percent

These projections confirm the general impression that Japan is the only Asia Pacific country that can say "no" to the United States on matters affecting the region. It also shows that, with China included, all the rest of Asia Pacific (without the United States) will have a combined weight approaching that of Japan. Here, "all the rest of Asia Pacific" includes the Asian NIEs, China, ASEAN, Australia, New Zealand, and Canada. To the extent that these percentages can serve as an indication of the distribution of economic power, they recommend a defensive coalition strategy for the

United States if it is out to protect its economic interests within the region. The strategy calls for strengthening bilateral relations with all Asia Pacific members, including Japan, and fostering the necessary multilateral institutions, or strengthening of existing ones (including APEC), so that the U.S. leadership can be strong enough to cope with any possible challenge within the region. Close U.S. bilateral relations will keep Japan's centripetal pull in the region to a minimum. In order to prevent South Korea and Taiwan from becoming Japanese economic satellites, the United States may even have to consider lending a helping hand to the unification of the Korean Peninsula and of the Chinese mainland with Taiwan. A united Korea may provide a strong enough economic base to deflect any Japanese pull to lock South Korea into Japan's economic orbit. The Chinese unification may prove useful for the creation of an alternative power center to both counterbalance Japan and remove the U.S.–Japan nexus as the magnet of major economic conflict in Asia Pacific. The PRC's potential at the macro level can be seen from its projected 6.4 percent share of world GDP by 2000, almost 2.5 times that of the four Asian NIEs (2.6 percent) projected for the same year (*ibid.*). Besides, China's average growth rates almost tripled those of Japan throughout the 1980s. Chinese reunification would mean the integration of three dynamic Chinese economies into one: the mainland, Hong Kong, and Taiwan. It would create, for the United States, that second power bloc to challenge Japan's heretofore unquestioned lead in Asia Pacific and, equally important, help stabilize U.S. relations with Japan in the U.S.– Japan–China strategic triad in the region.

The above discussion is premised upon the assumption that, as much as the United States needs Asia Pacific to be on its side as an economic counterweight to an economically overbearing European Community, the United States will also have to be prepared to face a formidable challenge posed by Japan from within the region. This premise necessarily reflects the ongoing U.S.–Japan trade conflicts unresolved since the mid-1980s.

In this second stage of the two-stage strategic scenario, the United States will have to be concerned more about the balance *within* Asia Pacific itself. In the first place, the Asia Pacific region will have caught up with Europe in GDP, share of total world trade, and possibly other dimensions including multilateral institution building (regional integration). Second, by the year 2050, China will most likely have caught up with Japan in economic power, as speculated above. The end result is that the United States will by then no longer view Asia Pacific as a necessary coalition partner in meeting the European economic threat. Indeed, it may be more worried about the dual threat from two, not one, regional economic superpowers: Japan and China. Within Asia Pacific, therefore, the United States will find itself in a triadic game situation recalling the one discussed before involving the three super trading blocs (from the 1990s through the early half of the twenty-first century). All the desiderata regarding coalition making in such a triadic game will then apply to U.S. relations with Japan and China. Without getting into great detail, I only wish to note that in the event of a parallel 4:3:2 distribution of power in the U.S.–Japan–China triad, the United States is most likely to have the weight of 4. In that event, the U.S. concern would be how *not* to be confronted with a Japan-China (3:2) alliance. As we have seen from the Vinacke-Arkoff experiment, there is a 67 percent chance that a 3:2 bond will form. The best strategy for the United States, under the circumstances, would be to try to play the "pivot" in a *ménàge a trois* game (Hsiung 1985, p. 128), maintaining an equidistant posture toward both wings.

■ THEORY AND INTERNATIONAL CHANGE

There are different ways to visualize and explain cataclysmic changes in the history of international relations. One is to place the changes in the context of long cycles, roughly 100 years apart (Modelski 1987). Another way is to group changes around certain "hegemonic wars," so called because by their gravity they determined "which state or states will be dominant and will govern the system" (Gilpin 1981, p. 15). Still another way is to agree with Arnold Toynbee (1931, p. 133) in his postulated twofold process of change. The first part of the process is the expansion of the center against the periphery, arousing the peripheral peoples. Then follows the second part of the process, the rise of the periphery and the weakening of the center by internecine power struggle.

Each of these three theories may have something to offer, but none is able to explain what is happening as our century gives way to the twenty-first. The long-cycle theory, although it does catch the long swings in history's movement in certain cases, seems too initutive in that it fails to offer a convincing explanation for why the long cycles occur the way they do. Moreover, the theory does not seem to explain if there are defining differences between cycles as they unfold, nor if there are any definitive, identifiable patterns in the transition from one particular cycle to the next. The hegemonic war theory may explain most of the epoch-making changes wrought by major wars of the past, including the Napoleonic and the Bismarckian wars and the two world wars. But the theory seems ill-equipped to offer an explanation for the precipitous changes in the last two decades of our time. The collapse of communism in Eastern Europe, the falling apart of the Soviet power, and the end of the Cold War—all happened without an international war. Toynbee's center-periphery interaction may account for the impact of the coming of the West to Asia Pacific and the latter's rise in the world hierarchy of wealth. But the Asia Pacific rise has happened and is happening *without* a debilitating power struggle in the center itself—unless the idea of "center" is stretched to include the bipolar conflict that just ended.

In sum, none of these existing theories seems as adequate as it claims in explaining, or even just describing, what is unfolding in the world at the end of our century and, more important, the significance it holds for world politics of the next century. An important reason, I submit, is that the kaleidoscopic changes in world politics are qualitatively different from all past international relations since 1648. The decisive difference is that all the cataclysmic changes of our time were wrought by primarily economic, only secondarily political, forces. Even the fall of communism came about under the crushing weight of massive economic failures at home against the backdrop of an attractive Western-dominated global economic structure (Collins and Rodrik 1991; Risse-Kappen 1991; Deudney and Ikenberry 1992). China has escaped the fate that befell its colleagues in Eastern Europe (including the Soviet Union) precisely because it introduced a successful economic reform in time and has not relented despite the Tiananmen disruptions.

The theories, therefore, need to make the necessary adjustments in order to regain their explanatory power. To wit, if we add the economic factor for change and substitute it for Gilpin's "hegemonic war," and if we substitute for Toynbee's "power struggle in the center" the factor of hegemonic decline in the strict economic sense, we may find a new way to account for what is happening in today's world. The extension of economic power (and consequently, in some instances, democracy) to Asia Pacific came both as a result of the latter's awakening to the earlier penetration by the West and as a price for U.S. hegemonic leadership since the end of World War II. The splintering of the global economic system (nominally still under the aegis of the General Agreement on Tariffs and Trade) into the three super trading blocs alluded to above is another outcome of U.S. hegemonic decline. The natural tendency for Asia Pacific and North America to close ranks results, by necessity, from the dictate of the balance of power in the new geoeconomic era. Finally, our century's most important bequest on the next is a new cycle in which a non-Western bloc (Asia Pacific) will compete on an equal basis with two Western blocs— one European and one [post-European] North American. This state of affairs makes a drastic break from past centuries, when the West dominated the entire Westphalian system.

At its dawn, the twentieth century opened on a Eurocentric stage; and at its close, the world seems set to return to a stage dominated by a rejuvenated and integrated European Community. Two epochal developments greeted the second half of our century: the advent of nuclear weapons, and the massive arrivals of postcolonial states. Both gained added importance because of the Cold War, in which the two contending superpowers threatened the world with a nuclear holocaust and scrambled to woo over the expanding ranks of the Third World. These two factors added to the strategic importance of geopolitics. With the end of the Cold War, both nuclear weaponry and the Third World lost much of their luster. In the new geoeconomic age, nuclear weapons will at best remain dormant. The Third World, especially Africa, seems headed toward oblivion—the prospects of their bid to seek a larger share of the world's wealth seem dismal, unless its members can act together in some unforeseen ways. Whatever the Third World nations do to improve their odds, it will probably result in an acute confrontation between North and South, the intensities of which the world has yet to witness. In the new century, the South-North conflict may well be the only fixation in international relations. Actually, with the withdrawal of the Soviet bloc, the South-North conflict will just be a South-West conflict.

In all this, Asia Pacific will have a unique dual role to play. First, its economic success story (to wit, its import-substitution and export-oriented strategy) will continue to hold out a model for all aspiring underdeveloped countries to emulate, although the international environment remains less supportive than during the Cold War. Second, in the event of an intensified South-West conflict, Asia Pacific, which both actively participates in the West-dominated global political economy and shares some of the anticolonial sentiments of the South, will be a natural intermediary. Already China has displayed much empathy for the crying demands of the Third World for a new international economic order, extolling the poor nations' right to development and right to subsistence.

The next century will probably see, initially at least, the European bloc leading all other regions. Before it catches up with Europe by 2010, Asia Pacific's claim to distinction will rest largely on its ability to serve as a mediator in the South-West conflict. But its success or failure to act as such depends very much on its economic clout, defined in terms of its sustained growth rates, percentage shares of world trade and of global GDP, and the extent to which it leads in high tech research and development. Thus, while the Pacific Era will not arrive until after 2010, Asia Pacific's significant role in world politics will gain increasing recognition long before that date, precisely for these reasons.

■ NOTES

1. "MITI Says Japan Offers Best Model for Economies in Emerging Countries," *Asian Wall Street Journal Weekly*, July 27, 1992, p. 7.
2. For data indicating the near-NIE status of these countries, see IMF, *World Economic Outlook* (Washington, D.C., May 1992), pp. 60–66. I am indebted to David Denoon for this information.
3. *Asian Wall Street Journal Weekly*, March 9, 1992, p. 3.

4. *Renmin Ribao* [People's Daily] (overseas ed.), January 23, 1992, p. 1.
5. *New York Times*, July 28, 1992, p. 6.
6. *New York Times*, June 15, 1992, p. D–1.
7. Pamela Baldinger. 1992. "Birth of Greater China," 19 *China Business Review* 3:13 (May–June).
8. "Changed Pattern of Taiwan Investments on the China Mainland," *The China Times* (Taipei), July 20, 1992, p. 3.
9. *The Economist*, July 25, 1992, p. 33.
10. *Central Daily News* (Taipei), June 10, 1992, p. 1.
11. Statistics provided by the Comptroller's Office, the Executive Yuan (Cabinet), Taiwan, ROC, as carried in *Qiao Bao* [The China Press] (New York), June 18, 1992, p. 2.
12. *China Times* (Taipei), July 20, 1992, p. 1.
13. *Qiao Bao* [The China Press] (New York), July 24, 1992, p. 4.
14. *Central Daily News* (Taipei), July 13, 1992, p. 2.
15. *New York Times*, June 15, 1992, p. 1.
16. For example, U.S. share of GDP for all OECD countries has dropped from 57 percent to 35 percent in 1960–1980, whereas the share of the largest three countries (the countries involved have also changed in the period) has dropped only from 65 percent to 62 percent. The corresponding figures for export share are 25 percent to 18 percent and 51 percent to 45 percent. The combined share of the United States, Germany, and Japan has risen slightly in both categories over the same period. See Snidal 1985, p. 603, n. 36.
17. *Financial Times*, January 20, 1992.
18. Richard Solomon. 1990. "Asian Security in the 1990s: Integration in Economics, Diversity in Defense," U.S. Department of State Dispatch. Washington, D.C., November 5, p. 248.
19. *The Economist*, October 26, 1991, p. 81.
20. *The Economist*, February 22, 1992, p. 48.
21. AFP dispatch from Paris dated August 9, 1992; carried by the *World Journal* (New York), August 19, 1992, p. 2.
22. *New York Times*, August 13, 1992, p. 1.

■ **REFERENCES**

Baker, James, III. 1991. "America in Asia," 70 *Foreign Affairs* 5:1–18 (Winter).
Balassa, B., et al. 1982. *Development Strategies in Semi-Industrial Economies.* Baltimore, MD: Johns Hopkins University Press.
Berger, Peter, and Michael Hsiao, eds. 1986. *In Search of an East Asian Developmental Model.* New Brunswick, NJ: Transaction Books.
Blair, John M. 1976. *The Control of Oil.* New York: Vintage Books.
Borthwick, Mark. 1992. *The Pacific Century.* Boulder, CO: Westview Press.
Byrd, William. 1991. *The Market Mechanism and Economic Reforms in China.* Armonk, NY: M. E. Sharpe.
Chan, Steve, and Cal Clark. 1992. *The Evolving Pacific Basin in the Global Political Economy.* Boulder, CO: Lynne Rienner Publishers.
Collins, Susan, and Dani Rodrik. 1991. *Eastern Europe and the Soviet Union in the World Economy.* Washington, D.C.: Institute for International Economics.
Deudney, Daniel, and G. John Ikenberry. 1992. "The International Sources of Soviet Change," 16 *International Security* 3:74–118 (Winter 1991–1992).
Fei, John, Gustav Ranis, and Shirley Kuo. 1979. *Growth with Equity.* New York: Oxford University Press.

Feldstein, Martin, ed. 1988. *The United States in the World Economy,* with an introduction by the editor. Chicago: University of Chicago Press.

Gilpin, Robert. 1981. *War and Change in World Politics.* London and New York: Oxford University Press.

Glickman, Norman, and Douglas Woodward. 1989. *The New Competitors.* New York: Basic Books.

Gray, Colin S. 1977. *The Geopolitics of the Nuclear Era.* New York: Crane, Russak, & Co.

Grieco, Joseph M. 1990. *Cooperation Among Nations.* Ithaca, NY: Cornell University Press.

Herz, John. 1976. *The Nation-State and the Crisis of World Politics.* New York: David Mckay.

Hofheinz, Roy, and Kent Calder. 1982. *The Eastasia Edge.* New York: Basic Books.

Hsiung, James C. 1985. "Sino–U.S.–Soviet Relations in a Triadic Game Perspective." In *Beyond China's Independent Foreign Policy.* New York: Praeger.

Hsiung, James C. 1992. "China in the 21st Century Global Balance: Challenge and Policy Response." In Chan and Clark, *The Evolving Pacific Basin.*

IBRD. 1991. *World Development Report.* Washington, D.C.: The World Bank.

Johnson, Bryan. 1992. "Forging Alliances to Bust into Japanese Market" *Backgrounder* No. 876. Washington, D.C.: Heritage Foundation.

Keohane, Robert. 1984. *After Hegemony.* Princeton, NJ: Princeton University Press.

Keohane, Robert, and Joseph Nye. 1977. *Power and Interdependence.* Boston: Little, Brown.

Kindleberger, Charles. 1986. *World in Depression.* Berkeley, CA: University of California Press.

Krickus, Richard. 1987. *Superpowers in Crisis.* New York: Pergamon-Brassey's.

Lake, David. 1984. "Beneath the Commerce of Nations: A Theory of International Economic Structures," 28 *International Studies Quarterly* 2:143–170.

Li Hong, 1992. "Developing Countries Fight for the Right to Subsistence," 35 *Beijing Review* 8:12–13; cf. also 35 *Beijing Review* 7:12–14.

Linder, Staffan. 1986. *The Pacific Century.* Stanford, CA: Stanford University Press.

Lockwood, William. 1964. "Economic and Political Modernization." In *Political Modernization in Japan and Turkey,* ed., Dankwart A. Rustow. Princeton, NJ: Princeton University Press.

McCord, William. 1991. *The Dawn of the Pacific Century.* New Brunswick, NJ: Transaction Books.

Modelski, George, ed. 1987. *Exploring Long Cycles.* Boulder, CO: Lynne Rienner Publishers.

Nakane, Chie. 1985. *Japanese Society.* Berkeley, CA: University of California Press.

Olson, Mancur. 1955. *The Logic of Collective Action.* New York: Schoken Books.

Rabushka, Alvin. 1987. *The New China.* Boulder, CO: Westview Press.

Risse-Kappen, Thomas. 1991. "Did 'Peace Through Strength' End the Cold War? Lessons from the INF," 16 *International Security* 1:162–188 (Summer).

Rosenau, James. 1989. "Global Changes and Theoretical Changes: Toward a Post-International Politics for the 1990s." In Ernst-Otto Czempiel and James Rosenau, eds., *Global Changes and Theoretical Changes.* Lexington, MS: Lexington Books.

Snidal, Duncan. 1985. "The Limits of the Hegemonic Stability Theory," 39 *International Organization* 4:579–614 (Autumn).

Spykman, Nicholas. 1942. *American Strategy in World Politics.* Hamden, CT: Archon.

Takahashi, Kamenkichi. 1969. *The Rise and Development of Japan's Modern Economy.* Tokyo: Jiji Press.

Thurow, Lester. 1989. "American Mirage: A Post-Industrial Economy?" *Current History* (January 1989).

Thurow, Lester. 1992. Paper given at Conference on the Role of Hi-Tech Inputs and Outputs in the 21st Century," Hong Kong, July 2, 1992; as reported in *The China Times* (Taipei), July 23, 1992, p. 11.

Toynbee, Arnold. 1931. *Survey of International Affairs 1930.* London: Oxford University Press.

UN. 1990. *World Statistics in Brief,* 13th ed. New York: United Nations.

UNCTAD. 1987. "Revitaliziang Development, Growth and International Trade." Report to UNCTAD VII. Geneva: UNCTAD.

Wade, Robert. 1990. *Governing the Market.* Princeton, NJ: Princeton University Press.

Wade, Robert. 1992. "East Asia's Economic Success: Conflicting Perspectives, Partial Insights, Shaky Evidence," 44 *World Politics* 2:270–320.

Waltz, Kenneth. 1979. *Theory of International Politics.* Reading, MS: Addison-Wesley Publishing Co.

Wei, Wou. 1992. *Capitalism, A Chinese Version: Guiding a Market Economy in Taiwan.* Columbus, OH: East Asian Studies Center, Ohio State University.

■ About the Editor and Contributors

James C. Hsiung is professor of politics at New York University. He is author and editor of fourteen books, including: *Asia and U.S. Foreign Policy*; and *U.S.–Asian Relations: The National Security Paradox*; *China in the Global Community*. His latest works are: *Beyond China's Independent Foreign Policy*; *Human Rights in Asia: A Cultural Perspective;* and *China's Bitter Victory: War with Japan, 1937–1945* (coedited with Steven I. Levine). He is an executive editor of *Asian Affairs*, consulting editor for *Asian Thought and Society*. Dr. Hsiung held visiting professorships from Taiwan and mainland China and holds honorary professor titles from a number of Chinese institutions of higher learning, including Jiangxi University (Nanchang) and Guangzhou Normal University (Canton). He is a consulting member of the Shanghai Academy of Social Sciences.

Peter Berton is professor emeritus of international relations and former coordinator of the Asia/Pacific Regional Studies Program at the School of International Relations, University of Southern California. He is also an associate of the Strengthening Democratic Institutions Project at the John F. Kennedy School of Government, Harvard University. He is editor of the *Far Eastern and Russian Research Series* and editor emeritus of *Studies in Comparative Communism*. His publications include *The Fateful Choice: Japan's Advance into Southeast Asia: 1939–1941* and *The Russian Impact on Japan* among many others. He served as associate dean, International Division, Waseda University, in Tokyo, and lectured extensively (in Japanese as well as in English) at universities and research institutes during 1987–1988.

Albert F. Celoza is a faculty member in social science at Phoenix College and is an adjunct professor in the Program for Southeast Asian Studies at Arizona State University. He also teaches international studies at the American Graduate School of International Management (Thunderbird). He was a member of the faculty in the College of Public Administration and the College of Arts and Sciences at the University of the Philippines.

Steve Chan is professor of political science at the University of Colorado (Boulder). He was a recipient of the Karl Deutsch award of the International Studies Association, a Pew faculty fellow at the Kennedy School of Government (Harvard University), and a Fulbright scholar in Singapore and Taiwan. His research interests include international relations and political economy. He is the author of seven books and numerous articles; among his most recent books are: *East Asian Dynamism*; *The Evolving Pacific Basin in the Global Political Economy: Domestic and International Linkages*, and *Defense, Welfare and Growth* (coedited with Alex Mintz).

Peter C. Y. Chow is associate professor of economics and coordinator for the M.A. in Management Economics Program at City College of the City University of New York. He was a visiting research fellow at the Hoover Institution, Stanford University, and at the University of California, Berkeley, before joining the faculty of CUNY. He is also a research associate at the National Bureau of Economic Research and on the doctoral-program faculty at the CUNY Graduate Center. He has written numerous articles; one of his most recent books is *Trade—The Engine of Growth in East Asia*.

Cal Clark is professor and head of the Department of Political Science at Auburn University. His primary teaching and research interests are international political economy and comparative public policy. He is author of many articles and *Taiwan's Development*; coauthor of *Flexibility, Foresight, and Fortuna in Taiwan's Development*; and coeditor of *State and Development* and *The Evolving Pacific Basin in the Global Political Economy* (with Steve Chan).

David B. H. Denoon is currently associate professor of politics and economics at New York University. He has served three times in the federal government as program economist, USAID, Jakarta, Indonesia (1978–1979); vice president of the U.S. Export-Import Bank (1978–1979); and deputy assistant secretary of defense (1981–1982). His most recent book, completed for the Council on Foreign Relations, is *Real Reciprocity: Balancing U.S. Economic and Security Policies in the Pacific Basin*.

Bernard K. Gordon is author of four books and many articles on foreign policy in the Pacific region and East Asia. He concentrates on Southeast Asia and Japan in connection with U.S. foreign policy and the international political economy. His newest book is *New Directions for American Policy in Asia*. He has worked in East Asia since the 1950s, most recently as visiting professor at Kobe University, Japan, in 1991–1992. He is professor of political science at the University of New

Hampshire and, in 1992–1993, a research fellow at the East-West Center (Honolulu), where he is writing a book on global trade issues.

Martin H. Sours is professor of international studies at the American Graduate School of International Management (Thunderbird). He was acting chair of the International Studies Department and was also interim vice president for academic affairs. He was an AID officer in Southeast Asia and held visiting professorships in South Korea, Japan, and Taiwan.

■ Index

■ About the Book

In today's post–Cold War world—with economic security a paramount concern—Asia Pacific is establishing an increasingly important role in global politics. This book assesses the potential power configuration of the region, exploring not only its new strategic position, but equally the parts played by its major actors: Japan, China, South Korea, Taiwan, the ASEAN members, Russia, and the United States.

Intraregional relations, the prospects for regional integration, and the implications of Asia Pacific's new strength for U.S. policy are also investigated. And, perhaps most important for IR theory, the book offers a coherent view of Asia Pacific's likely role in twenty-first century world politics.